HANDBOOK OF SYSTEM AND PRODUCT SAFETY

Prentice-Hall, Inc., Englewood Cliffs, N. J.

Willie Hammer

Professional Engineer

HANDBOOK OF SYSTEM AND PRODUCT SAFETY

ISBN: 0-13-382226-5

Library of Congress Catalog Card Number: 72-2683

Printed in the United States of America.

PRENTICE-HALL INTERNATIONAL, INC., *London*
PRENTICE-HALL OF AUSTRALIA, PTY. LTD., *Sydney*
PRENTICE-HALL OF CANADA, LTD., *Toronto*
PRENTICE-HALL OF INDIA PRIVATE LIMITED, *New Delhi*
PRENTICE-HALL OF JAPAN, INC., *Tokyo*

contents

foreword

I have known of Willie Hammer and his work for a long time. His education, experience, capabilities and interests have made him a prolific authority on safety matters. The outstanding feature of his writings is that they are not vague dissertations on the need for safety efforts, but practical guides which can be used by designers, managers, and procedural personnel. He is a highly respected authority on System Safety.

When I am asked for a quick and simple explanation of System Safety I usually reply "organizing to put your hindsight where your foresight should be in the identification and management of risks." The engineering executive who requires his staff to exercise the contents of this book will surely be in a very favorable position to do this. Of course, as in most successful technical endeavors, especially if they are new and unique, an intuitive and imaginative engineering sense coupled to a practical background is a necessary complement to System Safety.

The term "safety analyses" has, in the past, often meant investigations of accidents to determine their causes so that corrective actions could be taken to prevent recurrences. This is a worthwhile endeavor but it occurs after the accident happens. No company or governmental agency can long justify the massive costs of such a process with risks of great magnitude. Activities such as those undertaken by NASA require operations to be as safe as practical the first time they are undertaken. Analyses must be undertaken long before any operation is to be conducted so that suitable safeguards are provided to the most practical extent possible for all foreseeable hazards. Assumptions should be reviewed periodically. Accepted risks should be rationalized and documented.

To ensure that the accident prevention effort is timely and effective, the analysis effort must begin as soon as a product, system or operation is conceived. It must be continued through development, design, test, and production. Suitable programs must be undertaken utilizing the best available analysis techniques. Until now, to the best of my knowledge, no book has been available which presents these techniques, and where or when they should be applied.

In these times of increasing public awareness of "product liability", the management of a concern producing hardware will be better able to defend its integrity and reputation if it follows the precepts and techniques in this book. It constitutes a major milestone in the furtherance of accident prevention.

Jerome Lederer
NASA Director of Safety (Retired)

preface

To a certain extent, the title of this book is a misnomer. The material it contains is not limited to System Safety and Product Safety, but can be applied beneficially to other areas of safety: industrial, motor vehicle, railroad, mine, or nuclear. Examples of problems and solutions have been cited from most of these areas. The similarities to System Safety and Product Safety problems and solutions will be readily apparent to any reader concerned with safety. In all likelihood, these examples will bring others to mind in the field in which he is interested. This is the major benefit of this book.

This book can be used in fields related to safety:

- Analyses can be made of environmental pollution problems which can result from accidental release of damaging materials.

- Casualty insurance companies may require that each product or operation to be insured be analyzed for hazards so they can be eliminated or necessary safeguards provided, in order that accident losses can be minimized.

- Trial lawyers in the liability field can use the techniques of this book to determine where negligence might have occurred in design of a product or in conduct of an operation. On the other hand, defense counsels may be able to show that a company exercised due prudence by carrying out an effective safety program.

The reader will find the book is oriented more towards System Safety than to Product Safety. There are two reasons: most of my experience has been as a System Safety engineer; and System Safety requirements are broader and more inclusive than those for Product Safety. The principles indicated in this book for System Safety will therefore apply also to the generally less demanding requirements of Product Safety.

System Safety covers such a broad area of interest, it is difficult to establish limits to the material to be covered. This is one of the fascinating aspects of being a System Safety engineer: he must be knowledgeable and concerned with such a wide scope of subjects, there is no opportunity for his work to become boring. In writing this book, the chief problem was holding its scope to a manageable size. If anyone considers that a subject was omitted or treated too lightly, the necessity for limiting the size of the book must be my excuse.

I have attempted to credit every person whose material I have used; any omission must be attributed to oversight, — and will, I hope, be forgiven. In many cases, permission to use material was not requested since it was extracted from documents in the public domain. I am sure such permission would have been granted if it had been necessary. I will therefore extend my thanks to authors of such material, as well as to those of copyrighted documents who did grant permission when requested.

I would also like to thank Mrs. Avis Dillard for assistance in the preparation of the manuscript, and especially Jerry Lederer for his Foreword.

Willie Hammer

Cerritos, California

chapter 1

THE NEED FOR SAFETY PROGRAMS

Injury or damage can result from four fundamental causes: material failure, human error, adverse characteristics of a product, or unusual environmental conditions. Recently, personnel concerned with accident prevention have become more and more convinced that injury or damage from any of these causes can be prevented or lessened through good design and planning.

Unfortunately, adverse attitudes frequently impede actions to improve safety. There appears to be an ingrained resistance to devices and procedures by which persons can safeguard themselves or others. This resistance takes various forms. There may be reluctance or outright opposition to change or to the slight added effort or cost a safeguard might require. Individuals or companies may refuse to learn from disasters of others or admit that they could not be afflicted similarly. There may even be pride in accomplishing without suitable protection any unusually hazardous activity. Frequently, the result is a recurrence of catastrophies until public indignation or massive economic loss forces corrective action. History provides numerous examples.

In 1785, Pilatre de Rozier, the first man to make an ascent in a balloon, planned to cross from France to England in a combination balloon that was to use hot air and hydrogen as the lifting agents. Hot air was produced by a fire under the open mouth of the balloon. Hydrogen had better lifting power, but was extremely expensive, leaked rapidly through the fabric cover, and was dangerous. De Rozier had been warned of hydrogen's flammability. He and a passenger took off and rose to 3,000 feet, where they were seen adjusting the fire. There was a blue flash and explosion as the hydrogen ignited. The passenger basket dropped and both men were killed.

In 1922, the worst aerial disaster up to that time occurred when the hydrogen in the semirigid airship *Roma* exploded, causing the deaths of 34 men. A contemporary weekly magazine* reported: "Air Service officers at Washington and at Langley Field, where the accident to the *Roma* occurred, accustomed as they are to taking risks daily, look upon this most recent disaster as incident to the development of aviation. 'It is merely a part of the day's work,' in the opinion of one of them. On the other hand civilian aeronautical authorities and newspaper editors call attention to the fact that the *Roma* disaster was preventable through the use of helium."

Fifteen years later, the zeppelin *Hindenburg* exploded and burned when its hydrogen leaked through the lifting cell fabric and was ignited by a spark. Thirty-six persons were killed; others were badly burned. With them died the lighter-than-air transportation industry.

The development of the parachute followed a similar series of events. The parachute was first conceived by Leonardo da Vinci about 1500. A square type was built in 1595 by Fausto Veranzio, a Venetian, for emergency descents from high towers, but found little use. The first practical parachute was used by André Jacques Garnerin in 1797, when he dropped from a balloon that had risen to an altitude of 3,000 feet. He performed the feat a number of times. Over the succeeding years, the parachute was improved until a light backpack was developed before the first World War. In that war, however, no Allied pilot was provided one, and the Germans started using them only shortly before the war ended. The reason given for failure to supply parachutes: pilots and other aircrew men might abandon the aircraft before it was absolutely

The Need for Safety Programs

* "What The Wreck of the *'Roma'* Shows." *Literary Digest,* 4 March 1922, page 11.

necessary to do so. Hundreds of men died in their planes or jumped to their deaths to avoid being burned to death.

From the start of the Industrial Revolution, equipment began to grow progressively more complex, involved the use of greater and greater amounts of energy, and increased potentials for accidents, injuries, and damage. Accident prevention failed to keep pace with technological growth, so the number of mishaps increased tremendously with passing years. Corrective action was taken only after a particularly severe accident occurred or through the continued efforts of an outstandingly determined and energetic crusader. These efforts led to legislation for industrial safety, mine safety, railroad safety, marine safety, and traffic safety.

A hundred years ago, Lorenzo Coffin carried on a crusade almost single-handedly to force railroads to adopt basic safety devices. After observing an accident in which a brakeman lost two fingers inserting a pin in the links that coupled railroad cars, he learned it was a common occurrence. Almost everyone who worked as a brakeman had lost fingers in this way. Many lost their lives applying brakes in bad weather or other adverse conditions. An automatic coupler and an air brake had been invented years before, but the railroads refused to adopt them because of their initial costs. Almost 20 years later, Coffin's persistence paid off: Congress passed the Railroad Safety Appliance Act. The railroads had to install basic safety devices. Employee accidents dropped sharply soon after, and passenger fatalities fell to almost nothing compared to the former rate. Oddly enough, the railroads soon became ardent proponents of safety measures when they found that those measures produced tremendous savings. There were reduced losses of equipment, fewer injuries and deaths, and operations could be carried on much more rapidly and with fewer interruptions of service.

In the past few years, two new types of safety have developed: *product safety* and *system safety*. The aim of both is the same: prevention of injury and damage. Product safety and system safety grew out of the need to reduce the tremendous losses that resulted from accidents every year. Injuries and deaths are deplored, but more frequently the economic factors constitute the motivating force that produces corrective action. Injuries and death constitute an important factor and a moral requirement when safety is considered, but they lack the broad applicability that use of the dollar provides as a measure. Other considerations include loss of function, especially in military systems, where mission capabilities, attrition rates, and the availability of operating units can be seriously affected by accidents. System safety was therefore developed by the military services.

Product Safety and System Safety

The Department of Defense revealed early in 1969 that its losses in Southeast Asia alone, up to 31 December 1968, were 1,246 fixed-wing aircraft and 982 helicopters through enemy action and 1,247 fixed-wing aircraft and 1,293 helicopters in accidents. The total cost for losses due to accidents was approximately $2.5 billion. This figure does not include material losses by the Department of Defense in other areas of the world; other types of equipment, such as submarines, missiles, or ground vehicles; or losses by other agencies of the government. During this

Military Losses

period, another accident resulted in the loss of one of two B-70's which had been built at a cost of $1.5 billion. Theoretically, therefore, the accident caused the loss of $750 million for the B-70, plus the loss of the aircraft that hit it, costs for death and injury to pilots, and other related costs.

From 1952 to 1966, the Air Force lost 7,715 aircraft in accidents (in which 8,547 persons, including 3,822 pilots were killed). Concentrated and sustained accident prevention efforts reduced the number of aircraft destroyed from 789 in 1952 to 262 in 1966. The loss rate dropped from 9.9 aircraft per 100,000 flight hours to 3.7 aircraft. If the 1952 loss rate had continued, 12,000 aircraft would have been destroyed during the 15 years. Similarly, monetary losses in 1966 would have been between $3.5 to $5.0 billion per year at the 1952 loss rate of $241 million per year. This figure is calculated on the fact that the cost of aircraft in 1966 was six to nine times that of comparable 1952 aircraft. These costs are shown in the following table. New aircraft, such as the F-111, F-14, and F-15, are even higher in cost. (Each F-15 may cost $12 million).

	1952		1966	
USE OF AIRCRAFT	AIRCRAFT	COST	AIRCRAFT	COST
Against ground targets	F-84	$237,247	F-105D	$2,136,668
Against other fighters	F-86E	219,457	F-4C	1,898,365
Against bombers	F-94C	534,073	F-106B	3,564,525

Harris lists a typical program for acquisition of a new aircraft by the Department of Defense.* It presumes that 10 combat and 2 training squadrons will each require 18 operational aircraft, a total of 216, as unit equipment. An attrition allowance of 3.06 per cent of unit equipment per operating year is projected over a five-year period. Attrition is generally another expression for losses through accidents. The study indicates that 33 aircraft will be lost in accidents and require replacement over the five years. In the case of fighters, an average cost of $6 million each can be presumed, with a total loss of $198 million over that time. The loss over an expected program duration of 13 years is estimated at 58 aircraft; value: approximately $348 million. Avoiding the loss of one aircraft a year would generate savings of $78 million.

Oddly enough, it was more the concern with unmanned systems, the intercontinental ballistic missiles (ICBMs), that led to the development of the system safety concept. Until then, the philosophy had been that a pilot was a daring individual who liked to, took pride in, and had to live with hazards. Otherwise, why was he a pilot? And that was the reason that he drew flight pay. Hazards due to failures were so common and pilots were so successful in bringing home sick aircraft that this became the accepted course of action, rather than eliminating or minimizing the causes of the failures. Since the pilot was the most versatile element in the system, he was taught to overcome a wide variety of in-flight problems that might occur. One of the first things a student pilot was taught was how to make a "dead stick" landing. In fact, as late as the mid-fifties, military pilots were often criticized by their colleagues if they abandoned an aircraft that lost its power. Instead of eliminating the deficiencies that caused emergencies, designers devoted

The Need for Safety Programs

* N. D. Harris, "Forecasting Military Aircraft," *Space/Aeronautics*, October 1968, pp. 54–63.

much time and effort to developing emergency procedures and equipment to be used when failures occurred. This overdependence on the pilot's ability precluded earlier application of accident prevention principles to the elimination of engineering deficiencies.

Advent of the ballistic missiles illustrated one outstanding fact: There was no driver, no pilot, no one aboard a missile when it was involved in an accident during flight. There was no human present who could generate the accident. It became obvious that the problem lay in the design and production of the missile.

Indeed, personnel have usually been considered the primary cause of accidents, even though they have also prevented accidents by taking corrective and timely action when equipment malfunctioned. Man is superb in such situations and cannot be surpassed in the ability to overcome unforeseen conditions and problems. A comparatively minor malfunction during flight of a missile, unlike a manned aircraft, frequently results in its complete destruction. Computers aboard missiles are no match for trained men when failures, damage, or other unprogrammed events occur.

It was apparent that many safety problems could be solved only by good design. The system safety (and product safety) concept is predicated on this principle: The most effective means to avoid accidents during system operation is by eliminating or reducing hazards and dangers during design and development.

Product safety was made a national issue when the number of deaths and injuries from automobile accidents reached the level of a major catastrophe that occurred each year. The federal government was provoked into establishing regulatory requirements for public and government safety. This regulator activity was then extended to other products, such as household appliances. Even more compelling were the increases in the number of liability suits generated because of accidents and in the size of awards and settlements that resulted.

Nonmilitary Accident Losses

Examples of tremendous losses can also be cited from nonmilitary activities. For years, annual nonmilitary losses have exceeded $20 billion. The data do not include accidental losses of government property (which is uninsured); commercial, general or corporate aviation; railroad vehicles, or shipping. The problems with which one industry, the railroads, have been plagued, and the losses entailed are shown in Fig. 1-1. One item is repeated here for emphasis: "In 1967, the latest year for which figures are available, accidents cost the nation's railroads $266.3 million in out-of-pocket expenses—a figure equal to *more than half of the net income of all U.S. railroads that year.*"*

A potential for even greater losses exists in the possibility of accidents involving jumbo jets. Insurance underwriters have estimated that "the 747, carrying 360 passengers in initial service, will have a probable loss potential of $55 million, and infinitely more in case of injury or damage to persons or property on the ground. If passenger loads grow to 500 or 1,000, the probable loss rises to $125 million."† Since the cost of the 747 itself is estimated at $20 million each, the passenger loss

* Italics by the author. Statement from the *Wall Street Journal*, 26 June 1969, p. 1.

† W. H. Gregory, "747 Looms as Insurance Test Case," *Aviation Week and Space Technology*, 2 January 1967, p. 25.

Rail Wrecks
Railroad Accidents Soar To Nearly 100 Per Day, But Blame Is in Dispute

New Government Regulation May Result; Speeds Cut; 'So Far We've Been Lucky'

A Stationary Engine Derails

By TODD E. FANDELL
Staff Reporter of **THE WALL STREET JOURNAL**

CHICAGO — "So far we've been lucky," says a top offical of a midwestern railroad. "One of these days we're going to wipe a whole town right off the map."

The man is talking about railroad accidents, and he isn't exaggerating. Already this year, Laurel, Miss., and Crete, Neb., were almost wiped off the map. In Laurel, a derailment resulted in explosions of tank cars that killed two people, hospitalized 33, demolished 54 homes and two factories and damaged 1,350 homes, four factories, six schools, five churches and 100 small businesses. Total damage was $3.5 million. In Crete, a derailment ruptured a tank car, which spread a deadly chemical mist over the town, killing nine persons and injuring 40.

Those figures are astonishing enough, but here are some more:

— There now are around 30,000 railroad accidents a year — approaching 100 a day. The number of accidents where damage to railroad property totaled $750 or more was 8,028 in 1968, up 83% from 4,378 in 1962, despite a decline in miles traveled.

— There now are about 15 derailments a day, compared with nine in 1964.

— Last year 2,359 persons were killed in railroad accidents and 24,608 were injured. In contrast, 351 persons died in airline accidents.

— And in 1967, the latest year for which figures are available, accidents cost the nation's railroads $266.3 million in out-of-pocket expenses—a figure equal to more than half of the net income of all U.S. railroads that year.

Some Causes

What's the matter? It depends on whom you talk to, but there apparently are several reasons for the rash of accidents. Negligence, faulty rolling stock and improper maintenance or defects in track are about equally to blame as the immediate causes of the accidents. But the underlying causes are in dispute or unknown.

"There is nothing being done in the way of research," says the president of one big road. He says he was appalled at the inadequacy of the answers he was given when he recently began a personal investigation into a costly rise in the number of derailments on his line. He says he would ask for the cause and be told it was a broken rail. But no one ever seemed to know how or why the rail broke. "To say the cause is a broken rail and drop it at that is ridiculous," he says. "But that's what we've been doing."

One reason rails are breaking is that roads are using bigger, longer, heavier and faster trains on the same old track and roadbeds. But why the tracks and roadbeds haven't been improved along with the rolling stock seems to be unanswerable. Unions blame the managements. The managements blame the unions and the Government. And the Government syas it doesn't know who's at fault — but that somebody better do something quick to halt the rise in wrecks.

Indeed, mounting public concern is likely to prompt Congress to give the Department of Transportation broad powers to establish and enforce comprehensive safety regulations for the railroads, which are the only major mode of transportation not covered by copious safety rules.

"Safety Can't Be Legislated"

Talk of such regulation doesn't sit well with railroad officals. "Safety can't be legislated," asserts Thomas M. Goodfellow, president of the Association of American Railroads. Other railroad executives say that instead of legislating safety the Government should let the roads raise rates so they could afford to buy better equipment and make more frequent repairs. In support of this argument, they say that richer roads have better safety records than the poorer ones.

The richer roads do, in fact, have better safety records. The well-heeled Union Pacific, for instance, had 4.2 accidents per million miles traveled in 1967. The loss-ridden Missouri-Kansas-Texas Railraod had the worst record that year, 33.3 accidents per million miles. The Katy's track is so bad that a few years ago an engine derailed while standing still.

On the whole, claims Harold C. Crotty, president of the Brotherhood of Maintenance of Way Employes, "rail and tie replacement work has been neglected and, as a direct consequence, railway accidents caused by track and roadway defects have increased."

Cutting Top Speed

Mr. Crotty says that a decline in maintenance of way workers to 88,000 from 251,000 in 1951 reflects a decline in inspection and maintenance standards. The roads reply that the drop in maintenance workers instead reflects improved work methods, materials and mechanization. And some road executives say they could afford to hire more maintenance workers were it not for union "featherbedding" practices in in other areas that eat up railroad money.

Wherever the blame rests, a number of roads are taking steps to cut down the accident rates. Some have ordered lower maximum speeds for freight trains. The Soo Line, for instance, has trimmed its freights' maximum speed to 40 miles an hour from 60. "It was one of a number of steps we took to do something short range about the accident problem while we stepped up study efforts to discover causes and long-term solutions," says a spokesman. A large Western road has cut its top speed to 50 from 70 miles an hour.

The cutting of speeds hasn't been publicized, and most industry officals don't like to talk about it. "That's rather embarrassing and sure won't help us in Washington," says one official, who fears legislators will interpret the moves as admission of unsafe conditions.

Fig. 1-1. Article from the WALL STREET JOURNAL, 26 June 1969.

could initially be $35 million and ultimately $105 million for one accident. The same article went on to indicate that even with lower accident rates than those of present commercial jet aircraft, aviation insurance losses for operation of 200 aircraft with an average load of 500 passengers could be in excess of $1 billion over a five-year period.

Figure 1-2 indicates some types of losses that can result from an accident. Not all are applicable to every organization or activity. Almost all of these can be evaluated in terms of dollar costs; in general these costs are readily determinable through normal accounting procedures. Replacement costs of the equipment lost, medical and legal fees, legal judgments, costs to correct deficiencies that caused the accident, and increases in insurance rates can be determined directly. Loss of public

Accident Costs

Figure 1-2

COST OF AN ACCIDENT

Personnel Losses

1. Death, injury, or shock to personnel involved in the accident

2. Time of personnel involved in rescue

3. Medical fees, such as for doctors, nurses, hospitals, ambulances

4. Disability costs of personnel badly injured

5. Rehabilitation costs for those who have lost limbs, mental abilities, or physical skills

6. Funeral expenses for personnel killed in the accident

7. Pensions for injured persons or for dependents of those killed

8. Loss of skills, experience, and training

9. Training costs and lower output of replacements

10. Lost time of other personnel, such as those involved with management or public relations

Equipment and Material Losses

12. Costs of rescue equipment required

13. Nonrecoverable expenditures of emergency and survival equipment

14. Replacement cost of vehicle or equipment that generated the damage

15. Replacement cost of other equipment, vehicles, or property damaged or lost

16. Recovery and salvage of damaged equipment and vehicles

17. Obsolescence of equipment associated with vehicle or equipment destroyed

Corrective Actions

18. Accident investigation and reporting

19. Actions required to correct deficiencies that caused an accident, including recall costs

20. Slowdown in operations while accident causes are determined and corrective actions taken

Other

21. Fees for legal actions related to product liability and safety

22. Loss of function, production, or income

23. Increased insurance rates

24. Loss of public confidence

25. Loss of prestige

26. Deterioration of morale

confidence can be estimated by a decrease in sales. An airline that suffers a series of crashes, no matter the cause or where the fault lay, can expect a serious drop in passenger bookings and revenues.

A few costs, such as loss of prestige or deterioration of morale are much more difficult to evaluate monetarily, but even these can sometimes be estimated. The public relations effort to restore prestige to the preaccident level can be measured. Deterioration of morale can be equated to dollar values in terms of reduced output, replacement costs of personnel who resign or are released, and higher absentee rates.

Two accidents involving helicopters of a California airline illustrate some losses that can result. The first accident occurred on 22 May 1968, when all 24 persons aboard a helicopter were killed; the second on 14 August 1968, when 21 persons died. Flight operations were halted immediately after the second accident, eliminating all income for a week. Operations were then resumed on a restricted schedule for another week, during which half the normal 118 flights per day were conducted. The manufacturer of the helicopters, among others, sent personnel to assist in the investigations of both accidents to determine the causes. On 16 August, the Federal Aviation Agency (FAA) issued an airworthiness directive, which grounded most of the same helicopters operated by other airlines until corrective action could be taken.

Some of the immediate effects, on which dollar values could be placed with little effort, included:

- A suit for $1,250,000 was filed on behalf of a widow and child of one passenger against the airline and the manufacturer within 48 hours after the second accident. The charge against the airline was that the helicopter had been negligently and carelessly operated. The manufacturer was sued because the helicopter had been negligently and carelessly designed and manufactured.

- A month later, another suit was filed for $2,000,000 on behalf of another widow and four children. Other suits on behalf of dependents of other passengers were also expected.

- On 21 August, another airline, a major company, postponed the purchase of five similar helicopters, produced by the same manufacturer, worth approximately $5,800,000.

- On the basis of the costs just mentioned, the replacement cost of each helicopter lost was $1,160,000.

- The total income for the airline during the previous year had been $4,500,000. If we prorate this amount over a week and a half, the loss of income due to cessation and restriction of operations was $130,500. In addition, the income lost while awaiting a new helicopter was substantial, especially since the company's entire fleet had formerly consisted of only six helicopters.

- The loss of confidence by the public in the safety of helicopters was such that the airline purchased and made arrangements for the use of fixed-wing aircraft over certain of its routes, and used helicopters only where fixed-wing aircraft were impracticable.

- On 11 October 1970, the airline ceased operations and initiated bankruptcy proceedings.

The amounts of the legal suits mentioned leads to the question: How much is a man's life worth? Almost everyone recognizes that there is a moral obligation to minimize any possibility of an accident that could cause injury or death. Unfortunately, funds available for development and production of a new system are generally limited so that judicious compromise must be made between mission requirements, cost, and safety. How much should be spent on any safety feature that would save a man's life? In a multimillion-dollar system, the expenditure of $10,000 to save a man's life would probably be agreed to immediately; a requirement to spend $5,000,000 for that purpose would be doubtful. Somewhere between these two extremes is a range of values in which doubt would exist as to whether or not the cost could be borne. The value of a man's life then becomes a matter of dollars and cents. There have been numerous ways in which this has been computed.

Eleven states have prescribed limitations on the amount a victim's dependents can collect if someone else is held liable for his death in an accident. Examples are: Colorado, $20,000; Illinois, $30,000; Kansas, $25,000; and Minnesota, $25,000. Other states with similar limitations are Massachusetts, Missouri, New Hampshire, Oregon, South Dakota, Virginia, and Wisconsin. (In many instances, these limitations have little value since the plaintiff will generally file suit in a jurisdiction other than these states. An automobile manufacturer could be sued in Michigan, California, New Jersey, or any other location where the car was designed, manufactured, assembled, or sold, or where the company was headquartered.) Other states have no limitations. Internationally, liabilities are sometimes limited by agreement among countries whose nationals could be involved. For example, current maximum liability for a passenger on an international airline is restricted by the Warsaw Convention to $75,000 per person (recently increased from $8,300).

Another aspect of these laws and agreements should be pointed out. Suits for accidental deaths are generally brought on behalf of surviving dependents, and the life of a person who has no dependents has little or no legal value. A baby is in this category in this respect (although suit may be brought on any of many other grounds), and so is a man or woman with no child, spouse, father, mother, or other person dependent on his support.

Awards made by courts are computed in a variety of ways. By one method, it is predicated on the total income a victim could have earned had he lived his full normal life expectancy, less his cost of living, and calculated on the basis of accrual of interest.* For example, a judgment of $10,000 per year for 20 years is $128,000 not $200,000. This is determined through use of an interest rate of 5 percent on the amount awarded and on the remaining principal as sums are withdrawn to provide $10,000 per year for 20 years.† There are other legal methods by which

---

* This assumes other damages are not awarded. In 1971, a California jury awarded $21,747,000 to the families of four men killed in the crash of a private aircraft and to the owner of the plane, for negligence in design of the plane's fuel system. Actual awards to the families were $2,000,000, $1,250,000, $1,000,000, and $165,000 for losses of the heads of their families, and $82,000 to its owner for the plane. However, punitive damages of $3,450,000 each were also awarded to the plaintiffs.

† J. Lederer, V. A. Taylor, and R. E. Glubiak, *Development of a Technique for Estimating the Cost of General Aviation Accidents* (New York, New York: Flight Safety Foundation, July 1966).

courts have computed the value of a man's life (or his injuries). In each case counsel for the plaintiff selects the method most advantageous to his client.

A report prepared for the Federal Aviation Agency in 1962 states that the average age of persons killed in commercial aircraft accidents is 40. It then makes the following calculations:

"For persons involved in fatal aircraft accidents, this (present value of his earning stream) amounts to an average of $210,000 for the year 1960. This is based on an average salary of $13,000 for an air carrier passenger, a yearly salary increase of $2\frac{1}{2}\%$, assets of $25,000 and 40 as the average age at death. Of this amount, $185,000 represents the loss to the economy in the form of decreased output."* (Oddly enough, the average age of 40 indicated in the report is precisely that of the helicopter passenger for whose dependents the first suit was brought.)

The date of the report should be noted. The tremendous increase in the sizes of claims undoubtedly will keep this average increasing continually. Two examples can be cited. The family of a man killed in an aircraft accident in 1963 later collected $1,250,000 in settlement of a suit against the manufacturer. In Chicago awards in the three liability suits brought to court in 1960 averaged $1,400 each; in 1966 one award was for $725,000 and the remaining seven averaged $34,000 apiece. The increase in average size of awards is indicative of what can be expected in the future.

Replacement Method   The life of a man with no dependents may have no legal value because of his lack of dependents, but his death could result in financial loss to an organization for which he has functional value and in which he must be replaced.

A man may therefore be considered as a subsystem. His loss can then be evaluated as the cost required to provide a comparable replacement. For example, the military services have had studies made on expenditures to recruit, train, feed, clothe, and otherwise maintain and pay a man; the indemnities that would accrue to his family; and other costs such as burial expense.

One study for the Air Force on a man's value was predicated on the investment required for him to reach his rank and capabilities, less the return to the government from years of service.† These costs are listed in Fig. 1-3. Recent changes in training costs, especially for flight-rated personnel, have produced changes that have increased these costs substantially, especially in the benefits that accrue to dependents. However, even at the time of this study, the basic cost of replacing a man depended chiefly on payments to his family and were a minimum of approximately $40,000.

This study has one major fallacy: A captain or lieutenant trained as a pilot has a value much higher than that of a senior officer. No value was placed on the experience accumulated over the years by each officer as he rose to higher and higher rank and command. Reasoning based on these results should logically conclude that it is uneconomical to expose a pilot, lieutenant, or captain to any hazard, especially combat,

The Need for Safety Programs

10

* G. Fromm, *Economic Criteria for Federal Aviation Agency Expenditures* (United Research Corporation, June 1962).

† C. Mathewson and C. Brenner, *Re-evaluation of USAF Injury and Fatality Cost Standards*, Report No. 63–16 (University of California at Los Angeles; March 1963).

COST OF USAF MILITARY FATALITIES*

RANK/GRADE	PILOT	OBS/NAV	OTHER
Colonel	$ 56,146	$ 56,146	$ 56,146
Lt. Colonel	54,003	56,003	56,003
Major	63,964	55,969	54,748
Captain	132,626	74,126	54,269
1st Lieutenant	228,543	99,453	55,595
2nd Lieutenant	274,524	102,144	46,642
Warrant Officer	41,013	40,623	40,290
Officer Candidate			1,464
Air Cadet			1,464
E7, 8, 9			42,357
E6			44,091
E5			44,936
E4			38,050
E3			21,047
E2			10,853
E1			10,817

* Mathewson and Brenner, *Re-evaluation of USAF Injury and Fatality Cost Standards,* Report No. 63-16; (University of California at Los Angeles: March 1963).

AVERAGES FOR MILITARY PERSONNEL

Type of Injury	Recommended value
Fatality	$35,000
Permanent Total Disability	82,000
Permanent Partial Disability	52,000
Temporary Total Disability	$50 per day
Nondisabling (Minor) Injury	$14 per injury

Figure 1-3

before the investment in his training is repaid. Lieutenant colonels and colonels are most expendable and should be used first. One way to measure the worth of experience would be to average the total pay the person received until the time of his death and increase it by a given percentage for each year of experience to reflect the rising costs of replacements.

In a later report, a Navy representative indicated that in 1966 the training investment to bring a naval aviator to the rank of Navy lieutenant commander or Marine major cost approximately $1,250,000.* Even more costly were the 10 years required to replace such a man with one of equal experience. Each day, an average of 0.7 lives of pilots and crew members

* R. E. Luehrs, "Human Error and Research Program (HEARP)," Paper presented at the 23rd Annual Meeting of the Advisory Group for Aerospace Research and Development (AGARD) Medical Panel, Toronto, Canada; Conference Proceedings No. 14 on Assessment of Skill and Performance in Flying (September 1966). p. 7.

were lost, with an additional loss in equipment of approximately $1,000,000. A few years ago, an accident involved losses expressed in thousands of dollars; now loss of a modern aircraft and crew is valued in millions of dollars.

Insurance Aspects

In some instances, the value of a man's life is indicated by the amount of insurance that would be payable on his death. Where he himself takes out the insurance, he is providing an expression of his estimate of his value to his dependents. In other cases, an organization of which he is a part makes an estimate of his value similar to that indicated in the preceding paragraph regarding replacement costs. The organization considers the man an asset and his loss would be to its detriment.

Injuries

In 1967, the average amount paid for a claim for bodily injury suffered as the result of an automobile accident was $1.583.[*] Lederer indicates that the average amount paid for an injury incurred in a general aviation (nonairline) accident is ten times as much, approximately $15,000.[†] This figure is predicated on data that serious injuries average $35,000, and nonserious ones, which are twice as numerous, $4,500. A common definition of serious injury is any injury which:

- Requires hospitalization for more than 48 hours, commencing within seven days from the date the injury was received
- Involves lacerations which cause severe hemorrhages, nerve, muscle or tendon damage
- Involves injury to any internal organ
- Involves second- or third-degree burns, or any burns affecting more than five percent of the body surface

Other ways to obtain dollar costs of injuries are from tables issued for workmen's compensation or in accident insurance policies for loss of limbs, eyes, or bodily functions.

A fatality may be considered the ultimate injury, but judgments to persons badly injured in accidents often far exceed awards to families for deaths of persons on whom they were dependent. Generally, these have occurred in cases of complete disability in which providers with dependents not only lose their abilities to earn incomes but would require complete and intensive care by others for the remainder of their lives. Awards in such cases have been increasing each year. In 1968, an injured man received an award of $1,750,000; his brother, injured in the same accident, received a lesser amount. The details are quoted in a letter from the attorney for the injured men, except that names have been deleted:[‡]

> The plaintiffs were injured due to a defectively designed platform. This
> was part of an experimental space program of NASA at Moffett Field. The

[*] *Insurance Facts,* (New York: Insurance Information Institute, 1970).

[†] J. Lederer, V. A. Taylor, and R. E. Glubiak, *Development of a Technique for Estimating the Cost of General Aviation Accidents* (New York: New York; Flight Safety Foundation, July 1966).

[‡] Letter from James F. Boccardo of Boccardo, Blum, Lull, Niland, Teerlink & Bell, San Jose, Calif., 6 May 1969.

platform was affixed to a concrete projection on the side of the building approximately 35 feet above the floor of the building and had a hinged section that could be drawn up into a vertical position when not in use and then lowered to a horizontal position to permit astronauts to walk across it and into a simulated space ship. The platform was designed to carry a load of some 3,000 pounds and collapsed under the weight of two men, who were plaintiffs in the action.

One received $178,000.00 and the other $750,000.00, both awards being in addition to all their medical expenses. The most seriously injured is a paralyzed, brain-injured individual who will require continuous hospitalization and medical care for the balance of his life expectancy of some 32 years. Medical evidence indicated that these expenditures would amount to $1,000,000, or more. Although normally the workmen's compensation carrier would be entitled to be subrogated to his award and be reimbursed out of his award, settlement was made with the compensation carrier, by the terms of which it waived any right to reimbursement, so that the net result was that the injured man received the jury's verdict of $750,000.00, plus his medical expenses, thus totaling $1,750,000.00. I believe this to be one of the largest awards in the country and exceeds an award of $1,400,000.00 which I received for a client in Santa Ana. Injuries were comparable in each case.

Liability was fastened on the engineers and architects who designed the platform. The evidence disclosed that the manner in which they designed the stops which would hold the platform in a horizontal position did not measure up to acceptable standards of good engineering and architectural practice, and that they were negligent in the manner in which they designed the platform. Evidence of engineers supported the plaintiff's position that the standard of care of an ordinarily prudent engineer and architect was not adhered to by the defendant.

In December 1970, a client represented by Mr. Boccardo and two associates won the highest award to date for injury: $3,650,000. The decision is being appealed.

Awards Versus Settlements

Data on costs of accidents are frequently difficult to establish by anyone not immediately connected with a specific case. A suit can be brought for a large amount, an award by a court or jury may be less, and this sum may be reduced or voided by a higher court on appeal. In many instances, a settlement takes place out of court for a sum far below that which a jury would have awarded. The amounts involved in such settlements are usually not made public. It is almost impossible, therefore, to compare the award a jury might have made if a settlement had not been made.

A unique occurrence, which permits a comparison to be made, took place in Los Angeles early in 1971. A man injured in a helicopter crash accepted a settlement of his claim (for $500,000) while a jury was considering his case. He agreed to accept $35,000; the jury's award, made almost at the same time, was announced as $180,000.

The loss that a company or its insurer may sustain can therefore depend on the financial circumstances of the plaintiff, whether he is willing and capable of waiting until his case can be tried, and his or his counsel's estimate of whether the verdict will be favorable and its size. Another uncertain factor is the attitude of the jury, each one being different. Juries appear to be increasing the sizes of their awards for numerous reasons, a prominent one being an antipathy for insurance companies who, they believe, will be the ones to pay.

Reducing Losses   Insurance generally does not repay the entire monetary loss resulting from an accident (intangible losses are rarely covered, and punitive damages may not be, since they are intended to punish the liable company, not the insurer.) However, the total losses that the insurance companies sustain because of accidents is tremendous. Awards made by courts or settlements of claims outside courts are increasing each year. It may be expected that insurance companies will take steps to minimize these types of losses as they did by requiring that boilers be designed, built, and periodically inspected and tested in accordance with the provisions of the American Society of Mechanical Engineers (ASME) Code For Power Boilers, or its equivalent.

Some possibilities of actions that the insurance companies might undertake include:

- More intensive analyses of risks involved with any product, system, or operation that they are asked to insure
- Requirements on manufacturers to conduct safety analyses of products they intend to market
- Setting insurance premiums for an industrial plant's operation by the effectiveness of the company's continuing safety program and the safety analyses it has undertaken

chapter 2

LIABILITIES FOR ACCIDENTS

When thou buildest a new house, then thou shalt make a battlement for thy roof, that thou bring not blood upon thine house, if any man fall from thence.— Deuteronomy 22 : 8

Today, the "houses" we build are more complex, the precautions that they require are much more intricate than the "battlements" of the Bible, and the possible injuries are much more serious. For many centuries, however, this precept was considered law only by a few religionists. But in the last few years civil laws for liability have begun to approach the Biblical admonition of taking adequate precautions to avoid accidents or of being liable for injuries. Two principal factors have generated this change: gradual modification of judicial opinion and passage of new legislation. To understand what these factors have meant, the changes will be pointed out. Pertinent terms are defined in Fig. 2-1.

Recent interpretations regarding liabilities for accidents indicate that judicial attitudes are not fixed and can change drastically to new attitudes. In this country, there are numerous legal doctrines and principles that have been held to be true in all or most of the states for a very long time. Some of these are cited in Fig. 2-2. However, it must

Figure 2-1

TERMS COMMONLY EMPLOYED IN PRODUCT LIABILITY

Care —   Great care: That high degree of care that a very prudent and cautious person would undertake for the safety of others. Common carriers, such as airlines, bus companies, and railroads, must exercise a high degree of care.

Reasonable care: That degree of care exercised by a prudent man in observance of his legal duties towards others.

Slight care: That degree of care less than that which a prudent man would exercise.

Express warranty — A statement by a manufacturer or dealer, either in writing or orally, that his product is suitable for a specific purpose, will perform in a specific way, or contains specific safeguards.

Implied warranty — The implication by a manufacturer or dealer that his product is suitable for a specific purpose by: (1) placing it on sale for that purpose, (2) advertising that it will satisfy that purpose, or (3) indicating in operating instructions that it will accomplish that purpose.

Liability — An obligation to rectify or recompense any injury or damage for which the liable person has been held responsible or for failure of a product to meet a warranty.

Negligence — Failure to exercise a reasonable amount of care or to carry out a legal duty so that injury or property damage occurs to another.

Negligence per se — No proof of negligence required since it involves acts or the omission of acts of which no careful person would have been guilty.

Privity — Privity indicates a direct relationship between two persons or parties, such as between a seller and buyer. If *A* manufactures a product that is sold to dealer *B* who sells it to consumer *C*, privity exists between *A* and *B* and *B* and *C*, but not between *A* and *C*.

Proximate cause — The relationship between the plaintiff's injuries and the defendant's failure to exercise a legal duty, such as reasonable care. Example: *A* playfully pushes *B* in a crowded space, so *C* is hit by *B*, loses his balance, falls, and is injured. *A*'s push is the proximate cause of *C*'s accident.

Strict liability — The growing concept that a manufacturer of a product is liable for injuries due to defects, without a necessity for a plaintiff to show negligence or fault.

Tort —   A wrongful act or failure to exercise due care for which civil legal action may result.

SOME FUNDAMENTAL LEGAL PRINCIPLES

PRINCIPLE	EXPLANATION
Exercise of due care	Every person has a legal duty to exercise due care for the safety of others and to avoid injury to another if possible.
Standard of reasonable prudence	A person who owes a legal duty must exercise the same care that a reasonably prudent man would observe under similar circumstances.
Foreseeability	A man may be held liable for actions that result in injury or damage only when he was able to foresee dangers and risks that could be reasonably anticipated.
Foreseeability for safe design	A manufacturer must be reasonably careful in designing and producing a product to avoid injuring others by exposing them to possible dangers, or he is liable for damages. Where hazards cannot be eliminated, he is obligated to warn any prospective user of inherent dangers or properties of the product.
Inherent danger of a product	A manufacturer must employ reasonable care to warn all prospective purchasers and legal users of hazards involved and of any inherently dangerous conditions in the product.
Obvious peril	A manufacturer is not required to warn prospective users of products whose use involves an obvious peril, especially those that are well known to the general public.
Responsibility for handling	A distributor, wholesaler, or retailer must exercise reasonable care in the handling and preservation of a product in their possession so that it will not later cause injury to a user.
Foreseeability applied to rescue	Any foreseeable act that places a rescuer in the same danger as an injured person the rescuer is attempting to aid is considered negligence by the person who commited the initial act.
Res ipsa loquitur (The thing speaks for itself)	The principle that occurrence of an accident is sufficient proof that negligence existed. For the principle to apply, the item causing the accident must have been under the sole control of the defendant; the accident would not have occurred if proper care had been exercised by the defendant; and there was no contributory negligence on the part of the plaintiff.
Dangerous instrumentality	A person who keeps, maintains, transports, or stores a dangerous creature, device or substance is liable for injury or damage, regardless of fault, even when he exercises due care.

Figure 2-2

PRINCIPLE	EXPLANATION
Fright without physical contact	At one time it was considered that a plaintiff could not recover damages unless injury was due to physical contact. This principle has been modified or repudiated over the years by many states to permit a plaintiff to collect damages for neurological or emotional disturbances that occurred without physical injury.
Joint tort liabilities	When an injury is caused by two or more persons, each of which failed in a legal duty, they are in joint tort. The degree of suffering from each injury may then be assessed against the plaintiffs individually in case of successive injuries, or jointly in a concurrent injury.
Contributory negligence	When an injured person's care for his own safety was less than that reasonable for a prudent man under existing conditions, he is considered negligent and the defendant will not be held liable.
Assumption of risk	A person who is aware of a danger and its extent, and knowingly exposes himself, assumes all risks and cannot recover damages even though he is injured through no fault of his own.

Fig. 2-2. Continued.

be pointed out that interpretations of these principles are being broadened more and more in favor of injured parties.

Privity

Even though the principles indicated in Fig. 2-2 had already long been established, injured persons or dependents of anyone killed in an accident had difficulty in even bringing a suit to court. This was because of the relationship known as the *privity rule.*

An early decision in an English accident case involving negligence (*Winterbottom* v. *Wright,* 1842) held there could be no liability unless there was privity. A direct relationship between the injured party and the party whose negligence was the cause of the accident had to exist. The legal decision that first began to destroy the rule of no liability without privity came in 1916 in the case of *MacPherson* v. *Buick Motor Company.* This landmark case was based on an accident caused when a wheel collapsed on the automobile in which the plaintiff was moving at a speed of approximately 25 mph. The plaintiff was thrown from the car and injured. He had purchased the car from a dealer, who had bought it for resale from the Buick Company. A subcontractor had supplied the wheels to the automobile manufacturer. Suit was brought against the manufacturer of the car.

The automobile manufacturer based its defense on the privity rule. The company had sold the car to the dealer, had no contract with the injured party, and was therefore not liable to the plaintiff. The dealer was not liable since he had not manufactured the car. Judge Benjamin Cardozo ruled, however, that the car manufacturer was responsible. He stated that the manufacturer had a duty to inspect the products for defects; failure to do so was negligence.

If the nature of a thing is such that it is reasonably certain to place life and limb in peril when negligently made, it is a thing of danger; and if to the element of danger there is added knowledge that the thing will be used by persons other than the purchaser, then the manufacturer of the thing of danger is under a duty to make it carefully.*

The decision stated that lack of privity should not affect a plaintiff's right to recover for his injuries. As a result of this decision, it became possible to bring suit against anyone in the chain of relationships from manufacturer to the ultimate seller.

MacPherson v. *Buick Motor Company* pointed up another fact: Suit can be directed toward a manufacturer for failure of a component produced by a subcontractor for installation in his equipment. A plaintiff may, and often does, sue for both negligence in design or manufacture and failure to maintain control of product quality.

Another major change in legal doctrine involved the formulation and expression of the idea of *strict liability.* Until 1963, a plaintiff in an accident suit had to prove either that a warranty affecting the well-being of a person had been breached or that negligence existed. In that year, the doctrine of strict liability was enunciated by the California Supreme Court. It has since been adopted by 20 or more other states. In rendering its decision, the California Supreme Court stated:

Strict Liability

The purpose of such liability is to insure that the costs of injuries resulting from defective products are borne by the manufacturer that puts such products on the market rather than by the injured persons who are powerless to protect themselves.

. . .

A manufacturer is strictly liable in tort when the article he places on the market, knowing it will be sold without inspection for defects, proves to have a defect that causes injury to a human being.†

The concept of strict liability, or liability without fault, has greatly reduced the need for the plaintiff to show negligence on the part of a manufacturer, assembler, or retailer. The courts have held that since the plaintiff generally does not have the technical capabilities necessary to prove a negligence existed, the burden of proof is on the manufacturer to show it did *not*. The plaintiff could recover damages if he could reasonably show that a product had a dangerous defect (in design, manufacture, or other aspect) when it left the manufacturer, was the cause of injury or damage, and that he himself was free from negligence in the use of the product. The manufacturer then had to *prove* that he was not negligent or that the user was negligent himself.

User negligence may sometimes constitute the basis of a successful defense against a liability suit if it can be shown that the accident was due to an error that was a violation of a proper warning or of reasonable prudence. The limits of "reasonable prudence" (Fig. 2-2) have been almost impossibly difficult to define with any degree of nicety. A person may be in a car hit by another car whose driver is at fault. If the person in the car that was hit suffers injuries whose severities could have been mitigated by use of seat belts, the award may be predicated on whether

* 217 N.Y. 382 (1916)

† Greenman v. Yuba Power Products, 377 Pac. 2d 897 (1963)

seat belts were available, and if they were, whether they were worn at the time of the accident. If they were not worn, the question arises as to whether the injured person should have known enough to wear them.

The scope of decisions on strict liability not only includes the activities of manufacturers in design, manufacture, advertising, and customer relations but applies also to architects and contractors. Martin points out that the distinguishing characteristics of architects and professional engineers have no effect on liability.*

Warranties

Consider an automobile manufacturer. After careful study, the reliability engineers reach the conclusion, and convince their company managers, that specific assemblies should not fail within 5 years or 50,000 miles of use. To attract customers, a warranty to that effect is provided with each new car sold. After a few years with this warranty program in effect, it is found to be too costly; assemblies are failing more rapidly than predicted. Later warranties are reduced to 2 years or 20,000 miles. Under either of these *express warranties,* the manufacturer will replace any part or assembly that proves defective during the stipulated period. This replacement generally is the limit of his liability.

The express warranty, or any change in express warranty, has nothing to do with the *implied warranty* that the product, by being offered for sale, is reasonably safe for use. The implied warranty for safety is *always* in effect. No express warranty need exist. The implied warranty is limited neither by the period during which the product is in use nor by the liability for damages or injury that may be assessed if an accident occurs. In another landmark case in 1959 (*Henningsen* v. *Bloomfield Motors*), the plaintiff recovered for damages and injuries by successfully claiming a breach of implied warranty of fitness and merchantability. There was no private contract and no attempt was made to prove negligence. Henningsen had purchased a car for his wife. As she drove it a few days later, a part of the steering system failed; she lost control, and the car hit a brick wall.

After *Henningsen* v. *Bloomfield,* it became apparent that every product placed on sale would have a warranty, implied if not expressed, that it is safe unless specific warnings are provided to indicate otherwise. Also, any defective product that could be dangerous subjects the manufacturer to liability even if he has exercised care in producing it or issued a disclaimer of liability in advance.

These conditions should be examined. Any manufacturer who indiscriminately claims his product is safe (by implication, by a specific advertising statement, or by other medium) renders himself extremely vulnerable to a suit should someone be injured.

Warnings of danger must be prominent and located where they cannot fail to be observed by the operator. Warnings in small print or in an instruction manual that the operator may or may not read have been considered inadequate.

The possibility of being held liable for a dangerous product even when care has been exercised in its production involves considerations often neglected. Automobile companies believed that they could not

* A. I. Martin, "Responsibility of Architects and Contractors On Third Party Claims: Employers Insurance of Wausau, Wausau, Wisconsin," *Electrical Construction Design,* Spring 1969, pp. 31–35.

RELIABILITY VERSUS SAFETY

A popular misconception is that by eliminating failures, a product will be safe. A product may be made safer by eliminating or minimizing failures, but there are other causes of accidents: dangerous characteristics of the product, human action, extraordinary environmental factors, or combinations of these. Mishaps often occur where there is no failure.

A product may have high reliability but be afflicted with a dangerous characteristic. The Final Report of the National Commission of Product Safety (June 1970) discusses numerous products that have been injurious because of such deficiencies. In by far the majority of cases, these injuries were the results of hazardous characteristics rather than failures. Examples include:

- A toy oven and a metal casting set with exposed hot surfaces that could burn children seriously

- A toy bazooka that deafened a playmate of the user

- Wringer-washing machines that killed a little girl and crushed hands and arms of users

- Power tools that caused injuries because of lack of effective guards against whirling gears, chains, teeth, blades, or flying fragments

- Baby furniture that caused strangulation of infants

- Floor furnaces with exposed hot surfaces on which children were burned

- Rotary lawnmowers that caused amputations and deep cuts and injuries from thrown objects

Among the most publicized examples of liability suits are those attributed to the hazardous performance of the Corvair so that under certain conditions accidents resulted. The rear end of the Corvair did not fail mechanically in any of the cases for which suit was brought; the claimants cited dangerous characteristics due to negligent design.

Figure 2-3

be held liable for accidents if they maintained strict quality control over their manufacturing processes. Generally, they could be held liable only for items that failed prematurely or in ways in which the warranties had indicated the items would not fail. Others considered that if reliability were high and failures minimized, liabilities would be avoided. Neither belief is correct. A product could be tested intensively and the failure rate be extremely low, but it could have a hazardous characteristic. A TV set might not fail but could give off X-ray radiation. An aircraft might not fail but could be involved in an accident because of an instability. A child's wooden building block would have an almost perfect reliability but be dangerous because its paint was toxic or because the child could be injured by the sharp corners. (See Fig. 2-3.)

Disclaimers of liability have been held invalid since they are unilateral actions on the part of the manufacturers. The purchaser is given no opportunity to rebut the disclaimer. Frequently it is contained in a document, such as an operator's manual, which the purchaser obtains only after he has entered into a contract of sale, giving him no chance to negotiate the conditions.

When a product fails to measure up to its warranty, the manufacturer

Warranties

21

or dealer is liable. In such cases, the plaintiff* must show that the defendant* did make such warranties and that the product failed to live up to them. The burden of proof is on the plaintiff. However, in many instances, manufacturers and dealers have found it good practice to accept any reasonable claim by a customer that the product did not perform properly or was otherwise deficient. In the interest of good public relations, efforts are made to satisfy the customer even when the failure or deficiency was due to such causes as improper installation, operation, or care.

It is becoming more and more the general rule that an express warranty is an aspect of reliability and that safety is an implied warranty. Safety features may also be cited in express warranties, but such citations are becoming fewer, since they increase the vulnerability of a manufacturer to claims for injury or damage.

The privity rule, that a manufacturer or dealer is responsible only to the next person in the chain of sales, had been usual with warranties, but with numerous exceptions, which also seem to be increasing. An automobile manufacturer sells cars to a dealer with the expectation that they will be resold. If a failure occurs that is covered by the warranty issued by the manufacturer, the customer can have the matter rectified at any of the manufacturer's dealers, not only the one from whom he purchased the car. Certain warranties extend for the lifetime of the car or for other specified periods and can be transferred if a resale takes place.

Negligence   The principal basis on which liability claims are made are accidents involving products that were negligently designed, produced, installed, or maintained so that injury or damage occurred. No warranties are necessary for claims of negligence to be made. Negligence may also extend to failure of a manufacturer to perform the duty of warning the potential user of any dangers in use of the product. A product may not be defective but may be inherently hazardous so that suitable precautions must be stipulated. This, in effect, requires a manufacturer to analyze the design of his product and the procedures for its use to ensure that latent defects that cannot be eliminated are adequately controlled and brought to the attention of the user.

Another form of negligence is failure to anticipate all possible uses or misuses. This foreseeability (Fig. 2-1) is an area open to diverse legal opinions. Wise mentions the case of a farmer who was injured when he used a claw hammer to drive a pin into a clevis when connecting a manure spreader to a tractor.† A chip of metal broke off from the hammer and hit him in the eye, resulting in his losing the eye. Defense claimed that the hammer was not being used as intended by the manufacturer; a ball peen hammer should have been used. The court ruled that the defendants had a duty to foresee that the hammer might be used in the manner in which the plaintiff had used it. In this respect, then—foreseeability—they neglected to use "due care."

Claims that negligence existed and that a design was defective can sometimes be denied by showing that good practices common to the

* Use of the word "plaintiff" or "defendant" implies their counsels and any other assistance that they may have in a legal action.

† C. E. Wise, "Products Liability," *Machine Design,* 28 March 1968, pp. 22–23.

industry were employed. Here, too, there are exceptions. Practices may sometimes be shown to have limitations that are good in most instances but are inadequate in others. On the other hand, deviations from established practice may not be considered negligent if it is shown that due and reasonable consideration was given to safety in making the change.

Charges of negligence can also be made against a manufacturer for components produced by a subcontractor. A contractor can be sued for negligence to construct a building properly so failure occurs because of the materials used; an architect-engineer, for inadequate or faulty design; or an operator, such as an airline, for improper maintenance or operation.

Changes in Legislation

The numerous changes in legislation in the past few years were mentioned as the second major factor affecting liabilities of manufacturers, distributors, retailers, and operations. Most of these laws are predicated on reasoning similar to the statement in the opening paragraph of Public Law 90–146,* which establishes a National Commision on Product Safety: "... the American consumer has a right to be protected against unreasonable risk of bodily harm from products purchased on the open market for the use of himself and his family."

This law implies that the manufacturer has the means to establish and determine the hazards that use of his product entails, whereas the consumer does not. It is therefore the responsibility of the manufacturer to ensure that the product is safe before it is released for sale to the public. If he does not, he will be liable.

Since this concept was adopted, numerous federal and state laws have been passed or proposed in rapid succession. There are so many of these laws that little more can be said of them here but that they apply to almost all products for homeowners and similar consumers. Automobile safety is another area (in this case, well-publicized) in which legislative action is being taken.

Federal and State Regulations, Laws, and Codes

There are numerous other federal and state safety requirements that are based on public laws that either prescribe specific criteria to be observed or indicate the responsibilities of departments and agencies to issue such criteria. Regulations and codes prepared, published, and monitored by these organizations cover such items as working conditions, design, operation, storage, transportation, and handling. Here again, violators may be held liable for injuries and damage and, in addition, for non-compliance even when there has been no injury or damage.

Federal departments and agencies are concerned with safety standards for interstate or international commerce, defense, or similar areas of national interest. State laws, regulations, and codes affect operations, facilities, and commerce within the state. One exception is that a company located in one state may be responsible for observance of the standards of that state for personnel whose duties lie even temporarily in another state.

The federal government is adamant in ensuring that state safety

*Public Law 90–146. 90th Congress, S. J. Res. 33; November 20, 1967.

23

Federal and State Regulations, Laws, and Codes

requirements are observed even on federal installations. Requirements are generally the same or similar. In other installations, the state may indicate that federal requirements will be observed or will not be exceeded. State laws are applied chiefly in the working conditions required in industrial plants and in motor vehicle transportation over its roads.

When a system is being developed for a federal agency, such as the Department of Defense, its safety standards are the most pertinent. In most cases, coordination between federal agencies ensures maximum compatibility of requirements. In this way, the criteria of the Interstate Commerce Commission (ICC), Federal Aviation Agency (FAA), U.S. Coast Guard, and other federal organizations are reflected in Department of Defense criteria.

Military service directives are basically for government of the organizations under the jurisdiction of the headquarters that prepared them. However, a company that accepts a government contract to develop a system may be affected in numerous ways by these directives:

1. A specific contractual requirement may require observance of its criteria in whole or part.

2. Necessity for compliance with another requirement may, in turn, require adherence to these criteria.

3. Operation of or at a military facility is contingent on observance of these directives.

4. Design and development of a system for a military service should permit the user to operate within that service's directives. This requires that the designer be familiar with these directives even when they are not stipulated as contractual requirements.

5. Where injury results from noncompliance, a plaintiff may use that fact as a basis for his suit.

Military Specifications and Standards

These are criteria that can be required by contract, directly or indirectly, for specific equipment, materiel, construction, methods of assembly, or services to be furnished. They may be specified directly by number or title; or by cross-reference in cited specifications and standards, in this way becoming requirements indirectly. Even when observance of specifications or standards is not stipulated directly or indirectly, their observance is generally advisable since they usually constitute good engineering practice based on past experience.

Military specifications and standards change as the services attempt to keep current with technical developments. Responsible personnel must therefore make certain that the criteria used are up to date.

Technical Codes and Standards*

Various technical societies and industrial associations have determined that manufacturers and operators of equipment and facilities should observe certain criteria. These organizations have developed recom-

Liabilities for Accidents

* A book which lists sources of standards which were current when it was published is: E. J. Struglia's, *Standards and Specifications—Information Sources*; (Detroit, Michigan; Gale Research Company, 1965).

TYPICAL ENGINEERING CODES AND STANDARDS

American Institute of Electrical Engineers (AIEE), *Recommended Practice for Electrical Installations on Shipboard.*

American Petroleum Institute (API), Recommended Practices:

RP-500, *Classification of Areas for Electrical Installations in Petroleum Refineries,*

RP-510, *Recommended Practice for Inspection, Repair and Rating of Unfired Pressure Vessels in Service in Petroleum Refineries.*

RP-2001, *Fire Protection in Refineries.*

RP-2003, *Protection against Ignitions Arising out of Static, Lightning, and Stray Currents.*

American Society of Mechanical Engineers, *Boiler and Pressure Vessel Code*:

Section I, *Power Boilers.*

Section III, *Nuclear Pressure Vessels.*

Section VIII, *Unfired Pressure Vessels.*

Instrument Society of America (ISA), Recommended Practices:

RP-12.4, *Electrical Instruments in Hazardous Atmospheres.*

National Fire Protection Association (NFPA), Standards:

No. 30, *Flammable and Combustible Liquids Code.*

No. 70, *National Electric Code.*

No. 77, *Static Electricity.*

No. 78, *Lightning Protection Code.*

No. 493, *Intrinsically Safe Process Control Equipment For Use in Hazardous Locations.*

No. 802, *Nuclear Reactors.*

Society of Automotive Engineers (SAE),

AIR 818, *Subsonic Aircraft Instrument Standards: Wording, Terminology, Phraseology, Environment and Design Standards for.*

ARP 767, *Impact Protective Design of Occupant Environment-Transport Aircraft.*

AS 439, *Stall Warning Instrument.*

American National Standards Institute (ANSI), Standards:

Z 16.1, *Injury Classifications.*

mended standards for design, production, and operation. These standards have been gradually adopted by insurance companies and then by local governments.

The degree of compliance with these standards determined insurance rates, so that economics accelerated their acceptance. Local governments often prohibited construction of buildings and other facilities or use of certain types of equipment or matériel within their jurisdictions unless the standards were met or waivers obtained. Some standards developed and adopted in this way were the Boiler Code and Code for Unfired Pressure Vessels of the American Society of Mechanical

Figure 2-4

Technical Codes and Standards

25

Engineers (ASME) and the National Electrical Code of the National Fire Protection Association (NFPA).

Federal and state governments and their various agencies found it advisable to stipulate the use of many of these codes, because of their broad acceptance, rather than to develop their own. The codes are frequently supplemented where they do not cover governmental needs completely. Conversely, only pertinent paragraphs of certain codes may be specified. Where a contract, specification, or standard does not require such codes, their use is generally acceptable unless an overriding requirement is indicated.

Some of the more common codes with safety connotations are listed in Fig. 2-4. Unless they are named specifically by a contract, specification, or standard, users should ensure that any code selected is applicable to the item with which they are concerned. For example, although their titles appear to indicate their applicability, neither the National Electric Code (buildings and related structures) nor the National Electric Safety Code (power transmission and communications equipment) apply to the design of such vehicles as railroad equipment, trucks, automobiles, missiles, aircraft or ships.

As pointed out in the Final Report of the National Commission on Product Safety, industrial standards are based on the desire to promote maximum acceptance within the industry. To achieve this goal, the standards are frequently innocuous and ineffective.

Good Engineering Practice

Requirements of codes, specifications, and standards are sometimes so broad that the designer has a wide choice in selection of equipment, components, arrangements, procedures, and other design features. A design suitable for certain operational and environmental conditions may be entirely unsuitable under others. Components could meet all design and operational requirements when new and clean, when operated by specially selected and trained personnel, or when given a great deal of care. Under other conditions, they may fail, cause accidents, injure personnel, and damage other equipment. The mark of a good engineer is the ability to design a system to preclude failures, accidents, injury, and damage when specific technical requirements do not exist or when conditions are less than optimum.

Good engineering practice is required in all design fields. Certain basic practices can be pointed out that should be followed in each; on the other hand, careful review must ensure that the design is suitable for the particular circumstances under which it is being used. Figure 2-5 illustrates some examples of good engineering practices in accident prevention.

The Legal Process of Discovery

Liabilities for Accidents

There is no sounder basis on which a plaintiff can rest his case, and no easier way for him to win it, than to prove that a contractual requirement, regulation, specification, standard, code, or good engineering practice regarding safety had been violated. Failure to observe stipulated measures without well-considered reasons would be pointed out as negligence.

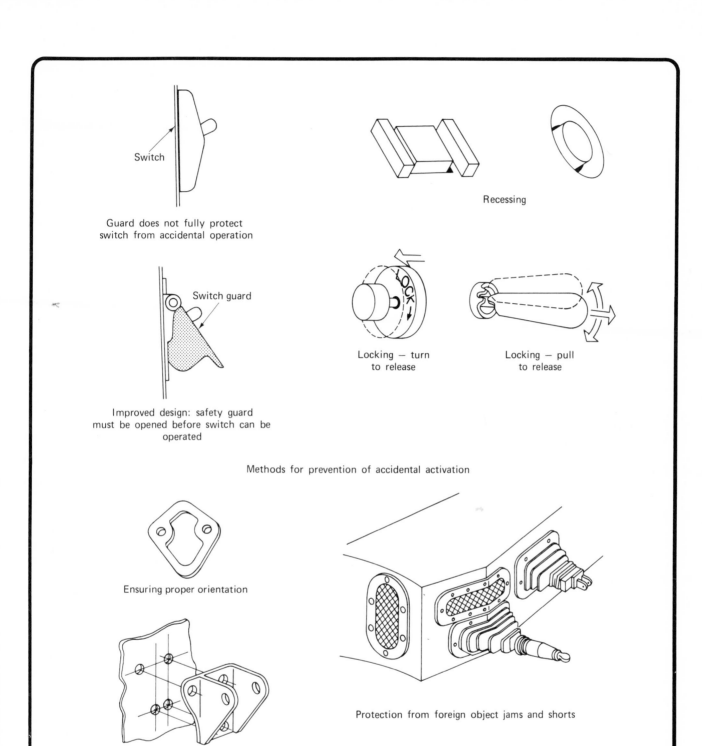

Switch

Guard does not fully protect
switch from accidental operation

Recessing

Switch guard

Improved design: safety guard
must be opened before switch can be
operated

Locking — turn
to release

Locking — pull
to release

Methods for prevention of accidental activation

Ensuring proper orientation

Protection from foreign object jams and shorts

Irregular pattern

Figure 2-5

The desire of a plaintiff to establish negligence has led to increased use of the procedure known as *discovery*. This legal process is predicated on the concept of determining as many facts as possible that are pertinent to a case before a trial begins so that the truth will be established to the best of everyone's abilities. It was found that a plaintiff frequently was aware that documents or data existed, usually in the possession of

The Legal Process of Discovery

the defendant, which would support his claims. Previously, unless those documents were identified precisely by title and a court order obtained for their release, the plaintiff had no access to them. In addition, it was disconcerting for a plaintiff to present the meager data that he may have had on a specific claim, only to be overwhelmed by the defense with masses of other data that he did not know were in existence, whose validity he had no opportunity to establish, and with no time to prepare a rebuttal.

Courts were adverse to plaintiffs searching indiscriminately for evidence for their claims under a court order with undefined limits; but with "*discovery*," the plaintiff may request all documents in specific categories. These categories cover documents that a reasonable person would ask for with good cause for a particular purpose in mind. It then became incumbent on the plaintiff to establish which categories fulfilled these requirements. All parties concerned had to be notified of the information required and the purpose for which it was to be used.

A good legal counsel can establish that almost any category of information and data relates to an accident and is essential to establish the truth of the claim by the plaintiff. He therefore has almost unlimited access to the defendant's files. Any indication that the defendant knew of any problems with his product would probably be revealed. Especially damaging would be any failure to show that he had attempted to take timely corrective action on any deficiency of which he was aware. Such facts in the hands of a skillful counsel can be extremely damaging to a defendant during a trial.

The case of *Hollerich* v. *The Boeing Company and Northwest Airlines* involved a Boeing 720B that crashed into the Everglades in February 1963, killing the 35 passengers and 8 crew members. Counsel for the plaintiff (the widow of a passenger) found that a Boeing engineer had written a memorandum, two months before delivery of the aircraft, expressing his opinion that the plane had a dangerous characteristic. The engineer had contended that the travel of the aircraft's stabilizer should be limited to 3.5 degrees, instead of the existing 4.4 degrees. This change was necessary to prevent pitchover if turbulence was encountered when the plane was controlled by the autopilot. No action was taken to correct the situation. The pitchover occurred as predicted in turbulence, and the aircraft crashed. The stabilizer was found at its maximum nosedown limit, 4.4 degrees. The plaintiff was awarded $2,000,000 in damages (later reduced to $1,250,000).

Counsel for the plaintiff stated:* "In the trial of this case in Illinois against the manufacturer and carrier, discovery by category (namely, *all* documents relating to the design, manufacture and production of the aircraft; *all* documents and inter-office memoranda relating in any manner to the occurrence) led to the discovery of most important and revealing documents." It may suffice to say that the documents referred to revealed a recommendation made for safety reasons by an engineer of the manufacturing company. The recommendation was submitted 60 days before delivery of the plane but was not carried out. Failure to take corrective action gave the attorney for the plaintiff an excellent opportunity to make his examinations of company personnel in court extremely damaging.

* J. J. Kennelly, "Litigation of an Aircrash Case against Manufacturer and Airline Which Resulted in Verdict for Two Million Dollars for Single Death, in *The Trial Lawyer's Guide* (Chicago, Illinois; Callaghan & Company, 1965), pp. 5–11.

Because of the important roles a safety effort and its records play in any defense against liability claims, some general rules have been formulated that should be observed by a manufacturer (or anyone else) who might face legal action. Records or other evidence should show that:

- The company maintained an organization specifically responsible for ensuring that safety was incorporated into the product during its design and production.
- The competence level (experience and education) of personnel involved in the safety effort was commensurate with the need.
- An effective product safety program actually existed. A current policy directive is beneficial as long as it can be shown that the assigned responsibilities had been carried out effectively.
- The program included undertaking analyses to detect hazards that might be involved in use of the product and ascertaining that effort had been made to eliminate the hazards, to minimize the possibilities of an accident, and to minimize the adverse effects an accident could produce. Records of the analyses and their findings should be maintained.
- Each revealed deficiency had been: (1) corrected, (2) was in the process of being corrected within a reasonable time, (3) provided with suitable safeguards, or (4) analyzed and found not to involve a safety problem. This provision is essential. It also applies to maintenance and other operations carried out by operators such as airlines or railroads.
- All safety devices designed or incorporated for hazards that could not be eliminated were actually provided. Any safety features for this product better than those normally provided for similar conditions should be pinpointed.
- All warnings and cautions constituting safeguards for potential users are prominent in operating instructions, maintenance documents, decals, plates, signs, or other locations.

Defense against Liability Suits

In February 1959, an airliner approaching La Guardia Airport in New York crashed into the East River, killing all 65 persons aboard. A conclusion of the accident-investigating board was that the pilot may have misread the altitude of the aircraft because of the design of the altimeter. The family of one of the passengers killed sued both the aircraft manufacturer and the company that made the altimeter. In this case (*Goldberg* v. *Kollsman Instrument Corporation**) the court would not hold the instrument company liable, stating: "Adequate protection is provided for the passengers by casting in liability the airplane manufacturer which put into the market the completed aircraft."

In neither *MacPherson* v. *Buick Motor Car Company* nor *Goldberg* v. *Kollsman Instrument Corporation* did the New York courts hold the subcontractors liable. In each case, liability was placed on the party that marketed the completed product. The necessity for suitable control and integration of subcontractors into a manufacturer's safety program

Liability of Subcontractors

* 191 N.E. 2d 81.

is evident. There have been cases in other states where parts suppliers have been held liable to the ultimate consumer.

Some manufacturers attempt to transfer to subcontactors and vendors the risks of losses from accidents caused by products the suppliers furnish. This is done by including an "indemnity" provision in a purchase order or other contractual document. In view of the tremendous losses which could result, suppliers should therefore be certain they understand the implications of such an agreement. Conversely, suppliers may want to protect themselves by stipulating on purchase agreements that they have not accepted such an obligation as a condition for entering into a contract.

Other Aspects of Liability

Personal injury liability suits now constitute the fastest growing area in the legal field. (Only a few outstanding examples of the legal aspects have been discussed in this book because changes in laws and legal interpretations having major impacts on the subject come about almost daily.) Awards for personal injury compensatory damges have been costly to defendants. In addition, the amounts for which courts have held manufacturers, carriers, public operators, and other corporate persons liable for punitive damages are sometimes even higher. Chapter 1 points out that in a liability suit a California jury had decided against an aircraft manufacturer in the total amount of $21,747,000. Of this, $4,415,000 was for personal injury, $82,000 for loss of a plane, and the remainder—$17,250,000—for punitive damages. Any company which has a record of consistently producing unsafe products or of failing to take corrective action when a product is reported unsafe, is especially vulnerable to a penalty for punitive damage. In July 1971, the State of Ohio sued the Penn Central railroad for more than $14 million in damages for "unsafe conditions" on its property in Ohio. A $110,000 fine would also be levied for each day of alleged continued violation of state laws.

Another development has been the increase in class action suits. This type of litigation is initiated on behalf of everyone who could suffer an injury from a deficiency in a product which caused an injury to one or more litigants. Such suits in amounts of $100 million and more are common.

Law of Safety Progress

A company which produces an unsafe product (or conducts an unsafe operation) must either correct the problem or suffer costly losses. The government may require corrective action, liability suits may be instituted, or the loss of customers who will not buy a product alleged to be unsafe will exert economic pressure for correction. Sometimes a product must be withdrawn from sale if its problems cannot be corrected. In cases where this is the company's sole or prime product, the company may never recover and will go out of business.

When a legal action or economic pressure is brought against one company, all other companies in the same or related fields will undoubtedly take action to ensure their products do not have similar failings. These improvements will take place even when no regulatory need exists. Gradually, because of improvements, withdrawals, or failures of the producers, the safety level of the remaining products of a specific type will improve. This can be stated as a law:

An unsafe product will bring on corrective action or drive its producer out of business, thereby raising the safety level of all such products.

Examples which illustrate this concept include:

1. In 1912, there were 33 fatalities for every 10,000 registered vehicles in the United States; the present rate is approximately 5 deaths per 10,000 vehicles.*

2. Most of the aerospace companies which produced dangerous airplanes during World War II, sacrificing safety for slight performance gains in speed, climb, or maneuverability, no longer produce airplanes. They have turned to other activities, producing missiles, experimental vehicles, or other equipment, or have terminated their aerospace activities entirely.

3. Commercial passenger aircraft and airline operations have improved so much that in 1970 no person was killed while a passenger of a scheduled airline.

Effective safety programs can reduce accidents and the injuries, damage, and litigation accidents will generate.

* *Accident Facts* (Chicago, Illinois; National Safety Council, 1968), p. 40.

chapter 3

THE SAFETY PROGRAM

To ensure that the end product of the company's safety effort actually achieves maximal results commensurate with desired performance, cost, and mission requirements necessitates a conscientious, effective, sustained, and integrated program. This program is management's responsibility. In addition, personnel as highly qualified in and as oriented toward accident prevention as others are in their disciplines are vital for technical accomplishment of the safety program. This concept is the basic charter for a system safety organization and the necessity for its engineers.

Other persons have responsibilities too. Specific responsibilities may be assigned by management to organizational elements with special interests. Every individual has a personal responsibility for prevention of accidents that could involve not only himself but others. However, personnel have a tendency to disregard or be careless of their safety responsibilities unless they are under almost continual surveillance by their supervisors. Any safety program that does not have the active participation of management is foredoomed to failure.

Management Participation

Some of the tasks with which management personnel may become involved in furtherance of a safety program include, but are not limited to, the following:

1. Preparing and issuing safety policies to be observed and carried out by all organizational elements, clearly delineating responsibilities, and ensuring adequate funding. This task also involves publication of directives and instructions requiring adherence to these policies and establishing the means by which management can ensure their directives are being observed. This can be done by conducting reviews and audits periodically to determine whether each organizational element is carrying out its designated tasks effectively, completely, and within programmed time and cost limits.

2. Establishing by directive a coordinated safety effort by designating organizational elements to carry out specific functions and tasks.

3. Ensuring that managers and supervisors at all levels understand the need for the safety program and their roles in its fulfillment.

4. Establishing means of liaison between safety elements of the company and their counterparts among its customers, subcontractors, and other outside agencies.

5. Ensuring that all personnel, managerial and technical, are aware of the progress of the program and of any problems that could affect its successful accomplishment.

6. Ensuring that suitable requirements are incorporated into contracts for procurement of goods and services from subcontractors and vendors that will involve them in the overall safety effort. This involvement may include such things as: providing data for analyses or studies; conducting analyses on subsystems, assemblies or components that they contract to furnish; providing information on hazards, and providing warning and caution notes to be incorporated in procedures, instructions, and

other operating documents; providing information on safety equipment required; and furnishing data on limitations of equipment they develop or provide.

7. Reviewing critically any requests for waivers or deviations from safety policies, standards, requirements, or practices, to ensure that they are made only when absolutely necessary and do not provide bases for less than optimally safe designs.

In addition to the managerial tasks listed, there are numerous others of a technical nature. These functions are generally carried out by the engineering disciplines involved in the development of a product or system. They may include:

Technical Tasks

1. Developing an overall plan to indicate required safety tasks, and by whom, when, and how they will be accomplished. The need for each task may have been established by a contractual requirement, company policy, design requirement, legal or regulatory code, or good engineering practice. It has been pointed out that many standards and specifications for military hardware stipulate that certain analyses, which are basically for accident prevention, are to be made for design purposes. Listings of such stipulations can provide an excellent guide to task requirements, by whom they should be accomplished, detail of effort to be undertaken, outputs to be generated, and time and cost for accomplishment.

2. Conducting analyses of the product or system, its mission, functions of its subsystems, environmental conditions, and other factors that could affect its safety and effectiveness.

3. Establishing safety criteria and practices to be observed by engineers during product or system development. These may be prepared in the form of checklists; may be references to required standards, specifications, or other documents; or may be lists of approved and prohibited practices.

4. Identifying required safety and protective equipment and devices and setting forth test requirements to verify these safety features.

5. Identifying safety critical production techniques and test and inspection requirements. Control must be ensured over production processes so that no changes are made without evaluating impact on safety of the product.

6. Reviewing designs, drawings, functional and wiring diagrams, and calculations to ensure that the criteria and practices established have been observed for each subsystem and the interfaces between them.

7. Completing any other analyses required by the customer or regulatory agency, or which company engineers believe advisable to ensure that hazards are eliminated or controlled. Suitable safeguards must also be provided if control of the hazard should be lost.

8. Conducting tests on critical items to determine principal modes of failure and means by which failures can be minimized. Data

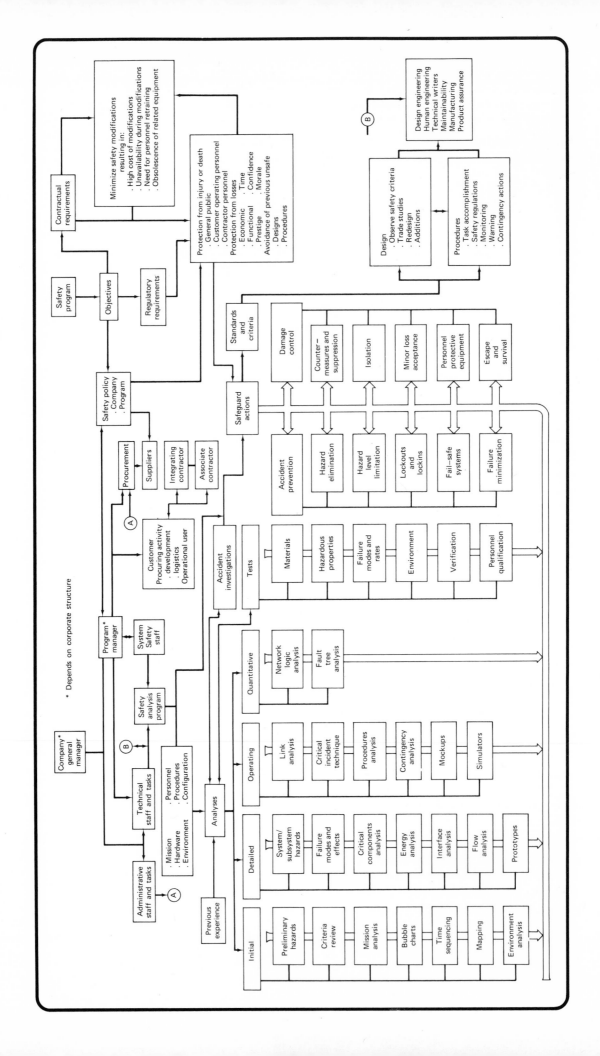

Fig. 3-1. Safety program model.

OTHER ENGINEERING ORGANIZATIONS INVOLVED IN SAFETY PROGRAMS

ORGANIZATION	NORMAL FUNCTIONS	SAFETY FUNCTIONS
Design Engineering	Prepares equipment and system designs that will meet contractual specifications for performance and mission accomplishment.	Conducts analyses of most appropriate and safest designs and procedures. Ensures that safety requirements in end item specifications and codes are met. Incorporates safety requirements for subcontractors and vendors in company specifications and drawings.
Human (Factors) Engineering	Ensures optimal integration of man, machine, and environment.	Conducts analyses to ensure well-being of personnel involved in equipment operation, maintenance, repair, testing, or other tasks in the proposed environment, especially to minimize fatigue and possible human error. Makes procedures analyses.
Reliability Engineering	Is concerned that equipment will operate successfully for specific periods under stipulated conditions.	Makes failure modes and effects analyses. Performs tests on parts and assemblies to establish failure modes and rates. Makes special studies and tests. Reviews trouble and failure reports, indicating any safety connotations.
Maintainability Engineering	Ensures that hardware will be in suitable condition for successful accomplishment of its prescribed mission.	Ensures that system or equipment will be kept at designed safety level by minimizing wear-out failures, through replacement of failed items, and by surveillance over possible degrading environments. Participates in analyzing proposed maintenance procedures for safety aspects.
Test Engineering	Conducts laboratory and field tests of parts, subassemblies, equipment, and systems to determine whether their performance meets contractual requirements.	Evaluates hardware and procedures to determine whether they are safe in operation, whether changes are required, or whether additional safeguards are necessary. Determines whether equipment has any dangerous characteristics or has dangerous energy levels or failure modes. Evaluates effects of adverse environments on safety.
Product (Field) Support	Maintains liaison between customer and producing company.	Assists customer on safety problems encountered in the field. Constitutes the major channel for feedback of field information on performance, hazards, mishaps, and near misses.
Production Engineering	Determines most economical and best means of producing the product in accordance with approved designs.	Ensures that designed safety is not degraded by poor workmanship or unauthorized production process changes.
Industrial Safety	Ensures that company personnel are not injured nor company property damaged by accidents.	Provides advice and information on accident prevention measures for industrial processes and procedures that are similar to those in system operations.
Training	Is concerned with improvement technical and managerial capabilities of all company personnel.	Ensures that personnel involved in system development, production, and operation are trained to levels necessary for safe accomplishment of their assigned tasks and can produce a safe system or product. Certifies workers on safety critical operations, especially for test operations.

Figure 3-2

obtained from these tests, especially when they are caused by designs that do not meet prescribed safety requirements, must be furnished to designers and analysts for their information.

Safety Program Model

A model of the factors that may be involved in carrying out a system safety program is presented in Fig. 3-1. Minor differences will exist in actual practice because of the different organizational structures. However, the model indicates broadly the process that takes place.

Because companies differ in size, organizational structure, products, and type of customer, the safety program and means for its accomplishment will vary too. The functions listed in the following paragraphs and in Fig. 3-2 will generally be undertaken in almost all cases; however, the units undertaking them may be known by other names or have multiple duties.

System Safety Engineering

Because System Safety engineering is a relatively new discipline, it frequently encompasses areas of interest that were formerly covered by other disciplines. Its members are not in competition with designers but complement and assist them in creating a safer product. Personnel of these other disciplines are obviously involved with safety to a limited extent because of the apparent needs encountered while carrying out their own tasks. Unfortunately, these people are the ones who most often oppose establishment of an organization devoted to safety alone. A System Safety organization can generate benefits to them by furnishing more detailed and intensive knowledge than they themselves are able to provide. The benefits that a System Safety group can produce are suggested by the functions, indicated in Fig. 3-3, that it generally undertakes.

Complex systems require a concentrated safety effort during development, without possibilities of degradation of that effort because of other requirements. The military services and NASA now stipulate that each major contractor must have a safety organization, program, and plan for any system or product that it will undertake to develop. This stipulation is to ensure that *one* organization within the contractor's management structure is delegated the function and responsibilities for accomplishment of the safety effort. It is similar to the emphases given maintainability, reliability, and other engineering disciplines. In this way, the safety effort will not be fragmented and will receive the same consideration as other areas of concern. These requirements make no stipulations regarding the title or location of the organization that will be responsible for safety. Some companies locate it organizationally on an equal level but separate from other disciplines. Others include it with (but not in) a related field, such as reliability engineering, in one management element.

Other Company Elements

Within any company, certain organizational elements are major participants in a system safety program (see Fig. 3-2). Although a safety department may have the responsibility for monitoring and ensuring that a safety program is carried out properly and effectively, it is not expected to carry out the entire program by itself. It must be a coordinated effort

FUNCTIONS OF SAFETY ORGANIZATIONS

1. Ensure that company safety policies are carried out by all personnel concerned.

2. Develop guidance by which the safety program will be carried out during design, development, production, test, transportation, handling, operation, maintenance, and repair.

3. Keep management informed on the safety program, its status, significant problems, deficiencies, or methods of improvement.

4. Review all safety requirements affecting the company product to ensure customer satisfaction. These requirements may be expressed in a contract, specification, federal or state law, transportation commission regulation, technical code, or good engineering practice. To focus attention on these safety requirements, the safety organization must know their contents, implications, and changes.

5. Review design, reliability, maintenance, production, test, quality assurance, transportation, human engineering, and training plans and criteria to ensure proper integration of safety activities into product development.

6. Are cognizant of new processes, materials, equipment, and information that might benefit the safety program. Recommend those safety developments that could be beneficial to the proper organization.

7. Analyze the product and its components to ensure that all hazards are eliminated or controlled to the greatest degree possible. Recommend containment measures to minimize damage that might result from an accident. Update analyses as development, testing and production proceed.

8. Review histories of hazards, failures, and mishaps in existing systems to ensure that design deficiencies are not repeated in the new system or product.

9. Participate in design preparations and reviews to ensure that incompatible or unsafe components, arrangements, subsystems, or procedures are not incorporated.

10. Participate in tradeoff studies to ensure that safety is not compromised by changes in mission, hardware, configuration, or procedures.

11. Monitor failure and incident reports to determine discrepancies, deficiencies, or trends that might affect safety. Make suitable recommendations for corrective action.

12. Prepare safety analyses required by the customer or his integrating contractor.

13. Determine the effects on overall safety of operations and failures of equipment being produced by associate contractors.

14. Develop safety analysis requirements, procedures, and milestones to be observed by subcontractors. Ensure that they understand all aspects of the safety program, the requirements imposed, and how their data and analyses will be integrated into the system effort.

15. Ensure that subcontractors' safety analyses are prepared and submitted and that their items will not degrade the safety of the company's product.

16. Ensure that safety training programs are adequate to meet organizational needs. Initiate action for improvement of such training.

17. Determine whether detection and warning devices, protective equipment, or emergency and rescue equipment are required for the system. Ensure that equipment selected is suitable for the specific hazard that might be encountered.

18. Ensure that safety warning and caution notes are incorporated in procedures, checklists, and manuals to warn personnel of hazardous conditions that might exist.

19. Disseminate information on hazards to other organizations that might be interested or affected.

20. Maintain liaison with safety organizations of the customer, associate contractors, subcontractors, other suppliers, consultants, and government safety agencies.

21. Serve on boards and committees dealing with industrial safety, bioenvironmental engineering, human engineering, and related fields.

22. Develop investigation plans for any mishaps involving the product.

23. Investigate mishaps involving the product while it is the responsibility of the company. Assist the user, at his request, in investigating mishaps that are the user's responsibility.

24. Ensure corrective action is taken to prevent recurrences of mishaps through similar deficiencies or practices.

Figure 3-3

by all elements concerned, the reason being that a system safety organization does not have enough personnel to make all the necessary analyses. To do so would require a unit larger and more knowledgeable than that necessary to design the system. It would require duplication of efforts undertaken by others and would be uneconomical. Inevitably, conflicts in approaches to solutions or requirements and problems would develop, necessitating resolution by higher management levels, a costly and wasteful procedure.

Subcontractors and Vendors

Any manufacturer is liable for accidents caused by defects in supplier products incorporated into his product. It is therefore necessary that subcontractors and vendors be integrated into the overall safety effort. Both agree to provide a prime contractor or other subcontractor with a specific product or service. Neither one has a direct contractual relation with the customer of the prime contractor. A subcontractor's or vendor's responsibility is to the contractor with whom he has made the agreement and who has specified what is to be supplied.

Subcontractors may be classified as major or minor. A major subcontractor is one who agrees to develop or produce an extremely large, complex, or expensive item. Major subcontractors may sometimes be requested to prepare safety analyses of the items that they are contracting to furnish. The information in these analyses is then incorporated into the overall effort of the prime contractor. A minor subcontractor develops or produces packages of lesser importance or size. A vendor supplies a component or small assembly. Minor contractors or vendors may be requested or required to provide safety information on the products that they agree to furnish and any hazards that may be involved. For example, vendors of components containing explosives generally must provide information on the characteristics of their products. Other data to be submitted may include such items as temperature or pressure limitations, possible hazards, failure modes, failure rates, and safeguards to be employed. More and more frequently, the Army is requiring from its contractors "Safety Statements," which must indicate hazards and safeguards provided, before any equipment is delivered to one of its test stations. This requirement is generally passed down to subcontractors by the prime contractor.

The prime contractor establishes the safety standards and criteria that he requires all subcontractors to meet for the matériel or services that they contract to provide. He must be certain that the requirements to provide safety information are stipulated in the contracts and that they are stated clearly. His safety personnel must ensure that the subcontractors and vendors understand how their safety analyses and other inputs will be incorporated into the overall system effort and how they will be prepared. Safety standards, criteria, compliance levels, and tasks are specified in procurement documents. The prime contractor's system safety organization ensures that subcontractor and supplier personnel prepare and submit safety analyses and other information as required and that the products furnished will not lower the safety of the overall system. The prime contractor may have to indoctrinate and train subcontractor personnel in accident prevention methods; assist or review trade studies involving safety; monitor the production and quality control methods of safety critical items; review results of tests on important components and assemblies; and review corrective actions taken because of failures, accidents, or other possible troubles.

The prime contractor can establish a safety program for his own organization, but in the efforts that he can require of subcontractors he is limited to those incorporated into contracts. In any case, a prime contractor can only indicate the technical tasks required; he cannot require their accomplishment by any specific organization of the subcontractor or that a safety organization be created. To ensure a complete, efficient, and effective safety program, a prime contractor must:

1. Prepare an overall system safety program to be accomplished by his own organization and a plan for tasks to be accomplished by the subcontractors.

2. Incorporate in subcontracts the required safety tasks. These will include such items as:

   a. Efforts that each subcontractor is expected to undertake;
   b. Analyses to be conducted on the portion of the system that each subcontractor has contracted to develop and data to be included;
   c. Formats to be employed;
   d. Dates on which analyses and other information are to be submitted.

3. Be certain that all contractors understand the effort that each must undertake, inputs to be made to the overall effort, and need for submission of inputs.

4. Conduct analyses of the total system and of the interfaces between end items being developed by different subcontractors. Analyses prepared by subcontractors are incorporated in the total system analysis. Preparation of an overall system analysis by the prime contractor does not relieve each subsystem contractor of any contractual responsibility for making his own analyses of problems that could be generated on his portion of the system by the outputs, normal or abnormal, from other portions.

5. Conduct trade studies with any affected subcontractors to reduce or eliminate any hazard that the output from a system produced by one subcontractor generates on that of another.

6. Recommend solutions to technical differences involving safety between subcontractors, especially during tradeoff studies.

7. Establish channels for flow of information between subcontractors where required to accomplish safety analyses. Information interchange should be as rapid and complete as possible.

8. Program and conduct meetings between his organization and subcontractors to review and integrate the safety effort and to exchange pertinent information.

The customer justifiably assumes that the product he procures will be safe. However, the level of safety may determine the cost of the product; or conversely, the price that the customer is willing to pay may determine the extent of a safety effort. A manufacturer generally intends to

Safety Program Manloads

follow current good engineering practice, commensurate with cost, to provide a safe product even where safety requirements have not been imposed by regulation or contract. It then becomes a problem to ensure that the customer's expectations equate with the manufacturer's practices. If the manufacturer is one with a policy and history of producing the safest system possible, at any cost, to maintain its reputation and excellent customer relations, there may be no problem. A marginal company and its customer may not be in accord as to what constitutes a usual safety effort that can be expected within the normal cost of the product. For a contracted system or product involving additional effort, safety requirements must be stipulated separately and additional funds provided. To make these stipulations, it is necessary that the additional tasks be recognized and the effort for their accomplishment determined. It is basic that any company creating a contracted product for a customer will attempt to minimize its costs and its efforts. Unless the tasks to be undertaken are specific and clearly defined, there will be different interpretations of what should be included in a safety program, and the program will suffer.

In any case, it is good practice, where a contracted effort is to take place, for the customer to require the contractor to indicate clearly the safety tasks that he proposes to undertake. Generalities should be avoided in such presentations, each task being defined as clearly as possible. If the customer decides that certain tasks are unnecessary or cannot be funded, he can indicate so. On the other hand, when additional tasks are required, even at a later date, such as for additional verification tests of safeguards, funds may have to be provided. Decisions on additional safety tasks that the contractor believes should be accomplished but that are not funded will remain his prerogative.

Delineation of safety tasks before a contract is entered into has numerous advantages:

- It indicates that both the contractor and the customer realize the magnitude of the safety effort to be undertaken.
- It ensures mutual understanding and agreement on the tasks that are to be accomplished.
- The cost of the safety program can be determined.
- The customer can make more intelligent decisions than when agreement must be made on the basis of an inadequately defined program.
- The tasks listed can provide the baseline against which accomplishment and progress of the program can be measured.
- Assignment of responsibilities for accomplishment of each task to an organizational element will avoid duplication while ensuring that no task is left undone.
- It ensures that each organizational element assigned a task will budget funds necessary for its accomplishment.
- Manloading required for the various tasks can be programmed so they can be done with most effective and efficient use of manpower.

The Safety Program

Many of the safety tasks were listed previously in broad terms in the paragraphs entitled Management Participation and Technical Tasks.

SAMPLE ENTRIES IN DETAILED SAFETY TASK AND MANLOADING LIST

TASK NO.	REQUIREMENT	TASK DESCRIPTION	RESPONSIBLE ORGANIZATION	ESTIMATED MAN-HOURS REQUIRED
1		Carry out specifically stipulated contractual requirements.		
1.1	Work statement	Prepare system safety program plan.	System safety	300
1.2		Prepare documents on contract data requirements list (CDRL).		
1.2.1	T023 — A1	Prepare transportation and storage data for explosive components.	Systems engineering	120
1.2.2	T037 — A3	Prepare range safety report.	Design engineering	120
1.2.3	W052 — A1	Prepare safety statement.	System safety	250
2		Carry out safety provisions of military standards and specifications.		
2.1	MIL—B—5087	Ensure that designs include electrical bonding and lightning protection and meet bond size and other criteria.	Design engineering	100
2.2	MIL—E—6051	Determine EMC criticality categories of system components, assemblies, and operation.	Design engineering	100

Figure 3-4

However, to ensure that all tasks are considered in detail so that necessary labor and costs are included, a form such as that in Fig. 3-4 can be employed. In some instances, two or more organizations may include provisions for accomplishment of the same task. Where review indicates that duplication is involved, and not that one complements the other, one submittal can be eliminated. It will also be found that a list developed for one program may require only minor modifications to serve for another.

The tasks can be listed under general headings such as those shown below. Figure 3-4 presents only a few of the headings and examples.

- Specifically stipulated contractual requirements
- Safety provisions of codes, regulations, standards, and specifications
- Safety analyses, including updates
- Documents, such as manuals, on safety matters required by the customer or by statute
- Reviews, trade studies, and similar activities
- Visits related to the safety effort, such as auditing supplier activities, liaison with the customer, and observing tests on critical safety items
- Training of personnel in safety matters,
- Data and reports related to the safety effort
- Test requirements
- Procedures and manuals for contractor and customer activities

Safety Program Manloads

43

Control of Program Tasks

To ensure that program tasks are accomplished in a timely fashion, it is necessary that adequate controls be established. These are usually maintained by the System Safety organization through use of a table on which entries can be made under headings such as the following:

Reference—Indicates the requiring document, such as the item specification or standard, contract requirement, regulation or code, including the pertinent paragraph number.

Task—A brief title of the effort required.

Description—Indicates type of effort, such as a design feature, study, or analysis.

Responsible Unit—The organization to accomplish the task.

Estimated Start and Completion Dates—Provide information on milestones.

Actual Start and Completion Dates—Provide information on program status.

Other Actions Required or Taken—Entries will identify special studies, research, or test data required, information necessary from the customer or other contractors, and other pertinent remarks.

Types of Analyses

The fundamental efforts in any safety program involve analyses of the product and the consequent actions taken to avoid or minimize conditions that could result in accidents. The two go hand in hand. Any analysis, no matter how good, is wasted unless action is taken to correct deficiencies or provide the safeguards determined necessary. Methods of analysis are presented in later chapters. Exactly which type should be employed for any specific program, hazard, piece of hardware, event, or mission depends on the discretion of the analyst. The selection of any type of analysis may be based on a contractual requirement, the point in time when the analysis is made, the detail expected, the need for quantitative values, and the type of item or operation to be undertaken.

It has been pointed out that analyses are conducted in many organizational elements. Designers analyze hardware to ensure that they are adequate to meet mission requirements. Information, data, and analytical techniques are frequently the same as those made to determine or resolve safety problems. For example, designers of pressure vessels calculate the required thickness of metal from the expected stresses and a safety factor. The safety analyst may either determine the safety factor from the matériel strength and the probable stress or may review and accept the designer's analysis. Conducting a separate safety analysis may therefore be redundant and time-consuming. If this duplication were required for all analyses, it would require a System Safety organization of tremendous size.

Design and System Safety engineering efforts must therefore be integrated to complement rather than duplicate one another. The design engineer is the logical one for the initial analysis. However, because a designer is generally biased toward his design, oriented toward requirements other than safety, or unduly optimistic, his work frequently must be monitored or reevaluated from the safety viewpoint to ensure that he has achieved the safest design possible and has not degraded safety because of other considerations.

A case in which safety could be jeopardized by other requirements would be the weight-reduction programs sometimes carried out by developers and manufacturers of aerospace vehicles. Frequently these vehicles begin to weigh more than expected in the original estimate or system requirement. The results would be reduction in performance, thus meaning penalties for the contractor. The contractor therefore may institute a campaign among his personnel for efforts to reduce weight and pay a reward for each pound saved. Personnel then become oriented toward weight reduction rather than safety, which is sometimes neglected; they may recommend changes that reduce strength and safety or may avoid the use of safety devices that would add weight.

Corrective and Preventive Actions

The ultimate purposes of an analysis program are to correct deficiencies and to provide information on safeguards required. Unless these corrective actions are taken, the analyses are worthless and wasted and protect no one. The means by which improvements in the safety posture of any product or system can be achieved are pointed out in Chapter 10. The degree to which these may be observed is generally limited by the funds available; it therefore becomes a management problem. Briefly, however, the actions that can be taken in a fully implemented program to correct deficiencies revealed by safety analyses include the following:

- Analysis results must be transmitted to the appropriate company elements, suppliers, or subcontractors for action.
- Tradeoff studies must be made to determine whether the hazard can be eliminated or minimized by redesign.
- Hazards and their possible adverse effects must be brought to the attention of the customer for acceptance or rejection. This information would permit decisions on whether the system could be operated on a calculated risk basis or whether additional safeguards must be provided. Information furnished should include: possible effects on the mission or on the operation, personnel, equipment, and facilities; comparative or probable frequency of occurrence; possible alternative, if any; and suggested methods of hazard control, minimization of damage, and personnel and system protection.

Verification and Testing

The old cliché, "The proof of the pudding is in the eating," derives from the same premise as verification and testing of components, assemblies, and systems. Tests may involve materials, hardware, personnel, processes, or combinations of these. They determine whether prescribed requirements have been met; compatibility of men with equipment and environment; adequacy of designs and procedures; and numerous other conditions, factors, and interrelationships that must be verified. Tests to develop information and data that can be integrated into the safety effort or to determine how effective analyses have been are of two broad types:

- Tests specifically for safety that are undertaken to determine the existence of hazards, whether analyses are correct, safe levels of stress or exposure, severity of damage resulting from an uncontrolled hazard, or suitability of safety equipment. Examples include testing such materials as plastics, oils, or solvents for flammability; testing halogenated hydrocarbons as fire extinguishants; determining initiation characteristics of explosives, the absorptive and adsorptive capabilities of gas-mask canisters, and radiation characteristics of high-frequency electronic tubes.

- Tests conducted for purposes other than safety but which generate data that can be incorporated into the safety program. Examples include: determining part failure rates; analyzing of field failures; testing strength or compatibility of new materials; determining interface problems between integrated assemblies; and making quality control analyses of items produced by subcontractors and vendors.

Either of these categories of tests can be applied to materials and hardware, personnel, or processes. For example:

1. Material and hardware tests can determine characteristics of materials, components, assemblies or systems; effects of environments, natural or induced; failure modes and failure rates; the effects of stresses and the reasons why parts failed; comparative differences between two or more materials or designs; and whether integrated portions of a product or system operate properly.

2. Personnel tests may involve two major categories: qualification testing and man-equipment integration assurance. Personnel who take part in critical functions during production, assembly, check out, test, transportation, and hazardous operations should be tested to ensure that they meet minimum levels of proficiency prescribed for their tasks and assignments. Whenever possible, such personnel should be certified, with renewals by test at regular intervals. Examples are proficiency tests in welding, driving, and crane operation.

    Tests are also conducted to ensure that men and equipment are properly integrated through prepared procedures. These tests determine the adequacies of personnel, hardware, and procedures during system operations under normal and abnormal conditions. They also determine whether hazards exist. These "run-through" tests determine the adequacy of human engineering aspects of designs, suitability of procedures, existence of hazards through incompatibilities of men and equipment, and effectiveness of analyses.

3. Process tests may first be accomplished in a laboratory to determine whether a process, such as one involving a complex chemical reaction, is hazardous. Temperature, pressure, and time limitations can be determined with small amounts of reactants under safeguarded conditions so there will be no

injury and little damage if control of the reaction is lost. After hazards and other affecting factors are determined, a larger operational test, such as a pilot plant, can be undertaken. If this is successful, a full-scale system can be built.

Information on failures is usually fed back to designers and other interested personnel. In some instances, failures may not occur, but tests may reveal the necessity for limiting conditions of operation. This type of information frequently fails to reach personnel who can benefit from it.

Tests should be conducted under conditions approximating those that will exist during actual operations and even during possible abnormal conditions. Oil may be tested for flash point or autoignition temperature while in a container. Under such conditions, it may exhibit low flammability characteristics. However, as a spray resulting from a high-pressure leak, it may ignite easily. Conversely, a plastic material in a thin film may ignite; as a fairly thick insulation around a cable, it will not.

Information and Documentation

The necessity for maintaining adequate records in the event a liability suit occurs has already been pointed out. In addition, other types of data are frequently necessary for the conduct of any major program. Information related to a safety program can be divided into four major categories: requirements, feedback, working papers, and outputs. Each of these is equally important.

Accomplishment and control of a safety program require that each organization undertaking any part of the effort have on hand or available copies of the appropriate portions of the contract, standards, criteria, and practices with which it must comply. In addition to mandatory requirements that it must meet, it should have a library of documents on subjects related to the system under development. These documents may include copies of books, manuals, magazine articles, reports, and technical papers relating to the tasks to be accomplished.

Much information can be derived from government agencies, research organizations, technical and scientific societies, other contractors, and knowledgeable individuals. Technical and scientific personnel of companies, even of competitors, are always willing as individuals to furnish information on subjects related to safety in which they too are interested. This is especially true when these personnel are queried regarding matters on which they have prepared papers for symposia. The one restriction is that they should not be asked to reveal proprietary information. One engineer commented that he had never been refused information that he had requested on a personal basis, within the proprietary limitation, even though he may never have met or spoken with the individual previously. On the other hand, a formal written request for information to another company frequently was unfruitful. During discussions with individuals, additional sources of information are often revealed.

A very common complaint by customers is that new systems frequently include designs, materials, or procedures found lacking and discarded previously by others because of adverse experiences. An example of feedback failure that resulted in an accident occurred when an aerospace company undertook tests involving gaseous oxygen under pressure in a titanium tank. The tank ruptured, killing some of the test personnel and injuring others. A government representative at the plant remarked that the managers, designers, and test personnel had not known of the incompatibility of titanium with gaseous oxygen. However, after the accident occurred, company safety personnel received 50 or more telephone calls, letters, and messages, some from their own employees, indicating numerous places in the literature where the incompatibility had been pointed out.

Designers would not knowingly incorporate deficiencies in new systems if they were aware the deficiencies had caused problems previously. Feedback of data and information on tests, operations, failures, mishaps, near misses, and corrective actions to designers and safety personnel therefore is essential in any accident prevention program. The problem is evidently in communication, negating any benefits in acquiring, analyzing, and storing data that could be beneficial if brought to the attention of interested personnel.

Information to be fed back can be divided into that from sources outside the company and that within the company itself. The first has already been mentioned. Information within the company may consist of material already drawn from the outside and information generated internally. Because safety covers so many fields and areas of interest, it is frequently difficult to establish a means of collecting and collating data. The chief problem has been that such attempts have endeavored to encompass too broad a scope. The method indicated in Chapter 5, using the coding system described under safety consideration trees, has been successful. A company is generally concerned with only specific systems, products, or programs. This specificity limits the data that can be useful. They can then be coded and filed according to the safety problem.

It is up to management to ensure that a suitable system is instituted and maintained for reporting failures of company products, determining causes, evaluating the data, and reporting the information derived to interested personnel and organizations. For example, safety hazards are frequently identified before they cause trouble, failure, or accidents. A hazard report should be submitted on any such problem, and a suitable procedure must be in effect to ensure that suitable corrective action is taken. Unless the system is well planned and carried out, ensuring that all who could benefit are informed, and suitable corrective action taken, even the effort of submitting the report will be worthless. Figure 3-5 indicates a procedure for submission and processing of hazard reports.

The last group of documents consists of those that may be required as end items specified by the customer, such as manuals, documented studies, and progress reports. Progress reports indicate how well the safety effort is proceeding. Unfortunately, they have a tendency to be overly optimistic. The customer would do well to employ the task control list described previously to ensure that all aspects of a safety program are being accomplished fully and on schedule.

Safety Program Monitoring and Review

To ensure that the safety program is adequate, complete, timely, effective, and efficiently done, managers must review it continually. (This review is in addition to the day-to-day control of program tasks carried out by the system safety organization.) The review determines whether com-

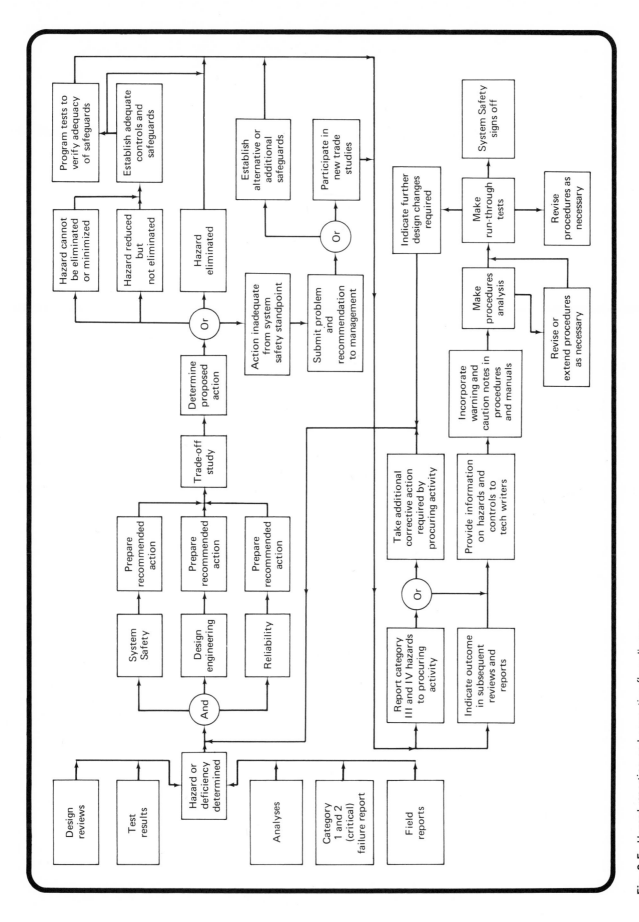

Fig. 3-5. Hazard reporting and correction flow diagram.

pany policies are being observed and contractual requirements met. If not, improvements must be instigated. Program reviews constitute the agency by which the managers assess:

- The conduct and status of activities within designated areas of responsibilities
- How well organizational elements under different managers are coordinating and integrating their activities toward achievement of a safe system or product
- How safe designs and procedures are through reviews of data from tests, operations, and other verification and demonstration processes
- Adequacy of subcontractor efforts
- Actions being taken to eliminate hazards or to provide suitable safeguards

Program reviews may be accomplished by managers, committees, or boards. A review should be a critique or evaluation by a person or group of persons of a problem, analysis, design, or proposed action studied or prepared by others. In this way, the matter under study is subjected to the scrutiny of persons oriented differently from those who made the original effort. Some reviews are conducted specifically toward evaluating various aspects of the system safety program. Others are interdisciplinary activities in which safety constitutes one portion.

In those reviews that are for safety purposes only, company management evaluates system, subsystem, and product designs; hazardous conditions; critical components; and system or product safeguards and protection. The management may determine whether safety standards, specifications, good engineering practices, and contractual requirements are observed and fulfilled. Safety management personnel may review analyses, designs of critical components and assemblies, test data, and operational procedures to establish their adequacy.

Interdisciplinary reviews involve the entire development program, in which system safety is only one aspect of the overall effort. These reviews are generally conducted by design or systems engineering personnel. Other organizations provide inputs and participate in presentations. These inputs indicate how their efforts and outputs comply with contractual requirements. Subjects of interest to safety personnel include review of safety provisions in standards and specifications, hazards that may be present in designs, methods of hazard control and other safeguards, and results of analyses. Reviews are generally held at major milestones in a development program, principally for the benefit of customer representatives. It is generally at such time that the customer may request changes in design, further analyses, additional verification tests, or more detailed information. Each review is made early enough to permit design changes to be incorporated before major commitments are made. Some types of review are indicated in Fig. 3-6. Other titles are frequently used for similar types.

Audits Audits are often undertaken to observe the conduct and progress of the system safety program. They establish whether stipulated contract requirements, management policies, established procedures, and good engineering practices are being fulfilled. Findings reveal where:

EXAMPLES OF TYPES OF REVIEWS

TYPE	INFORMATION REVIEWED
Concept	Requirements concerning mission, performance, environment, and other related factors, such as safety are reviewed. Approaches proposed for meeting these requirements, advantages and disadvantages of each approach, and the preferred solution are indicated. Background material derived from tradeoff studies, design analyses, feasibility studies, and laboratory investigations are discussed. Expected problems for the proposed approach are pointed out, with methods for their control.
Definition	Requirements and designs are reviewed in relation to the ability of the proposed product or system to meet stipulated objectives.
Preliminary design review (PDR)	Is conducted on initial designs. Takes place prior to or soon after initial details of the design are established. Safety personnel participate by providing an initial analysis of hazards, methods of control, other safeguards to be incorporated, analyses conducted and their results, analyses in process or contemplated, and other significant information available when the PDR is held.
Critical design review (CDR)	Is an extension and updating of the PDR as design proceeds. Additional reviews are made of detailed designs, analyses, and problem areas similar to those at the PDR. Safety analyses, results of component and subsystem tests (and especially of failures), progress in hazard elimination, and provision of safeguards developed since the earlier review are covered. Items discussed at the PDR that resulted in requests for additional studies are generally brought up again at the CDR. Reports on progress are presented if the study is still under way, or reports on findings if it has been completed.
Prototype or first article configuration inspection (FACI)	The proposed design is reviewed before the prototype is built. Updated or newly completed analyses, tests, and tradeoff studies are presented. Items left open for determination at the CDR are discussed.
Flight readiness review (FRR)	Is conducted to check readiness of principal items and their support equipment. Is generally accomplished immediately prior to the first flight of a missile or aircraft to ensure that procedures have been developed and reviewed for the test, that necessary data have been provided to the test sites, and that no outstanding problems remain uncorrected. Flight objectives are considered. Similar reviews are held for subsequent flights.
Preproduction review	Problems determined or encountered during tests and inspections are reviewed to determine the best solutions to be incorporated into production models. This is the last complete review of the product or system prior to acceptance of its design.

- Problems exist in accomplishment of the program
- The causes of problems lie and recommended solutions
- Management can most effectively and economically make improvements
- Further guidance is required for implementation of the safety program
- Redirection is needed
- Additional assistance or manpower is necessary
- Further training should be provided

Figure 3-6

Audits may be made by managers, members of their staffs, or members of the safety organization. Safety audits may be made of

Safety Program Monitoring and Review

51

activities undertaken by the various organizational elements of the company or of suppliers under contract; they should be a continuing activity. Special attention should be given to components, equipment, designs, or procedures that constituted problems in the past, that previous audits or reports indicated as troublesome, or that may be unusually critical safety problems. Audits within the company can be made to determine:

- How efficiently and effectively the safety program is being carried out
- Whether organizational elements are cooperating in its accomplishment
- The status of all tasks and whether they are being accomplished within prescribed time limits
- Whether specific hazards, tests, or especially stringent requirements are given special attention and effort

Suppliers' efforts may be audited to ensure that designs, quality of materials, or items that they are providing will not degrade safety; that stipulated safety analyses are being conducted; that problems affecting safety are being brought to the attention of their own managers and those of the contractor they are supplying; and that no changes in design or production methods have been made without contractor approval.

Safety audits should be accomplished by safety organization personnel, personnel experienced in safety matters, or interdisciplinary teams or managers accompanied by safety personnel. To ensure that all aspects of safety are covered during a visit, it is generally advisable to employ checklists on critical items to be reviewed and audited. However, auditors must ensure that their observations are not limited to those items on the checklists.

To ensure that audits are effective, findings should be reported in writing with requests for corrective action and a response by a specific date. The response should indicate the corrective action to be taken and the expected date by which it should be completed. Periodic progress reports should be made until the deficiencies have been eliminated. Subsequent audits should then determine whether the corrective action actually has been accomplished and is satisfactory.

Accident and Failure Investigations

Accident and failure investigations are undertaken to determine the causes of problems so that corrective actions can be taken to prevent or minimize recurrences. At one time, investigations constituted the chief means by which safety was incorporated into a product or system. Information on the causes of accidents and failures was furnished system designers so they would avoid similar errors or problems and so they could incorporate suitable safeguards. In this way, a body of acceptable and unacceptable practices was accumulated. Results were frequently collected under the title, "Lessons Learned." Sources of information about accidents on which designs and practices can be predicated are listed in Fig. 3-7.

Unfortunately, in many instances information on accident or failure causes, good practices, or "Lessons Learned" never reaches the de-

Figure 3-7

REPRESENTATIVE LIST OF ORGANIZATIONS
THAT FURNISH INFORMATION ON ACCIDENTS

U.S. Air Force

Directorate of Aerospace Safety
The Deputy Inspector General for Inspection and Safety
Norton Air Force Base, California 92409

U. S. Army

U.S. Army Board for Aviation Accident Research
Fort Rucker, Alabama 36360

U.S. Navy

U.S. Navy Safety Center
U.S. Naval Air Station
Norfolk, Virginia 23511

U.S. Coast Guard

Department of Transportation
U.S. Coast Guard
13th and E Streets, N.W.
Washington, D.C. 20005

National Aeronautics and Space Administration

Lewis Research Center
21000 Brookpark Road
Cleveland, Ohio 44135

Department of Transportation (DOT)

National Transportation Safety Board
Department of Transportation
Washington, D.C. 20591

National Safety Council

425 N. Michigan Avenue
Chicago, Illinois 60611

Flight Safety Foundation

468 Park Avenue South
New York, New York 10016

National Fire Protection Association

60 Batterymarch Street
Boston, Massachusetts 02110

Manufacturing Chemists' Association, Inc.

1825 Connecticut Avenue, N.W.
Washington, D.C. 20009

signers. The same problems are then incorporated into new products, and accidents similar to those in the previous products recur. No organization can afford to determine the inadequacies of its new products by waiting until they are involved in accidents. It becomes a vital function of the safety organization to mitigate this lack by ensuring that the designers do know about accident causes involving similar systems, products, materials, or processes.

Accident and Failure Investigations

53

Investigations are still being used as a means to determine causes of accidents and failures before deciding on corrective actions. Failures are generally concerned with matériel; accidents may also involve personnel to a great degree. Corrective measures therefore may require changes in design, procedures, or both; provision of additional safeguards; more intensive training or supervision; better quality control during manufacture or maintenance; or more frequent system monitoring and testing. An investigation may determine whether the product was at fault, making its manufacturer liable, or if the accident was due to circumstances outside his control, such as incorrect usage. It may indicate whether a company and its suppliers have met contractual requirements. On the other hand, investigation may show a company was not at fault in an accident in which persons were injured or matériel and property damaged.*

Accidents at company facilities are industrial accidents; investigations are generally carried out by the safety and industrial hygiene staff of the company involved. Tests of a new product or system may result in accidents injurious to company personnel or damaging to company equipment and facilities. Although the responsibility for investigation is generally that of the safety and industrial hygiene staff, System Safety personnel and system designers are also interested in accident causes of the product or system with which they are concerned. Reports of accidents should therefore be furnished organizations responsible for system design to ensure that the deficiencies generating the accidents are eliminated.

Investigations of accidents in a manufacturer's plant or on his facilities are his responsibility, and since accidents do occur in spite of all precautions, suitable procedures should be developed for these investigations. Quick response to the need for investigation requires that suitable plans and procedures be developed for use if an accident occurs. These plans should include assignments and responsibilities of personnel in any investigation.

Investigation of accidents at customers' plants, at facilities under their jurisdictions, or during their conduct of operations are their responsibilities. However, a customer may require technical assistance in determining accident causes. Most Department of Defense contracts for $10,000 or more contain a section regarding the contractor's role in helping investigate accidents involving its product or personnel. Incorporation of this clause into a contract is the basis on which payments will be made to the contractor for help provided. In many cases, the customer may require that persons who will provide the assistance be designated by name, position, phone number, address, and technical area long before operations begin during which an accident could take place. These assignments must be kept current for immediate use. The designated person can then be contacted directly to proceed as rapidly as possible to the scene of the accident, should one occur. Where there have been no previous assignments, a customer may request assistance through a field support engineer or other designated contact. The manager responsible for making assignments will generally provide the person best suited to assist. His selection will then depend on the type of accident, assistance requested, the system or subsystem involved, and the technical problems that might be present.

* An excellent description of the conduct of an accident investigation is contained in Morton M. Hunt's "The Case of Flight 320," *The New Yorker,* 30 April 1960, pp. 119–122.

Near misses occur much more frequently than accidents, but reports on their occurrences are much less frequently submitted, chiefly because reporting procedures are generally lacking. The Federal Aviation Agency requires that both accidents and flight hazards be reported. These flight hazards include those cases in which an accident appeared imminent or possible. Until recently, the numbers of such reports were limited because flight personnel involved in such incidents were afraid that action might be taken against them for infractions of rules of which they were not aware. Lately, however, the policy of the FAA to desist in taking punitive action for such reported near misses has tended to increase the number of reports.

Reports on near misses, either in writing or as determined by interviews (see Critical Incident Technique in Chapter 8), are an important source of information on both designs and procedures. Furthermore, they indicate problems that could result when either the design or the procedure is inadequate or wrong for the operations being undertaken. They indicate the involvement of personnel in hazardous situations, as causative agents, entities to be safeguarded, and as corrective factors by which an accident was avoided.

Near Misses

When a customer, such as the government, contracts for a system or when a manufacturer decides to develop a product, consideration must be given to the cost of the safety program. This cost, in turn, is dependent on the risk involved: How much of a loss can occur if there is no safety program or only a very limited effort? If the product or system is never involved in an accident, some people may consider the funds expended as wasted. In most cases, avoidance of even one major accident will repay the cost of the safety effort. A major problem is the impossibility, in most cases, of establishing with any degree of certainty how much a safety program has saved or what its lack has cost.

System Safety Program Costs

Risk is an expression of probable loss over a specific period of time or over a number of operational cycles. It can be indicated by the probability of an accident times the loss in dollars, lives, or operating units that could occur. This concept of risk involves consideration of the frequency at which mishaps could occur and the possible damage levels. With no damage possible, the system or product is inherently safe, even with matériel or personnel failures, and there is no risk. If the inconvenience of having failures or errors that make the system inoperative creates no other problems, the frequency of occurrence may not matter. On the other hand, since the magnitude of injury and damage generated by a nuclear detonation could be so great, its probability of accidental occurrence must be reduced to an absolute minimum. Between these two examples are other combinations of frequency and loss.

Knowledge of risk involved permits the person responsible for an operation to decide whether the danger can be accepted, must be reduced, requires protective measures be incorporated, or whether the operation must be canceled. He may then be able to determine whether probable losses over a period of time are bearable, be able to decide on amounts that can be spent justifiably on accident prevention measures to reduce losses, and be able to make comparisons between accident rates and losses for different but similar systems.

Risk

Mathematically, risk can be expressed by:

$$\text{Risk} = DM_T = DMN$$

where $\quad D$ = loss per mishap

$\quad M$ = mishap rate, experienced or predicted

$\quad N$ = total length of time, number of periods, or number of operational cycles during which the mishaps occurred or could occur

$\quad M_T$ = number of mishaps

For example, an aerospace system has a planned life cycle of 10 years, during which each of 50 vehicles may be operated 1,500 hr per year. Operations of similar systems indicate that losses due to accidents average $7,000 each. Accidents occur 3.5 times per 10,000 hr of operation. If the cost of the new system is three times that of the old, what will be the risk (expected loss) per year?

$$\text{Risk} = 3 \times 7,000 \times 3.5 \times 10^{-4} \times 50 \times 1500 = \$551,250 \text{ per year}$$

Risk determination and prediction has provided the concept on which insurance has been based for hundreds of years. Cases in which complete loss of equipment result can be evaluated comparatively easily. More complex problems exist in evaluating possible losses where there is a range of damage that can occur. For example, the probability of a mishap to an aircraft can be estimated or determined from past experience. However, the possible losses can vary from damage to a wing tip to complete destruction of the aircraft. For any detailed evaluation, it is necessary to employ subjective probabilities in which the probability of any specific level of damage occurring is further dependent on the probability that, first, an accident will occur and, secondly, that it will involve a specific type and level of damage. The insurance company could categorize as follows the probability of each level of damage of an aircraft valued at $100,000 if an accident should occur:

Damage ($) (1)	Average ($) (2)	Probability* (3)	(2) × (3)
1– 1,000	500	0.10	50
1,000– 10,000	5,500	0.75	4,125
10,000– 20,000	15,000	0.07	1,050
20,000– 30,000	25,000	0.03	750
30,000– 40,000	35,000	0.02	700
40,000– 50,000	45,000	0.015	675
50,000– 60,000	55,000	0.005	275
60,000– 70,000	65,000	0.004	260
70,000– 80,000	75,000	0.003	225
80,000– 90,000	85,000	0.002	170
90,000–100,000	95,000	0.001	95
		1.000	$8,375

* Assumed values

The table is predicated on the premise that when a mishap occurs there will be damage. Mishaps from all causes may occur at a rate equal to 3.0 per 100,000 hr of flying time. The number of losses between $1,000 and $10,000 will therefore be:

$$3.0 \times .75 = 2.25 \text{ per } 100,000 \text{ hr}$$

The total monetary loss for damages between $1,000 and $10,000 for 100,000 hr of flying time can be expected to be:

$$2.25 \times 5,500 = \$12,375.$$

The average loss for any mishap can be approximated by the summation of the average or each loss category times its probability. The result in this case is $8,375. Expectations are therefore, that 3.0 mishaps will take place every 100,000 hours with an average loss of $8,375 per mishap, and a total dollar loss of $25,125.

Various attempts have been made to measure the safety level of a product or system through analysis of past accident statistics. In some instances, rates per unit of hours or of total losses have been used. Neither one of these is entirely satisfactory. Risk, the product of rate and loss, provides a better measure of the impact of accidents. For example, the Air Force computes accident statistics on the basis of rates. According to this method, two aircraft loss rates for a specific year were:

Safety Index

U-10 . . . . .27.6 aircraft per 100,000 hours of flight
F-105 . . . . .27.4 aircraft per 100,000 hours of flight

Statistically, the rate of loss of the F-105 is almost equal to that of the U-10. However, the F-105 cost $2,100,000 and the U-10, $55,200. If we recompute on the basis of rates times monetary loss:

	RATE	×	LOSS	=	INDEX
U-10	27.6		55,200		$ 1.52 $\times 10^6$
F-105	27.4		2,100,000		57.5 $\times 10^6$

The material loss to the Air Force of an F-105 is therefore 38 times as significant as that of a U-10. This can be exemplified further by the two following tables that show the significance of aircraft losses listed first by rate only and then by risk level.

MISHAP RATES ALONE

AIRCRAFT	RATE	SIGNIFICANCE RANK
	(per 100,000 hours)	
A-1	34.0	1
O-1	19.7	2
F-106	9.4	3
H-43	6.0	4
C-123	4.8	5
T-28	3.9	6
B-47	2.2	7

Risk indices such as those shown above and in the table on the top of page 58 can serve a number of purposes:

- This ranking method shows where the greatest effort should be applied to minimize loss of resources.

- Past experience can provide a measure of future probable losses for cost effectiveness studies, planning, and budgeting. For

RISK

AIRCRAFT	RATE	LOSS	INDEX	SIGNIFICANCE RANK
F-106	9.4	$3,560,000	33.46×10^6	1
A-1	34.0	414,000	14.08	2
B-47	2.2	1,900,000	4.18	3
C-123	4.8	680,000	3.26	4
H-43	6.0	304,000	1.82	5
O-1	19.7	30,000	0.59	6
T-28	3.9	142,000	0.55	7

example, a loss index for an aircraft may be $1,710,000 per 100,000 hr. If it is estimated that these aircraft will fly 300,000 hr during a specific period, a loss of $5,130,000 can be expected during that time.

- Values obtained in these ways can be used in tradeoff studies to determine approximately how much could reasonably be spent on safety equipment and other protective devices. The person making the decision to accept or reject a specific level of risk must consider all pertinent factors. Although he may be determined to make the system as safe as possible, he generally must keep expenditures within the limit of available funds. Efforts to increase the safety of any product must therefore be predicated on probable losses that would result because accidents were possible. To obtain support for the safety effort and to indicate where the effort can be best concentrated, risk data are required.

Risk Versus Cost Investment in a safety program is justifiable from an economic standpoint only when risk exceeds cost. Mathematically, some of the interrelationships can be expressed as follows:

$$C_E = \text{cost of safety effort}$$
$$C_A = \text{dollar loss in a mishap}$$
$$M = \text{mishap rate, actual or predicted}$$
$$N = \text{number of periods or cycles}$$
$$M_T = \text{number of mishaps}$$

1. Loss during a life cycle:

   Total loss = Number of mishaps × Average loss per mishap
   $$= M_T C_A = M C_A N$$

2. Loss rate during a specific period
   $$= \text{Mishap rate} \times \text{Average loss per mishap}$$
   $$= M C_A$$

The overall value to an organization of a safety program equals the cost of the mishap prevention effort and of losses.

$$\text{Value over a period} = C_E + M_T C_A$$

$$\text{Or as a rate} \qquad = \frac{C}{N} E + M C_A$$

The Safety Program

Increased cost of added safety effort can be justified only by decreasing the mishap number or rate, severity, or both. The product of these two factors must exceed any added cost to be economically justifiable. A comparison of two efforts for the same system would show.

1. Savings during an entire life cycle would

$$= M_{T_1}C_{A_1} - M_{T_2}C_{A_2} + C_{E_2} - C_{E_1}$$

2. Rate of savings would

$$= M_1 C_{A_1} - M_2 C_{A_2} + \frac{C_{E_2}}{N} - \frac{C_{E_1}}{N}$$

$$= M_1 C_{A_1} - M_2 C_{A_2} + \frac{1}{N}(C_{E_2} - C_{E_1})$$

chapter 4

BASIC CONCEPTS OF HAZARDS

Accidents have been occurring since time immemorial, and personnel have been concerned with their prevention for almost as long. Unfortunately, even though the subject has been discussed continually, the language involved still lacks clarity and precision. From a technical standpoint this is especially frustrating since it results in a lack of communication and understanding and contributes to the difficulty in solving problems. Any discussion of hazards and hazard analyses must be preceded by explanations of terms, their precise meanings, and interrelationships.

Explanation of Terms

The following explanations are the author's attempt to define more precisely terms that are widely used but often in diverse ways.

Hazard—A hazard is a condition with the potential of causing injury to personnel, damage to equipment or structures, loss of matériel, or lessening of the ability to perform a prescribed function. When a hazard is present, the possibility exists of these adverse effects occurring.

Danger—Danger expresses a relative exposure to a hazard. A hazard may be present, but there may be little danger because of the precautions taken. A high-voltage transformer bank, such as those in power transmission systems, has an inherent hazard of electrocuting someone as long as it is energized. A high degree of danger exists if the bank is unprotected in the middle of a busy, inhabited area. The same hazard is present even when the transformers are completely enclosed in a locked underground vault. However, there is almost no danger to personnel. An aboveground installation with a high fence and locked gate has a danger level between these two.

Numerous other examples can be cited, showing how danger levels differ even though the hazard is the same. A person working on a very high structure is subject to the hazard that he could fall to his death. When he wears an anchored safety harness, the danger is reduced but is still present since the harness might break.

Damage—Damage is the severity of injury or the physical, functional, or monetary loss that could result if control of a hazard is lost. An unprotected man falling from a steel beam 10 ft above a concrete pavement might suffer a sprained ankle or broken leg. He would be killed in a similar fall from 300 ft. The hazard (possibility) and danger (exposure) of falling are the same. The difference is in the severity of damage that would result if a fall occurred.

Safety—Safety is frequently defined as "freedom from hazards." However, it is practically impossible to eliminate all hazards completely. Safety is therefore a matter of relative protection from exposure to hazards: the antonym of danger.

Risk—Risk is an expression of possible loss over a specific period of time or number of operational cycles. It may be indicated by the probability of an accident times the damage in dollars, lives, or operating units.

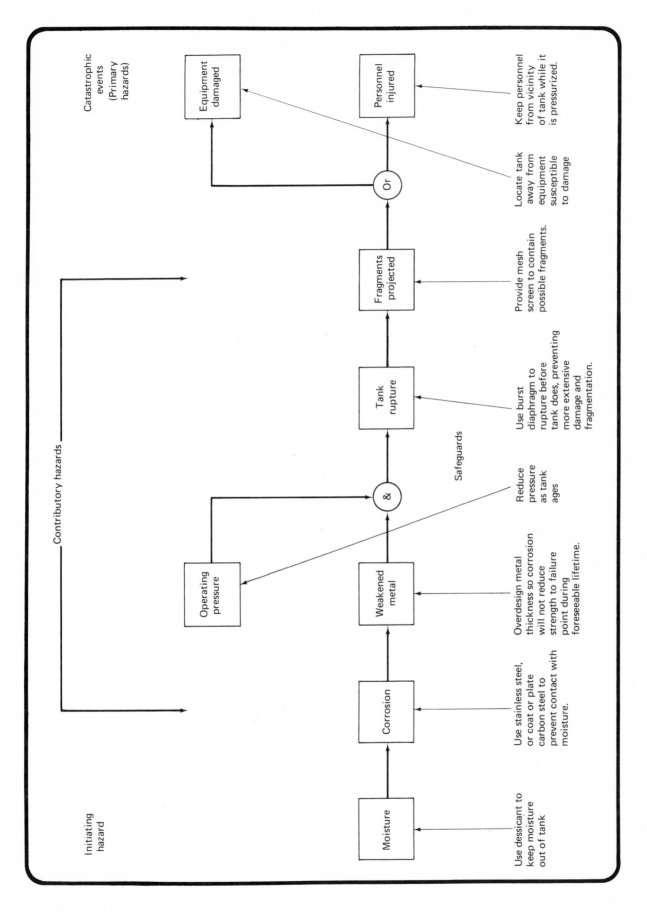

Fig. 4-1. Sequences of events that could cause injury and damage from a rupture of a pressurized steel tank, and possible safeguards.

Primary, Initiating, and Contributory Hazards

Determining exactly which hazard is or has been directly responsible for an accident is not quite as simple as it seems. Consider a high-pressure air tank made of ordinary, unprotected carbon steel. Moisture can cause corrosion, which reduces the strength of the metal, which ruptures and fragments under pressure (See Fig. 4-1.). The fragments hit and injure personnel and damage nearby equipment. Which hazard—moisture, corrosion, reduced strength, or pressure—caused the failure? (Figure 4-1 also illustrates how safeguards can be provided to prevent the mishap and to contain any possible injury or other damage.)

In this series of events, the moisture started the degradation process, which finally resulted in the rupture of the tank. If the tank had been of stainless steel, there would have been no corrosion; moisture would not have been a problem; and there would have been no damage.

Rupture of the tank, which caused the injury and other damage, can be considered the *primary* hazard. The moisture started the series and can be called the *initiating* hazard; the corrosion, loss of strength, and the pressure are *contributory* hazards. The primary hazard is often indicated by other names: catastrophe, catastrophic event, critical event, critical hazard, and single failure. It can be seen that a primary hazard is one that can directly and immediately cause one of the following:

- Injury or death
- Damage to equipment, vehicles, structures, or facilities
- Degradation of functional capabilities (disruption of power transmission service)
- Loss of matériel (accidental release of large amounts of oil or chemicals)

Determining Existence of Hazards

Each system or product has certain inherent hazards. However, each system or product will have only a limited number of primary hazards and a larger number of initiating and contributory hazards. A list of possible primary, initiating, and contributory hazards in a specific system or product can be developed in two ways. Past experience is the principal one but may not contain all possibilities. For example, although nuclear weapons have been involved in accidents, there has never been an accidental nuclear detonation. Experience data alone would indicate no possibility of such a detonation. Theoretically, such a mishap is possible, but the danger (probability) of its occurrence is low because of the controls imposed. Experience can provide an excellent base, which can be extended with theoretical possibilities. Or the process can be reversed by considering first all theoretical aspects and then adding all possible information available from past experience.

The Appendix was prepared in this last way. It lists a wide variety of hazards, with their possible causes and effects. This table can be used as a reference or a check list when an analysis is being made. The basic problem areas are shown in Fig. 4-2a, which can be employed as a rough check sheet. The component, assembly, product, system, task, or operation under consideration is noted in the column headings. Each hazard is considered, and a decision made on whether it can affect or be generated by the entry at the head of the column. A mark is then entered for the applicable hazard. On a separate sheet, the alphanumeric combination for column and line is shown with detailed information

Subsystem/operation _____

		Unit or task	(1)	(2)	(3)
HAZARD					
Acceleration and motion	A				
Chemical reactions	B				
Dissociation	C				
Oxidation	D				
Replacement	E				
Contamination	F				
Corrosion	G				
Electrical	H				
System failure	I				
Inadvertent activation	J				
Shock	K				
Thermal	L				
Explosion	M				
Fire	N				
Heat and temperature	O				
High temperature	P				
Low temperature	Q				
Changes	R				
Impact and shock	S				
Leakage	T				
Moisture	U				
High humidity	V				
Low humidity	W				
Power source failure	X				
Pressure	Y				
High pressure	Z				
Low pressure	AA				
Changes	BB				
Radiation	CC				
Thermal	DD				
Electromagnetic	EE				
Ionizing	FF				
Ultraviolet	GG				
Structural damage/failure	HH				
Stress concentrations	II				
Stress reversals	JJ				
Toxicity	KK				
Vibration and noise	LL				

a.

Possibilities of injury
by subsystem or operation

Subsystem/operation _____

			Unit or task	(1)	(2)	(3)	(4)	(5)	(6)
	TYPE OF INJURY								
Mechanical	Cuts	A							
	Punctures	B							
	Bruises	C							
	Broken bones	D							
	Particles in eyes	E							
Burns	Electrical	F							
	Thermal, heat	G							
	Thermal, cold	H							
	Radiation	I							
	Chemical	J							
Pressure	Acceleration	K							
	Crushing, fluid	L							
	Crushing, soild mass	M							
	Pinching	N							
	Noise and vibration	O							
	Dysbarism	P							
Shock	Electrical	Q							
	Pressure wave	R							
	Physical contact	S							
	Physiological	T							
	Trauma	U							
	Cold immersion	V							
Toxicity	Asphyxiation	W							
	Organic damage	X							
	Respiratory sys.dmge.	Y							
	Circulatory sys.dmge.	Z							
	Dermatosis	AA							
Others	Heat exhaustion	BB							
	Wind chill	CC							

b.

describing the problem. A similar type of checklist can be made for possible injuries (Fig. 4-2b).

For products and systems that have been or are in operational use, the hazards and required safeguards may already be known. Proposed systems can often be analyzed through synthesis of information known about its subsystems and components. A new electrical product, such as a household appliance, must be studied for possibilities of shock, high temperatures that could cause burns, and fire.

Fig. 4-2. Hazards that may affect or are produced by subsystems or operations.

Worst-Case Conditions A system or product will be exposed in its operational lifetime to environments, processes, conditions, and loads of varying magnitudes. The stresses and effects produced will differ at various times. All of these and their interrelationships must be analyzed for the worst-case conditions that could exist, the most serious hazards, and the most damaging effects that could be produced. (See the discussion on foreseeability in Chapter 2.) Differences in the magnitudes of damage may be due to such reasons as:

1. Design strengths of materials may have been predicated on data from laboratory tests under specific conditions, such as normal room temperature and pressure at sea level. Operational conditions differing drastically from these temperature variations may produce greatly increased stresses, reduced strengths, or both. Each possible condition of a hazard that changes in magnitude with temperature should therefore be analyzed to determine whether operational requirements will be met. The same is true of all other affecting factors. If this procedure is not followed, a condition may result that will create a failure and an accident. In such cases, it may be necessary to prescribe limits to the hazard to ensure that a worst-case condition does not occur.

2. The point in time at which a problem, such as a failure, occurs may generate a worse effect, more serious accident, or greater damage than at other times. Failure of the first-stage motor igniter during launch of a large missile or space booster from the launch pad would leave it sitting there. A similar failure immediately after launch would result in a fallback and complete destruction. Losing control of a missile immediately after lifting from a pad could be much more damaging, since it is completely loaded with propellant, than loss of control far down range. Each operation and hazard must therefore be investigated for the point in time when loss of control could generate the maximal adverse effect.

3. The most damaging accident can be produced from one having an extremely low probability of occurrence. Conversely, the greatest danger of a mishap may be at a time when minimal damage is likely. Both factors, *probability* and *severity*, must be analyzed to determine the worst-case conditions involved in operation of the system over an extended period, because any probability is based on occurrence of a specific event during an extremely large number of identical operations. When that large number of operations is undertaken, the event (for example, an accident) whose probability has been calculated will generally occur in numbers approximating the value determined by theory. The resultant effects and damage may then range from zero or other minimal amount to an unknown maximum.

In analyses of possible mishaps in which a nuclear device or system could be involved, the term *Maximum Credible Accident* is frequently seen. It is employed to indicate the worst-case condition that can reasonably be expected to occur. The probability may be extremely low, but not so low that it would be impracticable to incorporate suitable safeguards in the system. The concept of Maximum Credible Accident can be illustrated by an example. An aircraft is to be developed to carry a thermal device using a radioactive isotope as the source of energy. The device is nonexplosive; the principal danger is the possibility that a fire could cause dispersion of the radioactive material in airborne products of combustion. The Maximum Credible Accident would be an aircraft crash severe enough to rupture the device and then a fire that would cause isotope dispersion. Since aircraft crashes and fires do occur, it is necessary to provide a container that will not rupture should the Maximum Credible Accident occur.

Study of the hazards in the Appendix shows that they can be divided into three broad categories:

Categories of Hazards

1. Inherent properties or characteristics of the equipment. These may be present in all products of a specific type or may be peculiar to a specific design. Such a product may cause injury, damage, or loss directly, constituting a primary hazard, or may initiate or contribute to an accident. A color television set, which presents a good picture and excellent sound, may give off X-radiation, which could injure nearby viewers. An aircraft crashed because of the characteristics of its control system. When the plane hit severe turbulence, the autopilot overcontrolled, causing an extreme noseover condition during which it dove into the ground. Some automobiles are unsafe under certain conditions that cause them to swerve violently, resulting in loss of control. In these cases, the products or their components have not failed, yet injuries and accidents have resulted.

2. Failures, matériel or human. The greatest number of accidents are due to failures. Human failures are much more common, but their causes and prevention present much more complex problems than do matériel failures. Man as a hazard is discussed in detail later. Much of the information on matériel failures for accident prevention is derived from considerations of reliability programs and their attendant test and operational data. Reliability of a part or product is defined as the probability of successful accomplishment of its mission over a specified time and under stipulated conditions. If the time or conditions are exceeded, failures are not considered as prejudicial to the product's reliability. Failures as safety considerations may therefore constitute a broader scope of interest than they do for reliability analyses.

3. Environmental stresses. Natural conditions can cause immediate injury or damage, can lead to long-term problems, or can place stress on design or human capabilities, thus leading to errors, failures, and accidents. Lightning strikes, hail, or heavy rain are examples of the first type of such environmental hazards. Rain that produces corrosion and high humidity that causes personal stress, discomfort, and errors are examples of the others. Many environmental hazards were previously considered "acts of God" about which little could be done. However, advances in knowledge of the environment and in technology have led to development of safeguards in design and procedures that in many cases have reduced the injurious effects of these natural phenomena.

Any product, system, or operation must therefore be studied for the existence of any of these three categories of hazards, individually or in combination. Hazards can be present, but under suitable control they will present little danger. Not all hazards can or will be eliminated. No aircraft could fly, no automobile move, and no ship put to sea if all hazards had to be eliminated first. Due consideration must therefore be given to all circumstances under which the hazard might exist. The various configurations in which a piece of equipment might be operated or employed, and handling or use to which it will be subjected by personnel of differing competency must be considered. In most cases where it has been established that a hazard exists, suitable safeguards can be provided. This is especially true in cases where a possible failure of matériel constitutes the hazard, since such failure will only occur in a limited number of ways. The product can then be made *fail-safe*, or protective devices or procedures can be provided. Unfortunately, where failure is due to human error, all-encompassing safeguards are more difficult to provide because of the unforeseeable unsafe acts in which personnel can become involved.

Man as a Hazard

Almost every mishap can be traced ultimately to personnel error, although it may not have been error on the part of the person immediately involved in the mishap. It may have been committed by the designer, production worker, maintenance man, or almost anyone other than the person present when the accident occurred. Pilots, especially those of the Air Line Pilots Association, have often protested (and rightly) statements of investigation boards that accidents were the results of pilot error. These findings were predicated on the previously mentioned premise that the pilot should be able to and must overcome any emergency. In many instances, the pilot was overwhelmed by failures due to causes beyond his control; failures could have been forestalled by incorporation of suitable precautions in the design stage.

The designer can do much to minimize the possibility of an emergency occurring through so-called "human error" on the part of others. Human error can be defined as any personnel action that is inconsistent with established behavioral patterns considered to be normal or that differs from prescribed procedures. They can be divided into two categories: *predictable* and *random*.

Predictable errors are those that experience has shown will occur under similar conditions. For example, it is known that a person will generally tend to follow those procedures involving minimal physical and mental effort, discomfort, or time. Any procedure contravening this basic principle is certain to be modified or ignored by the persons supposed to carry it out.

Random errors are nonpredictable and cannot be attributed to any specific cause beforehand because of their uniqueness. For example, a person may be highly competent as an operator but may be annoyed by a fly or mosquito. Swatting at it, he hits a critical control or piece of sensitive equipment. There are fewer types of random errors than there are predictable errors, and even this number is being reduced as experience increases. If swatting flies or mosquitoes becomes a common problem, it becomes a predictable cause for which suitable precautionary measures can be provided. In any case, precautionary measures to minimize the effects that random errors can produce are generally the same as those for predictable errors. The one major difference is that general safeguards may be provided for *all* random errors, while a specific safeguards may be provided for a predictable error.

Errors can also be categorized as *primary* or *contributory*. Primary errors are those committed by personnel immediately and directly involved with the equipment, the operation, and the mishap. Contributory errors result from actions on the part of personnel whose duties preceded and affected the situation during which the results of the error became apparent. In either case, error is generally due to:

- Failure to perform a required function (omission). A step is left out of a procedure, intentionally or inadvertently, or there is failure to complete the sequence. In some instances, intentional omissions may be due to procedures that are overlengthy, badly written, or in defiance of normal tendencies and actions.

- Performing a function not required, including repeating a procedure or procedural step unnecessarily, adding uncalled for steps to a sequence, or substituting an erroneous step (commission).

- Failure to recognize a hazardous condition requiring corrective action.

- Inadequate response to a contingency.

- Wrong decision as a solution to a problem that arises.

- Poor timing, resulting in a response that is too late or too soon for an adverse situation.

Design Errors

The philosophy that accident prevention begins during system or product concept and development rightly implies that the designer is responsible for many accidents. Figure 4-3 indicates that the majority of failures in missile electronic systems is principally due to inadequate design. The designer may not only commit errors but be guilty of omissions in failing to incorporate desirable features as safeguards that would have prevented accidents or protected personnel. When a designer cannot eliminate a hazard or the possibility of an accident completely, he must attempt to minimize the possibilities that other personnel will commit errors generating mishaps. In effect, the designer, through foreseeability, must attempt to make the system "idiot-proof," although he knows he will always be subject to the inevitability of Murphy's Law.*

Errors that can eventually damage or destroy an operational system or its equipment and that can injure or kill the operators can be generated as early as the time the system is first conceived. Pilatre de Rozier's proposal to use hydrogen as a buoyancy agent in the presence of an

---

* There are hundreds of whimsical versions of "Murphy's Law," each containing a grain of truth that makes them sadly applicable. Four versions are:

- Any task that can be done incorrectly, no matter how remote the possibility, will someday be done that way.
- No matter how difficult it is to damage equipment, a way will be found.
- Any item that can fail can be expected to fail at the most inopportune and damaging time.
- Instructions will be ignored when the most dangerous and complicated task is being accomplished.

ELECTRONIC SYSTEM FAILURES*

MODE CATEGORY	PERCENTAGE OF TOTAL	PROBABLE RESPONSIBILITY
Transients	17.1	D
Excessive current	10.7	M or I
Damaged	9.2	I
Shorts	6.9	M or I
Poor bond — opens	6.7	M or I
Low safety margin	5.2	D
Thermal expansion-contraction	4.8	D
Broken semiconductor crystals	4.6	D or M or I
Improper material	4.6	D or M or I
Improper switching time	4.3	D
Tolerance buildup	4.0	D
Wrong procedure	3.7	I
Contacts burned-welded	3.4	D or M or I
Parameter change	2.8	M
Excessive epoxy	2.8	M
Contamination	2.3	M
Poor heat sink	1.2	D
Corrosion	1.2	D
Cold solder joints	1.2	M
Miscellaneous	3.1	D or M or I

D for design and system problems; M for manufacturing and quality; I for improper operation by the user.
Survey based on 5,000 samples.

Figure 4-3

open fire was doomed. He was told so by persons familiar with the characteristics of hydrogen, but he ignored their warnings.

Most design errors are more subtle. The word "error" in such cases includes more than a mistake. It also includes any design that is technically practical but improper and inadequate for the conditions under which it is to be operated. For example, all the controls on a panel may be well chosen for their intended individual functions. However, their arrangement on the panel may invite errors by the operators or unacceptably increase operator reaction times. Inabilities to act or respond properly may generate difficulties for the operators.

A design error can also be one that violates normal tendencies and expectancies. People expect that on a vertically numbered instrument, the higher value numbers will be at the top; on a dial, they expect values to increase clockwise. A design can place undue stresses on the operator. Instead of being provided with means to avoid contamination of an environment, the user may be required to wear burdensome respiratory protective equipment. Other fatigue-producing designs are those that fail to eliminate glare, inadequate lighting, vibration or noise, undue strength requirements for activation of controls, unusual positions in which to operate, or proximity of hot surfaces. A person who must

Basic Concepts of Hazards

70

work close to heat-radiating equipment in a humid environment may perspire so much that his efficiency is badly affected. If too close to the hot equipment, he must be on guard constantly to avoid burning himself. This tension reduces his efficiency even more because of the psychological stress imposed.

Figure 4-4 indicates numerous causes of errors that can be committed by operators and the measures that designers can utilize to eliminate or minimize them. Certain of these measures are almost mandatory in any design; that is, they constitute good engineering practice and cost little more to provide. Other measures are more costly and are provided only when a procuring or regulatory activity requires their incorporation. Each of these measures can help alleviate the problem of error somewhat, although probably not entirely.

Production Errors

Manufacturing errors can ruin any design. These can sometimes be minimized by providing special care and attention to critical components during their production and assembly into larger units. A critical items list is often prepared for this purpose from a comprehensive analysis of the system's components and functions.

During assembly personnel can introduce additional errors that could later cause failures and problems for operators. Failures to torque fluid connections tightly enough so they loosen and leak are common. Overtorquing them may cause them to crack and also to leak. Failures to keep electrical connectors clean, dry, and free of wire strands can cause short circuits when the system is energized. Scratches, dents, corrosion, tool marks, and other rough finishes will create stress concentrations that could result in structural failures under operational loads.

Maintenance and Repair Errors

Failures to lubricate moving devices, or to replace parts when scheduled or when they show signs of deterioration are examples of these types of errors. Mistakes in reassembling equipment that has been disassembled can be similar to those that often occur when initial assembly is made during production.

Maintenance and repair errors sometimes involve the same mistakes that occur during manufacture and those that occur during operations. In effect, maintenance and repair personnel are often subjected to greater hazards than operators, consequently, their errors can involve them in more injurious accidents. For example, failures to depressurize pneumatic systems have caused fatalities to repairmen. Personnel who worked on high-voltage electrical equipment or lines without first de-energizing them have been electrocuted. Many of the causes of error indicated in Fig. 4-4 are especially significant and applicable to maintenance and repair personnel.

Operations Errors

As the name implies, these errors can occur during operation of a system and are principally procedural and control types. Procedural mistakes taking place during normal operations can generate abnormal situations leading to accidents. An operator can activate a circuit inadvertently, fail to close a valve or to shut off a pump, or forget to set the brakes when parking a vehicle on an incline. Procedural errors are especially critical during contingencies when an emergency already exists. Personnel

ERROR PREVENTION THROUGH GOOD DESIGN

CAUSES OF PRIMARY ERRORS	PREVENTIVE MEASURES (TAKEN BY DESIGNER OR METHODS ENGINEER)
1. Improvising procedures that are lacking in the field	1. Provide adequate instructions.
2. Following prescribed but incorrect procedures	2. Ensure that procedures are correct.
3. Failure to follow prescribed procedures	3. Ensure that procedures are not too lengthy, too fast, or too slow for good performance, and are not hazardous or awkward.
4. Lack of adequate planning for error or unusual conditions.	4. Provide backout or emergency procedures in instructions.
5. Lack of understanding of procedures	5. Ensure that instructions are easy to understand
6. Lack of awareness of hazards	6. Provide warnings, cautions, or explanations in instructions.
7. Untimely activation of equipment	7. Provide interlocks or timer lockouts. Provide warning or caution notes against activating equipment unless disconnected or disengaged from load, or other damaging conditions.
8. Errors of judgment, especially during periods of stress	8. Minimize requirements for making hurried judgments, especially at critical times, through programmed contingency measures.
9. Critical components installed incorrectly	9. Provide designs permitting such components to be installed only in the proper ways. Use assymetric configurations on mechanical equipment or electrical connectors; use female or male threads or different-sized connections on critical valves, filters, or other components in which direction of flow is important.
10. Exceeding prescribed limitations on load, speed or other parameter	10. Provide governors and other parameter limiters. Provide warnings on: exceeding limitations, inadequate strength of stressed parts, use of excessive mechanical leverage.
11. Lack of suitable tools or equipment	11. Ensure that need for special tools or equipment is minimized; develop and provide those that are necessary; stress their need in instructions.
12. Interference with normal habits	12. Ensure that recognition and activation patterns are in accordance with usual practices and expectancies.
13. Lack of data on which to make correct or timely decisions	13. Ensure that response time is adequate for corrective action; if not, provide automatic corrective devices.
14. Hampered activities because of interference between personnel	14. Ensure that space is adequate to perform required activities simultaneously.
15. Inability to concentrate because of unsafe conditions or equipment	15. Ensure that personnel must not work close to unguarded moving parts, hot surfaces, sharp edges, or other dangers.
16. Error or delay in use of controls	16. Avoid proximity, interference, awkward location, or similarity of critical controls. Locate control close to readout. Locate readout above control so hand or arm making adjustment does not block out readout instrument. Ensure that controls are labeled prominently for easy understanding.

Figure 4-4

17.	Error or delay in reading instruments	17	Ensure that instruments are labeled and designed for easy understanding; do not require reader to turn head or move body; and that visibility problems due to glare or lack of light, legibility, viewing angle, contrast, or reflections are avoided. Provide direct readings of specific parameters so operator does not have to interpret.
18.	Inadvertent activation of controls	18.	For critical functions provide controls that cannot be activated inadvertently: use torque types instead of push buttons. Provide guards over critical switches.
19.	Controls activated in wrong order	19.	Place functional controls in sequence in which they are to be used. Provide interlocks where sequences are critical.
20.	Control settings by operator not precise enough	20.	Provide controls that permit making settings or adjustments without need for extremely fine movements. Use click-type controls.
21.	Controls broken by excessive force	21.	Ensure that controls are adequate to withstand maximum stress an operator could apply. Provide warning and caution notes for those devices that could be over stressed.
22.	Failure to take action at proper time because of faulty instruments	22.	Provide procedures to calibrate instruments periodically, or provide the means to ensure during operation that they are working correctly.
23.	Confusion in reading critical instruments because of instrument clutter	23.	Make critical instruments most prominent or locate in easiest-to-read area.
24.	Failure to note critical indication	24.	Provide suitable auditory or visual warning device that will attract operator's attention to problem.
25.	Involuntary reaction or inability to perform properly because of pain due to burns, electrical shock, puncture wound, or impact	25.	Insulate or guard against hot surfaces, "live" electrical conductors, sharp objects, and hard surfaces.
26.	Fatigue	26.	Avoid placing on operator severe and tiring physical and mental requirements such as loads, concentration times, vibration, personal stress, awkward positions.
27.	Vibration and noise cause irritation and inability to read meters and settings or to operate controls	27.	Provide vibration isolators or noise elimination devices.
28.	Irritation and loss of effectiveness due to high temperature and humidity	28.	Provide environmental control. Prevent entrance or generation of heat or moisture from external sources or from internal equipment or processes.
29.	Loss of effectiveness due to lack of oxygen, or to presence of toxic gas, airborne particulate matter, or odors	29.	Prevent generation or entrance of contaminants into the occupied space. Provide suitable life support equipment. Avoid presence near occupied areas of lines or equipment containing hazardous gases or liquids.
30.	Degradation of capabilities due to extremely low temperatures	30.	Ensure that design provides for adequate heating or insulation, protective shelter, equipment, or clothing.
31.	Fixation or hypnosis	31.	Avoid procedures or designs that require visual concentrations for long periods of time. Avoid humming equipment. Provide alternate reference points. Provide procedures to relieve monotony.
32.	Disorientation or vertigo	32.	Provide adequate reference points or means to maintain orientation.

Figure 4-4 continued.

| 33. | Slipping and falling | 33. | Incorporate friction surfaces or devices, guard rails, access hole covers on floor openings, or protective harness in designs. |
| 34. | Inattention | 34. | Avoid long intervals between procedural steps. Provide female voice on audio devices to attract attention. Provide bright, colorful, and pleasant work areas. |

Figure 4-4 continued.

are extremely susceptible to committing error at such times since they are almost always in a state of shock. The disruptive effect of such shock will depend on the training of the individual, his reflexes and temperament, the type and severity of the contingency, reaction time available, complexity of the operations that he must perform, and numerous other factors. The ability to make decisions is generally impaired, no matter how calm the individual may appear. At such times, there is an increased propensity for making errors.

Control errors can occur even when a procedure is carried out in the stipulated sequence. Indicators can be read incorrectly; setting adjustments can be inaccurate; a wrong push button can be punched in performance of a prescribed procedure; control of a vehicle can be lost due to excessive speed; one airplane can be taxied into another plane; or too sharp a turn on a wet pavement can cause an automobile to skid. There can be an excessive delay in operating controls, or the operator can overcontrol a piece of equipment. In some instances, an operator can become so irritated because of an inability to make a fine adjustment, to get an adequate response, or simply because of high environmental temperature and humidity that he may "slam" the controls violently. Such action can be as damaging as an inadvertent error.

Two-Man Concept To minimize the possibility of human error in accomplishing any procedure involving a nuclear device, the Department of Defense has developed the "Two-Man Concept." Two or more persons, each capable of undertaking the prescribed task and of detecting that incorrect or unauthorized procedures have been employed, are involved. One person accomplishes a step in a procedure and the other checks his actions to make sure the step has been accomplished correctly. Thus, the possibility of error is reduced and system reliability is ensured. It is not necessary that both persons have "equal" knowledge; it is only necessary that each has the capability of detecting and ensuring that the action of the other has been correct and authorized.

Man Versus Machine Accidents attributable to human error are basically similar. Information on human error as a causative factor in accidents can be determined from different areas of investigation in psychology, physiology, accident analysis, industrial operations, and other sources. The information can then be evaluated, adapted, and used for new systems being developed. Unfortunately, although the basic causes of accidents are alike, personnel have generated a myriad of variations that plague any safety effort.

Accidents rarely involve willful violations of procedures or a desire to cause a mishap. They are generally due to situations in which human capabilities are inadequate and overwhelmed by a need to respond rapidly to an adverse situation. These inadequacies can be permanent or transient. Physical limitations or inadequate training can be considered permanent inadequacies. Transient inadequacies can be temporary losses of capabilities because of long hours of activity with inadequate rest, lack of understanding between personnel, or external physiological or psychological pressures. More important is the need to make an extremely rapid decision while suffering temporarily from shock due to a sudden and unexpected emergency. Man cannot be excelled in his abilities to cope with unusual and unforeseen situations. However, even this capacity is limited and easily impaired.

A human being is subject to such a magnitude of variables of varying degrees in different situations in which different possible responses can produce different effects that all possible combinations cannot be foreseen. The problem is compounded by the fact that each of these combinations is different for almost every individual. The designer would find it impossible to produce a system that would be applicable to every individual's case. Analysts have found it almost impossible to determine with any degree of certainty whether any specific person will or will not cause an accident.* Therefore, when designing a system, the designer must provide for as many possible combinations as foreseeable by assuming that man is a subsystem that can malfunction in certain ways.

Man as a subsystem can have precisely defined and measured capabilities. Limiting conditions that must not be exceeded if accidents are to be prevented are available. In handbooks the vast amount of such information is based on man as a machine, as a structure, as a biological organism, as a chemical process, as a sensing device, as an activating agency, and as a power source.

He has often been compared to a machine, a comparison that does man little justice. Figure 4-5 compares specific abilities. The total weight of machines required to perform the many functions that man can accomplish would probably exceed 1,000 times the weight of a man's body. He is a highly efficient organism, able to accomplish many functions that machines cannot. Man can reason inductively, mentally reaching far beyond the abilities of any existing computer. He can adjust to unusual situations, improving conditions where necessary to overcome unforeseen difficulties in the way of successful accomplishment.

The capabilities of his senses can equal or exceed those of manufactured equipment. No simple machine can determine odor, taste, or color, or their gradations with the versatility of a human. The ear can detect sound with an amplitude of vibration as small as $1/30$ of the

---

* "How to Pick Women Who Can Drive Cars," (The *Literary Digest* 5 April 1924) ; p. 58 published a means of determining a woman's abilities as a driver:

> The fullness of the bony ridge in the eyebrow region is said to be an unmistakable sign of a woman' driving ability. Same with the ear in which the central section is larger. A firm mouth, with closed lips is credited with indicating carefulness, while full lips and a partly open mouth belong to impulsive persons. If the crown of the head appears rounded, its owner is not very cautious, but if the back of the head at the crown is wider across, caution is well represented.

CAPABILITIES: MAN VERSUS MACHINE

MAN	MACHINE
Can reason and make decisions inductively.	Has no inductive capability.
Can follow a random and variable strategy.	Always follows the programmed strategy.
Can improvise and exercise judgment based on memory, experience, education, and reasoning.	Is better at routine functions.
Can make judgments and take action when preset procedures are impossible.	Programs for all conceivable situations, such as emergencies, and corrective or alternative actions are impracticable.
Can adapt his performance since he learns by experience, education, and reasoning.	Cannot learn other than those facts and capabilities that it is programmed to learn.
Has high ability to reason out ambiguities and vague statements and information.	Is highly limited if input lacks clarity.
Can interpret an input signal accurately even in the presence of distraction, high noise level, jamming, or masking.	Can have performance degraded by interference so it may fail entirely.
Can fill in lacking portions himself to supplement superficial training.	Pertinent facts and programming must be present and complete for accomplishment of function.
Can undertake new programs without extensive or precise programming.	Reprogramming must be as complete and precise as initial programming.
Can sometimes overcome effects of failure of one part of his nervous system through use of other parts.	Electronic systems will sometimes fail completely if only a single circuit element fails.
Can maintain himself or require comparatively little care.	Maintenance is always required and increases with system complexity.
Is small and light in weight for all functions that can be performed, and requires little power.	Equivalent capabilities are generally heavier, bigger, and with high power and cooling requirements.
Is in good supply and inexpensive for most functions.	Complexity and supply is limited by cost and production time.
Can override preset procedures and plans if necessary or preferable.	Can accomplish only preprogrammed actions within their designed capabilities.
Can add reliability to system performance by his ability to make repairs on associated equipment.	Generally has no repair capabilities.
Can detect and sometimes correct his own mistakes.	Machines make few mistakes once their programs have been checked out. Programs frequently have self-check routines.
Can sometimes tolerate overloads without complete failure; in other cases, performance deteriorates slowly.	Even small overloads can cause complete breakdown or disruption of operations.
Has high performance flexibility.	Performs only tasks for which it was built and programmed.
Performance can be degraded by fatigue, boredom, or diurnal cycling.	Performance will be degraded only by lack of calibration or maintenance.
Long repetitive tasks will impair performance.	Performs repetitive or precise tasks well.
Can refuse to perform even when capable of doing so.	Will always respond to proper instructions except when there is a malfunction
Can detect low-probability events impracticable in machine systems.	Many unexpected events cannot be handled adequately because of the size and complexity of the equipment required.
Can exert comparatively small force. Generally cannot execute a large force smoothly or for extended periods.	Can exert large forces smoothly and precisely for for almost any periods of time.
Is not adapted to high-speed search of voluminous information.	Searching of voluminous information is a basic function of computers.

Figure 4-5

Is interested in personal survival.

Is emotional in relations with others and in stress situations.

Performance may deteriorate with work-cycle duration.

Great individual differences can take place in performances by different personnel.

Has certain sensing abilities machines do not have: smell and taste.

Quickly saturates capacity for accomplishing diversified functions.

Lacks consciousness of personal existence.

Has no personal relations or emotions.

Performance is impaired relatively little with long work cycles if maintenance has been adequate.

Only very minor differences in performances will take place by similar types of machines.

Range of abilities generally extends outside human limits for those abilities it does have: can see into infrared and ultraviolet.

Can be designed to accomplish a large number of functions at once. Ability to do each rapidly increases its ability to do many sequentially. Can frequently do many simultaneously.

Figure 4-5 continued.

diameter of a single molecule. The eye is equally sensitive, having the ability to detect as few as six quanta or photons of light. Some of the capabilities of man's senses are listed in Figs. 4-6 to 4-8. Intensity range of each sense indicates the lowest and highest points between which these abilities generally exist. Discrimination indicates a change within these limits that would be detectable by the average person.

PARAMETER	VISION	AUDITION	TOUCH	VESTIBULAR
Sufficient stimulus	Light-radiated electromagnetic energy in the wavelengths from 400 to 700 mμ (violet to red)	Sound-vibratory energy, usually airborne 20 cps to 20,000 cps	Tissue displacement by physical means >0 to <400 pulses per second	Accelerative forces Linear and rotational accelerations
Spectral range	120 to 160 steps in wavelength (hue) varying from 1 to 20 mμ.	~ 3 cps (20 to 1000 cps) 0.3 percent (above 1000 cps)	$\frac{\Delta pps}{pps} \simeq 0.10$	
Dynamic range	~ 90 db (useful range) for rods = 0.00001 mL to 0.004 mL; cones = 0.004 mL to 10,000 mL	140 db (0 db = 0.0002 dyne/cm^2)	~ 30 db, 0.01 mm to 10 mm	Absolute threshold $\simeq 0.2°$ /sec/sec
Amplitude resolution $\left[\frac{\Delta I}{I}\right]$	contrast = $\frac{\Delta I}{I}$ = 0.015	0.5 db (1000 cps at 20 db or above)	0.15	~ 0.10 change in acceleration
Acuity	10 arcminutes	Temporal acuity (clicks) $\simeq$ 0.001 sec	Two-point acuity = 0.1 mm (tongue) to 50 mm (back)	
Response for rate for successive stimuli	~ 0.1 sec	~ 0.01 sec (tone bursts)	Touches sensed as discrete to 20/sec	~ 1 to 2 sec nystagmus may persist to 2 min after rapid changes in rotation
Reaction time for simple muscular movement	~ 0.22 sec	~ 0.19 sec	~ 0.15 sec (for finger motion, if finger is the one stimulated)	
Best operating range	500 to 600 μ (green-yellow) 10 to 200 foot-candles	300 to 6000 cps 40 to 80 db		1 g acceleration directed head to foot
Indications for use	1. Spatial orientation required. 2. Spatial scanning or search required. 3. Simultaneous comparisons required. 4. Multidimensional material presented. 5. High ambient noise levels.	1. Warning to emergency signals 2. Interruption of attention required 3. Small temporal relations important. 4. Poor ambient lighting. 5. High vibration or g forces present.	1. Conditions unfavorable for both vision and audition. 2. Visual and auditory senses.	1. Gross sensing of acceleration information.

Figure 4-6

MAN'S SENSES AS INFORMATIONAL CHANNELS: A COMPARISON
OF THE INTENSITY RANGES AND INTENSITY DISCRIMINATION ABILITIES
OF THE SENSES*

| SENSE | INTENSITY RANGE | | INTENSITY DISCRIMINATION | |
	SMALLEST DETECTABLE	LARGEST PRACTICAL	RELATIVE	ABSOLUTE
Vision	2.2 to 5.7×10^{-10} ergs	Roughly, the brightness of snow in the midday sun, or about 10^9 times the threshold intensity	With white light, there are about 570 discriminable intensity differences in a practical range	With white light, 3 to 5 absolutely identifiable intensities in a range of 0.1 to 50 ml.
Audition	1×10^{-9} ergs/cm^2	Roughly, the intensity of the sound produced by a jet plane with afterburner or about 10^{14} times the threshold intensity	At a frequency of 2,000 cps, there are approximately 325 discriminable intensity differences	With pure tones about 3 to 5 identifiable steps
Mechanical vibration	For a small stimulator on the fingertip, average amplitudes of 0.00025 mm can be detected	Varies with size of stimulator, portion of body stimulated and individual. Pain is usually encountered about 40 db above threshold	In the chest region a broad contact vibrator with amplitude limits between 0.05 mm and 0.5 mm provides 15 discriminable amplitudes	3 to 5 steps
Touch pressure	Varies considerably with body areas stimulated and the type of stimulator. Some representative values: Ball of thumb— 0.026 erg Fingertips— 0.037 to 1.090 ergs Arm—0.032 to 0.113 erg	Pain threshold	Varies enormously for area measured, duration of stimulus contact and interval between presentation of standard and comparison stimuli	Unknown
Smell	Widely variant with type of odorous substance. Some representative values: Vanillin—2×10^{-7} mg/m^8 Mercaptan (C_2H_5SH)—4×10^{-5} mg/m^3 Diethyl/Ether ($C_2H_5OC_2H_5$) 1.0 mg/m^3	Largely unknown	No data available	No data available
Taste	Widely variant with type and temperature of taste substance. Some representative values: Sugar—0.02 molar concentration Quinine Sulfate— 4×10^{-7} molar concentration	Not known	No data available	No data available

Figure 4-7   78

| | INTENSITY RANGE | | INTENSITY DISCRIMINATION | |
SENSE	SMALLEST DETECTABLE	LARGEST PRACTICAL	RELATIVE	ABSOLUTE
Temperature	Sensation of heat results from a 3-second exposure of 200 cm^2 of skin at rate of 1.5×10^{-4} gm-cal/cm^2/sec	Pain results from a 3-second exposure of 200 cm^2 of skin at a rate of 0.218 gm-cal/cm^2/sec	No data available	No data available
Kinesthesis	Joint movements of 0.2 degree to 0.7 degree at a rate of 10 deg/min can be detected. Generally, the larger joints are the most sensitive	Unknown	No data available	No data available
Angular acceleration	Dependent on the type of indicator used 1. Skin and muscle senses 1 deg/sec^2 2. Nystagmic eye movements 1 deg/sec^2 3. Oculogyral illusion 0.12 deg/sec^2	Unconsciousness or "blackout" occurs for positive "G" forces of 5 to 8 G lasting 1 second or more Negative forces of 3 to 4.5 G cause mental confusion, "red-vision" and extreme headaches lasting sometimes for hours following stimulation	No data available	No data available
Linear acceleration	In aircraft—0.02 G for accelerative forces and 0.08 G for decelerative forces	For forces acting in the direction of the long axis of the body, the same limitations as for angular acceleration apply	No data available	No data available

Figure 4-7 continued.

Judgment

Another outstanding capability of man is his ability to exercise judgment. He can assemble data from various outside sources, correlate these with information drawn from past experience and education, reject inconsistencies or incompatibilities, and quickly arrive at a logical conclusion. He can do all this without first being programmed to undertake such actions. The most complex computers can perform only those specific operations for which they have been programmed and for which they have been fed information coded in a particular form. Man is inventive, can improvise in cases of necessity, and even override previous training and instructions if the need arises. He can continue to do many of these things even when he has been injured or suffered the loss of one of his organs, such as an eye or an arm. Some machines would be completely disabled by the loss of even one component.

Mobility

Man is mobile in ways no single machine can duplicate. He can cross level terrain with little trouble and still jump over obstacles; climb trees, stairs, and cliffs; crawl through a hole of limited size; and swim a river or lake. His ability to do all of these activities without complicated changes in his structure is unsurpassed.

Man Versus Machine

A COMPARISON OF THE FREQUENCY RANGES AND FREQUENCY
DISCRIMINATION ABILITIES OF SOME OF THE SENSES*

SENSE	WAVELENGTH OR FREQUENCY RANGE		WAVELENGTH OR FREQUENCY DISCRIMINATION	
	LOWEST	HIGHEST	RELATIVE	ABSOLUTE
Vision (hue)	300 mμ	1,500 mμ	At medium intensities there are about 128 discriminable hues in the spectrum	12 to 13 hues
Interrupted white light	Unlimited	At moderate intensities and with a duty cycle of 0.5, white light fuses at about 50 interruptions per second	At moderate intensities and with a duty cycle of 0.5, it is possible to distinguish 375 seperate rates of interruption in the range of 1 to 45 interruptions per second	No greater than 5 or 6 interruption rates can be positively identified on an absolute basis
Audition (pure tones)	20 cps	20,000 cps	Between 20 cps and 20,000 cps at 60 db loudness, there are approximately 1,800 discriminable steps	4 to 5 tones
Interrupted white noise	Unlimited	At moderate intensities and with a duty cycle of 0.5, interrupted white noise fuses at about 2,000 interruptions per second	At moderate intensities and with a duty cycle of 0.5, it is possible to distinguish 460 seperate interruption rates in the range of 1 to 45 interruptions per second	Unknown
Mechanical vibration	Unlimited	Unknown, but reported to be as high as 10,000 cps with high intensity stimulation	Between 1 and 320 cps, there are 180 discriminable frequency steps	Unknown

Figure 4-8

The Biochemical Machine

As a machine, man has other advantages. His body is a highly efficient engine, using food as fuel and oxygen from air as an oxidizer to produce power. It will adjust its heat output in accordance with demands and input. It will store excess energy as fat, and draw upon it when input is lacking. His body will reproduce and, to a great extent, repair itself.

Unfortunately, man also has problems. As a mechanical structure, he can go only so far, lift only so much, sense only so rapidly, and react only so quickly and effectively. His sensory systems have definite limitations. Every human response to a situation involves perception, decision, and response. Difficulties and accidents result from any demand for abnormal uses of a person's senses, quick decisions based on inadequate or overwhelming information, excessively rapid responses, or physical capabilities that he does not possess.

In many instances, he does not provide the same care for the superb mechanism that is his body as he provides for a piece of equipment. During the Industrial Revolution and during the sweatshop days at the beginning of the century in this country, equipment was valued more highly, cared for more tenderly, and guarded more zealously than were its human operators. This situation has been alleviated somewhat, but the lack of consideration for the needs of the human body is still apparent. It is said that a dog being fed canned food has a more balanced diet than his master. An automobile is generally checked more often than its owner.

The human body's structure, operations, and sensory system effectivity are directly related to how well its biochemical medium is maintained. Violations cause inefficient operations of the whole system. The body needs oxygen, without which life cannot be sustained; depriving the body of even small amounts of oxygen can affect it adversely. Various contaminants, such as carbon monoxide, deprive body tissues of oxygen nourishment so that they are prevented from performing their normal functions. Toxic materials are introduced primarily through the respiratory or gastrointestinal systems. Solvents, such as those that exhilarate and cause the deaths of "glue sniffers," constitute one class of these substances. Ethyl alcohol, the primary constituent of intoxicating beverages, will upset the body's biochemical balance, acutely disrupting basic body functions or reducing their effectiveness. This reduced effectiveness makes the person susceptible to errors even when the amount of alcohol ingested is small.

Fatigue due to changes in the body's biochemical balances through accumulation of toxic wastes is another types of disruption. The efficiency of a tired body is reduced; the probability of error is increased; and the detection of any errors that may have been committed is less acute. Long or irregular hours or strenuous effort are causes of fatigue. Bodies adapt to physiological cycles of work and rest, and disruption of these cycles contributes to fatigue and inefficiency (Fig. 4-9). Both illness and medication reduce the body's efficiency, causing chemical imbalances, fatigue, and inability to perform physical functions. It is essential therefore that all illnesses of personnel and medication for personnel who operate critical equipment be under medical control.

Man is motivated. In most cases, this motivation constitutes an advantage since it creates a drive toward successful accomplishment of a mission. Man frequently exceeds his own normal abilities and the abilities of others when motivated by esprit de corps, patriotism, love, hate, revenge, sex, competition, prestige, hunger, fear, pride of accomplishment, financial rewards, and numerous other reasons. When they act to man's benefit, these are advantages no machine can derive. When they are detrimental, the equanimity of the machine is an advantage.

Motivation

Aptitudes, desires, feelings, and motivations provide other limiting or distracting variables that must be considered in ensuring efficient operations. An eager, well-motivated individual who is undistracted by personal problems or stresses can outperform a distracted or poorly motivated person, other things being equal. Persons with emotional imbalances often remain potential sources of difficulty; they frequently make errors through minor omissions or other acts leading to inefficiency or accidents. Related to human error is the broader aspect of human reliability. Human error has the connotation of a person performing an unintentional act. Human reliability includes, in addition, those intentional acts contrary to policy, instruction, and good practices.

A few persons are disturbed emotionally. Screening systems must be developed to avoid their employment in critical positions. Some emotionally disturbed persons may not be eliminated, whereas others may become disturbed after screening. It therefore becomes necessary that the designer provide adequate safeguards to ensure that they do not create a catastrophic situation, intentionally or through error, if they should be critically situated. Procedurally, an arrangement such as that in which the Two-Man Concept is employed can be directed by the management element responsible.

Man Versus Machine

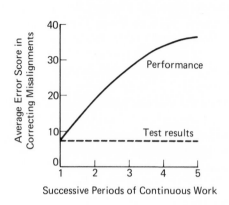

Successive Periods of Continuous Work

DIFFERENCE BETWEEN PERFORMANCE AND CAPACITY[*]

In many kinds of human activity, performance deteriorates as work is continued even though it can be shown with tests that there has been no change in capacity. Difference is attributable to high motivation in tests but lowered motivation in actual work situations.

TYPE OF WORK DETERMINES THE LENGTH OF TIME AN OPERATOR CAN EFFICIENTLY PERFORM HIS DUTIES[†]

Type of work	Recommended Time Limits
Task that requires low level of motor skills, is highly repetitive, and devoid of critical decisions.	Up to 12 hr.
Highly redundant task using standard procedures, moderate responsibility, and limited manual precision.	Up to 8 hr.
Heavy, continuous physical labor interspersed with suitable recess.	Up to 6 hr.
Fairly responsible, decision-making task on a continuous but random basis.	Up to 4 hr.
Critical but monotonous vigilance task.	Up to 2 hr.
Extremely accurate motor skill with critical reaction time — no time to relax	Up to 30 min.

NOTE: The time limits suggested above are subject to variations including proper insertion of rest periods or changes in task routines. Work-rest cycles are normally based on a 24-hr. day and, as such, will reflect variations during this period. It is important to consider the normal variations in planning critical tasks; i.e., efficiency normally drops off about 10 am, and once again in midafternoon, followed by an end spurt just before the worker knows his work period is over. Although we are normally oriented to an 8-hr. workday, with 8 hours for sleep, people can adapt to other cycles quite easily.

Figure 4-9

82

Psychologically, everyone is different, being of different origins, upbringing, and experience. Each is affected to a different degree by the same processes and stresses. Each varies in aptitude, desire, feeling, motivation, and emotion. Psychological criteria must be developed for personnel assigned to specific tasks. Standards and procedures must be set for their selection. Environments must be arranged for their well-being. Methods of training must be developed.

Hazards and Accidents

Not all dangerous characteristics, matériel failures, or adverse environmental conditions cause accidents, even when they are present. In numerous instances, accidents have been avoided by timely corrective actions, accomplished automatically through fail-safe product designs or through the timely and correct response of personnel present. By listing the various combinations of factors that could be involved, the designer can provide a general mathematical expression for the probability of an accident occurring under specific circumstances. These factors are shown below. Unfortunately, reliable data are lacking for most of the factors in the expression. However, such data are being developed little by little.

Let each of the following represent the probability:

F = of all matériel failures occurring under foreseeable conditions
$= F_A + F_M + F_O$

F_A = of those failures occurring that will result in accidents (no corrective action possible)

F_M = of those failures occurring that will result in accidents unless possible, timely corrective actions are taken

F_O = of those failures occurring that will not cause an accident under any circumstances

H_M = of any correctable human failures occurring that could cause or permit an accident: wrong decision, inadequate response, lack of corrective action, wrong action

H_A = of any irreversible human failure occurring that could cause or permit an accident

H_S = of proper action taken as required: correct decision, suitable response, proper corrective or preventive action

C_A = of the product having an adverse characteristic that could cause injury, damage, or loss without matériel failure or error

C_F = of the product having an adverse characteristic that could cause matériel failure

C_H = of the product having an adverse characteristic that could cause human failure

N_A = of the product encountering an adverse, extraordinary environmental condition that could cause injury or damage without failure or error

N_F = of the product encountering an adverse, extraordinary environmental condition that could cause product failure (includes conditions not normally considered under F because they are too improbable or unforeseeable)

N_H = of the product encountering an adverse, extraordinary environmental condition that could cause human failure

Then the probability of an accident will be:

$$= H_A(1 + C_H + N_H) + F_A(1 + C_F + N_F) + F_M(1 + C_F + N_F)(1 - H_S)$$
$$H_M(1 + C_H + N_H)(1 - H_S) + (C_A + N_A)(1 - H_S)$$

In effect, the four principal terms of this expression indicate when an accident is possible:

1. $(1 + C + N)$ shows that the failure, human or matériel, could be: an inherent problem (shown by the 1), due to the adverse characteristic of another product (C), or due to an unforeseen, detrimental environmental condition (N).

2. An irreversible error or noncorrectable failure, no matter the cause, will result in an accident: $H_A(1 + \ldots)$.

3. A correctable error or failure, no matter the cause, will result in an accident unless suitable action is taken: $(1 - H_S)$.

4. Harmful product or environmental characteristics will cause injury or damage unless preventive action is taken: $(C_A + N_A)$ $(1 - H_S)$.

chapter 5

FUNDAMENTALS OF HAZARD ANALYSIS

Hazard analysis is the investigation and evaluation of:

- The interrelationships of primary, initiating, and contributory hazards that may be present
- The circumstances, conditions, equipment, personnel, and other factors involved in safety of a product or the safety of the system and its operation
- The means of avoiding or eliminating any specific hazard by use of suitable designs, procedures, processes, or material
- The controls that may be required for possible hazards and the best methods for incorporating those controls in the product or system
- The possible damaging effects resulting from lack or loss of control of any hazard that cannot be avoided or eliminated
- The safeguards for preventing injury or damage if control of the hazard is lost

The general procedure for carrying out a hazard analysis is illustrated in Fig. 5-1.

Accident Analysis

Originally, analyses were attempts to reconstruct causes of especially damaging accidents. Corrective actions were then taken to prevent or minimize recurrences. These corrections eventually found their way into specifications, standards, codes, regulatory requirements, and good engineering practices. Valuable as the results derived in this way may be, it is an inefficient and costly method of determining the types of hazards that could be present. No organization responsible for development, production, or operation of a product or system can long sustain any series of accidents as the means of determining possible problems.

To a safety engineer, an accident is an indicator that his safety program has failed in some respect. The consequences of some accidents are so devastating that analyses must be made beforehand to ensure that they do not occur under any preventable circumstances. An accidental nuclear detonation is in this category. Analyses therefore have been undertaken to provide suitable safeguards against such an occurrence. Theoretical cause and effect relationships in conjunction with past experience have been employed for the purpose. Gradually, the requirement for such analyses has been extended to include other types of adverse events that could generate extensive damage.

Types of Hazard Analyses

Numerous types of hazard analyses are in use or have been proposed. many are similar, differing only in the names given by the organization developing them. One problem in studying a system or product is determining which basic method best applies to any specific design or situation. No one method is universally superior to all others or even applicable to all types of analysis. There are certain ones that are in common use because of their broad applicability, but even these have disadvantages. Any complete analysis will therefore require use of at least two methods. For this reason, it is advisable to indicate all methods of analysis that appear to be usable and some cogent applications. In the past, failure to categorize these methods properly has resulted

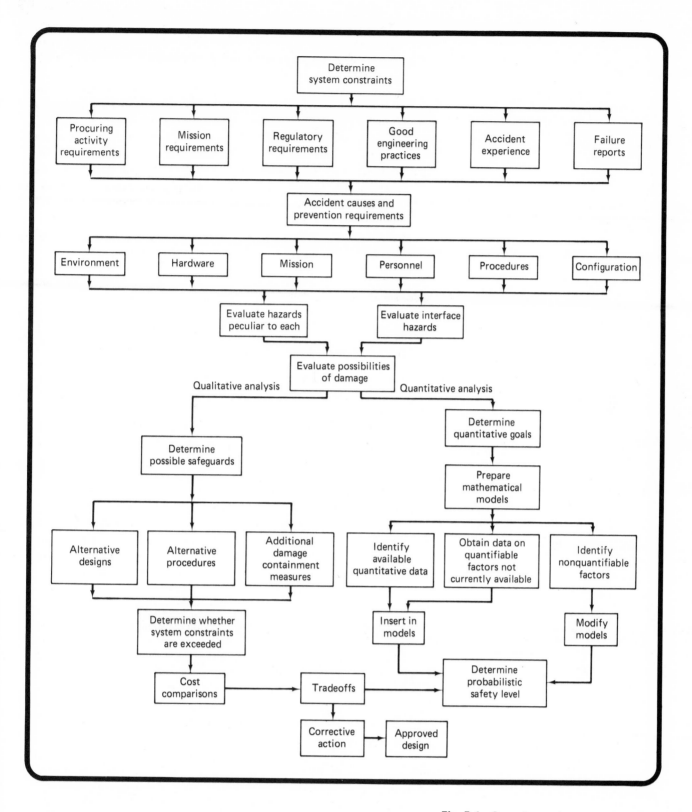

Fig. 5-1. General procedure for an analysis.

in confusion; that is, similar methods have been given different names, confusing personnel interested in selecting the one best suitable.

Classification by this method is predicated on the point in time at which the analysis is made. A *predesign* analysis determines and evaluates those hazards that might be present in a system to be developed. It may

Predesign
and
Postdesign Analyses

provide the basis for preparation of specifications, standards, and other criteria to be followed in design, and it may indicate undesirable characteristics, conditions, and practices to be avoided.

Studies in the predesign stage may reveal specific precautions that must be observed and incorporated into the system. They may determine the suitability of particular pieces of hardware, materials, or proposed procedures. In accordance with the system safety concept, it is in the predesign period that discovery and resolution of problems can be accomplished most effectively and economically and with the least amount of friction. Designers are understandably unhappy when members of other organizations point out after the equipment is designed or selected that requirements exist of which they, the designers, knew nothing. Safety is a specialized discipline; designers may be unaware of information, such as hazards or best safety practices, known to safety engineers, unless it is provided them before design or selection begins.

A *postdesign* analysis determines whether selected equipment and procedures meet the standards and criteria established as a result of the predesign analysis. Unfortunately, standards and criteria are often lacking prior to design, are inadequate, or have not been observed well. In other cases, the safety effort may have been initiated after designs have been prepared. The analyses must therefore be undertaken to determine potential hazards, as would otherwise be done in the predesign stage. Here, however, the design selected must be examined for the dangerous effects that could be produced by normal and abnormal environments, operating conditions, procedural errors, presence of inherent hazards, and possible failure modes. Evaluations must be made to determine whether designs that do not provide the best in safety should be modified or redone. The problem becomes even more troublesome after production has begun on items that are less than satisfactory from a safety standpoint, since changes may be extremely costly.

One thing should be emphasized here. The accomplishment of either a predesign or postdesign analysis does not preclude the need for the other. Each accomplishes specific results so that both can be used advantageously in a safety effort.

Qualitative Analyses

A hazard analysis, predesign or postdesign, can also be designated as *qualitative* or *quantitative*. A qualitative analysis is a nonmathematical review of all factors affecting the safety of a product, system, operation, or person. All possible conditions and events and their consequences are considered to determine whether they could cause or contribute to injury or damage. A qualitative analysis must precede a quantitative analysis. Any mention of a quantitative analysis therefore infers that a qualitative analysis will also be made.

There is no regard for the probability of occurrence of any specific event, such as an accident, in a qualitative analysis. The end object is to achieve maximum safety by eliminating, minimizing, and controlling *all* hazards, regardless of probability of occurrence. Conclusions of a qualitative analysis may be used as the basis on which needs for design or procedural changes can be predicated. However, considerations of cost and mission requirements may limit accomplishment of all preventive and corrective measures. Quantitative evaluations may then be necessary to establish frequencies of occurrence, either probabilistically or relativistically, magnitudes of risks, and costs involved.

A question that frequently arises when hazards and dangers are present in any situation is: How safe is it? The "it" in this case referring to a system, product, vehicle, structure, or operation. Attempts have been made to develop rating systems that could provide a good indication of safety or, conversely, its danger. These methods can be divided into those that are *relativistic* and those that are *probabilistic.*

Relativistic Methods. Relativistic methods can also be sub-divided. One type of analysis includes a rough frequency with which a specific adverse event has occurred with existing, operational items. Ratings are based on past experience with similar systems, assemblies, or components or are based on results obtained during early testing of portions of the system under development. Each hazardous condition is rated in accordance with the following list to indicate past performance and to govern the degree of care that must be exercised with the new system or product:

1. Remote—No record of past occurrence in similar systems
2. Random—Has occurred once in the histories of items reviewed
3. Seldom—Has occurred two or three times
4. Chronic—Has occurred more than three times

Safety Factors and Safety Margins. One of the earliest numerical methods of indicating safety levels was by using safety factors. This was originally a relativistic method. It provided a rough indication of the ratio by which design stresses or loads could be exceeded without failure. A container or structure with a safety factor of 5 was considered safer than one with a lower value. A safety factor is the ratio of the strength of an item to the stress that it must withstand. Although not expressed in probability terms, safety factors have been shown to involve probability distributions. This has led to redefinition of terms and modification of its application. Instead of nominal values for strength and stress to determine the factor or to meet one that was stipulated, minimum strength and maximum stress are used. This, in turn, led to another concept: the *safety margin,* or difference between minimum strength and maximum stress. Safety factors and safety margins are discussed in much greater detail in Chapter 10.

Numerical Ratings. The third relativistic method involves the use of assigned numerical ratings. A scale is selected to divide the range of possible adverse events into a limited number of classes: say 4, 5, or 10. Each hazardous condition, event, or operation is then assigned a number according to the class it most closely approximates. The criteria for rating indicate whether the highest numbers are the safest or most dangerous categories. In some instances, all the assigned values are then added. The totals can then be compared to similar totals for other systems or situations. Figure 5-2 indicates how safety connotations of maintainability tasks may be scored. Cooper ratings of aircraft characteristics involve having pilots indicate on a scale of 1 to 10 their opinions on how well an aircraft performs.

This type of rating has inherent disadvantages. The values assigned depend on the personal opinions of the raters themselves; these opinions are dependent on their individual abilities, education, and experience. Other raters might establish entirely different values. For example, ratings

SCORING MAINTENANCE TASKS*

PROTECTIVE DEVICES

This item encompasses equipment design provisions for self-protection against damage to component or parts after a malfunction has occurred. If a system has protective devices such as fuses, circuit breakers, relief valves, rupture discs, etc, the equipment can then be considered protected from further damage as well as aiding in the isolation of the malfunction. If no provisions have been made for the inclusion of protective devices within a system, further damage and increased repair time could be a direct result.

SCORING CRITERIA

1. To be scored when automatic shutoff devices protect parts or components from further damage after a malfunction occurs in a critical area. A typical example of such malfunction would be if the bias supply fails, and B+ voltage is automatically cut off by circuit breakers, fuses, or relay action;

2. To be scored when automatic shutoff devices do not protect parts or components from further damage, but visual indicators or audible alarms warn personnel of the situation;

3. To be scored when a critical malfunction occurs, and parts or components are not protected by automatic shutoff devices, indicators, or alarms. Involves malfunctions that damage parts or components because automatic shutoff devices or alarms were not provided.

CHECKLIST

Protective Devices:

1. Equipment was automatically kept from operating after malfunction occurred to prevent further damage (this refers to malfunction of such areas as bias supplies, keep-alive voltages, etc) 4;

2. Indicators warned that malfunction has occurred 2;

3. No provision has been made . . . . 0.

SAFETY (PERSONNEL)

This item determines if the maintenance action requires personnel to work under hazardous conditions, such as being in close proximity to high voltage, high pressures, radiation, toxic fumes, high temperatures, etc, or working on elevated structures such as scaffolding.

SCORING CRITERIA

1. To be scored when the maintenance action did not require personnel to work under hazardous conditions. The maintenance action did not require precautions to be taken, since the task was not associated with high pressures, moving parts, etc.

2. Applicable when precautions were taken due to hazardous conditions causing slight delays in maintenance action. A typical example would be when the task required that filters must be cleaned with volatile solvents requiring some degree of caution;

3. To be scored when precautions taken due to hazardous conditions would cause excessive delay to the maintenance action. Such precautions would be the use of SCAPE suits when working in areas that may be contaminated with oxidizer, or when working in areas in close proximity to high voltage, etc.

CHECKLIST

Safety (Personnel):

1. Task did not require work to be performed in close proximity to hazardous condition (high voltage, radiation, moving parts, etc) 4;

2. Some delay encountered due to precautions taken   2;

3. Considerable time consumed due to hazardous conditions . . . . 0.

Figure 5-2

by designers could indicate a system to be much safer than the ratings given by maintenance or operations personnel. In some instances, attempts have been made to have ratings made by a panel composed of personnel with different interests and abilities. Here again, however, ratings of another group could be much different, since ratings are based on personal opinion. The possibilities of even closely duplicating ratings by independent raters are remote except when there is a large number of raters.

The other major disadvantage is its limited use. The fact that a system has a safety level of 85 out of a possible 100 would mean nothing in itself. It must be compared to either the same, but modified, system or to another that is very similar.

The chief advantage in such a method is in obtaining opinions of personnel regarding safety of equipment, conditions, or procedures.

Fundamentals of Hazard Analysis

Rating can be applied beneficially to the Critical Incident Technique discussed in Chapter 8. When various personnel consistently rate a specific operation as hazardous, it indicates that further investigation and corrective action are necessary.

Probabilistic Analyses. This type of quantitative analysis is a determination of the safety level of a system, subsystem, or event in which the result is generally expressed in probability terms. In any case, a quantitative safety analysis must be based on a qualitative analysis. Numerical values are then applied. A probability analysis may be accomplished in a number of ways, depending on the desired end result.

A *probability* is the expectancy that an event will occur a certain number of times in a specific number of trials. Probabilities provide the foundations for numerous disciplines, scientific methodologies, and risk enterprises. Actuarial methods employed by insurance companies involve predictions of future occurrences based on past experience. Reliability engineering has developed complex methods for the evaluation of probabilities that hardware will operate successfully. (See Fig. 5-3.) Statistical quality control, maintainability, and system effectiveness are other applications of probabilities in engineering. Little by little, the need for numerical evaluations of safety levels has generated an increase in the use of probabilities for this purpose.

The concept underlying this use of numerical evaluations is that the safety level of a system, subsystem, or operation can be indicated by determining the probability that mishaps will be generated by specific hazards or combinations of hazards whose presence has been established through qualitative analyses. Probabilities may be derived from experience data on operations of similar systems, preliminary tests, synthesized combinations of values, or extensions of all of these. The quantitative expression may include not only the expected rate at which the hazard will cause accidents, but also the severity of damage that could result, or both. The application of probabilities in terms of reliability is discussed in Fig. 5-3.

The probability of damage or injury is not synonymous with the probability of success or failure upon which reliability is based. The equations presented in Chapter 4 express the fact that many failures will not result in accidents. The expression "fail-safe" itself is an indication that conditions and situations exist in which equipment can fail and no damage or injury result. Conversely, there are many situations in which personnel are injured using equipment designed and manufactured with high reliabilities.

Many persons who have been concerned with accident prevention for a long time sometimes object to the use of probabilities as indicators of safety levels or safety goals. These objections are based on many reasons:

1. A probability, such as reliability, guarantees nothing. Actually, a probability indicates that a failure, error, or mishap is possible, even though it may occur rarely over a period of time or during a considerable number of operations. Unfortunately, a probability cannot indicate exactly when, during which operation, or to which person a mishap will occur. It may occur during the first, last, or any intermediate operation in a series. For example, a

FUNDAMENTALS OF RELIABILITY

Reliability is the probability that a piece of equipment or component will perform its intended function satisfactorily for a prescribed time under stipulated environmental conditions. Unreliability is the probability of failure. Reliabilities are expressed either as decimals or percentages. When reliability (R) is expressed as a decimal, unreliability (Q) is its complement and equals $1 - P$. The reliability of an operation or test can therefore be established from: R = 1 − (No. of failures/No. of items at the start of the operation or test).

The frequency at which malfunctions occur is called the failure rate, λ. It is measured by the number of failures for each hour of operation or number of operations. Five failures in 1,000 hours of operation would constitute a failure rate of 0.005 per hr. The reciprocal of the failure rate is the mean time between failures (MTBF). The mean time between failures for a failure rate of 0.005 per hr is 200 hr.

Equipment failures are of three types: (1) Early failures, which occur during the "debugging" or "burn-in" period due to poor assemblies or to weak, substandard components that fail soon after startup of a system. These are gradually eliminated with decrease in the early failure rate until the overall failure rate reaches a fairly constant level. This fairly constant level is attributable to random failures. |(2)| Random, or chance, failures result from complex, uncontrollable, and sometimes unknown, causes. The period during which malfunctions are due chiefly to random failures is the useful life of the component or system. (3) Wearout failures begin when the components are past their useful life periods. The malfunction rate increases sharply due to old age and to some random failures. Failure rates plotted against time for a large number of similar components produce the bathtub curve. Although reliability determinations are usually predicated on the useful, or random, failure period, the use of a constant failure rate concept is an over − simplification that has been undergoing modification lately.

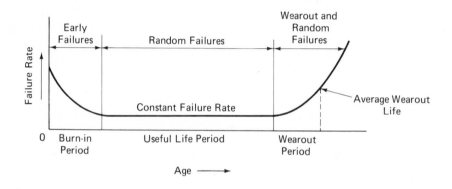

BATHTUB CURVE

According to the concept of constant failure rate, during the useful life of a large number of similar components, approximately the same number of failures will continue to occur in equal periods of time if failed items are replaced continually. The constant failure rate can be described mathematically by an exponential function. When failed items are not replaced, the number of failures during any period will decrease since there are fewer remaining items that can fail. The mathematical expression indicating the probability (or reliability) that components in a constant failure rate system will operate successfully to the end of a time period is the exponential law of reliability: $R = e^{-\lambda t} = e^{-t/T}$; where R is the reliability, e = 2.718, λ is the failure rate, t is the operating time, and T is the mean time between failures (MTBF).

The ratio, t/T, between required operating time (t) and mean time between failures (T) is of extreme importance according to the exponential law of reliability. When t equals T, whether each is one minute or 1,000 hours, reliability is 0.368 (36.8 per cent). To increase reliability, it is necessary that the t/T ratio be decreased. When the mean time between failures is increased, the failure rate (which is its reciprocal) is also reduced.

The reliability of a complex system depends on the individual reliabilities of its components. If the operation of the system requires that all components operate satisfactorily at the same time, it is said to be a series system. In a series system, overall reliability is equal to the product of the individual reliabilities of the components:

$$\text{System Reliability, } R_s = R_1 \times R_2 \times R_3 \times R_4 \ldots$$

This is called the Product Law of Reliability. In the event that each component of a six-component system has a reliability of 90 per cent, the overall reliability is: $R_s = 0.9^6 = 0.53$ (53 per cent). A system made up of 24 such series components would have an overall reliability of only 8 per cent. Complex electronic systems are made up of thousands of components. To keep the reliability as high as possible and to minimize the effect of the Product Law, other means are employed, such as the use of extremely high reliability components, parallel redundant systems, standby systems, and operations under optimum conditions.

Figure 5-3   92

Where components are numerous, increasing individual reliabilities even a small amount can increase the overall reliability tremendously. A piece of equipment having 50 components in series, each having a reliability of 0.98, has an overall reliability of 0.36. Increasing each individual reliability to 0.99 raises the overall reliability to 0.60, an increase of 66.7 per cent. However, the cost for each item with the higher reliability may be 600 to 1,500 per cent greater.

Parallel redundant arrangements perform the same function at the same time even though the output of only one is required for the system to operate successfully. Both components must fail for the system to fail. The probability of simultaneous failures is the product of the individual failure probabilities of each operable arrangement. For example a component has a reliability of 81 per cent; the probability of failure is 1 − 0.81, or 0.19. The probability of two failures in a parallel redundant system is (0.19)(0.19), or 0.036. System reliability is then 1 − 0.036, or 0.964 (96.4 per cent). A doubly redundant system using three similar components in parallel would have an overall reliability of 99.3 per cent. Redundant systems also have disadvantages. They increase cost, weight, volume, complexity, and maintenance. To retain the advantages of such systems, there must be a means to detect failed items and a system to ensure that they are replaced as soon as possible after failure.

Another means to increase reliability is to have standby or idling units that take over only when and if an operating units fails. To be effective, failure detection and switchover devices are necessary to activate the standby unit at the proper time. The little-used duplicate unit wears out at a much lower rate than the operating unit and does not require replacement as often. One unit may sometimes be the standby for any one of many components.

This method also has disadvantages. The failure detection and switchover devices do not have 100 per cent reliability, so there is a possibility switchover may not be accomplished successfully. The standby unit itself may fail. Like parallel redundant systems, standby systems increase cost, weight, volume, maintenance, and complexity. Standbys are used in critical systems, especially for such facilities as electrical power for hospitals. Standby generators back up commercial power supplies or operating generators, and batteries sometimes back up the standby generators. Overall reliabilities of such electrical systems are extremely high.

Improving environmental operating conditions can also increase reliability. Parts are rated for specific conditions and stresses. Failures of electronic equipment increase with increased operating temperatures. Reducing operating temperatures prolongs the lives of electronic parts and thereby increases their reliabilities. Many computer units are provided with cooling units for this reason. Other environmental conditions that can be controlled to reduce failures are: humidity, shock, vibration, corrosive atmospheres, erosion, radiation, and friction.

Tests to establish reliability, especially of complex components or systems, are usually expensive, making a minimum of tests desirable. On the other hand, true probabilities are based on results from infinite or extremely large-sized samples. When only a few items are tested, the results may not be truly representative. Tossing a normal coin two or three times may result in heads each time. This may lead to the erroneous assumption that the result will always be heads. The next three tosses may all be heads again, all tails or combinations of heads or tails. With more and more tests, the average probability of a head (or tail) will be found to approach 0.50. The problem then arises as to how much confidence can be placed on past results to predict future performance. The term confidence level is used for this purpose. If it is believed that any prediction of future performance will be wrong no more than five times out of a hundred, the confidence level is 95 per cent. Tables have been prepared to indicate the relationships between test results, reliability, and confidence. One such table is shown below in abbreviated form:

MINIMUM RELIABILITY (%)	CONFIDENCE LEVEL 90%	95%	97½%	99%	99½%
75	8	11	13	16	19
80	11	14	17	21	24
85	15	19	23	29	33
90	22	29	35	44	51
95	45	59	72	90	103
96	57	74	91	113	130
97	76	99	122	152	174
98	115	149	184	229	263
99	230	299	370	460	530

NUMBER OF TESTS THAT MUST BE PERFORMED WITHOUT A FAILURE

TO PROVIDE A SPECIFIC MINIMUM RELIABILITY AT ANY

CONFIDENCE LEVEL

It has been found that most assemblies and systems actually do not have constant failure rates, especially when the system does not have many components that are similar or have similar characteristics such as large mechanical units. Instead of being exponential, the distribution of failures may be Gaussian, Weibull, gamma or log normal. The chief difference is in establishment of failure rates. Means of improving reliability as indicated above remain the same.

Figure 5-3 continued.

In a constant failure rate system, the probability of failure of a component near the end of its useful life is no greater than at the beginning or any part of that period. Where the cause of failures is wear-out, the probability of a malfunction increases with the life of the component. Reliability decreases progressively and depends on the exact time that wear-out begins. In a constant failure rate system, the reliability decreases with overall time of use but not during the period of use, of the component. In many systems, the failure rate is assumed to be almost constant since continuing, regular maintenance is supposed to keep equipment in optimal operation condition. Components are not supposed to operate longer than their useful life periods, so that wear-out failures will not occur. By this concept of regular maintenance and replacement, the life of the equipment is endless; reliability is not degraded; and there will be no increase in failures. However, it has been found that components and equipment begin to wear out as soon as they begin to operate. Because of this fact, modification of the concept of constant failure rate and use of other failure distributions is necessary.

Figure 5-3 continued.

solid propellant motor developed as the propulsion unit for a new missile had an overall reliability indicating that two motors of every 100,000 fired would probably fail. The first one tested blew up.

2. It is morally unjustifiable to permit a hazard to exist unless maximum effort is applied to eliminate it, control it, or limit any damage that it could possibly produce, no matter how high the probabilistic safety level. The loss of the *Titanic*, considered the safest ship in the world at the time, during its maiden voyage can only be blamed on the fact that hazards were ignored because the ship was considered so safe. Use of a numerical goal may also result in designers working to achieve that goal only, and proceeding no further, even where additional corrective action could be taken.

3. Probabilities are projections determined from statistics obtained from past experience. Although equipment to be used in programmed operations may be exactly the same as that with which the statistics were obtained, the circumstances under which it will be operated will probably be different. In addition, variations in production, maintenance, handling, and similar processes generally preclude two or more pieces of equipment being exactly alike. There are numerous instances in which minor changes in methods to produce a component with the same or improved design characteristics as previous items have instead caused failures and accidents. If an accident has occurred, correction of the cause by a change in design, material, procedures, or production process immediately nullifies certain of the data.

4. In other instances, data may be valid but only in special circumstances. Statistics derived from military or commercial aviation sources may indicate that specific numbers of aircraft accidents due to bird strikes take place every 100,000 or million flying hours. On a broad basis involving all aircraft flight time, the probability of a bird strike is comparatively low. At certain airfields, such as Boston, the Midway Islands, and other coastal and insular areas where birds abound, the probability of a bird-strike accident is much higher. The same reasoning holds that generalized probabilities will not serve well for specific, localized areas. This applies to other environmental hazards such as lightning, fog, rain, snow, and hurricanes.

5. *Reliability* is the probability of successful accomplishment of

Fundamentals of Hazard Analysis

94

a mission within prescribed parameters over a specific period of time. It may become necessary to operate equipment outside those prescribed parameters and time limits. Replacement parts for equipment vital to an operation may not be available. The high reliability designed into the equipment could be degraded and result in an increase in failure rates.

6. Human error can have damaging effects even when equipment reliability has not been lessened. A common example is the loaded rifle. It is highly reliable, but people have been killed or wounded when cleaning, carrying, or playing with them.

7. Probabilities are predicated on an infinite or large number of trials. Probabilities, such as reliabilities, for such systems as missiles are frequently based on small samples that result in low confidence levels. This problem especially occurs with the first pieces of hardware produced for a new system. These pieces are not governed by the constant failure rate criterion on which most reliability calculations are based, but on the infant mortality or wear-in portions of the curve where much higher failure rates can be expected.

Safety Analysis Program

Experience has shown that no single method of safety analysis is universally applicable to all systems, products, events, and conditions. This is especially true for a complex system involving the use of different types of equipment and devices with variations in design and varied operational procedures. In addition, it is necessary to ensure that all possible preventive and corrective measures are brought to the attention of those persons responsible for taking corrective action and that corrective action is taken.

A safety analysis procedure that past efforts have shown to be the most effective for complex systems requires preparation of four principal items: safety models, safety analysis tables, detailed safety studies, and narrative summaries. They are generally prepared roughly in that order, although simpler products may not require accomplishment of all. Most of the types of analyses discussed in later chapters will fall into or employ one or more of these items.

Modeling

Modeling is a technique that is finding increasing use in safety programming and hazard analysis as well as in other scientific, technical, and management applications. It is especially effective in qualitative analysis for the insight it provides into cause and effect relationships. Modeling involves presentation of all parameters in a program, situation, project, system, process, theory, or analysis to organize and indicate logically all factors and their interrelationships. The word "model" can be interpreted in different ways, but generally there are three types of models: *iconic, analog,* and *symbolic.*

An iconic model is a visual representation closely resembling the system or any of the parts that it describes. In one interpretation, it is the simulation of a system by one that is very similar but generally on a smaller scale. For example, a model airplane is a much smaller representation of an aircraft. On the other hand, a model of the DNA molecule is thousands of times the actual size. In both cases, the models are physical, three-dimensional representations. Other iconic models include photographs and sketches and the mock-ups and simulators that can be employed for system development and safety analyses. Iconic models are generally the easiest to conceive, and to construct, since they represent the original so closely.

An analog model represents one property or set of properties by another. Common analogs include use of electric currents and voltages to represent water flow and pressure. Force or weight can be indicated by deflections, minute amounts of current, or water pressure. Other common analogs are maps to represent terrain, flow charts to indicate how a process is accomplished, or a graph to indicate relationships between two measurable factors.

A wider usage of the word "model" has developed with systems analysis, operations research, computer programming, and similar efforts. A symbolic model represents a system or relationship by a series of mathematical equations, electronic or electrical network diagrams, functional block diagrams, logic trees, computer programs, set or series of symbols, or combinations of these and other representations.

Symbolic models have the least physical resemblance to the system or situation being described. They can be used effectively to indicate the relationships between abstract factors, whether quantifiable or not, between physical factors, or between all of these. They can be used to determine the effects that can be generated by a change in any of the factors or in the interrelationships. Figure 5-4 is such a symbolic model.

Models are effective because they include the elements and factors similar to real systems and obey the same rules of behavior. Knowledge of how a system, its subsystems, and affecting factors should act and interact can be synthesized from knowledge of how individual variables performed in the past. Because of the similarities, two or more models can be prepared and compared to determine differences, advantages and disadvantages, costs, outputs, and other factors.

The validity of a model in representing a real system can often be established by inserting known values and observing whether a known result or output occurs. If the model is valid, it can be applied where there are unknown factors and results. If previously known factors and results are unavailable, assumed values can be employed and the results reviewed to establish whether they are reasonable and within acceptable limits. Many theoretical situations can be simulated in this way. In hazard analysis, the outcome of contingencies resulting from various actions can be determined.

Models permit easy understanding and recognition of the factors in a process, program, or procedure. Related factors can be rearranged to produce the best possible arrangement. The result of changing one factor can often be established before the change is made. This permits experimentation with various tradeoff possibilities before a final selection is made. Alternative decisions can be explored without risk of equipment loss. Changes made at low cost in this way can permit an optimal design to be selected before actual, costly construction begins. Any error recognized in a model can be corrected much more easily and cheaply than in the actual hardware. High-penalty deficiencies, which must be corrected after a product is produced, can often be minimized this way.

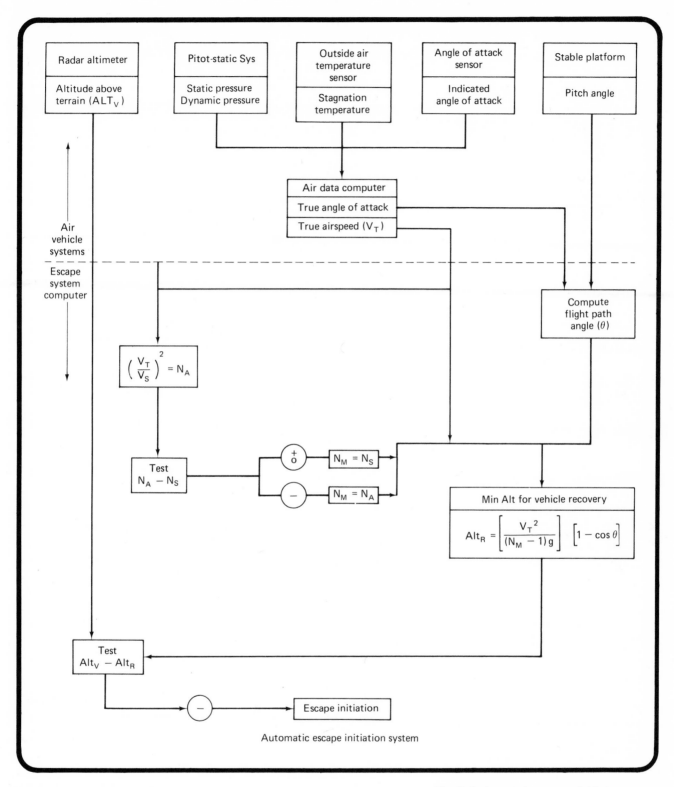

Fig. 5-4. Automatic escape initiation system. J. O. Bull, E. L. Serocki, and J. Schor, *Investigation of Crew Escape Concepts for VTOL and Low Altitude Dash Vehicles,* Air Force Flight Dynamics Laboratory, Wright-Patterson AFB, OHIO: (AD 815-210); 1966; p. 16.

Safety Consideration Trees

One principal use of modeling in hazard analysis is in development of logic trees and networks. Figure 5-5 presents such a safety consideration tree for a submarine. Figure 5-6 shows all the factors that could result in failure of a wet-cell battery. The general procedure for preparing such trees involves the following steps:

1. The primary hazards that could generate injury, damage, loss of function, or loss of matériel are determined. Each type of product or system has a limited number of primary hazards. These constitute the top levels of the trees; all other factors contribute to or affect these top-level items.

2. Factors contributing to the top-level events are listed as they come to mind. The analyst lists everything that he believes could have an adverse effect on the product or system. No effort is made at this time to consider frequency of occurrence or severity of damage. The list can be developed from theoretical considerations of possible hazards, from results of past failures of equipment, or from knowledge of problems with similar systems or subsystems.

3. Items on the preliminary list are rearranged according to the effects that they will produce. Generally, this rearrangement is done best by continuing the trees down through additional cause and effect levels. In some instances, certain conditions or events may be included in more than one tree or branch. Contributory events in these trees are interrelated through OR or AND gates.* OR relationships are considered to exist between any branches of a tree unless an AND gate is shown. No symbol is used for an OR gate.

4. Any other events that consideration indicates should be included are then added to the trees. It will generally be found that listing the affecting factors will conjure up other factors in a process of reiteration and refinement. Additional levels of events are listed gradually. The number of levels depends on the depth and detail of analysis desired. In many instances, trees will eventually reach levels involving failures of specific components for which analyses prepared for reliability studies are, or should be, available. The results of such analyses may be utilized to avoid duplication of effort. Otherwise, an analysis may be undertaken by the safety organization or other appropriate unit.

Each block in the tree is coded for correlation with the safety analysis tables. In addition, these code numbers can be used to prepare a data file. The file would contain information relating to that factor, results of analysis and tests, comments, operational data, and any other pertinent facts.

Safety Analysis Tables

A model presents a graphic display of various interrelationships between applicable factors and little else. Supplementary information must be provided. One means of doing this is in a suitable table. In most of the analyses requiring their use, tables generally have certain main headings,

* See Fig. 9-1 for explanations of logic gates.

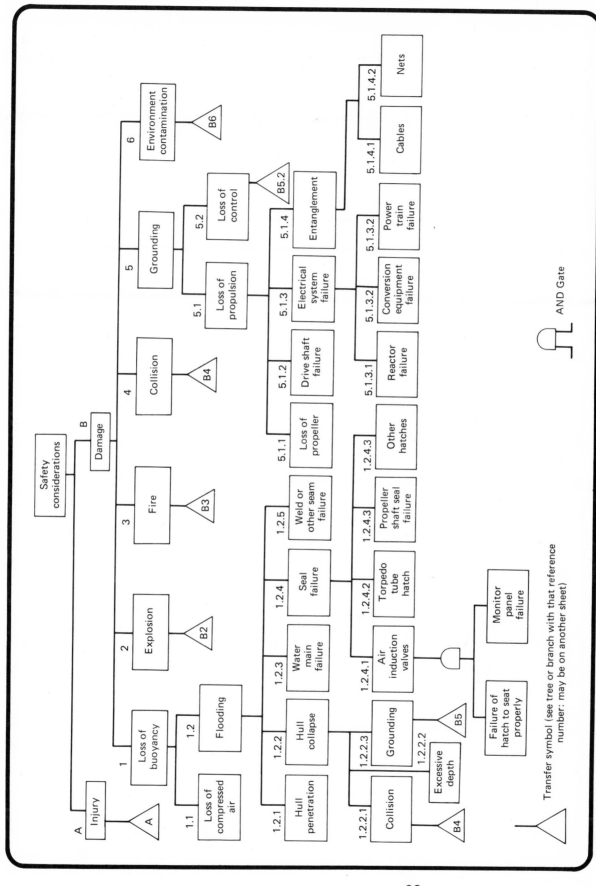

Fig. 5-5. Safety considerations for a submarine.

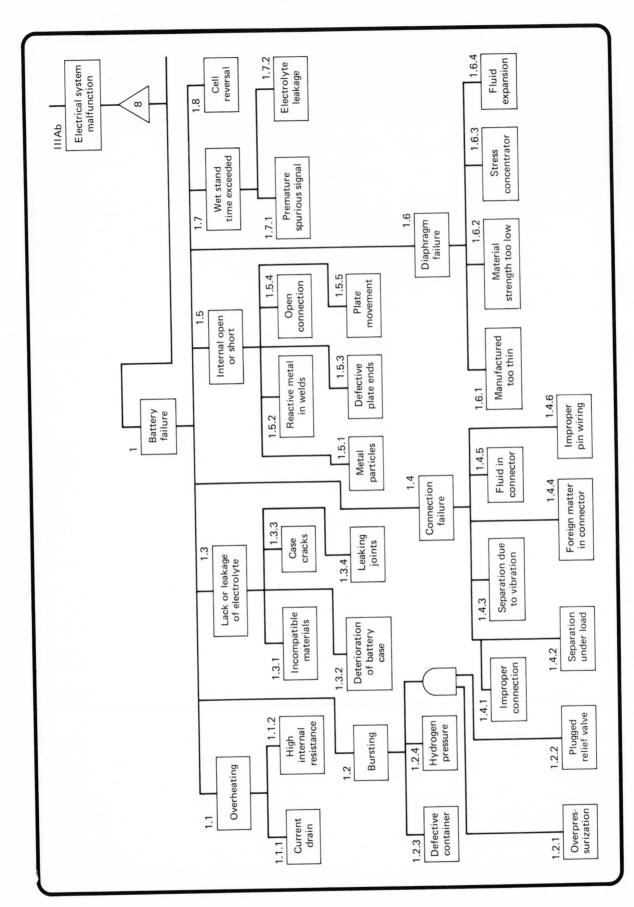

Fig. 5-6. Logic tree indicating causes of battery failure.

which may be further broken down into more subordinate headings if amplification of detail is required. These main headings are:

Hazard—An environmental condition, operational event, personnel action, matériel failure, or other factor

Cause—Includes those factors that could generate or contribute to the hazard

Effect—Includes the result generated by the hazard or its cause

Corrective and Preventive Measures—Actions that could be or should be or have been taken

Other information often included may be: the most critical time the hazard could occur, time available for corrective response, relative frequency of occurrence, hazard level, office responsible for taking corrective design action, and any pertinent remarks on controlling conditions or related studies. Figure 5-7 is one version of such a table, but it has been modified as an efficiency measure. This table does not list causes or effects. The model accompanying this table indicates the cause and effect relationships more clearly than they can be presented in a table. The coding of the blocks in the models and the entries in the tables makes for easy comparison.

Detailed Safety Studies

The model and the table lack details and must be supplemented. Studies may then be made to review and investigate in depth those problem areas, conditions, and events indicated by the model and table. Tables of data or lengthy descriptions of characteristics of dangerous materials or components can be prepared, analyzed, and presented in such studies. For example, the model and table may indicate that fire is a hazard in the system being analyzed. The detailed study can list the materials being considered for use, their flammabilities, flash points or ignition points, and other pertinent data. A study may be made by a design engineer on a pressure vessel to establish required metal characteristics, dimensions, and strength; safety factors and safety margins; and proof and burst pressures for test. Operating restrictions, acceptable hazard limits such as radiation levels, monitoring and warning devices, and needs for personnel protective equipment can be determined. Advantages and disadvantages of the various options in selection of a design, material, or procedure can be presented for tradeoffs and management decisions.

These studies may be prepared for a specific product, project, or program, or may be reports prepared for general use which can be applied to a particular case. Searches of technical literature frequently produce reports, magazine articles, papers presented at scientific and engineering symposia, and other publications that can contribute to a problem's solution. Many of the methods of analysis indicated in subsequent chapters are detailed studies.

The procedure for conducting a detailed study includes preparing the following:

- Statement of the problem or the hazard to be studied.
- Scope of the study, with an indication of the results to be achieved.

III Ab— ELECTRICAL SYSTEM FAILURES

REFER NO.	CONDITION, EVENT OR CAUSE	RELATIVE FREQUENCY	PREVENTIVE OR CORRECTIVE MEASURES	ANALYSES ORG. – STUDY NO.	REMARKS	ACTION TAKEN
1.	Battery failure	Chronic	There is only one battery in the missile for operational purposes. (A few are provided with instrumentation batteries.) It therefore constitutes a component through which a "single-point" failure could cause loss of a missile. If redundancy is impracticable, the battery must be an extremely high reliability item. It should be considered a critical item.	84.59 – Newell, FMEA; 11/11/67	Design Engineering to prepare specifications for battery which will ensure item of highest possible reliability is obtained for output required. Reliability Engineering to develop quality assurance test plan to ensure that manufacturer is maintaining high level. Advise manufacturer battery is critical item.	Battery has been designated a critical item with need for high quality control and special handling. Test engineering advised of need for rigid quality control. Manufacturer advised of problem areas indicated by these trees and tables. Requested to report on measures being taken to minimize possibilities of failure.
1.1	Overheating	Remote	Use current limiters to ensure any possibility of excessive current drain over extended periods is avoided. Ensure battery capacity is adequate to carry any load under all foreseeable conditions.	84.50 – Hochman RQM 87326; 7/21/68	Safe procedure for removal of battery from missile required. Should contain contingency provisions in case battery is defective. Design Engineering to prepare mission profile to determine required battery loads.	Measures to be taken by Design Engineering have been incorporated into design standards and into checklists for review personnel. See Standard No. XX-OO and checklist on Electrical Systems.
1.1.1	Excessive current drain					
1.1.2	High internal resistance					
1.2	Bursting	Random	Minimize any type of overheating which could cause gas or electrolyte expansions in case. Maintain battery within prescribed temperature limits. Procedures for assembly and before installation of battery should ensure relief valve operates properly.		Battery manufacturer to be requested to indicate temperature limits on the battery. Technical writers to insert in procedures warning and caution notes on assembly and installation of battery, on maintaining battery temperature within prescribed limits, and testing of relief valve. Manufacturer to be requested to indicate how he intends to maintain high quality level of cases and relief valves.	Manufacturer will fasten a plate indicating temperature limits and warning to avoid exceeding them. Instructions indicating criticality and need for tight control have been furnished quality assurance personnel. Warnings and caution notes on installation of battery have been included in maintenance procedures.
1.2.1	Overpressurization					
1.2.2	Plugged or faulty relief valve		Maintain close quality control of cases and relief valves.			
1.2.3	Defective manufacture of container		Preventing excessive drain will prevent cell reversal and generation of hydrogen gas.			
1.2.4	Hydrogen produced by cell reversal pressurizes container or ignites					
1.3	Lack or leakage of electrolyte	Chronic	Ensure cell container is not cracked before filling. Ensure reservoir is full. Handle with care to avoid container damage. Ensure fill caps are secure after filling. Avoid incompatibility of materials which could cause corrosion and lead to leakage. Ensure brazed joints in manifolds and other parts are leaktight. Use helium or dye leak tests to ensure overall tightness. Investigate machine methods of brazing, since present manual methods could result in wide variations and poor quality products.		Battery manufacturer to be requested to explain test methods he intends to use to ensure there is no leakage of electrolyte. Periodic audits should be carried out to ensure quality control is effective.	Manufacturer will use dye leak tests to ensure integrity of cases and electrolyte reservoir before filling.
1.3.1	Incompatibility and attack of seals, joints, diaphragms, and other components					
1.3.2	Deterioration of battery case with age					
1.3.3	Cracking; minor fault developed into a crack due to vibration or flight load					
1.3.4	Joints not leaktight					
1.4	Terminal or connection failure	Chronic	Inspect during installation to ensure connections are made properly. Ensure no physical load is on connection. Ensure connector halves are clean, contain no debris, corrosion, solder, cut wire, or dirt. Seal to prevent entrance of moisture, KOH, or other foreign material. Make connections tight to prevent loosening by vibration. Ensure pins are wired correctly by having individual pin assemblies checked visually, and the entire connector tested electrically. Inspect for bent pins prior to assembly. No undue force to be used to mate the halves of the connector.	Design analysis 81-XX, dated 5/12/68, analyzed necessary length and clamping required.	Design Engineering to ensure leads are long enough and clamps designed to avoid loads on connections. Manufacturing Engineering to establish that designed lengths are adequate. Technical writers to incorporate steps for inspection for cleanliness, bent pins, and deleterious materials in procedures. Procedures also to include warning and caution notes to make connections correctly, tight and sealed, and to avoid forcing of connector parts during assembly.	Lead lengths confirmed by Manufacturing as adequate. Warning and caution notes incorporated into manuals and checklists for operational procedures.
1.4.1	Connection improperly made					
1.4.2	Physical load causes separation					
1.4.3	Vibration causes separation					
1.4.4	Foreign matter in connector halves					
1.4.5	Moisture of KOH in connector					
1.4.6	Improper pin wiring					

Figure 5-7

- Past history and trends. This section provides the background for the study, indicating when and how the hazard began or was first encountered, the problems that it has generated, and problems that can be expected in the future. Reference can be made to organizations concerned with the hazard and its problems, contacts that were made, and general references that also provide background material.

- Hazard sources and causes. This portion of the study contains information on all sources that could generate the hazard, the conditions under which the hazards would occur, and related information. Sources of the hazard should also indicate whether they occur during or are the result of normal operating procedures or result from accidents. The types of accidents generating the hazard or any related problems should be noted, with examples from past experience if they have occurred previously.

- Effects that could be generated. Effects may be immediate or protracted. Since many of these effects may have been established by prior experience, observations, or tests, any reports pertinent to the subject should be indicated.

- Preventive measures. Safeguards that could be incorporated or adopted to prevent or minimize occurrences of the hazard or loss of its control should be indicated here. Such measures are indicated in general terms in Chapter 10 of this book.

- Damage minimization. General methods for damage minimization if an accident should occur are also discussed in Chapter 10.

- Corrective measures. The means by which damage can be overcome and the system, equipment, facility, or site restored to its initial state can be indicated. If persons are involved, methods of treatment can also be indicated.

- Costs and risks. The economic impact of the hazard is considered, including discussion of the losses that the hazard could generate and the costs of preventive or corrective measures to avoid, eliminate, or minimize damage. Risks, with evaluations of probable losses, can be compared to costs for providing safeguards.

- Other affecting factors. In some instances, it may not be practicable to make certain changes or to incorporate specific safeguards. Conditions which preclude incorporation of safeguards may be political factors, lack of time, criticality of weight or space, or magnitude or nature of a factor that permits only limited control. Any such additional information should be provided here. If the material to be presented is lengthy enough, separate sections could be used.

- Recommendations. Actions recommended by agencies concerned with the hazard are shown here. Generally, this step necessitates review of governmental or other mandatory requirements, standards, and criteria. The responsibilities of all parties concerned are pointed out, especially those responsible for taking action on the recommendations. Further studies and tests that should be undertaken; changes in requirements, designs and procedures; and research and development programs should be indicated.

Safety Analysis Program

Some studies may not require evaluation of all these factors; others are limited only to findings of causes, effects, and methods of elimination or control of a specific hazard. One factor frequently omitted is cost. (Many engineers evidently do not consider this proper for a technical subject.) Such omissions are often detrimental to the effectiveness of the study, since management decisions on a course of action to be followed are generally predicated on cost.

Safety Narrative Summary The summary is produced last but generally introduces each portion of the analyses covered by a model and table, and by detailed studies. The summary provides information which supplements that contained in those media. It presents and points out items of special concern, further studies to be made, recommendations for actions to be taken, and other applicable comments. It is especially useful to inform managers of possible problem areas and to indicate where added safety efforts should be directed. A summary applying to the model in Fig. 5-6 and table in Fig. 5-7 is shown in Fig. 5-8.

The need to maintain records of safety analyses in the event of a liability suit can be satisfied to a great degree through use of models, tables, studies, and narratives. Furthermore, this method can provide the basis on which some other types of analysis can be accomplished logically and systematically. These analyses are pointed out in the following chapters.

Figure 5-8

SAMPLE NARRATIVE TO ACCOMPANY
SAFETY CONSIDERATION TREES AND SAFETY ANALYSIS TABLES
III Ab — ELECTRICAL SYSTEM FAILURES

1. Batteries. The missile batteries consist of the tactical battery, which supplies all electrical power during flight for operational units, a destruct battery, and an instrument package battery. Chief concern is with the tactical battery, since loss of power from this source will produce complete electrical failure and loss of the missile. In certain instances, this type of failure may constitute a more serious problem than an explosion of a major system, such as a second-stage motor. For example, a motor explosion in flight would cause debris to be thrown along the line of flight, generally to land on the range. A power failure would cause loss of guidance so that the missile could change its flight path until it heads off-range. If the destruct system does not work, the missile could land where it might cause considerable damage even without a warhead.

Failures of the battery could occur at various times after installation in the missile. The following events are some possibilities. The events asterisked have occured with missiles, although they may not have been due to battery failure.

   • Spurious signals or stray currents could activate the electroexplosive device, charging the battery prematurely and permitting it to run down.*

   • The battery may not be activated properly even with a correct firing signal. Failure before launch would probably be detected, causing an abort.*

   • Failure during flight would result in either automatic destruct or destruct by the range safety officer.* However as just mentioned, failure to destruct might then generate additional damage.

The battery must therefore be designated a critical item. Past histories of flights of similar missiles should be examined by Design, Reliability, and System Safety engineers to determine whether the number of aborts and failures due to this cause would warrant redesign to include a redundant power system. Redundancy could be provided through use of:

   • A second battery, either in parallel or standby

   • A small generator driven by gas produced by combustion of a solid-propellant grain

- A small second battery and wind generator

In any case, the safety consideration tree indicates that many of the conditions causing battery failure can be optimized only through close control of internal design and manufacture. It is therefore necessary that:

- Design Engineering personnel establish specifications for this battery to permit only minimal deviations from acceptable conditions. These design conditions should provide the basis for battery procurement.

- Reliability Engineering personnel establish reliability levels and test requirements to ensure that batteries meet the highest practicable system flight requirements.

- Quality Assurance personnel conduct tests to ensure that stipulated requirements on the battery supplier are met.

- The supplier be required to indicate: the provisions incorporated in his batteries to minimize failures due to modes indicated in the safety consideration trees, quality control procedures for a critical item, and results of production tests.

In addition to Design Reliability, Procurement, and Quality Assurance activities to provide a high reliability critical item, it is also necessary that suitable procedures be written for field use. Normal procedures should indicate all the measures to be taken and precautions to be observed during transportation, handling, inspection, test, installation, check out, and removal of the batteries. Contingency procedures should indicate clearly those actions to be taken in the event a battery shows damage from an unknown cause, one is dropped, inadvertent activation of the electroexplosive device occurs, the case cracks or ruptures, overheating occurs, or other adverse events. These procedures should be:

- Developed initially by Design Engineering division or the supplier.

- Edited and verified by the Technical Writing department.

- Reviewed by Human Engineering personnel for human factors, such as proper procedural steps, review of weight lifting requirements, space availability, and warning notes.

- Reviewed by System Safety Engineers for hazards, provision of necessary safeguards, and other accident prevention factors.

- Reviewed by Field Support Engineering and Maintainability Engineering divisions to ensure that the procedures are compatible with customer practices.

2. Voltage out of Limits. . .

Figure 5-8 continued.

chapter 6

INITIAL
ANALYSES

Certain types of analysis are beneficial only during specific periods in development of a product or system. Others can be effective at any time. This chapter discusses those methods that could be used during development or in early planning stages. This qualification does not diminish the benefits that certain of them can provide even at later periods, up to and including operational use. Lack of space precludes presentation of the numerous variations to which some of these methods have been subjected for specific applications. Design and safety engineers and other analysts can adapt them for their own particular needs.

Preliminary Hazard Analysis

According to Greek mythology, King Minos of Crete imprisoned Daedalus and his son, Icarus. Daedalus, a "skillful artificer," made wings of feathers, flax, and beeswax with which he and Icarus could escape to Greece. Before they flew off, Daedalus warned his son:

> My boy, take care
> To wing your course
>   Along the middle air:
> If low, the surges
>   Wet your flagging plumes;
> If high the sun
>   The melting wax consumes.*

This warning was probably the first hazard analysis. (The son failed to follow his father's advice and flew too close to the sun. The wax melted, the wings came apart, and Icarus fell into the sea.) Today we would call it a *Preliminary Hazard Analysis*. This type of analysis consists of making a study during concept or early development of a product or system to determine the hazards that could be present during operational use.

The Preliminary Hazard Analysis helps establish the courses of action to be taken. Its principal advantages are that:

1. Its results may help develop the guidelines and criteria to be followed in product or system design.

2. Since it indicates the principal hazards as they are known when the product is first conceived, it can be used to initiate actions for their elimination, minimization, and control almost from the start.

3. It can be used to designate management and technical responsibilities for safety tasks and used as a checklist to ensure their accomplishment.

4. It can indicate the information that must be reviewed in codes, specifications, standards, and other documents governing precautions and safeguards to be taken for each hazard.

This type of analysis is of special importance where there is little similarity to previous products or systems so that experience on hazards is lacking. For this reason, the Preliminary Hazard Analysis was first

Initial Analyses

108 * Ovid (Publius Ovidius Naso), *The Metamorphoses*, (Rome, Publisher Unknown, 8 A.D.)

required as a review to be made of hazards that could be present in new missile systems. When this type of analysis was initiated in safety programming, missiles containing highly hazardous features were in operation. Four out of 72 operational Atlas F ICBM launch silos (costing approximately $12 million each) were destroyed by accidents in rapid succession. The multiplicity of hazards possible with high-energy systems were of special concern with those missiles that were to use liquid propellants. Exotic, highly reactive, toxic, and destructive fuels and oxidizers were being evaluated for possible use. Designs and operational procedures differed in major characteristics. During test and operation it became apparent that certain materials, products, and systems were much more dangerous compared to others, especially in the hands of field operational personnel. The Preliminary Hazard Analysis was developed to attempt to forestall unnecessary use of hazardous materials, designs, or procedures and to ensure that adequate safeguards are incorporated when the use of hazardous materials cannot be avoided.*

For new products or systems similar to those already in operation and from which much experience has been gained, the Preliminary Hazard Analysis is less important. Experience can provide a great deal of information on actual problems. The analysis just provides only slightly more information, generally including theoretical situations during which additional hazards could exist.

The Preliminary Hazard Analysis is normally a cursory review of safety problems. At the stage at which it should be undertaken there is usually little information on design details and even less on procedures, which are written after designs are formalized. For the detailed analyses, the system/subsystem analyses, described in the next chapter, are used to evaluate designs, and the analysis shown in Chapter 8 is used for procedures review. Although cursory, the Preliminary Hazard Analysis requires review of the same information on mission requirements; performance capabilities; operational sequences; environments to be encountered; and codes, regulations, specifications, and standards as more detailed and comprehensive analyses. The analyses presented in the following sections of this chapter can therefore be used at any stage of product or system development.

The simplest type of Preliminary Hazard Analysis is shown in Fig. 6-1. Entries are predicated on a review of the wings created by Daedalus and his analysis of the hazards involved. The chart shows that Daedalus could have taken steps to ensure that Icarus did not fly too high. In present-day accident investigation practice, findings would indicate supervisory error as a contributory accident cause. Daedalus knew Icarus was a headstrong youth and should have kept him under close surveillance. Furthermore, Daedalus failed in his design to provide safeguards, such as a flaxen leash by which he could have restrained Icarus.

To ensure that all possible hazards are listed and evaluated, a model such as those in Figs. 5-5 and 5-6 can be used. To determine what factors could constitute problems, numerous sources can be used. Known

Analysis Procedure

---

* The hazards of liquid-propellant systems require safeguards whose inconvenience frequently outweigh the advantages in performance that they provide. For this reason, these systems have given way to the much safer solid propellants in most military missile systems.

PRELIMINARY HAZARD ANALYSIS

IDENTIFICATION: _____ MARK I FLIGHT SYSTEM _____

SUBSYSTEM: _____ WINGS _____   DESIGNER: _____ DAEDALUS _____

HAZARD	CAUSE	EFFECT	HAZARD CATEGORY	CORRECTIVE OR PREVENTIVE MEASURES
Thermal radiation from sun	Flying too high in presence of strong solar radiation	Heat may melt beeswax holding feathers together. Separation and loss of feathers will cause loss of aerodynamic lift. Aeronaut may then plunge to his death in the sea.	IV	Provide warning against flying too high and too close to sun Maintain close supervision over aeronauts. Use buddy system. Provide leash of flax between the two aeronauts to prevent young, impetuous one from flying too high. Restrict area of aerodynamic surface to prevent flying too high.
Moisture	Flying close to water surface	Feathers may absorb moisture, causing them to increase in weight and to flag. Limited propulsive power may not be adequate to compensate for increased weight and drag so that aeronaut will gradually sink into the sea. Result: loss of function and flight system. Possible drowning of aeronaut if survival gear is not provided.	IV	Caution aeronaut to fly through middle air where sun will keep wings dry or where accumulation rate of moisture is acceptable for time of mission.

Figure 6-1

troubles and accident causes or the list of hazards in the Appendix can be used. It will be found that the logic tree, such as that in the model can be developed easily in this way as one factor generates ideas of other factors in cause and effect relationships.

The table to be prepared can be more comprehensive than that in Fig. 6-1*. The form can be extended to include columns and information on governing criteria, organizations responsible for ensuring that safeguards are provided for specific hazards, tests to be undertaken to demonstrate safety, and other proposed and necessary actions.

* The column headed "Hazard Category" is required by MIL-STD-882 to provide a rough measure of hazard present: "Hazard level. A qualitative measure of hazards stated in relative terms. For purposes of this standard the following hazard levels are defined and established: Conditions such that personnel error, environment, design characteristics, procedural deficiencies, or subsystem or component failure or malfunctions:
   (a) Category I—*Negligible* . . . will not result in personnel injury or system damage.
   (b) Category II—*Marginal* . . . can be counteracted or controlled without injury to personnel or major system damage.
   (c) Category III—*Critical* . . . will cause personnel injury or major system damage, or will require immediate corrective action for personnel or system survival.
   (d) Category IV—*Catastrophic* . . . will cause death or severe injuries to personnel, or system loss."

Initial Analyses

The benefits of this categorization are doubtful. Much time is wasted in attempting to establish that a particular problem is in a low hazard category when it would be better to try to eliminate or minimize the problem.

In most instances, the following basic steps are undertaken for a Preliminary Hazard Analysis:

- Review problems known through past experience on similar products or systems to determine whether they could also be present in the equipment under development.

- Review the mission and basic performance requirements, including the environments in which operations will take place.

- Determine the primary hazards that could cause injury, damage, loss of function, or loss of matériel.

- Determine the contributory and initiating hazards that could cause or contribute to the primary hazards listed.

- Review possible means of eliminating or controlling the hazards, attempting to use the highest possible method listed in Fig. 10-1, compatible with mission requirements.

- Analyze the best methods of restricting damage in case there is a loss of control of a hazard.

- Indicate who is to take corrective action, and the actions that each will accomplish.

The Preliminary Hazard Analysis should be superseded by more detailed types of analysis as soon as possible. For simple products or those with known problems, the Preliminary Hazard Analysis may be circumvented and the detailed analyses begun immediately. However, the other aspects and advantages of the Preliminary Hazard Analysis must not be neglected.

Criteria Review and Analysis

Specifications, standards, codes, and safety regulations are excellent sources of information on hazards and methods for their elimination or control for systems, hardware, procedures, and personnel. These requirements and other data were originally generated to avoid recurrence of accidents or of other past problems or of situations that careful consideration showed could develop into problems unless suitable precautions were taken. They can therefore produce definite benefits in a safety program. Such specifications can:

- Provide guidelines for engineers to follow during system development. For example, the National Electric Code contains information on designs of circuits, pointing out features to be incorporated and others to be avoided. It indicates hazardous atmospheres for which special safeguards are required (summarized in Fig. 6-2), overload protection for circuits and electrical equipment, and safety devices for personnel protection.

- Provide information on hazards to be avoided, controls for those that cannot be eliminated, and containment measures where loss of control could cause injury or damage. Stipulations that such protection is required or should be incorporated suggest immediately that hazards for which the protection is necessary may exist in the system being studied. Possibilities of the presence of those hazards must therefore be investigated and evaluated.

- Indicate those analyses and other development efforts that also

	CLASS I	CLASS II	CLASS III
	Locations where flammable gas or vapor are or may be present in air in quantities sufficient to produce explosive or ignitable mixtures	Locations where a combustible dust may be present	Locations where ignitable fibers or flyings are present but are not in air in ignitable amounts
Division I	(1) Hazardous concentrations exist continuously, intermittently, or periodically under normal operating conditions. (2) Hazardous concentrations may exist frequently because of repair or maintenance operations or because of leakage. (3) Hazardous concentrations may be caused by breakdown or faulty operation of equipment or process with simultaneous failure of electrical equipment.	(1) Combustible dust in explosive or ignitable quantities may be in the air continuously, intermittently, or periodically under normal operating conditions. (2) Mechanical failure or abnormal operation of equipment may produce such mixtures, as may also an ignition source through simultaneous electrical failure. (3) Electrically conductive dusts may be present.	Easily ignitable fibers or materials producing combustible flyings are handled, manufactured or used.
Division II	(1) Flammable liquids or gases present are normally in closed containers or are in systems from which they can escape only by accidental rupture or breakdown or by abnormal equipment operation. (2) Hazardous concentrations normally prevented by mechanical ventilation may become hazardous through ventilating equipment failure or by abnormal operation. (3) Spaces adjacent to Division I locations to which hazardous concentrations of gas may be communicated unless prevented by positive-pressure clean air ventilation, and safeguards against ventilation failure.	(1) Quantities of combustible dusts are not likely to be thrown into ignitable suspensions during normal equipment operations but may interfere with safe dissipation of electrical equipment heat. (2) Dust deposits on, in, or near electrical equipment may be ignited.	Easily ignitable fibers are stored or handled (except manufacturing processes).
Groups (Atmospheres containing:)	A — acetylene B — hydrogen, or gases or vapors of equivalent hazard such as manufactured gas C — ethyl-ether vapors, ethylene or cyclopropane D — gasoline, hexane, naphtha, benzine, butane, propane, alcohol, acetone, benzol, lacquer solvent vapors, or natural gas	E — metal dust, including aluminum, magnesium, and their commercial alloys, and other metals of similarly hazardous characteristics F — carbon black, coal, or coke dust G — flour, starch, or grain dusts	

Figure 6-2

constitute accident prevention tasks. Determining and programming all such tasks can produce a baseline from which the extent of the work load required in the overall safety program can be established and progress later measured.

- Determine whether the documents incorporated into contracts contain costly requirements, unattainable safety stipulations or levels, or impracticable conditions.

Procedure Analysis of specification documents can be divided into three major efforts, each directed toward the end result to be achieved:

Initial Analyses
- Determination of hazards and corrective measures
- Preparation of checklists

112
- Establishment of design tasks and standards

Figure 6-3 presents a few military specifications and some of their safety connotations. A complete table would include not only all applicable specifications, but standards, regulations, and codes as well. These can be derived from contractual and legal documents. In many cases, it will be found that specifications refer to other criteria whose provisions then become obligatory. Even where a specification or standard is not mandatory, it may be reviewed for pertinent information.

Review of these criteria can begin with either those relating to a specific system or to a specific condition. These can then be used to establish hazards that could affect or exist in the product or system.

As specifications, standards, and codes are being reviewed, checklists can be prepared. This is another effective means of review for hazards that could exist in a product or its operation and of seeing that a design meets stipulated requirements. Checklists may assist designers in ensuring that adverse features are not incorporated into the equipment and that those that cannot be avoided or eliminated are provided with

Checklists

Figure 6-3

EXAMPLES OF SAFETY REQUIREMENTS IN MILITARY SPECIFICATIONS

NUMBER	TITLE	SERVICE	SAFETY PROVISIONS
MIL–E–5007	*Engines, Aircraft, Turbojet and Turbofan; General Specification for.*	DOD	Requires that "Fail-safe design shall be incorporated with the objective of eliminating the possibility of catastrophic failure" of the compressor and turbine, in which case rupture can occur. Contractor must study all possible failure modes. Blades should fail first rather than discs; bearing or lubrication failure should not cause parting or decoupling of the shaft. Has requirements on fatigue life; against ingestion of sand, ice, birds; on fire protection. Has reliability requirements: capabilites and analyses.
MIL–P–5518	*Pneumatic Systems, Aircraft; Design, Installation and Data Requirements for.*	DOD	Indicates measures that will be taken to prevent damaging ignitions and explosions due to combination of air and lubricant or other combustible materials. Requires submission of explosion hazard report. Other safety provisions include: system to be as simple and foolproof as possible; safety essential services to be provided emergency devices; isolation of critical systems. Although title indicates this specification is for aircraft systems, it is sometimes cited for use with missiles.
MIL–W–8160	*Wiring, Guided Missile, Installation of, General Specification for.*	DOD	Wires and devices should minimize possibility of smoke in missile. Wires and cables shall be supported and separated from lines containing flammable liquids, gases, oxygen, and their associated equipment. Has other requirements regarding added insulation, support, bends, separation from high-temperature equipment.
MIL–S–8512	*Support Equipment, Aeronautical, Special; General specification for.*	DOD	States that the safety of personnel and operating utility shall be primary considerations in design. Includes special safety features and requirements relative to guards, sharp edges, electrical shock, fire prevention, safetying, smoke and fumes, heat, explosive atmospheres, etc.
MIL–B–8584	*Brake System, Wheel, Aircraft; Design of.*	DOD	Requires provision for an emergency brake system.
MIL–A–8591	*Airborne Stores and Associated Suspension Equipment; General Design Criteria for.*	DOD	Requires that all electrical components shall be explosion-proof, requires fail-safe design of compressor and turbine cases, and sets requirements for safe operation under emergency conditions.

suitable safeguards. Such lists are effective in refreshing a designer's, reviewer's, or operator's memory. They can extend a designer's or reviewer's knowledge of governing criteria by guiding him to features that must be included to satisfy stipulations in mandatory standards or specifications or that should be included because they are good engineering practice. Safety engineers or other reviewing personnel may also benefit from checklists by ensuring that designers have avoided specifically prohibited or poor practices and that mandatory requirements have been satisfied.

Checklists can be prepared simply by rephrasing the applicable requirement as a question. The questions may be listed in two ways. A series can be prepared from a specific specification, standard, code, or regulation, with the number of the pertinent paragraph in parentheses after the question; or a series can be developed relating to a product, component, hazard, or subject. The numbers of the document and paragraph are then entered in parentheses after each question to identify the source. A considerable number of checklists can be developed in this way, each identified numerically. The list of specifications, standards, and codes can then include cross-references to the related checklists.

Including the source from which it was derived is especially helpful in eliminating the occasional arguments between designers and reviewers about the necessity for incorporating or omitting a design feature. When the designer can be shown or can note for himself that the checklist item is based on a firm requirement and not just an opinion or desire of the reviewer, he is more apt to make changes gracefully.

Some checklists are provided with column spaces in which entries can be made regarding the status of the checklist item. These columns may be designed to enter a mark when the item has been satisfied, to provide a "Yes" or "No" entry, or to permit comments such as expected completion data, adequacy of a design or procedure to satisfy the checklist items, or similar remarks.

Checklists may be prepared from information derived in a variety of ways, including:

- Specifications, standards, manuals, manufacturers' instructions, and other documents
- Lists of precautionary measures that personnel experienced with similar operational systems had previously found necessary or advisable
- Results of testing that indicate limitations and problems or practices and features to be avoided
- Trouble and failure reports, results of accident investigations, or other information in the feedback process
- Theoretical considerations of possible hazards, failures, or adverse conditions that could generate mishaps

A problem often arising in preparation of checklists is the level of detail and the number of items to be included on a list. When standard lists are derived from handbooks* or similar sources, many entries may

* *Air Force Systems Command Design Handbook* DH 1-6, *System Safety*, contains a large number of checklists that can also be employed as design standards.

not be applicable to the product or system under study. Lists prepared by the methods indicated above would be more productive; but even these can be lengthy unless entries are made judiciously.

The checklist format may consist of a series of questions or statements arranged as sequentially as possible within similar areas of review. These sequences may involve dealing first with the largest assembly being reviewed first, and then with smaller and smaller units.

When a safety program is carried out, it is necessary to ensure that the stipulations of the requiring documents have been observed. Ignorance of the existence of these requirements or failure to accomplish them until the customer or a regulatory agency found that they were lacking have proved very costly to some companies. To ensure accomplishment, the safety organization can monitor the responsible design unit, such as design or test engineering.

To preclude differences in opinion after a design is accomplished, it is advisable to provide the designer with a copy of the checklist before a design is entered into. This list can be incorporated into any procedures and standards the design engineering organization might have. Having to change a design to eliminate an adverse or inadequate feature is much more costly than avoiding it in the first place.

Analysis of such requirements is a vital part of an integrated safety program. The methodology indicated here ensures that maximum benefit is derived from information in documents developed from past experience and that control is maintained over safety tasks accomplished by personnel other than those in the safety organization.

Mission Analysis

Another early step that should be taken in analyzing a product or system is to determine its intended functions and the conditions under which it will be required to carry them out. For a product or system, this step necessitates analysis of its mission; similarly, a subsystem must be analyzed for its contribution to mission accomplishment. The mission is the culminating operation and fundamental reason for which the product or system is required, conceived, developed, produced, tested, and maintained. However, to ensure that hardware and personnel achieve the operating configuration that permits the mission to start as planned, careful consideration must be given to all prior activities, processes, and conditions that could degrade the overall effort.

Mission of a system must therefore be redefined as an all encompassing term including all activities of a completely developed operational system: manufacturing, transportation and handling, field preparation and check out, maintenance and repair, operational use, and all other support functions required throughout the life cycle of the system could be adversely affected or could affect others. All conditions of design, performance, procedure, and environment that could be hazardous must be analyzed to be sure that:

1. Successful accomplishment of the mission is not affected or prevented.
2. Injury or damage is not generated during successful accomplishment of the mission by a hazardous characteristic of the product. For example, sonic booms during a supersonic flight could cause destruction of glassware and other brittle objects.

Procedure   Mission analysis generally starts with examination of the contract performance requirements and other support documents. In some instances, a contract may have been entered into only after a prior study of the feasibility of the system, desirable characteristics, operational limitations and requirements, and other factors involved. Generally, such a study will review all pros and cons and may contain comments on conditions or hazards that would relate or contribute to safety.

In many cases, these documents do not in themselves indicate the possible hazards; instead, the hazards will have to be determined from the mission requirements themselves. For example, a requirement that a missile be carried under the wing of an aircraft from which it is to be launched will generate environmental conditions and hazards different from those of a ground-based launch.

Profiles   The second step is detailed examination of the function and operation of the system and of each proposed major subsystem, individually and as interfaced with other subsystems. This step involves reviewing sequences of performances of system and subsystem and noting environments in which they take place. This review can be accomplished through use of a mission profile in which the operation cycle required for a successful mission is divided into segments. Each segment is usually selected to extend from the point in time at which a major change occurs in configuration, environment, or other factor to a second major change. For example, the operational cycle through which a large passenger aircraft might pass could involve: ground operations (refueling, passenger loading, stores replacement), taxi-out, takeoff, climb, level flight, descent, approach, landing, taxi-in.

Figure 6-4 indicates this cycle as it is applied to one specific process to be analyzed: the handover of ground control of a flight as it passes from checkpoint to checkpoint. It illustrates the various zones under the jurisdictions of different controllers and the limits of their responsibilities. The accompanying table summarizes some functions of the controller of each zone and the problems that he may encounter. A similar diagram can be used to indicate the various ambient conditions, such as pressure and temperature, and other data for further analysis.

One phase of the entire cycle may require more detailed analysis than others. For example, statistics indicate that slightly less than 60 per cent of all commercial aircraft accidents occur during the landing sequence. Figure 6-5 represents the last portion of this sequence leading to final touchdown of the aircraft. Each event or sequence shown here can be analyzed even further. These analyses can review hazardous conditions, procedures followed or to be followed by the crew, the use of flight instruments during landing, effects of critical component failures that could occur at such times, and actions to be taken in an emergency.

Other profiles may be prepared to indicate changes in specific parameters (acceleration, altitude, dynamic pressure). Data obtained during or as results of actual performances can be recorded. Data may also be obtained from environmental or other ground tests and correlated for similarity with the flight data. Where ground test data show good correlation with actual flight results, similar agreement can generally be expected between ground test and flight performance data for a vehicle not yet flown.

Initial Analyses

116

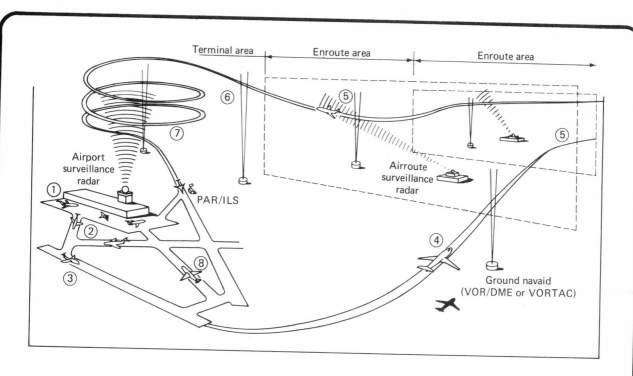

CONTROLLER POSITION	FUNCTION	PROBLEMS
① Take off clearance delivery	IFR route clearance confirmation to pilot via radio	Much talking in coordination of enroute control and others in terminal facility
② Ground control	Gate position to takeoff runway; taxi instructions using visual and radio data	Excessive communications and coordination. May not see taxi traffic due to visual blockage or perspective distortion
③ Local control	Takeoff instructions and altitude assignment; visual and radio data	Needs daylight radar display. Requires excessive coordination data on traffic handovers
④ Departure control	Transfers aircraft from terminal to enroute control using radar and radio	Requires altitude and aircraft identity to correlate range-azimuth radar display. Needs automatic handoff of radar target to enroute control
⑤ Enroute control	Enroute check point progress and handover to next enroute or terminal area	Requires good weather information as well as altitude/identity of aircraft and its flight plan
⑥ Approach control	Preliminary landing instructions and air terminal operations status; feeds holding pattern	Requires good position data and ability to keep tabs on penetrations of uncontrolled aircraft
⑦ Local control	Retrieve aircraft from holding pattern and feed into landing pattern	Requires improved data on runway visibility and wind shear to evaluate hazard conditions
⑧ Ground control	Taxi position and ramp assignment, usual visual, radar and voice data	Runway surveillance radars perform marginally; not tailored to job. At night, must discern aircraft against 5000—10,000 acres of ground with many lights

Figure 6-6 indicates data obtained during the interval shortly after lift-off of a space vehicle. These data for each parameter are plotted in seconds against time from lift-off. The shaded, diagonal rulings indicate a break in time during which the parameters are considered to continue from the values at the beginning of the rulings. The operational phases through which the vehicle passes are shown in the middle of the diagram. Other environmental data are shown qualitatively above the operational phases to indicate how they fit into the time profile and affect the quan-

Fig. 6-4. Air traffic flow: Handovers from checkpoint to checkpoint. P. G. Thomas, "Air Safety—Controlling Air Traffic," *Space/Aeronautics*, May 1968, p. 77.

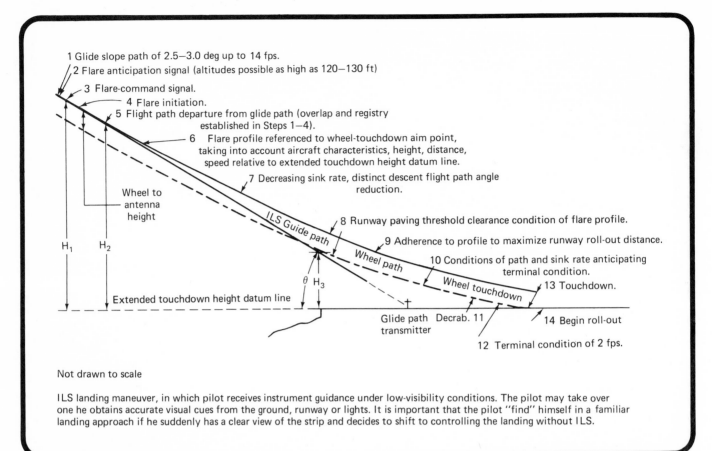

1 Glide slope path of 2.5–3.0 deg up to 14 fps.

2 Flare anticipation signal (altitudes possible as high as 120–130 ft)

3 Flare-command signal.

4 Flare initiation.

5 Flight path departure from glide path (overlap and registry established in Steps 1–4).

6 Flare profile referenced to wheel-touchdown aim point, taking into account aircraft characteristics, height, distance, speed relative to extended touchdown height datum line.

7 Decreasing sink rate, distinct descent flight path angle reduction.

Wheel to antenna height

ILS Guide path

8 Runway paving threshold clearance condition of flare profile.

9 Adherence to profile to maximize runway roll-out distance.

Wheel path

10 Conditions of path and sink rate anticipating terminal condition.

Wheel touchdown

13 Touchdown.

H_1 H_2

θ H_3

Extended touchdown height datum line

Glide path transmitter

Decrab. 11

14 Begin roll-out

12 Terminal condition of 2 fps.

Not drawn to scale

ILS landing maneuver, in which pilot receives instrument guidance under low-visibility conditions. The pilot may take over one he obtains accurate visual cues from the ground, runway or lights. It is important that the pilot "find" himself in a familiar landing approach if he suddenly has a clear view of the strip and decides to shift to controlling the landing without ILS.

Fig. 6-5. ILS landing maneuver. G. B. Litchford, "The 100-Ft. Barrier," *Astronautics and Aeronautics,* July, 1964 p. 59.

titative data. The differences in heights of the qualitative plots are merely to indicate that changes in magnitude take place. Much of this information is provided in the data blocks below the figure. This data could have been plotted quantitatively to illustrate correlations between the various parameters. Series of tests with different payloads and flight paths indicate that these variables caused little change in the other parameters for this type of vehicle. Values for these parameters can therefore be adapted or extrapolated for new arrangements.

Values obtained from a profile can be used to determine possible problems and their magnitudes. They can determine whether proposed or stipulated product or system constraints might be exceeded, design strengths that will be required for expected stresses (especially for any spikes or unusual transient loads), and adverse conditions that might degrade performance. For example, severe vibrations could damage electronic assemblies unless suitable safeguards are provided.

The exact instant or time interval when a specific parameter reaches a prescribed level could also be established. For example, a minimum sustained acceleration may be required for missile motor staging or warhead arming. When acceleration is less than the preset level or duration, staging or arming is inhibited.

Bubble Charts

Bubble charts find wide use for analyses involving sequences of events. They can therefore be helpful tools for safety analyses, especially for those involving series of operations. In some instances, the bubbles

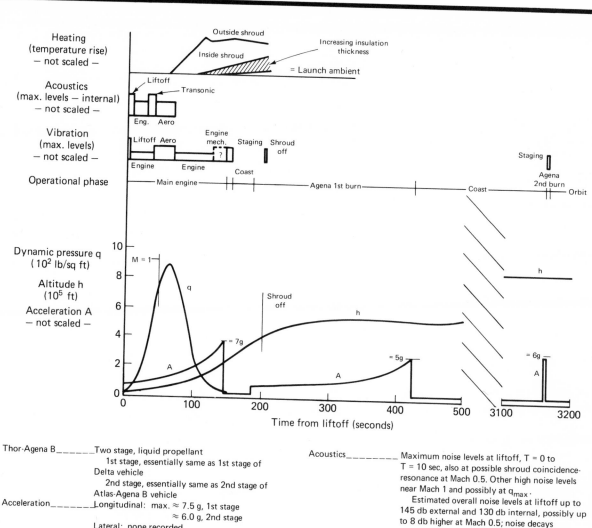

Thor-Agena B _____ Two stage, liquid propellant
1st stage, essentially same as 1st stage of Delta vehicle
2nd stage, essentially same as 2nd stage of Atlas-Agena B vehicle

Acceleration _____ Longitudinal: max. ≈ 7.5 g, 1st stage
≈ 6.0 g, 2nd stage
Lateral: none recorded

Altitude _____ At end of boosted flight, T = 3160 sec:
≈ 851,000 ft

Dynamic Pressure ___ Maximum ≈ 900 lb/sq ft at T = 66 sec

Vibration _____ Highest vibration input (low and high frequency) at liftoff, other low frequency vibrations at staging; high frequency vibration peak at Mach 1 to q_{max}. Possible low frequency longitudinal mode, resulting from engine mechanical system, existing for about 20 sec prior to 1st stage (main engine) cutoff. This mode may give up to ± 2.8 g-peak at 16 to 22 cps.

Acoustics _____ Maximum noise levels at liftoff, T = 0 to T = 10 sec, also at possible shroud coincidence-resonance at Mach 0.5. Other high noise levels near Mach 1 and possibly at q_{max}.

Estimated overall noise levels at liftoff up to 145 db external and 130 db internal, possibly up to 8 db higher at Mach 0.5; noise decays rapidly after q_{max} (T = 66 sec).

Noise spectra peak at 150 to 300 cps external and about one octave higher, internal.

Heating _____ External temperature at junction of nose cone and cylindrical section rises ambient up to T = 60 sec, to about 300°F at T = 110 sec, then decreases slowly. Temperature inside shroud at same point rises slowly from ambient, to 100° to 230°F, depending on the thickness of the insulation. The shroud is ejected at T = 200 sec, carrying most of the heat input with it.

Spin _____ Not used during powered flight.

Pad environment prior to T = 0 ____ Probably air-conditioned on pad, but may be unprotected at times.

Typical Thor-Agena B payloads (NASA only); capability—1600 lb to 300-mile orbit:

POGO (S–50)   1000 lb, 4 ft diam. by 10 ft long
Echo–2   650 lb
Nimbus   650 lb, 5 ft diam. by 10 ft long
Alouette (S–27; Canadian)   300 lb
POGO in shroud   1400 lb, 5.5 ft diam. by 18 ft long
Nimbus in shroud   1100 lb, 5.5 ft diam. by 16 ft long

Frequency, Sinusoidal (cps)	Peak (g)
Longitudinal	
8-16	± 1.5
16-22	± 2.8
22-100	± 1.5
100-250	± 2.2
250-400	± 3.3
400-2000	± 5.0
Lateral	
5-100	± 1.0
100-400	± 1.5
400-2000	± 5.0

Fig. 6-6. Representative launch profile for THOR-AGENA-B vehicle (POGO profile; payload, 1000 lb.).

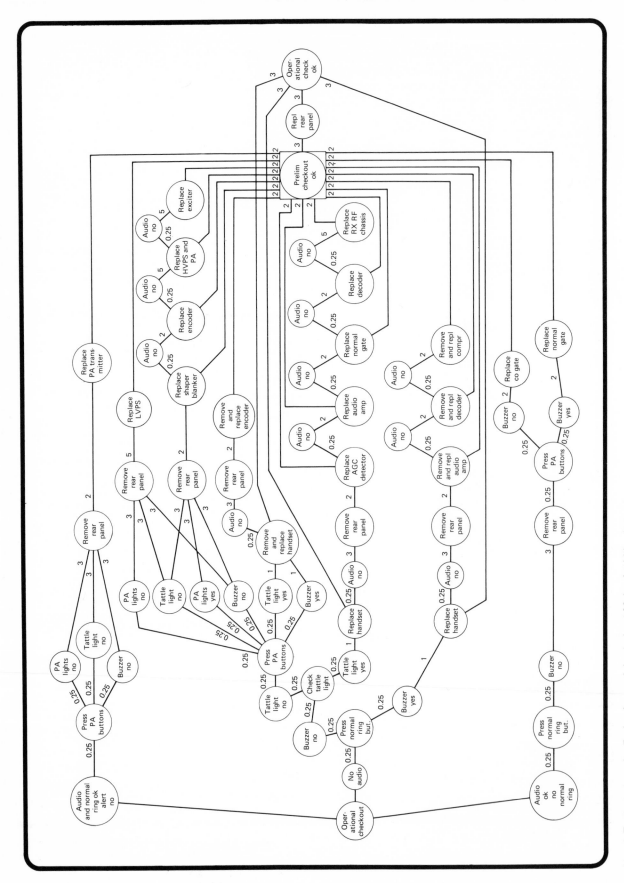

Fig. 6-7. Technique for Evaluation and Analysis of Maintainability (TEAM).

represent events simply arranged in the orders and relationships in which they are expected to occur. In others, periods of time are noted on the lines connecting the bubbles (Fig. 6-7) or events can be plotted against a time scale. In one technique, times between events are noted on the lines connecting the bubbles; time to accomplish the event is indicated in the bubble, where a cross-reference is also made to a table containing a full description of the event.

Time Sequencing. I have proposed a method, Time Sequencing,* using bubble charts for the systematic presentation and evaluation of operations and hazards as they might occur over a period of time. Instead of putting durations of time on the connecting lines between the bubbles, the events are plotted on a time scale. The lines between the bubbles can be shown to be activities or operations for which probabilities can be established.

An operation can be segmented into groups of sequenced events, each of which can then be evaluated for any possibilities of accidents. Whether an accident can occur and the damage that could result from an accident may be affected by the time at which a malfunction occurs. A component failure while a missile is still on a launch pad may leave it inert and harmless. Failure of the same component when the missile is 5 to 10 feet off the ground could be catastrophic. Damage to surroundings from an accident will also depend on the time and location of the missile when the mishap occurs. The potential damage and the probability of such damage occurring will change as the missile configuration and location change with time. Any evaluation of hazards, danger, damage, and risk must therefore include a time analysis to determine the critical periods and operations in the life of a system.

This method is based on the principle that every operation can be shown on a chart. These operations will occur in a series or in simultaneous series of operations. The point at which a specific action will begin in any sequence can be illustrated. From the plot, much information can be derived. The events following inadvertent activation of a system or subsystem at times other that those for which it was programmed can be noted easily. Subsequent actions can be traced. If there is an indication that such inadvertent activation could result in an accident, special safeguards might be incorporated to prevent the untimely occurrence or to minimize any subsequent effects if it does occur.

Bubble charts and sequencing of events and operations can be employed beneficially to:

- Provide a graphic, easily recognizable layout of the interrelationships between functions of various components and subsystems as they contribute to progressive operation of the entire system.

- Show sequences of events that will follow if inadvertent activation takes place at one of the initiating points of the system.

- Simulate the effects of failure of any component on subsequent events.

- Determine the probability of failure of any sequence.

- Identify those points and times during which personnel may have

* W. Hammer, "Numerical Evaluation of Accident Potentials," Paper presented at the Institute of Aeronautics and Astronautics Symposium on Reliability and Maintainability, New York (July 1966), pp. 494–500.

contact with the system and cause accidents through performance errors.

- Note events and activities during which personnel can be injured or damage occur to the system.
- Determine actual use time of components and sub-assemblies during an operation, exercise, or test.
- Determine mishap causes during accident investigations by relating the time the malfunction began to specific components that were operating at those instances or to specific operations that were taking place just then.

Mapping Problems that could develop because of the locations or proximity of units, lines, and hazards can frequently be revealed through mapping. Mapping is usable for distances that can be measured in inches, such as when plotting electrical conductors to determine whether electromagnetic coupling could take place, to thousands of miles, when the limits of safety of a missile or rocket firing range are indicated. It can also be used for such purposes as determining:

- Distances between fuel lines and ignition sources, such as those on hot engines. The dangers existing when these are in close proximity are evident. Leakage of fuel from a poor connection or ruptured line onto a hot surface could result in a fire. Many of these dangers can be recognized from drawings that show the locations of connections, lines, engines, spark-producing devices, and similar hazards. In such cases, lines can be designed with a minimal number of connections, or connections could be placed where leakage would not hit the hot spot, or a means of isolation could be provided to separate the fuel lines and the hot spot.
- Separation of fuels and oxidizers. In a similar way, mapping can indicate whether adequate distance or other means of separation exists between a fuel and oxidizer. Here again, lines carrying these materials could leak and come in contact with each other, with disastrous results. Leakage is especially hazardous when the two substances are hypergolic and will ignite without an outside source of ignition. Locations of tanks in storage farms can be reviewed: to ensure that adequate separation exists so that leakage of either fuel or oxidizer will not result in contact with the other substance; to determine the necessity for dikes or containment walls to hold liquids if a tank should burst; and to determine whether leakage could endanger personnel or facilities along channels down which liquids would flow.
- Danger areas for personnel, structures, and equipment. Figure 6-8 is a layout of facilities near a missile launch pad; it indicates limits of danger if a missile should explode. Control points beyond which personnel must not pass to avoid exposure and injury of an explosion occurs during launch are also shown. Similar maps can be prepared to show the danger zones behind an operating jet engine; areas where noise levels could be injurious and pro-

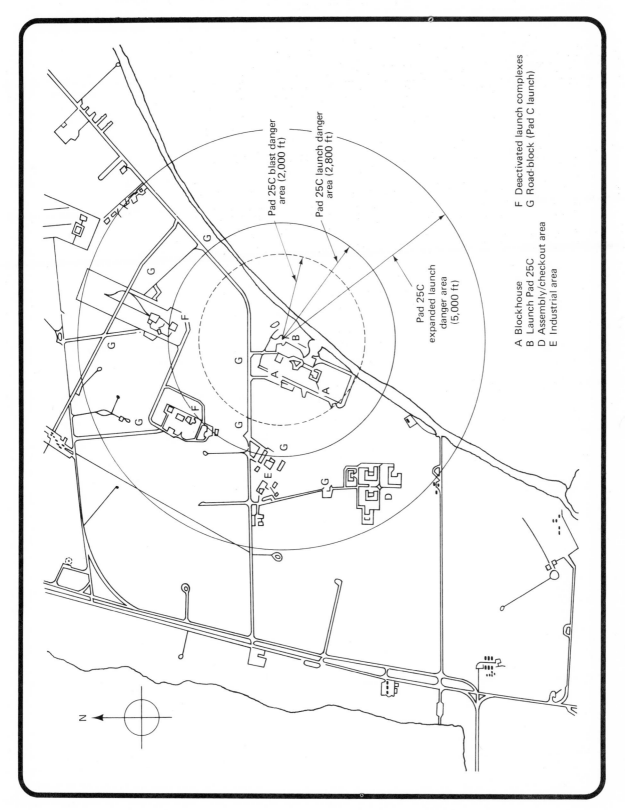

Fig. 6-8. Pad launch and blast danger areas, Air Force Eastern Test Range.

Pad 25C blast danger area (2,000 ft)

Pad 25C launch danger area (2,800 ft)

Pad 25C expanded launch danger area (5,000 ft)

A Blockhouse
B Launch Pad 25C
D Assembly/checkout area
E Industrial area

F Deactivated launch complexes
G Road-block (Pad C launch)

123

tective devices should be worn; and areas where hard hats, face shields, and similar equipment are required.

- Hazard contours. Contours may be plotted to indicate the existence of such hazards as radiation or noise levels. Electromagnetic radiation contours have been plotted for such locations as aircraft carrier decks to determine danger areas for electro-explosive devices.

Noise Level Contours

Another example of the numerous applications of hazard mapping is illustrated in Fig. 6-9. Here the problem was in establishing noise level contours for various types of Short-Take-Off-and-Landing aircraft (STOL) whose use in serving large cities was being investigated. The upper left diagram indicates the noise levels that can be detected at various distances from different types of aircraft. These noise level data are then used to prepare the diagram at the upper right. The dotted portions show the noise levels at various distances from an aircraft making an approach and landing. The heavy lines show noise levels as an aircraft takes off and makes a maximum turn to avoid restricted areas or to proceed on to another destination.*

The contours established in this way can then be plotted on a map of a proposed landing site. Natural and structural obstructions and restricted areas can also be shown. The analysis can then evaluate whether a safe route for the aircraft can be established while maintaining an acceptable noise level in inhabited areas. In Fig. 6-9, one site is being evaluated. The report from which this material was drawn also investigated other sites in that city, sites in other cities, and noise effects of other types of aircraft.

Failure Plotting

Figure 6-10 illustrates another use of mapping for safety analysis. The Bullpup (AGM-12) is an air-to-ground missile launched from fighter-bomber aircraft. The launch aircraft flies in a direction that, on the chart, would be up Sector 6 toward the center of the circles. The missile is guided toward the target after launch by radio transmissions from the aircraft in accordance with signals initiated by the pilot.

Control of the missile is frequently lost due to such problems as transmitter or receiver failure, exhaustion of the compressed air that activates the flight control surfaces, or electrical failure. The chart illustrates that most missile failures followed a ballistic trajectory, impacting along or adjacent to the initial line of flight of the aircraft.

Occasionally, firepower demonstrations would be given to visitors to indicate the missile's capabilities. At one time, grandstands provided for viewers were located approximately a mile from the target and approximately 1,000 feet from the extended line of flight through the target. Command personnel began to doubt the safety of the viewers in the grandstands. The plot of reported failures and impact points confirmed these suspicions. The lines along which aircraft flew prior to launch were readjusted and the grandstand was moved.

Use of this type of failure plot was proposed for another purpose. Some ranges into which Bullpups were launched for practice purposes

Initial Analyses

124

* D. W. Hayward *et al., Study of Aircraft in Short Haul Transportation Systems,* (Published by the Boeing Company for NASA, 1967).

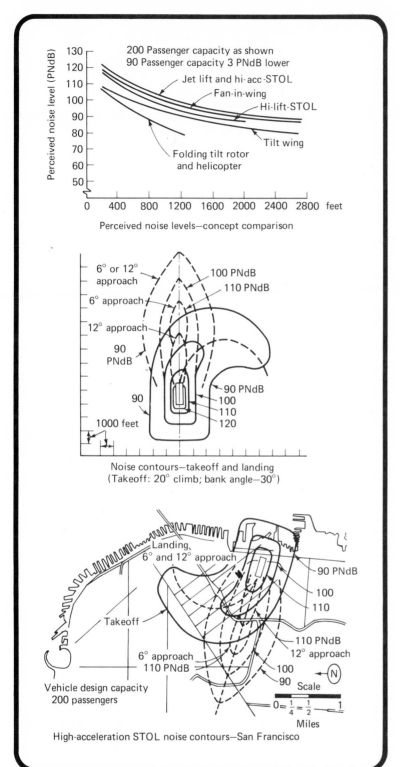

130
120
110
100
90
80
70
60
50

Perceived noise level (PNdB)

200 Passenger capacity as shown
90 Passenger capacity 3 PNdB lower

Jet lift and hi-acc-STOL
Fan-in-wing
Hi-lift-STOL

Tilt wing

Folding tilt rotor
and helicopter

0   400   800   1200   1600   2000   2400   2800   feet

Perceived noise levels—concept comparison

6° or 12°
approach

6° approach

12° approach

90
PNdB

90

1000 feet

100 PNdB
110 PNdB

90 PNdB
100
110
120

Noise contours—takeoff and landing
(Takeoff: 20° climb; bank angle—30°)

Landing
6° and 12° approach

Takeoff

6° approach
110 PNdB

Vehicle design capacity
200 passengers

90 PNdB
100
110

110 PNdB
12° approach

100
90   Scale

N

0 = ¼ = ½   1

Miles

High-acceleration STOL noise contours—San Francisco

Fig. 6-9. Mapping noise levels. (High acceleration STOL, 200 passenger capacity shown; 90 passenger capacity 3 PNdB lower.)

were comparatively small. A failure plot could be used as an overlay on a range map drawn to the same scale. It would become immediately evident whether any failures would result in impacts off-range or whether there were hazards to facilities or inhabited areas. It could be used to determine the best lines of flight and missile launch point limits to minimize the possibility of an accident if a failure after launch occurred.

Mapping

125

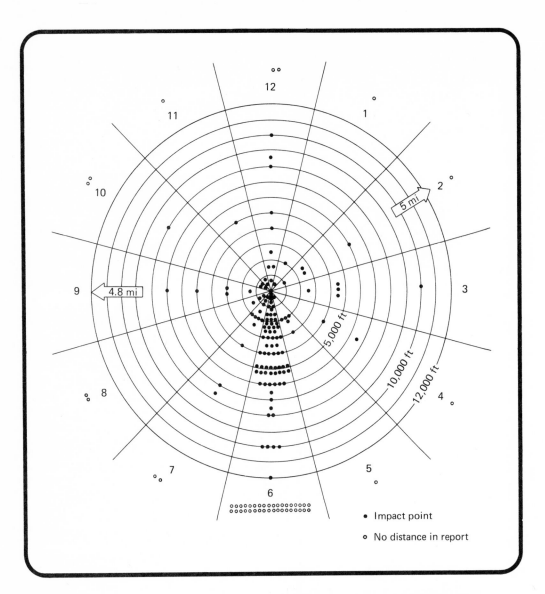

Fig. 6-10. Impact points of Bullpup failures.

Accident Mapping

Figure 6-11 is an application of hazard mapping to analyze accidents involving fires with Army helicopters. Although this mapping was used in accident analysis, it is undoubtedly an effective way of studying new designs to determine whether similar hazards would exist.

Study of the seven helicopters shown indicated that 8.4 per cent of the major helicopter accidents during the six years from July 1957 to June 1963 involved fires.* Ninety per cent of the fires were generated by the initial impact of a crash or immediately thereafter. In 80 per cent of the fires, ruptured fuel cells and broken fuel lines caused spillage or leakage of gasoline, which ignited when it hit a hot surface, such as the engine exhaust. Although the fire accidents constituted 8.4 per cent of the major accidents, they caused 42 per cent of the injuries and 62 per cent of the deaths. Twenty-seven fatalities were attributed to thermal

Initial Analyses

126

* Emil Spezia, *United States Army Helicopter Accidents Involving Fire,* United States Army Board For Aviation Accident Research, Report 1–64 (Fort Rucker, Alabama) (AD 658 080)

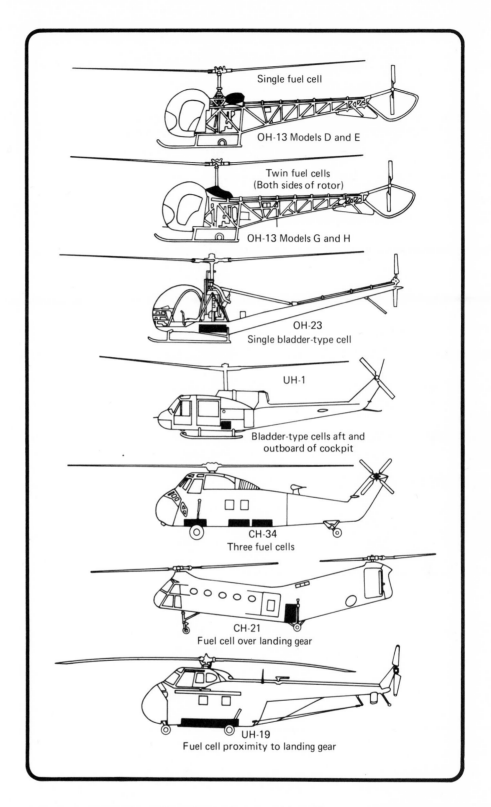

Single fuel cell

OH-13 Models D and E

Twin fuel cells
(Both sides of rotor)

OH-13 Models G and H

OH-23
Single bladder-type cell

UH-1

Bladder-type cells aft and
outboard of cockpit

CH-34
Three fuel cells

CH-21
Fuel cell over landing gear

UH-19
Fuel cell proximity to landing gear

Fig. 6-11. Location of fuel cells [black] in various helicopters.

injuries; of these, 10 were in accidents in which persons would probably have survived if there had been no fire.

Fixed-wing aircraft accidents involving ground impacts generally occur with forward movement. Helicopter behavior in a crash is much different. Most helicopter crashes involve hard, almost vertical, impacts and then roll-overs. As a result, there is a high thermal injury and fatality

127

rate. In major accidents, the helicopter generally rolls over and lies on its side. At least one of the personnel exits is then blocked; in some helicopters, it may be the only exit out of the cargo space. Secondly, the fuel tank may come to rest in a position where its remaining fuel spills onto the hot engine below it, as shown in Fig. 6-11. In addition, the layouts indicate the protection afforded the tanks against rupture after any hard impact.

The model OH-13 D and E series helicopters differ from the G and H series in one respect that significantly effects their tendency to burn. The D and E series have one 29-gallon metal tank above the engine, aft of the rotor mast, which is also above the engine. On the other hand, the cells of the G and H series extend outside the airframe. The airframe provides protection for the cells in the D and E series. Lacking this protection, the G and H fuel cells are more frequently ruptured by hitting the ground, broken rotor blades, pieces of mast linkage, and by wires or other external objects they might hit. Even more critical because of the tank location is the inherent hazard from spillage during roll-over. Because of their situations, one of the two tanks will almost always be above the hot engine onto which any remaining fuel can spill. This may be either from a vent, a fill opening, a ruptured seam, or a loose connection. G and H series helicopters burned in 11 per cent of their major accidents compared to 3.4 per cent for the D and E series.

Another helicopter of somewhat similar design is the OH-23. However, the location of the fuel cell under the cockpit floor and the outer skin of the fuselage offer much more substantial protection. As can be expected, the OH-23 had a much lower fire rate than the OH-13 G and H. Only one OH-23 caught fire in 10 roll-overs, and that one was due to an extremely hard landing that ruptured the fuel tank. Much lesser impact forces are necessary to cause leaks, spills, ruptures, and ignitions in the OH-13.

The construction of the UH-1 is even better. A layer of energy-absorbing honeycomb surrounds the lower portion of the fuel cells, which, in addition, are reinforced and self-sealing. Accidents involving fires of the UH-19 and CH-21 were principally due to fuel cells being punctured when the landing gear broke and penetrated the fuselage after impact. The gasoline was then ignited either by a spark, a hot surface, or by an electrical source.

Other analyses that were made or could have been made with similar plots include:

1. Determination of possibilities that a tank or line leak could permit fuel to hit an ignition source, such as the hot engine, exhaust manifold, or electrical system, even when there had been no impact or roll-over. Each of these ignition sources would be plotted in relation to the fuel tanks, lines, connections, vents, and fill openings.

2. Locations of openings through which personnel could evacuate the aircraft in an accident, and especially for worst-case conditions that might occur during roll-over.

Other Uses of Mapping

On 14 December 1961, a train struck a bus loaded with schoolchildren near Greeley, Colorado, killing 20 and injuring the remaining 16 and the driver. Harold R. Willis has suggested a procedure for analyzing the dangers that could be encountered as a bus made its rounds, picking up and delivering children, to minimize the possibilities of such accidents.* Mapping complements the procedure, which is summarized below, as an excellent method of hazard analysis. Public authorities would then approve or disapprove the analysis after review or recommend changes. A vehicle route will endeavor to have a minimum number of hazard points, or authorities will take measures to reduce the hazards at certain points by suitable control measures. After the route is approved, drivers will be provided with copies of the analysis with indications of where the hazards exist and with instructions for dealing with these hazards. The procedure consists of considering:

1. The stops each conveyance makes and any hazard at each stop

2. The safe speed along each portion of the route

3. Traffic flow rate during times that the conveyance must traverse the route

4. Traffic signs to be placed for the safety of children when the bus is loading and unloading

5. Special hazards along the bus route

    a. Dangerous cross streets

    b. Railway crossings:

    No railway crossing will be used unless the school bus driver has at least one mile of unobstructed view of the track and no other route is available.

    All rail crossings used by school buses will be clearly marked for the attention of the train crewmen at least one mile down the track from the crossing. The train will slow to 25 mph at that point. The marking of the point will be the joint responsibility of the state and the railway company.

    The state will inform each railway company of crossings that school buses will use at least 30 days before the route is to be used.

    All school buses will be required to stop at least 40 ft from the railway crossing. The driver will determine that the track is clear and record the stop on a trip record sheet before proceeding.

6. Dangerous hills, analyzed for seasonal hazards

7. Dangerous corners, particularly where views are obstructed

8. Dangerous bridges

9. Bumps or dips of significant proportions

10. Locations of fire stations

11. Parking lots, industrial plants, or other locations where heavy traffic concentrations might exist

12. Any other condition considered to be a hazard by the Highway Safety Department or any other responsible person or organization

* Harold R. Willis, *Human Error—Cause and Reduction,* paper presented to the Joint Meeting of Midwest Human Factors Society and National Safety Council (Chicago: Martin Company, 1962).

In another use of mapping, fire zones and fire defense routes are shown. Such maps have been employed extensively for chemical plants where hazardous processes are involved. High temperature and high-pressure equipment are spotted in relation to other critical equipment that could be damaged or activated if control of a process is lost. In addition, access routes can be plotted for emergency equipment and personnel in the event a fire or explosion takes place.

Emergency evacuation routes, safety zones, and protective structures can also be mapped. These are especially useful when incorporated into contingency procedures to indicate to personnel the routes that they should take to safety and the areas and structures that would be considered safe. Engineers who develop or analyze such procedures can utilize maps to ensure that routes are feasible, are the shortest possible, involve no obstructions, and that the interval required to move from an area of danger to one of safety is possible under conditions that could exist.

Maps can be used for micrometeorological analyses: They can illustrate directions of prevailing winds and areas and facilities that could be affected by contaminants. A liquid oxygen plant was subject to reboiler and compressor explosions. Investigation revealed that acetylene released into the atmosphere from a nearby plant was windborne to the compressor intakes. The acetylene accumulated until it reached amounts that reacted explosively. Similar plots can be employed to determine possible effects if a toxic, corrosive, or flammable gas were released by accident, through an operation such as a rocket launch or as exhaust from a chemical process in an industrial plant.

Environment Analysis

The environment in which a mission is to take place, in which hardware is to exist, and in which personnel must function is one of the basic factors affecting safety. Environments can be divided into:

- Natural
- Induced
- Controlled
- Artificial
- Free
- Closed
- Combinations of these

Natural

A natural environment is one unaffected by the actions of man and is characteristic of a specific location and time. The qualification regarding time is important in many instances. Winds may blow over a point near the coast in one direction during the day and in the opposite direction at night. Land masses may be colder than water in winter and warmer in summer; the water will then have an equalizing effect.

A chart illustrating natural environmental conditions at various altitudes is presented in Fig. 6-12. A safety analysis on all aspects of system operation must consider these factors. Many airports are located in areas that would not have been selected if proper analyses had been

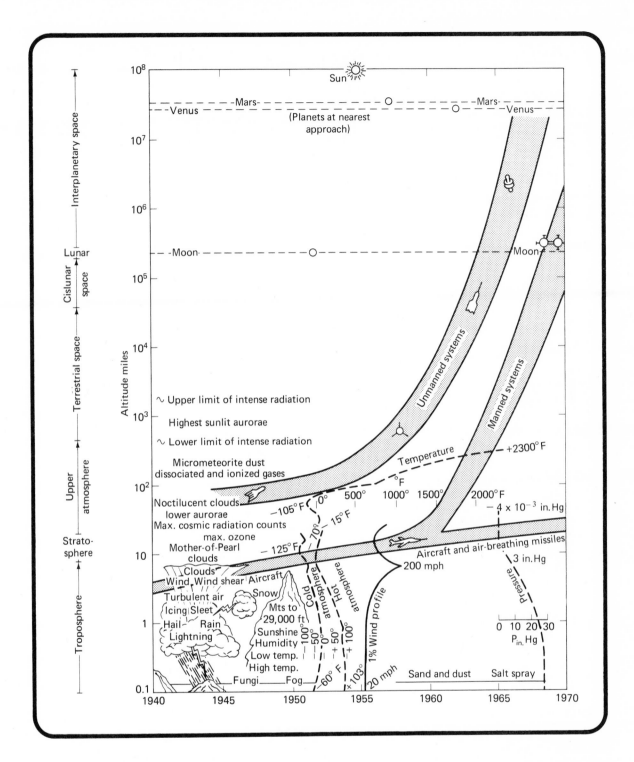

Fig. 6-12. Some natural environments at various altitudes. E. C. Theiss et al, *Handbook of Environmental Engineering,* ASD Technical Report 61–363 (Wright-Patterson AFB, Ohio: Aeronautical Systems Division: p. 1–11 (AD 272 272)

made of environmental conditions. Studies may have been made of prevailing winds to determine in which directions the runways should be laid out. However, little attention was given to factors such as updrafts or downdrafts, which occur when winds are deflected vertically by embankments and hills or when convective currents are generated by differences in temperature.

Sometimes a city wants to locate an airport on cheap, unwanted land, so the officials responsible simply neglect many safety considerations. In one case, a site was selected near a water bird sanctuary. The

Environment Analysis

131

land was low, frequently covered by fog, and, at certain times of year, was marshy. Three grave problems are immediately apparent to anyone knowledgeable in flight safety: bird strikes, limited visibility, and the possibility of aircraft hydroplaning on flooded surfaces.

Environment analysis is first required to determine the natural conditions that could constitute primary, contributory, or initiating hazards. Figure 6-13 lists many such conditions, some of which can be pointed out briefly here:

1. Solar radiation—Causes burns, blindness, and sunstroke.
2. Temperature—Extremely low temperatures can cause wind chill, frostbite, and freezing; high temperatures cause dehydration and heat exhaustion.
3. Pressure—Low atmospheric pressure may result in anoxia; high pressures under water cause narcosis; changes in pressure cause dysbarism.
4. Moisture—Causes corrosion, condensation inside electrical connectors, and shorting of circuits.
5. Wind—Causes toppling of structures.

A natural environment can include combinations of factors. Each can be damaging individually or can increase or decrease the effect of another. During a hot summer day, an exposed material can be subjected to solar radiation, high temperature, and blowing sand that could cause it to degrade rapidly. Some possible combinations and their interrelationships are also shown in Fig. 6-13.

Induced   Next to be considered is induced environment, one in which an action generates conditions not normally found in a natural environment. Some induced environmental factors are illustrated in Fig. 6-14.

- A high-speed aircraft moving through the atmosphere generates friction. The air immediately adjacent to the skin of the aircraft is heated to a temperature far above the one normally existing at that altitude.
- The shock waves (sonic booms) induced by a supersonic aircraft can break windows and other frangible objects.
- Smog caused by exhausts emitted from automobiles, heating plants, refineries, and industrial processes can irritate the eyes and lungs, reduce visibility, poison vegetation, annoy people so they are more likely to make errors and cause accidents, and reduce the amount of solar radiation received by the surface of the earth.
- Extensive concrete surfaces or large buildings can create abnormally hot temperatures during the summer because of their abilities to absorb heat. Whirlwinds (wind-devils) may form on such concrete surfaces, while the buildings may block passage of air that could cool lower areas.
- When a fabric-covered aircraft with a large surface area, such as a zeppelin, passes through air, it can generate tremendous amounts of static electricity. Discharge of accumulated electrical charges caused the destruction of the *Hindenburg.*

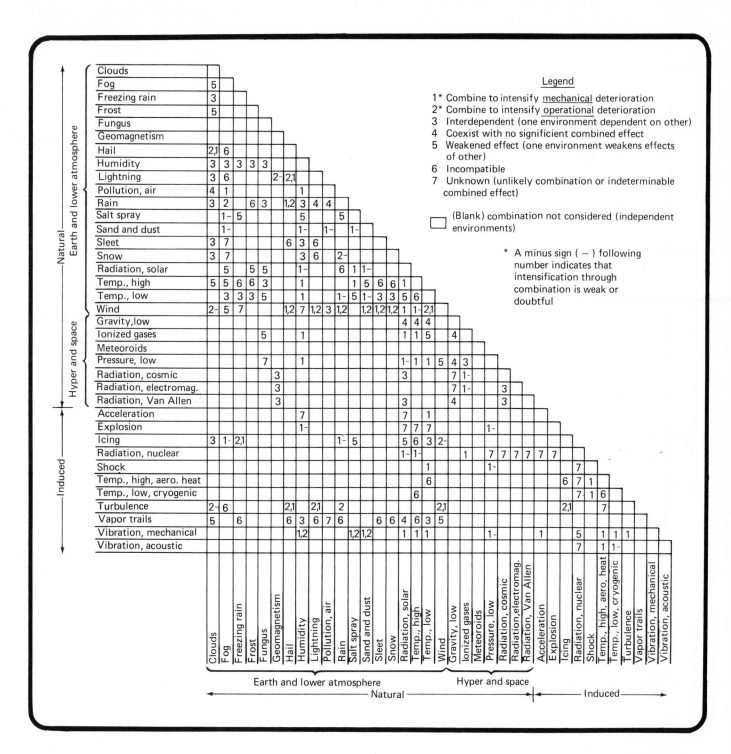

Fig. 6-13. Qualitative relationships of combined environments. E. C. Theiss et al. *Handbook of Environmental Engineering,* ASD Technical Report 61–363 (Wright-Patterson AFB: Aeronautical Systems Division, 1961) p. 3–46 (AD 272 272).

133

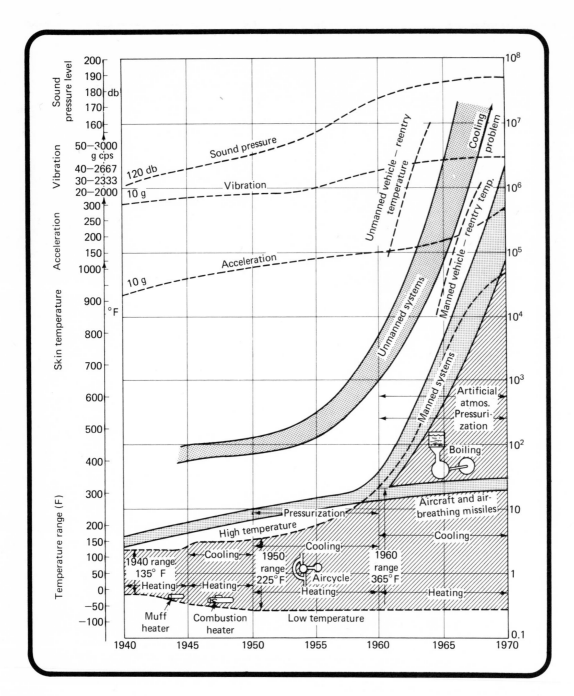

Fig. 6-14. Trends in induced environments. ECC. Theiss et al, *Handbook of Environmental Engineering,* ASD Technical Report 61–363 (Wright-Patterson AFB: Aeronautical Systems Division, 1961) pp. 1–11 (AD 272 272).

Controlled   A controlled environment exists when one or more parameters of a natural environment are limited or modified to make it suitable for occupancy.

- Air conditioning is an extremely common example. Air is heated or cooled, filtered, and dried or humidified to meet desired levels.

Initial Analyses

- The cold, purified air at high altitudes is compressed for use in aircraft engines, and compressed and heated for use in crew and passenger cabins.

134

- A person in protective clothing breathes through a gas mask canister which removes any harmful gases, vapors, or particles that may be present in the atmosphere around him.
- Air entering spaces where materials susceptible to moisture are stored is dried by being passed through dessicants or over cooling coils.

Artificial

An artificial environment is one created to exist within, but neither derives from nor forms part of, the natural environment. An artificial environment may be either of two types. Air at breathable pressure and temperature is provided when the person is in a totally foreign environment that would be lethal unless artificial conditions were provided. The crew of a submerged submarine exists in an artificial environment since the air of which it is composed differs from the water outside that constitutes the natural environment. In the second type, the environment is foreign to a person but is determined and created because of hostile outside conditions. A deep-sea diver supplied with a pressurized mixture of oxygen and helium is in this category.

An artificial environment differs from one that is controlled. The controlled environment inside a passenger aircraft at high altitude has the same relative composition as that outside, except for air pressure and temperature. A pure oxygen atmosphere supplied by internal sources would constitute an artificial atmosphere. Other examples of artificial environments include:

- Oxygen and helium or nitrogen mixtures in space capsules
- Nitrogen or other inert gas in a container for long-term protection of a material that deteriorates in the presence of air
- Underwater storage of substances that react in air, such as phosphorous, lignite, or subbituminous coal

Free

A free environment is one in which movements of air masses are unrestricted. Natural or man-made obstacles, such as hills or high buildings, may divert the flow of air but do not otherwise prevent intermixing with other masses. The science of micrometeorology is concerned with the movement of free air over limited distances.* At one time, this limit was approximately 6 to 10 feet above the ground and within a radius of 500 to 1000 feet. However, concern with movements of air and its pollutants from boiler plant and chemical process stacks has resulted in studies involving greater heights and distances.

Closed

A closed environment is one in which movement of air is restricted, and intermixing with a free environment is generally accomplished through mechanical means. A closed environment may become extremely hazardous under adverse conditions; the presence of a small amount of toxic gas in such a location often becomes lethal, whereas little harm would be done in a free environment. A common example is death due to carbon monoxide poisoning in closed, parked automobiles in which the engine is kept running to provide heat. Children have suffocated in

* For an introductory discussion, see the author's article, "What an Engineer Should Know About Micrometeorology," *Heating, Piping and Air Conditioning*, May 1965, pp. 101–105.

refrigerators and trunks in which they hid while playing or in closed cars in which their parents left them while shopping. In 1964, 53 men died in minutes, mostly due to carbon monoxide poisoning, as a result of a fire involving 93 gal of hydraulic fluid in a Titan II silo. This accident in a closed environment can be compared to those involving fires in above-ground tank farms where millions of gallons of petroleum products have burned without injury to anyone.

Long- and Short-Term Effects

Environmental effects can be categorized as immediate or long-term. Immediate effects include interference with operations or material damage. Heavy rain can stop flight operations or make them hazardous because of possible hydroplaning of aircraft. Flooding can damage electrical equipment by causing it to short out. High humidity can cause environments to become unbearable for personnel.

Long-term effects can involve slow chemical or nuclear reactions that also generate damage or loss of ability to function. Moisture can cause corrosion that, over varying lengthy periods, can ruin equipment. Condensation can occur to such an extent that leaching of soluble materials can degrade and change the characteristics of mixtures.

Changes in environment can produce long- and short-term effects; exactly which will occur depends on the equipment and material affected. Changes in temperature cause expansion and contraction of metals. The metallic objects or structures can fail either immediately, if the stresses generated are greater than the strengths of the restraints on the metal, or after a time, because of fatigue effects. Campus pointed out how very large steel beams, some of them thirty feet in length, failed longitudinally through their webs because of changes in temperature while still in a warehouse. The beams had high residual stresses, which had been produced internally during manufacture of the beams. The changes in temperature caused them to fail along lines of maximum stress.*

Ffield showed the effects of solar heating on the hull of an LST during different times of day (Fig. 6-15).† The changes in temperature with their attendant stresses occur in both the external structure and in the interior bulkheads. The same report also points out that greater temperature differences, stresses, and problems exist in refrigerator ships. More gradual effects occur when a ship moves from a tropic to a frigid zone or vice versa. The complex interrelationships between stresses due to changes in temperature, structural loads on the hull, vibration, brittleness, and rigidity of welds as compared to riveted joints, produced a rash of hull failures of welded ships built during World War II.

Similar environmental stresses result from solar radiation on other types of vehicles and structures, such as space boosters on a launch pad or aircraft at high altitudes. Space boosters with cryogenic liquids in their tanks are subject to problems of temperature differences that are even more severe than those with refrigerator ships. In such cases, there are multiple effects that can be generated by environmental changes: evaporation of cryogenic liquids, expansion of the liquid and

* F. Campus, "Effects of Residual Stresses on the Behaviour of Structures," in *Residual Stresses in Metals and Metal Construction,* ed. W. R. Osgood (New York: Reinhold Publishing Corp., 1954), pp. 1–21.

† P. Ffield, "Some Notes on Typical Residual Stresses in Welded Ships," also *Residual Stresses in Metals and Metal Construction,* pp. 45–74.

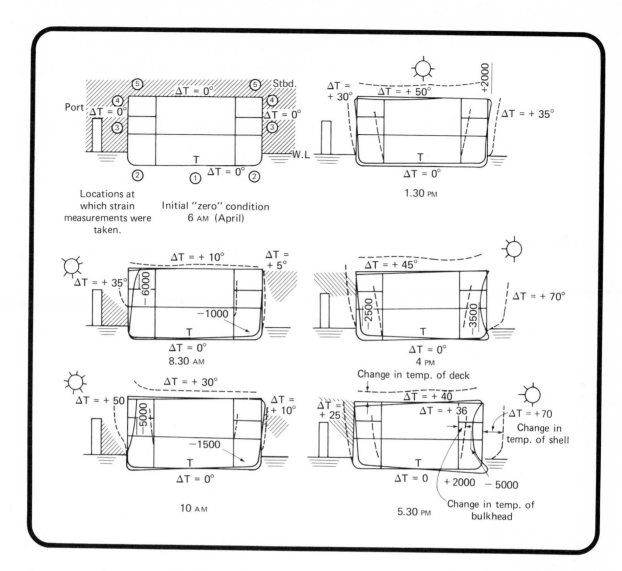

Locations at which strain measurements were taken.

Initial "zero" condition 6 AM (April)

1.30 PM

8.30 AM

4 PM

Change in temp. of deck

10 AM

5.30 PM

Change in temp. of bulkhead

gas, increased pressure and stresses, expansion of metals, and reduction in strength of the metal. Careful consideration must therefore be given to effects generated by both a specific level of environmental stress, such as high or low temperature, and also to the changes in the environmental stresses.

Furthermore, environmental factors in combination may generate effects totally different or of different magnitudes than they would individually. It is also necessary therefore to explore these factors and the stresses generated individually and in combination with all other factors and stresses.

Analysis of environmental problems may be done by:

- Reviewing mission requirements to determine which of the preceding types of environments will exist.

- Reviewing the list of hazards in Fig. 6-13 (or in the Appendix) that could exist or be generated in each of these types of environment.

- Determining the level of each parameter that might be reached

Fig. 6-15. Thermal stress patterns due to changes in ambient temperature (LST hull). All stress changes (psi) in fore and aft direction. Tension (+) plotted outboard of normal hull configuration. Compression (−) plotted inboard. T + temperature change, not actual temperature. P. Ffield, "Some Notes on Typical Residual Stresses in Welded Ships," in *Residual Stresses in Metals and Metal Construction,* ed. W. R. Osgood (New York: Reinhold Publishing Corp., 1954) pp. 70–71.

Analysis Procedure

Environment Analysis

137

in each environment. This procedure may be done by preparing mission profiles based on previous experience, conducting tests to establish data, or extrapolating known data to theoretical situations.

- Establishing by test the effects of various environments on materials, components, systems, personnel, and operations.
- Reviewing possible means of controlling the environment, hazards, or damaging effects.
- Determining the most suitable artificial environment for a specific mission.

Analyses and Tests   Theoretical analyses have a definite place in environmental analyses, but these are predicated heavily on tests and experience because of the multiplicity of variations that could exist in almost every situation. For example, one of the commonest and most damaging environmental problems is corrosion and resultant metal failures. The degree to which a part may corrode is dependent on such factors as the composition of its metal, the size and arrangement of its crystals, the heat treatment to which it was subjected, the surface finish, presence of any stress concentrators, any stresses imposed, length and duration of vibrations to which it was subjected, protective coatings or films, humidity present, temperatures at which it exists, salt air or other similar conditions to which it has been exposed, orientation of a crack or other surface defect to moisture or dirt, and numerous others. Rather than evaluate each of these factors and their interrelationships, it is frequently much simpler to make environmental tests of the items in question under conditions approximating those expected during system operation. If enough tests are made, minor differences will become unimportant and can be disregarded. Major affecting factors and their end effects will then become apparent. Decisions can be made on material suitability based on these factors.

Some attempts have been made to treat environments mathematically, but the results frequently lack dependability. In micrometeorology at least 30 equations have been developed to determine how high and far emissions from tall chimneys and ground release points will travel. However, results have been found to be rough approximations even over extremely short distances. Better results have been obtained through wind tunnel tests of physical models of structures and the terrain on which they are to be built. Use of such models before the structures are built permits analysts to determine: directions in which buildings, equipment, and air intakes should be oriented; requirements for wind control devices, whether nearby populated areas would be affected by stack effluents or accidental releases; and need for exhaust cleaning or neutralizing systems. In some instances, such as at rocket or propellant test sites, investigations are first conducted during which controlled amounts of dispersants are released under metered wind and temperature conditions. Downwind concentrations are then measured and evaluated. Large-scale operational tests will be permitted only when atmospheric conditions are such that the indicators evaluated by the controlled tests imply that the operation will be safe.

Initial Analyses   Testing is expensive and any technique or process that can reduce costs is highly desirable. Tests under actual field conditions might require

SIMPLE ENVIRONMENT FACTORS		Ther	Chem	Em	Rheo	Elas	Str	Stn	Cln
High temperature	Th	D	I	I	D	D	O	I	I
Low temperature	Tl	D	I	O	D	D	D	I	I
Changing temperature (thermal shock)	Tc	D	I	O	O	O	I	D	O
High pressure	Ph	I	I	I	I	O	I	D	I
Low pressure	Pl	I	I	I	O	O	I	D	I
Changing pressure (pressure shock)	Pc	I	O	I	O	O	O	D	O
Ionizing radiation	Ri	I	I	D	I	I	I	O	O
Mechanical interference (sand, dust, ice)	Im	I	O	I	I	I	I	I	D
Relative acceleration, steady or cyclic (includes vibration)	Ar	I	O	I	O	O	I	D	O
External electric or magnetic fields	Fd	I	I	D	O	O	O	I	O
Abnormal chemical surroundings	Cs	I	D	I	I	O	I	O	I
Aging	Zt	O	I	O	I	I	I	I	O

SIMPLE UNIT PARAMETERS

Column headers (diagonal): Thermal state / Chemical state (composition) / Electric-magnetic state / Rheological state / Elastic state / Structural state (crystal structure, polymerization) / Strain state / Cleanliness state (dirt, corrosion products, etc.)

O. SUP unaffected in all cases. Example — age on thermal state.

I. SUP affected in some cases. Example — electric field on thermal state.

D. SUP affected in all cases. Example — temperature on thermal state.

transporting equipment and personnel to desert, arctic, or tropical sites and then waiting until environmental conditions were suitable. This is extremely time-consuming and expensive, especially if tests must be conducted in more than one type of climate. Some field testing must undoubtedly be done, but anything reducing its necessity or duration may save time and money.

One means employed to eliminate some testing on the effects of

Fig. 6-16. Effect of environmental stresses on specific parameters.

Environment Analysis

139

environment is computer simulation. This simulation is predicated on two basic facts. First, materials and parts will react in definite ways to environmental stresses. Second, those stresses can be established that will reflect the environments encountered by the materials or parts. Natural environments have certain general characteristics of temperature and humidity; for example, a desert is hot and dry. Other characteristics, like pressure change with altitude, are common to all climates. Induced environments can be established from theoretical considerations or past experience, such as the data indicated on the flight profile in Fig. 6-6.

Arnold has described how information on actual or stipulated environments is employed in a computer simulation process.* Environmental factors, listed in Fig. 6-16 are plotted against some of the material or process parameters that might be affected. The two are compared by computer techniques. Figure 6-16 relates the action that a single environment factor (SEF) will have on a simple unit parameter (SUP). The factors and parameters shown here were chosen for a specific case (ordnance material), but others can be employed where required.

The computer is furnished data on real environments, such as a desert and its related single environmental factors: high temperature, low temperature, solar radiation and mechanical interference (sand, dirt, dust). Other conditions are indicated, such as whether the equipment was provided with an overhead shelter. The computer is programmed to compare information on environments to physical and chemical characteristics material and equipment. Effects are then established.

The computer can also be programmed to form all possible combinations of environmental factors acting simultaneously to affect each unit parameter. In such cases, each of the single environmental factors is analyzed by the computer for effects on each simple unit parameter. Another matrix is then prepared to indicate whether there are any mutual effects. If one of the effects is 0, there will be no combined effect; two I terms or an I and D will indicate a possible, but not certain, effect; whereas two D terms means a combined effect will occur. This methodology can be extended to as many environmental inputs as desired. Results may then approximate those shown in Fig. 6-16.

* J. S. Arnold, "Computer-Calculated Environments," *Machine Design*, 25 April 1963, pp. 126–130.

chapter 7

DETAILED ANALYSES

Product or system hazards are of three principal types: those that affect or are generated by the subsystems, those that are due to their interfaces and interrelationships, and those that affect or are generated by the total, integrated system.

Every product or system must have certain basic subsystems; other types of subsystems may be peculiar to a specific product or system. The fundamental subsystems are:

- *Power*. Operation of any system requires the expenditure of energy. The source of power may be man, draft animal, hydraulic, electric, pneumatic, mechanical, chemical, solar, compressed gas, or other means.

- *Structural*. This subsystem supports, unites, and frequently protects the other subsystems. The skeleton of a man; chassis of an automobile or truck; frame of a building, equipment cabinet, or motor; fuselage of an aircraft; and motor case of a missile are examples. In its protective capacity, the structural subsystem may keep an adverse external environment from its contents or permit a suitable internal environment to be maintained.

- *Control*. The operation of each subsystem must be controlled. Control is maintained either by fixed parameters designed and built into the system through the use of devices adjusted to operational requirements before each operation begins, or by adjustments during operation.

- *Sensor*. A sensor may be a sentient creature or device that reacts to a specific condition or event. It senses the environment, outputs, inputs, and other factors required to inform the operator of the status of the system or subsystem.

- *Operator*. The operator may be a person, animal, computer, or device responsive to needs or signals. The operator, even when inanimate or limited in capacity, is the brain of the system. When the operator is a person or computer, the information fed in from its own or related sensory equipment is analyzed for suitable control decisions. There is no analysis with a device that reacts to a prescribed condition or event, only automatic response. An animal may be conditioned to respond, act instinctively, react to suitable stimuli, or make extremely simple decisions.

- *Communications*. As the operator constitutes the brain, so the communications network is the nervous system. Through it goes all the information the system and subsystem receive from their environments; input, output, and operational data; and control signals. Electrical wiring, mechanical linkages, hydraulic and pneumatic lines, sound, and electromagnetic pulses are some of the links making up communication media. Without communications, the system and its subsystems would be inoperative; with defective communications, confusion and error result.

Some of the other subsystems that may be required or are beneficial for specific systems include:

- *Propulsion*. Any vehicle or system that must be mobile requires a means by which motion is accomplished. Wheels, belted treads, rollers, propellers, jets, or rockets are examples. The means may be separated from the power supply to which it is connected, such as on an automobile. In other systems, as in a rocket or air-cushion vehicle, the power supply and means of motion are the same.

- *Environmental control.* When personnel must exist in environments different from those to which they are normally accustomed or best suited, an environmental control system is necessary or advisable. Environmental control is necessary when the ambient atmosphere is unsuitable because of composition, temperature or pressure, or presence of pollutants. Control is advisable for conditions that may be bearable in emergencies but that would increase personnel efficiencies and reduce errors through increased comfort.

Subsystem Analysis

Initial system and subsystem analyses may be conducted systematically through use of charts correlating hardware, hazards, personnel, and other factors. In a pamphlet, "System Safety Hazard Analysis,"* prepared by the author (of this book) for the U.S. Air Force, one method for reviewing subsystems was indicated. The pamphlet was originally developed for use with missile and space systems. These systems were categorized according to subsystems and major components that each might contain, as indicated in Fig. 7-1. A form (Fig. 7-2) was devised to correlate hardware, hazards, and operational time segments during which the hazards could exist. An analyst can develop similar forms to suit his particular needs.

In some instances, major components are also listed as subsystems. For example, a Unit Cooling System is shown as a major component under "Guidance," but it is also shown as a subsystem entitled "Cooling Units." As a major component, its hazards are related to the subsystem of which it forms a part. As a subsystem, it is broken down into components that can be evaluated further. A reviewer could categorize these into even greater detail if he believes it advisable.

The columns on "Detection and Warning" and "Protective Equipment" are additional check items for the reviewer. "Desirable" indicates it is generally advantageous to make provisions for this equipment. Notes can be entered under "Included" regarding whether provisions actually have been made for this specific system.

After subsystems are analyzed, operational time periods must be reviewed to determine how critical the effects of any hazard might be at any time in the life cycle of the system. For example, during transportation of a liquid-propellant missile, the propellants usually are not present and fire hazards from this source are nonexistent. Similarly, acceleration is no hazard during storage of a missile, whereas corrosion might be a problem. Subsystem review sheets therefore contain space for notes regarding periods during which a specific hazard might be critical to the system. The following list is a broad breakdown of opera-

* A condensed version can be found in: W. Hammer, "Progressive Qualitative Hazard Analyses," AIAA Paper No. 67–935, paper presented at the American Institute of Aeronautics and Astronautics (AIAA) 4th Annual Meeting and Technical Display, Anaheim, California (23–27 October 1967).

MISSILE AND SPACE SUBSYSTEMS

AUXILIARY POWER AND PROPULSION UNITS

RATO units
Independent liquid-propellant units
Independent solid-propellant units (strap-ons)
Units using prime propulsion system propellants
Gas-driven pumps and power supplies

COOLING UNITS

Heat sources and sinks
Coolant or refrigerant
Insulation
Tanks, piping, and connections
Power supply
Starting, control, and regulation

ELECTRICAL SYSTEMS

Power source
Loads (motors, lighting, etc.)
Wiring and connectors (incl. umbilicals)
Switching gear
Circuit protection

ELECTRONIC SYSTEMS (OTHER THAN GUIDANCE)

Navigation systems
Launch systems
Communications systems
Countermeasures
Surveillance systems
Checkout
Telemetry and display
Warhead enable and firing
Destruct
Unit power supply
Unit cooling
Unit overload protection
Unit wiring and connectors

EXPLOSIVE DEVICE UNITS

Initiators
Gas generators
Stage separation
Launch ejectors
Jettison ejectors
Panel or canopy removers
Warheads
Fuel and oxidizer valves
Destruct systems
Thrust termination
Infrared sources (flares)

FACILITIES AND GROUND EQUIPMENT

Transportation equipment
Loading and unloading equipment
Propellant handling equipment
Maintenance and check out equipment
Assembly equipment and facilities
Compressed gas equipment
Environmental control units
Launch control centers
Launch pads

Launch silos
Utilities equipment and facilities
Storage facilities
Disposal equipment and areas
Fire-fighting and emergency equipment

FLIGHT CONTROL

Autopilot
Attitude control actuators
Thrust vector control
Vernier motors
Unit pneumatic system
Unit hydraulic system
Unit electrical system

GUIDANCE

Programmer
Reference units
Launch computer
Missile computer
Sensors
Target seekers
Terrain clearance system
Irdome or radome
Unit power supply
Unit cooling system
Unit overload protection
Unit wiring and connectors

HYDRAULIC SYSTEMS

Pressure sources
Fluid
Tanks and accumulators
Pressure regulators
Piping and valves
Filters
Connectors and umbilicals

LIFE SUPPORT SYSTEMS

Atmosphere control
Ecological systems
Temperature and humidity control
Fire protection
Suits
Escape and rescue
Radiation protection
Impact protection
Sensing equipment
Cabin sealing
Oxygen and water storage

LUBRICATION SYSTEMS

Lubricant
Pressure sources
Tanks and accumulators
Piping and valves
Filters

Figure 7-1   **144**

PNEUMATIC SYSTEMS

> Pressure sources
> Fluid
> Tanks and accumulators
> Piping and valves
> Pressure regulators
> Filters
> Connectors and umbilicals

PRIME PROPULSION SYSTEM

> Fuel
> Oxidizer
> Tankage
> Pressurization
> Pumping units
> Piping and valves
> Filters
> Metering systems
> Combustion chamber
> Ignition systems
> Thrust termination system
> Nozzle
> Space propellant settling system
> Motor case

SAFETY SYSTEMS

> Safe-and-arm devices
> Malfunction detecting and warning systems
> Leak and vapor detectors
> Emergency and rescue equipment
> Fire detectors
> Fire suppression systems
> Interlocks
> Temperature and pressure indicators
> Shutdown and abort systems
> Protective clothing
> Respiratory protective equipment

STRUCTURES (MISSILE AND VEHICLE)

> Fuselage or body
> Wings
> Interstage structure
> Control surfaces
> Engine mounts
> Doors, hatches, and other openings
> Fairings
> Launch gear

Figure 7-1 continued.

tions into time segments through which a missile or space system may pass. By its generality it indicates that some segments may not be applicable to some systems.

- Packaging and transportation to launch facility
- Handling on launch facility, emplacement, loading or unloading on launcher
- Storage of components, subsystems, or complete missiles
- Assembly and test
- Alert
- Maintenance and check out
- Launch
  + Ignition
  + Lift-off or separation from carrier
  + Emergency escape
  + Hold or abort
- Flight
  + Boost
  + Staging
  + Cruise and glide
  + Maneuver and rendezvous
  + Flight termination
  + Impact or landing
  + Escape and rescue
  + Recovery

The pamphlet was prepared for Air Force personnel as a checklist to evaluate system safety efforts by contractors. Many contractors found the information useful in establishing the types of problems that might

Subsystem Analysis

145

SUBSYSTEM: PRIME PROPULSION SYSTEM (LIQUID PROPELLANTS) (LIQUID PROPELLANTS: STORABLE, CRYOGENIC) (SOLID PROPELLANT) (HYBRID)

MAJOR COMPONENTS

1. Fuel*	2. Oxidizer*	3. Tankage	4. Pressurization	5. Pumping Units	6. Filters
7. Piping and Valves	8. Metering System	9. Combustion Chamber	10. Ignition System*	11. Thrust Termination System*
12. Nozzle *	13. Space Propellant Settling System		14. Motor Case*	

*This item is also applicable to a solid propellant or hybrid propulsion system.

HAZARD	COMPONENTS POSSIBLY AFFECTED	DETECTION AND WARNING		PROTECTIVE EQUIPT.		CRITICAL OPERATIONAL SEGMENTS
		DESIRABLE	INCLUDED	DESIRABLE	INCLUDED	
Acceleration	1,2,4,5,8,13					Launch Flight
Contamination	1,2,6,8					Packaging, Maintenance, Launch, Alert, Flight
Corrosion	3,4,5,6,7,8,9,10,11,14			x		Transportation, Storage, Alert
Dissociation, Chemical	1,2,10					Storage, Alert
Electrical	8,10,11	x				Test, Maintenance, Launch, Flight
Explosion	1,2,4,9,10,11,12,14			x		Alert, Launch, Flight
Fire	1,2,6,9,10,12	x		x		Storage, Alert, Launch, Flight
Heat and Temperature	1,2,4,8,9,10	x		x		Transportation, Storage, Alert, Launch, Flight
Leakage	1,2,3,4,5,7,8,11	x				Alert, Launch, Flight
Moisture	1,2,5,6,7,8,10			x		Storage, Alert, Launch, Flight
Oxidation	1,11					Storage, Alert
Pressure	3,4,5,7,8					Transportation, Storage, Alert, Test, Launch, Flight
Radiation	1,2,10	x				Storage, Alert, Launch, Flight
Replacement, Chemical	1,2					Storage, Alert
Shock and Impact	1,8,10,11,14					Transportation, Assembly, Launch, Handling
Stress Concentrations	3,4,5,7,9,11,12,14					Transportation, Handling, Assembly, Launch, Flight
Stress Reversals	3,4,5,7,9,11,12,14					Transportation, Assembly, Launch, Flight
Structural Damage	3,4,5,7,9,11,12,14					Transportation, Handling, Assembly, Launch, Flight
Toxicity	1,2,10,11	x		x		Alert, Launch, Flight
Vibration and Noise	3,4,5,8					Transportation, Launch, Flight
Weather and Environment	1,2,10,11			x		Transportation, Storage, Alert, Launch

146

Figure 7-2

exist in the systems that they were developing and in checking their own designs.

Figure 4-2 also indicates how a subsystem and its major constituent assemblies can be checked against hazards and whether operations, failures, environmental conditions, or other factors could result in various types of injury. In actual practice, these forms can be used by reviewers as checklists, and also by designers, vendors, field personnel, and others. Each of these persons can be issued the forms with instructions to review each component, assembly, subsystem, or operation with which they are concerned and to note whether the item could generate any of the hazards. Designers at the lowest component level could begin the process, and their comments would be reviewed by safety personnel and supervisors and designers at the next higher assembly level.

This method can also be employed for effective control of subcontractors and vendors and to obtain information on hazards and safety problems that could be encountered with the items that they will furnish. Again, each manufacturer can be provided with a set of forms and instructions for checking his product. They could also be required to indicate the measures that they intend to take or have taken to minimize any problem. They can also include any stipulations that they believe advisable for designers of the next higher assemblies in which their items are to be incorporated, any warning and caution notes for maintenance and operations personnel, and any other pertinent data such as limitations on inputs and environments.

Procedure

A product, system, or subsystem analysis is a process of reiteration as more and more information becomes available. In its initial stages, it is similar to a Preliminary Hazard Analysis. As the hardware is developed, more intensive analyses, such as Failure Modes and Effects or network logic analysis can be used. The initial hardware hazard analyses may be accomplished by preparing or reviewing applicable portions of the following:

- · • The mission analysis, to determine performance requirements and possible hazardous environmental conditions.
- • A functional flow diagram indicating the various subsystems.
- • A brief description of each subsystem in accordance with the functional flow diagram. This description should indicate the proposed functions, the principle on which it operates, input characteristics and limitations, and intended output characteristics and levels.
- • A list of hazards that could affect each subsystem and the damage that could be generated. Each hazard in the Appendix is reviewed to determine whether the subsystem would either be affected by the hazard or would generate the hazard. A suitable entry is made in a review chart such as that shown in Fig. 4-2 or 7-2.
- • Detailed descriptions of the findings on separate sheets to explain any problem areas. Entries on this sheet should be coded to those on the chart by the alphabetical designation of the hazard and the numerical designation of the subsystem hardware. There may be multiple cause and effect relationships under a single alpha-

Subsystem Analysis

147

numeric designation. Information on these relationships can be entered under suitable subheadings.

- Failure Modes and Effects Analysis to establish affecting conditions and environments and to determine those modes of failure that could occur and the problems that they could generate.

- Review of hazards that could affect the system and those generated by the various assemblies to determine whether they could cause injury to personnel. Use of Fig. 4-2 or a similar method of coding and providing detailed descriptions on separate sheets, as described previously, can be used.

- An interface analysis, which investigates the effects that subsystems can have on each other, and their physical compatibilities. This analysis can be prepared in accordance with later sections of this chapter.

- Descriptions of materials that have not been employed previously for purposes intended in the subsystem under development. These materials are then reviewed to determine the problems that might be involved in acceptance of new materials or applications of known materials for new uses.

- A review to determine whether other hazards exist that could affect or be generated by the total product or system.

Each step should also indicate a possible preventive or corrective measure. This measure may be prepared concurrently with each part of the analysis or after all hazards are determined.

Failure Modes and Effects Analysis

This is a method developed by reliability engineers to determine problems that could arise from malfunctions of hardware. Extensions in applications have resulted in other titles that reflect the modifications from the basic method. In each case, however, the fundamental technique remains the same. The Society of Automotive Engineers designates the method as Failure Modes, Effects and Criticality Analysis (FMECA), whose accomplishment is broken down into two steps: Failure Modes and Effects Analysis (FMEA) and Criticality Analysis (CA).* (Criticality analyses are discussed in the following section.) System Safety engineers prepare a Fault Hazard Analysis (FHA) based on Failure Modes and Effects Analysis. The chief difference between the two is scope; the FHA includes only those items whose failures could result in an accident.

In Failure Modes and Effects Analysis, as many components, assemblies, and subsystems as possible are analyzed for failure causes and their possible effects. Analyses are made to determine those factors that could prevent a piece of hardware or a system from accomplishing its intended mission. This goal of successful accomplishment requires that the design, material, and production methods selected for each component and assembly of components be studied to ensure that possibilities of failure are minimized. It ensures that items with the highest reliabilities are selected and designs are such that the system will survive and operate even if individual items fail. To this end, each part and the effects that its failure would generate are analyzed. To establish the

Detailed Analyses

* Design Analysis Procedure for Failure Modes, Effects and Criticality Analysis (FMECA), SAE Aerospace Recommended Practice ARP 926, 15 September 1967.

magnitude of each possible problem, it is also necessary to determine the probability of a failure.

Failure Modes and Effects Analysis is therefore concerned almost entirely with equipment, ways in which its components could fail, the effects that could be generated, and estimated failure rates. These failure data provide the bases for determining where changes can be made most advantageously to improve the probability that a design will function successfully. Hazards and the possibilities of damage are related to failures only; they rarely involve investigation into damage or injury that could arise if the system operated successfully.

Each failure is considered individually, as an independent occurrence with no relation to other failures in the system except the subsequent effects that it might produce. Generally, a Failure Modes and Effects Analysis is first accomplished on a qualitative basis. Quantitative data may then be applied to establish a reliability or failure level for the system or subsystem. Four failure modes are considered:

- Premature operation of a component
- Failure of a component to operate at a prescribed time
- Failure of a component to cease operation at a prescribed time
- Failure of a component during operation

These limitations are due to the fact that the definition of reliability is: *the probability of successful accomplishment of a mission within a specified time and under specified conditions*. Narrow adherence to this definition restricts analysis to the parameters imposed by the definition.

The objectives of a Failure Modes and Effects Analysis that relate to safety include the following:

- Systematic review of component failure modes to ensure that any failure produces minimal damage to the system.
- Determining the effects that such failures will have on other items in the system and their functions.
- Determining those parts whose failures would have critical effects on system operation, thus producing the greatest damage, and which failure modes will generate these damaging effects.
- Calculating probabilities of failures of assemblies, subsystems, and systems from the individual failure probabilities of their components and the arrangements in which they have been designed. Some components have more than one failure mode. The probability that it will fail at all is therefore the total probability of all failure modes. One or more of these may be modes that can generate accidents, whereas the others will not. Each mode must therefore be considered separately.
- Establishing test program requirements to generate failure mode and rate data not available from other sources.
- Establishing test program requirements to verify empirically obtained reliability predictions.
- Providing input data for tradeoff studies to establish the effectiveness of changes in a proposed system or to determine the probable effect of modifications on an existing system.

- Determining how probabilities of failure of components, assemblies, and subsystems can be reduced through use of high-reliability components, redundancies in design, or both.
- Eliminating or minimizing the adverse effects that assembly failures could generate, and indicating safeguards to be incorporated if systems cannot be made fail-safe or brought within acceptable failure limits.

In its original usages, Failure Modes and Effects Analysis determined where improvements in component life or design were necessary; and because failure intervals and probabilities were estimated, maintenance periods and requirements could be established. It has proven effective for both purposes. Deficiencies can be eliminated or minimized through design changes, redundancies, incorporation of fail-safe features, closer control of critical characteristics during manufacture and use, and identification of areas requiring close control and extra care at subcontractors' or users' facilities.

Effects of human actions on the system are generally not included in Failure Modes and Effects Analyses; these effects are considered as the province of Human Engineering. Bioenvironmental engineering is another area of investigation considered only from the standpoint of analyzing equipment required for environment control for failure modes and rates.

Procedure To conduct a Failure Modes and Effects Analysis, it is first necessary to know and understand the mission of the equipment, the constraints within which it is to operate, and the limits delineating success and failure. Once these basics are known, analysis of the equipment can begin. Information and data are recorded on forms such as that shown in Fig. 7-3. There are numerous variations of this form; each organization undertaking an FMEA generally prepares its own.

- The system is divided into subsystems that can be handled effectively.
- Functional diagrams, schematics, and drawings for the system and each subsystem are then reviewed to determine their interrelationships and those of their component subassemblies. This review may be done through the preparation and use of block diagrams. The block diagram can be assigned reference numbers to permit coordination with the items on the functional breakdown tables.
- A complete component list is prepared for each subsystem as it is to be analyzed. The specific function of each component is entered at the same time.
- Operational and environmental stresses affecting the system are then established. These are reviewed to determine the adverse effects that they could generate on the system or its constituent assemblies and components.
- The significant failure mechanisms that could occur and affect components are determined from analysis of the engineering drawings and functional diagrams. Effects of subsystem failure are then considered.

Detailed Analyses

150

FAILURE MODES AND EFFECTS ANALYSIS

1. SUBSYSTEM _____   2. DWG. NR. _____   3. PREPARED BY _____   4. DATE _____

ITEM	FAILURE MODES	CAUSE OF FAILURE	POSSIBLE EFFECTS	PROBABILITY OF OCCURRENCE	CRITICALITY	POSSIBLE ACTION TO REDUCE FAILURE RATE OR EFFECTS
Motor case	Rupture	a. Poor workmanship b. Defective materials c. Damage during transportation d. Damage during handling e. Overpressurization	Destruction of missile	0.0006	Critical	Close control of manufacturing processes to ensure that workmanship meets prescribed standards. Rigid quality control of basic materials to eliminate defectives. Inspection and pressure testing of completed cases. Provision of suitable packaging to protect motor during transportation.
Propellant grain	a. Cracking b. Voids c. Bond separation	a. Abnormal stresses from cure b. Excessively low temperatures c. Aging effects	Excessive burning rate; overpressurization; motor case rupture during otherwise normal operation	0.0001	Critical	Carefully controlled production. Storage and operation only within prescribed temperature limits. Suitable formulation to resist effects of aging.
Liner	a. Separation from motor case b. Separation from motor grain or insulation	a. Inadequate cleaning of motor case after fabrication b. Use of unsuitable bonding material c. Failure to control bonding process properly	Excessive burning rate Overpressurization Case rupture during operation	0.0001	Critical	Strict observance of proper cleaning procedures. Strict inspection after cleaning of motor case to ensure that all contaminants have been removed.

Figure 7-3

- The failure modes of individual components that could lead to the various possible failure mechanisms of the subsystem are identified. Basically, it is component failures that produce ultimate failures of entire systems. However, since some components may have more than one failure mode, each mode must be analyzed for the effect on the assembly and then on the subsystem. This procedure can be done by tabulating all failure modes and listing the effects produced by each.

- All conditions which affect a component or assembly should be listed to indicate whether there are special periods of operation, stress, personnel action, or combinations of events that would increase the possibilities of failure or damage.

- The hazard category, as defined by the procuring activity, may be indicated. Reliability categories differ from those prescribed for System Safety (see Chapter 6).*

- Preventive or corrective measures to eliminate or control the hazard are then listed. If the analysis reveals that failure can cause injury or death, notes may be entered regarding provision of safeguards.

- Probabilities of occurrence of each component failure may be entered. Initially, they may be estimated from generic rates that have been developed from experience and published in documents such as MIL-HDBK-217A.† Figure 7-4 is a sample of such generic rates. Data can be obtained from information centers that collect and collate such information. Figure 7-5 indicates some sources of failure rate data. Almost every large manufacturing company, especially in electronic fields, has files of data on reliability and failure rates of the components, assemblies, or devices that it produces. Subcontractors or suppliers can be requested or required to furnish data on the items that they contract to provide.

- Probabilities of failure of subassemblies, assemblies, subsystems, and systems can then be computed in accordance with the arrangements indicated in the block diagrams.

- Some analyses then proceed to determine the criticality of components and the effects that failure will have on the mission. Such determinations are entered into more detail in the section on Critical Component Analysis.

The component level to which a Failure Modes and Effects Analysis should be conducted is sometimes a problem. Judicious compromise is

---

* The four reliability categories are generally:
    Catastrophic—Any failure that could result in deaths or injuries or prevent performance of the intended mission.
    Critical—Any failure that will degrade the system beyond acceptable limits and create a safety hazard; (could cause death or injury if corrective action is not immediately taken).
    Major—Any failure that will degrade the system beyond acceptable limits but can be adequately counteracted or controlled by alternate means.
    Minor—Any failure that does not degrade the overall system performance beyond acceptable limits—one of the nuisance variety.

† Department of Defense, Military Standardization Handbook: *Reliability Stress and Failure Rate Data for Electronic Equipment,* MIL-HDBK-217A; (Washington, D.C., 1965).

PART CLASS AND TYPE FAILURE RATES*
(FAILURES PER 10^6 Hrs.)

	MINIMUM	AVERAGE	MAXIMUM
ELECTRON TUBES			
Clamping diodes and small signal diodes, triodes, tetrodes and pentodes			
165°C bulb temperature	0.324	0.836	2.38
220°C bulb temperature	0.202	0.559	2.80
Power Output and Current Passing triodes, tetrodes and pentodes			
165°C bulb temperature	0.970	2.92	7.12
220°C bulb temperature	0.600	1.66	8.40
Miscellaneous types			
SEMICONDUCTORS			
Diodes	0.10	1.0	10.0
Transistors	0.10	3.0	12.0
Microwave Diodes	3.0	10.0	22.0
RESISTORS	0.05	0.18	0.50
MIL–R–11, fixed composition	0.0035	0.0048	0.16
MIL–R–10509, fixed film	0.070	1.5	9.9
MIL–R–11804, fixed power film	0.93	1.2	1.96
MIL–R–93, fixed accurate wirewound	0.87	1.4	2.4
MIL–R–26, fixed power wirewound	0.0060	0.050	0.14
MIL–R–22684, general purpose film	0.11	0.27	0.90
MIL–R–27208, variable lead screw	37.0	52.0	100.0
MIL–R–55182, established reliability film	0.0011	0.64	10.0
MIL–R–94, variable composition	0.10	0.12	0.26
MIL–R–19, variable wirewound	0.88	1.4	2.4
MIL–R–22097, variable non-wirewound	29.0	41.0	80.0
CAPACITORS			
MIL–C–25, quality paper	0.0011	0.11	4.0
MIL–C–5, mica	0.0003	0.054	20.0
MIL–C–10905, button mica	0.018	0.052	2.0
MIL–C–81, variable ceramic	0.004	0.030	3.20
MIL–C–62, aluminum electrolytic	0.090	0.48	6.0
MIL–C–3965, wet slug tantalum	0.010	0.36	5.8
MIL–C–3965, glass sealed wet slug tantalum	0.0010	0.034	0.92
MIL–C–3965, tubular foil tantalum	0.043	0.22	3.6
MIL–C–3965, rectangular foil tantalum	0.22	0.67	17.5
MIL–C–26655, solid tantalum	0.005	0.058	1.1
MIL–C–39003, solid tantalum	0.00002	–	10.0
MIL–C–27287, mylar	0.0010	0.0035	0.46
MIL–C–14157, paper plastic	0.0001	0.029	10.0
MIL–C–11272, porcelain and glass	0.0014	0.025	1.2
MIL–C–19978, polystyrene	0.0020	0.010	1.8
MIL–C–14409, piston trimmer	0.010	0.065	10.0
MIL–C–92, air trimmer	0.004	0.030	3.20
MIL–C–20, general purpose ceramic	0.0020	0.018	3.0
MIL–C–11015, general purpose ceramic	0.0020	0.020	2.5
TRANSFORMERS, MAG AMPS, INDUCTORS AND COILS	0.20	0.30	20.0
O, Q Insulation	0.20	0.70	20.0
A, R	0.20	0.34	20.0
B, S	0.20	0.20	20.0
H, T	0.20	0.20	20.0
C, U	0.20	0.20	1.00
ROTARY ELECTRICAL DEVICES			
Motors	0.60	5.0	500.0
Other Rotary Devices			
CONNECTORS	0.01	0.10	10.0

Figure 7-4

	MINIMUM	AVERAGE	MAXIMUM
RELAYS	0.0002	0.01	0.27
SWITCHES	0.02	0.2	0.75
INTEGRATED CIRCUITS	0.05	0.40	1.0

NOTE: Minimum, average, and maximum failure rates refer to failure rates for various stress levels. Maximum would be the failure rate at maximum rated thermal and electrical stress, etc.

Figure 7-4 continued.

RELIABILITY DATA SOURCES

SYSTEM NAME AND ACRONYM	ADDRESS	TYPE OF DATA
Air Force Engineering and Logistics Information System (AFELIS)	Headquarters, Air Force Logistics Command Wright-Patterson Air Force Base Dayton, Ohio 45433	Information on all types of parts in Air Force inventory
Apollo Parts Reliability Information Center (APIC)	Marshall Space Flight Center Huntsville, Alabama 35812	Reliability, qualification, and evaluation of electrical, electronic and associated mechanical parts.
Chemical Propulsion Information Agency (CPIA)	Applied Physics Laboratory Johns Hopkins University 8621 Georgia Avenue Silver Springs, Md. 20910	Data on liquid propellants, motors, and components; solid fuels, cases and motor parts
Defence Documentation Center (DDC)	Cameron Station, Building 5 5010 Duke Street Arlington, Virginia 22314	All types of data from military contracts; bibliographies issued
Electronic and Mechanical Component Reliability Centers (ECRC and MCRC)	Battelle Memorial Institute 505 King Avenue Columbus, Ohio 43201	Summaries of parts tests on electronic and mechanical parts
Failure Rate Data System (FERADA)	U.S. Navy Fleet Missile Systems Analysis and Evaluation Group (FMSAEG) Corona, California 91720	Compilation of failure rate data and publication of results
Interservice Data Exchange Program (IDEP)	Air Force IDEP Office (SAMSO) Air Force Unit Post Office Los Angeles, California 90045	Exchange of parts-test data and summaries
	Navy IDEP Office (Code E–6) U.S. Navy FMSAEG Corona, California 91720	
	Army IDEP Office (AMSMI–RBP) Army Missile Command Huntsville, Alabama 35809	
Inter–NASA Data Exchange (INDEX)	Headquarters, NASA 600 Independence Avenue, S.W. Washington, D.C. 20546	Failure and performance data on items used by NASA
Parts Reliability Information Center (PRINCE)	Marshall Space Flight Center Huntsville, Alabama 35812	Printouts of reliability data from tests on NASA items
Reliability Analysis Center (RADC)	Rome Air Development Center Griffis AFB, New York 13440	Reliability data on microelectronic and semiconductor devices

Figure 7-5

154

necessary since the work load could be overwhelming for a system of even moderate size. It appears reasonable to investigate a system down to the level at which accurate failure data is available or can be obtained. For example, if the system should involve a diesel engine for which failure data is available, carrying the analysis to the parts level would generally be unnecessary. However, it may be determined that the failure rate for such an engine is too high. It may then be advisable to analyze the failure modes and rates of the various parts to determine which should and could be improved. More detailed analyses may also be required if failure of a part or subassembly could create another dangerous condition. For example, loosening of a connection on the fuel inlet line to a gasoline engine could permit fuel to be sprayed on a hot surface where it might ignite.

This technique is extremely effective when applied to analysis of single units or single failures. Its inadequacies have led to the development of other techniques, such as Fault Tree Analysis, which it complements excellently. A subsystem may have failure modes that do not result in accidents; failure rates related to those safe modes must be eliminated from determination of accident probabilities. The problem of identifying exactly which failures contribute to the occurrence of a specific catastrophe were overcome to a great extent by use of logic methods. Fault Trees, in their original usages, were diagrams indicating how the data developed by Failure Modes and Effects Analysis should be interrelated to arrive at a specific event. In many instances, the reverse process is now being employed: A logic analysis establishes those events, failures, or successful operations that could contribute to an accident. A Failure Modes and Effects Analysis then studies in detail those conditions that could cause failures, the modes in which failures could take place, and preventive or safety measures to be taken.

The second major deficiency in this method is the inadequate attention generally given to human error problems because of the concentration on hardware failures. Since every system involves the use of personnel to some degree, and errors constitute a major percentage of all accident causes, this is a significant omission in any safety study.

Until recently, analyses were based almost entirely on components and their modes and rates of failure. Rough estimates of reliability were made from the number of components in the system. However, studies of system failures have shown that a much greater number are due to connector problems rather than to the components themselves.

Although environmental conditions are considered in establishing the stresses that could cause hardware to fail, the probabilities of occurrence of such environmental stresses are rarely used. Instead, a usage factor is incorporated for the type of system application, such as shipboard, aircraft, or missile use. Another factor is applied for reduction of theoretical reliability that could result from substandard manufacture of assembly. This factor is extremely rough even over a large sample, since some items may suffer little damage during production, whereas others may be damaged so badly that they fail soon. Oddly enough, in spite of all those factors affecting a system but whose probabilities of occurrence can only be estimated imprecisely, reliability engineers carry out their calculations to six or seven significant figures.

Such concentration of precision in mathematical portions of the

Failure Modes and Effects Analysis frequently detract from the more important effort of determining methods of eliminating or reducing failures and accidents.

Criticality Analysis   Certain components or pieces of equipment in any system are especially critical to its mission, operation, and the well-being of its operators. For this reason, they should be given special attention and analyzed more fully than others. Just which components are critical can be established through experience or as the products of other analyses. The experience may have been either with generic types or with specific items that created problems in previous or existing systems similar to the one being developed.

A component or assembly may be critical because it is inherently hazardous by its very nature. Experience or tests may have shown it to be sensitive, damaging, or both. These components generally have high energy-release rates and can generate extensive damage if their release is excessive or uncontrolled. Electroexplosive devices, highly flammable liquid propellants, and tankage and combustion systems are in this category. Such items may sometimes be subjected to Energy Analysis.

Major effort must also be applied to safeguard those items that could produce injury, damage, or system degradation through *single-point* failures. A single-point failure is one in which an accident could result from one component loss, human error, or other single untimely, undesirable event.

There are numerous examples of designs that can produce single-point failures. One source of power may supply electricity for operation of both critical and noncritical equipment, such as for both hospital operating rooms and also equipment that could be dispensed with temporarily during an emergency. Overloading noncritical circuitry could cause failure of the entire system. To eliminate such a possibility, various means can be employed to ensure that power will always be available for critical needs. The critical circuits could be separated from the others, eliminating the possibility that the latter could cause failure. A standby source could be provided to supply both critical and non-critical equipment. An emergency source, circuit, or both could be installed for the critical equipment only.

Single-point failures in especially critical instances can be avoided both by redundancy and through fail-safe designs. The American Society of Mechanical Engineers (ASME) long ago stipulated that water flowing into a power boiler should pass first under the disk of a feedwater valve, not over it. In the event that the disk becomes separated from the valve stem, incoming water under the disk will lift it from its seat so flow will continue. The boiler will not be starved of water. In addition, since the feedwater line or valve could be blocked by other causes, large installations frequently use two feedwater lines, each with its valve in the fail-safe configuration. This precaution eliminates the chance of a failure which could cause an extremely damaging accident.

Similarly, the Air Force Eastern Test Range (AFETR) states that the capacitor bank for any ordnance fired by an exploding bridgewire (EBW) will have a dual bleed system. Two bleed resistors ground the capacitor bank in parallel. If one fails, the other will permit charges on

Detailed Analyses

156

the capacitor to bleed off. No charges can accumulate to create a potential high enough to fire an EBW prematurely. If only one bleed were installed and should fail, the capacitor bank could be energized by stray currents. When the ordnance firing circuit was closed, the capacitors would discharge and cause an untimely, premature detonation.

Criticality is rated in more than one way and for more than one purpose. MIL-STD-785, *Requirements for Reliability Programs (for Systems and Equipment)*, includes those items as critical whose failures would: affect safety, prevent mission accomplishment, require special handling, impose unbearable maintenance loads, require long resupply or procurement lead times, or involve high replacement costs. Other items sometimes considered critical are those under development that may generate problems if they should fail but as yet have limited reliability history. The Society of Automotive Engineers (SAE) in *Aerospace Recommended Practice 926* categorizes criticality of failure modes as:

Category 1—Failure resulting in potential loss of life

Category 2—Failure resulting in potential mission failure

Category 3—Failure resulting in delay or loss of operational availability

Category 4—Failure resulting in excessive unscheduled maintenance

Criticality ranking may be used to determine:

- Which items should be given more intensive study for elimination of the hazard that could cause the failure and for fail-safe design, failure rate reduction, or damage containment.

- Which items require special attention during production, require tight quality control, and need protective handling at all times.

- Special requirements to be included in specifications for suppliers concerning design, performance, reliability, safety, or quality assurance.

- Acceptance standards to be established for components received at a plant from subcontractors and for parameters that should be tested most intensively.

- Where special procedures, safeguards, protective equipment, monitoring devices, or warning systems should be provided.

- Where accident prevention efforts and funds could be applied most effectively. This is especially important since every program is generally limited by the availability of funds.

Criticality ranking can be accomplished in many ways. The method described by the Society of Automotive Engineers in *ARP 926* is made an extension of Failure Modes and Effects Analysis (FMEA) and the two are then designated Failure Modes, Effects, and Criticality Analysis (FMECA). In the procedure for criticality determination, the criticality number for any component is indicated by the number of failures of a specific type expected during each million operations occurring in a critical mode. The criticality number, C_r, is calculated by:

$$C_r = \sum_{n=1}^{i} (\beta \alpha K_E K_A \lambda_G t \times 10^6) \qquad n = 1, 2, 3, \ldots, j$$

where C_r = criticality number for the system component in losses per million trials

n = the critical failure modes in the system component that fall under a particular loss statement

j = last critical failure mode in the system component under loss statement

λ_G = generic failure rate of the component in failures per hour or cycle

t = operating time in hours or number of operating cycles of the component per mission

K_A = operational factor that adjusts λ_G for the difference between operating stresses when λ_G was measured and the operating stresses under which the component is going to be used

K_E = environmental factor that adjusts λ_G for difference between environmental stresses when λ_G was measured and the environmental stresses under which the component is going to be used

Note.—For simplified uses, omit K_E, K_A, and use λ_G as the estimated failure rate for the given failure mode and operating condition.

α = failure mode ratio of critical failure mode. The failure mode ratio is that fraction of λ_G attributable to the critical failure mode.

β = conditional probability that the failure effects of the critical failure mode will occur, given that the critical failure mode has occurred. Values of β should be selected from an established set of ranges:

FAILURE EFFECTS	TYPICAL VALUE OF BETA
Actual Loss	100%
Probable Loss	> 10% to < 100%
Possible Loss	> 0% to 10%
None	0%

10^6 = factor that transforms C_r from losses per trial to losses per million trials, so C_r will normally be greater than one.

Unfortunately, this method requires a great deal of effort when used in this form. The SAE indicates how it can be simplified. However, it still does not consider one vital aspect of criticality that could be generated by a failure: possible damage. A very simple method of criticality determination that can be used is merely to multiply the probability of failure by the damage that could be generated. Another method entails ranking by:

$$CR = P_L \times Q \times F_R$$

where CR = criticality ranking

P_L = probable damage resulting from a specific failure mode

Q = probability of component failure (1 − reliability)

F_R = ratio of occurrence of a specific failure mode

A specific component can have more than one mode of failure, with only certain ones possibly causing damage or injury. F_R is the ratio of those failures that could generate a specific damage level to the total number of possible failures. These failure ratios can be determined for new systems from manufacturers' data on failure modes, network analyses, tests, or combinations of these sources of information.

Criticality rankings are generally expressed as probabilities but may also be indicated in other ways. In some instances, they are designated in categories from 1 to 10 to show the principal items that could generate problems or as letters starting with the top of the alphabet. These last two methods are often not based on probabilities but reflect experience, especially with subsequent systems.

Ranking does not complete a critical component analysis. Evaluations must also be made to establish the preventive and corrective measures that should be taken and the safeguards to be incorporated if the hazard that could be generated by critical component failure does pass out of control.

Because of the broad variety of components that can be considered critical, no preferred method of analysis can be indicated. A number of specific types can be employed, depending on the system. Logic trees, network analysis, or Failure Modes and Effects Analysis can be used to determine items that would be critical or designs in which single-point failures could occur. A container whose function is to hold a highly pressurized gas can be subjected to any number of different analyses to ensure that its design strength is adequate for the purpose.

Data submittal requirements in Armed Services contracts frequently stipulate that lists of critical items be furnished the procuring agency. These items can be listed on work sheets for Failure Modes and Effects Analysis, which have been provided with a suitable space and method for indicating criticality ; or they can be listed on abbreviated work sheets such as that shown in Fig. 7-6.

		CRITICAL ITEMS LISTS			
ITEM	NUMBER	MODE OF FAILURE	FAILURE PROBABILITY	EFFECT ON MISSION	CRITICALITY RANKING WITHIN SUBSYSTEM (0 to 10)
Identify by name.	Part and detail drawing number	List all possible failure modes.	List a probability for each mode.	Abort, degradation of performance, damage etc.	List numerically.

Figure 7-6

One concept of accident prevention is predicated on the idea that energy flow is the fundamental cause of accidents. At such times, energy is transferred or lost in uncontrolled, undesirable manners. Safety of a system can therefore be evaluated and improved by analyzing:

1. Sources of available energy existing in a system or subsystem or in its environment
2. Means of reducing and controlling the level of energy
3. Means of controlling the flow of energy

Energy Analysis

Energy Analysis

159

4. Methods of absorbing free energy to prevent or minimize damage should loss of control occur

This concept can be shown to have a good basis in fact by comparison with some of the accident prevention measures listed in Fig. 10-1.

ACCIDENT PREVENTION	ENERGY CONCEPT
1. Hazard elimination	1. Eliminate unnecessary sources of energy.
2. Hazard level reduction	2. Keep energy level as low as practicable by controlling factors such as pressure, temperature, voltage, velocity, or radiation.
3. Lockouts and lockins	3. Isolate energy sources from regions where they could initiate damage.
4. Passive fail-safe systems	4. If a failure occurs, reduce the energy level to zero.

It can be seen that proponents of energy control for accident prevention have a substantial basis for their concept. Canale has attempted to show that the magnitudes of free energy that could cause damage can be indicators of the safety levels of systems.[*] Leimkuhler indicates that the damage that could result during transportation of nuclear material is dependent on vehicle mass and velocity and therefore on energy.[†] Each of these proposals, and of others more esoteric, is based on a limited application, contains no provision for incorporation of factors such as human error, or is so difficult to apply that it is presently impracticable. However, where a situation involves one of the limited applications, energy analysis can be extremely useful.

TNT Equivalency   Energy exists in many forms, such as thermal, electrical, radiation, chemical, kinetic, and nuclear energy. Practical energy analyses generally are limited to consideration of one, two, or at most three of these forms at a time. One attempt to indicate the magnitude of a hazard by energy comparisons is indicated in Fig. 7-7. In this case, TNT equivalency is the parameter to which the energy of compressed air in a container is compared.

TNT equivalency is predicated on the fact that 1 lb of TNT contains 1,600,000 ft-lbs of chemical energy, which is released as thermal energy in an explosion. This explosion causes a shock wave as the gas generated is heated, expands, and reacts against the surrounding atmosphere. Similarly, a mass of confined, compressed gas exerts pressure that tends to rupture its container. If rupture occurs, an adiabatic process takes place in which the energy of the compressed gas is converted into expansion work and kinetic energy. The energy that the gas contained is indicated by:

$$\text{Energy (ft-lbs)} = E = 144 \frac{P_1 V_1}{n-1} \left[1 - \left(\frac{P_2}{P_1} \right)^{(n-1)n} \right]$$

where P_1 and P_2 = initial and final pressures (psia)
V_1 = initial volume (cu ft)
n = ratio of specific heats

[*] S. Canale, "System Safety Measurement and Control," paper presented at the 6th Reliability and Maintainability Conference, New York (July 1966).

[†] F. F. Leimkuhler, *Trucking of Radioactive Materials* (Baltimore: Johns Hopkins Press, 1963).

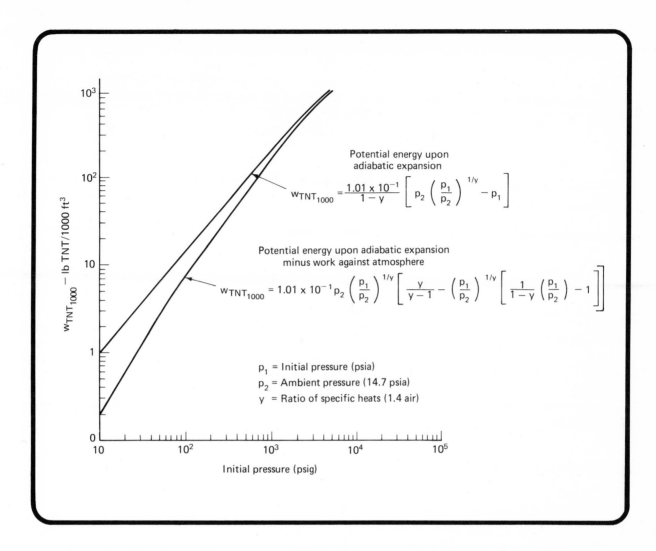

The graph shows:

Potential energy upon adiabatic expansion

$$w_{TNT_{1000}} = \frac{1.01 \times 10^{-1}}{1-\gamma}\left[p_2\left(\frac{p_1}{p_2}\right)^{1/\gamma} - p_1\right]$$

Potential energy upon adiabatic expansion minus work against atmosphere

$$w_{TNT_{1000}} = 1.01 \times 10^{-1} p_2\left(\frac{p_1}{p_2}\right)^{1/\gamma}\left[\frac{\gamma}{\gamma-1} - \left(\frac{p_1}{p_2}\right)^{1/\gamma}\left[\frac{1}{1-\gamma}\left(\frac{p_1}{p_2}\right) - 1\right]\right]$$

p_1 = Initial pressure (psia)
p_2 = Ambient pressure (14.7 psia)
γ = Ratio of specific heats (1.4 air)

y-axis: $w_{TNT_{1000}}$ — lb TNT/1000 ft³
x-axis: Initial pressure (psig)

The energy contained in the gas divided by 1,600,000 ft-lbs indicates the number of pounds of TNT that would release the same energy in an explosion. This number of pounds is the TNT equivalency of compressed gas. Figure 7-7 shows the TNT equivalencies of 1,000 cu ft of air (and gases with the same ratio of specific heats) at various pressures. One curve shows this relationship if the gas release occurred in a vacuum; the other, if the expanding gas had to work against a surrounding atmosphere at 14.7 psia. To determine the total equivalency, multiply the volume of gas in cubic feet and divide by 1,000.

TNT equivalencies are useful since equations have been prepared indicating overpressures that will develop at various distances by specific weights of TNT. The most publicized use is in rating nuclear detonations. Energy releases here are in thousands (kilotons) or millions (megatons) of *tons* of TNT.

Energy available in a TNT explosion is produced almost instantaneously even if it is not confined. In a rupture of a pressure vessel, much energy is utilized in breaking the container, which may not fragment, depending on the material of which it is made. In addition, the rupture process is not instantaneous since the container will generally yield and stretch somewhat before it ruptures. If rupture occurs without fragmentation, the energy converted to generating a shock wave is often assumed to be proportional to the ratio of crack area to total projected

Fig. 7-7. Comparison of TNT equivalences based on adiabatic expansion with and without work against atmosphere. R. A. Bourdreaux, "TNT Equivalencies for Moderately Pressurized Tanks," paper presented to the Hazards Working Group Meeting, Interagency Chemical Rocket Propulsion Group, New Orleans, La. (7–9 December 1969) p. 99.

Energy Analysis

161

area. In any case, peak side-on (static) overpressure produced, P_s, would be:

$$P_s = \frac{4120}{Z^3} - \frac{105}{Z^2} + \frac{39.5}{Z}$$

where $Z = r/W^{1/3}$
$\quad\quad\quad r$ = distance (ft)
$\quad\quad\quad W$ = weight of TNT (lb)

Face-on (total + kinetic) pressure, P_f, is:

$$P_f = \frac{2P_s(102.9 + 4P_s)}{102.9 + P_s}$$

Tables of face-on pressures at which damage or injury will occur have been determined through field tests. These are listed in Fig. 7-8. Analyses such as the preceding one can determine at what range damage or injury will occur; or within a specific distance, the magnitude of damage. Safe limits within which personnel or critical equipment will not be permitted during an operation that could generate an explosion can be determined. The limits shown in Fig. 6-8 were established in this way, as were the quantity-distance criteria in various explosive safety manuals.

PRESSURE EFFECTS AT VARIOUS OVERPRESSURES (psi)

0.2	Limit for uncontrolled area; no significant damage to personnel or facilities
0.4	Limit for unprotected personnel
0.5 to 1	Breakage of window glass
0.75	Limit for windowless, ordinary construction
1 to 2	Light to moderate damage to transport-type aircraft
3	Exposed man standing face-on will be picked up and thrown; very severe damage, near total destruction to light industrial buildings of rigid steel framing; corrugated steel structures less severely damaged
3 to 4	Severe damage to wooden frame or brick homes
4 to 6	Complete destruction of aircraft or damage beyond economical repair
5	Possible ear damage; exposed man standing side-on will be picked up and thrown; complete destruction of wooden frame or brick homes; severe battering of automobile and trucks
6	Moderate damage to ships
6 to 7	Moderate damage to massive, wall-bearing, multistory buildings
7	Possible internal injuries to human beings
9	Complete destruction of railroad boxcars
10 to 12	Serious damage to and sinking of all ships
12	Possible lung injuries to exposed personnel
20 to 30	50 per cent probability of ear drum rupture
25	Probable limit of thermal injury

Figure 7-8

162

How damaging can specific weights of TNT or differences in pressure be? An example can be cited as an indication. On 10 January and 8 April 1954, two BOAC de Havilland Comets exploded shortly after leaving the airport at Rome. The explosions occurred at approximately the time when the aircrafts reached their cruising altitude of about 30,000 feet. At first, the violence of the explosions led to the belief that bombs had been placed aboard the aircraft. However, investigation of their stopovers in Rome disclosed that sabotage was impossible. Further investigation indicated that in each case metal fatigue had started a crack in the top of the fuselage at an opening where an aerial for an automatic direction finder (ADF) protruded. Cabin pressure then caused the crack to extend rearward, tearing out a section of the aircraft. The difference between the cabin and ambient pressures was slightly more than 8 lbs per sq in. The total area involved produced forces and stresses as damaging as those that would have resulted from the explosion of 500 lb of high explosive.

Heat-generating and heat-flow processes are also frequently subjected to energy analyses. Some examples are: **Heat**

- Heat balances of human environments such as aircraft cabins, protective clothing, space capsules, and similar enclosed spaces. Solar radiation, aerodynamic heating, combustion processes, and electrical losses are means by which tremendous amounts of heat are generated. Failure to provide insulation, absorption, and dissipation of heat and control of temperature may cause these environments to become unbearable and uninhabitable.

- Heat balances of electrical and electronic equipment. Excessive heat and temperature may cause degradation and failure of material, ignition of combustibles, melting of solder in connections, and may shorten the lives of electronic components.

- Expansion of gases, liquids, and metals. Where expansion of these is restricted, stresses may develop that could cause bursting of containers; overflow and loss of fluids; distortion of parts, equipment, or structures; or cracking of coatings.

A generalized procedure can be established for an energy analysis. Briefly, this involves determining: **Procedure**

1. Sources and reservoirs of energy and the magnitudes of energy present and available to generate damage or injury. The magnitude of energy present depends on the level of energy per unit and the number of units present. For example, the hazard that a compressed gas container presents depends on both the gas pressure and its volume.

2. Whether the energy requirements of the product or system and the stored energy level and volume are the minima for the required purpose, or whether they could be reduced so that a lesser hazard exists.

3. Whether a less hazardous type of energy source could be substituted.

4. Primary hazards that could initiate sudden, inadvertent release of the stored energy. For a combustible mixture or explosive, such hazards would be any possible ignition sources.

5. Factors that could contribute to the primary hazards, such as corrosion, penetration, or other weakening of a pressure vessel.

6. Damage or injury that could result from release of stored energy. This possibility of stored energy release may require analysis of the limits to which the effects would extend.

7. Safeguards to maintain the stored energy in its controlled state. These safeguards may include maintaining measurable parameters below specific levels; i.e., by using a relief valve to limit pressure, thermostatic control to limit temperature or rise in temperature, or a circuit breaker to limit current.

8. Isolation measures to prevent increase in energy level from outside sources; for example, shielding from the sun's rays or other heat generators or shielding to eliminate electromagnetic coupling.

9. Measures to contain outputs from the energy source or reservoir that could cause injury or damage, such as wire mesh screens to stop fragments if a tire being tested under pressure should fail.

Interface Analysis

The purpose of interface safety analysis is to ensure that incompatibilities between units of a system do not generate hazards that could result in accidents. The analysis must establish not only that separate units can be integrated into a viable system but also that the normal operation of one will not impair the performance or safety of another or of the entire system. The various relationships that must be considered can be categorized principally as *physical* or *functional*.

1. *Physical.* Two units might each be built well and operate properly during separate tests but may not fit together because of dimensional differences. A black box with one dimension more than 12 inches will not fit into a space slightly under that length. An example can be cited of physical incompatibilities causing fatalities. Two men were assigned to inspect repairs at the inside bottom of a 30-ft vertical tank. The tank normally held pressurized gaseous oxygen. To reduce the danger of fire in this type of atmosphere, the tank was filled with nitrogen. The two men were to wear backpacks containing compressed air for their respiratory needs. They were to enter the tank through a manhole in the top and descend to the bottom by ladder. The manhole had been designed according to industry standards. Dimensions were adequate for an unencumbered man but not for one with a backpack. In order to pass through the manhole, the first of the two men decided to remove the backpack and face mask; then the other man would pass them through, and he would don them while he stood on the ladder. Unfortunately, when this procedure was attempted, the first man was overcome almost immediately from lack of oxygen and fell from the ladder. The second man immediately entered without his respiratory equipment to attempt a rescue. He also collapsed soon after

Both died. The accident would not have occurred if the manhole had been large enough to allow a man wearing a backpack to go through.

Other examples of problems that have arisen because of physical interface incompatibilities include:

a. Damage to missiles being loaded or unloaded on aircraft as they hit the structure because of inadequate clearances

b. Injury to flight personnel during emergencies when arms and legs failed to clear the cockpit during ejection

c. Inadequate capacities of safety or relief valves for systems that they were selected to safeguard

Another problem frequently arising is the inability to join or mate parts that should fit together. Misalignment of holes is a common example. Bolts to join the two units cannot be inserted through both holes. Assemblies must not only mate properly but be easily separable when required for maintenance or transportation. The mating process must also be such that assembly errors will be impossible, have an extremely low probability of occurrence, or will generate no problem if a mistake is made. Means by which errors can be eliminated include the following (see also Fig. 2-5):

a. Asymmetrical parts to be fitted or arrangements of bolt holes.

b. Keyed connections that must be assembled with the correct polarization.

c. Different sized or differently keyed connectors for circuits or lines to prevent cross-connections.

2. *Functional.* The possible outputs of one unit will constitute the inputs to a downstream unit. Damage to the downstream unit may result when the output of the upstream one differs from that programmed. Conditions that could occur can be categorized as:

a. Zero output. The unit fails completely. (Other failures due to interconnections may occur so that the input unit does not receive the output of the upstream unit. These include a connection failure at either end or a break or short circuit in the connecting line. These failures are considered later in this chapter.)

b. Degraded output. There is a partial failure so that designed or programmed output is not achieved. Partial clogging of hydraulic unit passages reduces fluid flow. This may cause decreased cooling effect, delay in activation of brakes or other hydraulically operated equipment, inadequate lubrication, and similar deficiency effects. Possibly the output of a unit may approach the prescribed limit. A downstream unit may be in a condition in which it would operate if output from the first unit were the designed nominal value but because of its own subnormal condition fails at the lower level.

c. Erratic output. This condition consists of intermittent or unstable operation. Chattering of relays or valves may cause surges in electric power or fluid flow.

d. Excessive output. A unit may overspeed due to a governor failure; the temperature of liquid produced may be too high because of a thermostat failure; or voltage may be excessive when a regulator fails.

e. Unprogrammed output. Inadvertent operation or erroneous outputs could cause damage to downstream units. One example is the interceptor fire control computer that generated output signals when none should have occurred. The signals activated parameter fuses in the missiles that the aircraft carried. If a launch had been attempted after this time, the missiles would have failed to guide to the target.

f. Undesirable side effects. Although its programmed outputs are within prescribed limits, a unit may also generate other outputs that could be damaging. An electrical or electronic assembly may perform its function but may generate excessive heat that can shorten the lives of adjacent units. A television set may generate its picture properly but emit radiation that could injure viewers.

3. *Miscellaneous relationships.* Units of a system must also be analyzed for any other possible effects that one could produce on another. When man is regarded as a subsystem, he can generate innumerable problems on other subsystems, human or material. Man's participation in accomplishment of a system mission can be evaluated effectively by Link Analysis, Procedures Analysis, and Contingency Analysis.

Other factors between subsystems also must be tested or studied for safety connotations. A fine metal filter may be an excellent means for removing foreign particles, but when inserted in a line in which petroleum products flow at moderate rates, it will cause static electricity to be generated in amounts that can be extremely dangerous. Other problems arising between units of a system include:

a. The possibility that a missile will hit the aircraft from which it was launched.

b. The possibility that an airfield has runways too short for the planes that will be landed or flown from there.

c. The possibility that an automobile can collide with another car, a structure, obstruction, or person. In this case, the automobile is a subsystem that must interface with all these other items in a transportation system.

The number of interfaces between units or subsystems can sometimes be staggering. It was mentioned under System and Subsystem Hazard Analysis that every system must have six basic subsystems, sometimes more. If only one parameter existed between each two, subsystems there would be 15 interfaces of two subsystems each. In some instances, there may be many more parameters and interfaces. (Consider the number of interfaces between all the automobiles and other components of a transportation system.) It may therefore be necessary to determine which ones exist in any system by sketching the subsystems in a block diagram and indicating the interfaces, and then determining which ones could cause damage. Each of the interfacing factors can be reviewed in the manner described previously under

System and Subsystem Hazard Analysis through use of Figs. 4-2 and 7-2. In each case, the column headings would consist of the subsystems.

Another effective means of establishing the relationships and interfaces between units is by Time Sequencing (Chapter 6). In this method, a system's operation is segmented sequentially to show the inputs that are required for each programmed event to occur. It can therefore be used to establish the inputs required from each contributory subsystem.

An interface analysis can also be undertaken by a combination network analysis and Failure Modes and Effects Analysis. The network analysis will determine what outputs will be generated if any specific component or components in a circuit fail. The Failure Modes and Effects Analysis will establish various ways in which components can fail and their effects on other components and the subsystem.

It is apparent that an interface analysis can be accomplished in numerous ways, the optimal method depending on the system and subsystems involved. However, a basic procedure can be established to accomplish an interface analysis. The following steps are recommended:

- Review the functions of the integrated system.
- Establish the various subsystems and where they interface.
- Establish the parameters that are outputs of one unit and inputs to a downstream unit. Outputs from one unit must sometimes be established from the downstream unit's requirements. It is necessary to know what type of inputs are required to ensure that they will be provided as outputs of the upstream units.
- Review prescribed or necessary limits for these parameters. These limits may be indicated by a procuring activity when different contractors are responsible for providing the interfacing units. The contractor is responsible for establishing these parameter limits when he produces both or all interfacing units. In certain instances, even these latter must meet certain restrictions, such as voltage, power levels, or pressure.
- Ensure that all possible outputs will remain within the prescribed limits even if a failure should occur within the unit. It may be necessary to simulate the effects that single failures or failures in combination could produce in outputs.
- Determine whether means are required to adjust differences in outputs and inputs for best performance. In such cases, means are also required to monitor the various parameters and to establish when desired performance is achieved.
- Establish the effects of natural and induced environments on the interrelated units and on the interface itself. Environmental factors may cause changes in outputs or overloads on the downstream unit so that a failure occurs.
- Determine whether the manner in which interfaces are to be made are the safest for the system. In some cases, routing different circuits through the same connectors may be practical and economical but not the best design from a safety standpoint because of the possibility of a short circuit in the connector.
- Determine whether the possibility exists of making the interface

connection incorrectly. If so, a connection design that makes incorrect assembly impossible should be provided.

• Determine whether special instructions, warnings or caution notes in assembly procedures are required to ensure that personnel are aware of any possible problems in making the interface properly.

• Establish by test and trial that interfaces can be made properly, that a subsystem will not affect other subsystems adversely, and that the integrated system works properly.

Flow Analysis Flow of fluid, energy, or both from one unit to another must be investigated for hazardous conditions. Flow may be confined and involve a fluid, such as water, fuel, lubricating oil, steam or air, or involve energy (electrical, electromagnetic, hydraulic or thermal). It may also be unconfined, such as radiation of heat from one body to another. It can be seen that flow analysis may constitute part of an interface analysis. It is described here separately because the most frequent, severe, and varied problems in any system are generally with the fluids and energy that must flow from one unit to another through confined passages. Some of the possible problems and their effects are indicated below.

1. The connection between two units may be faulty. For example, explosions of jet fuels in the tanks of bomber aircraft occurred because electrical bonding between parts was missing. The flow of fuel in the supply line to the combustion chambers of the engines, the spraying of fuel into the chambers, and the combustion process itself all generate static electricity. The current produced this way flowed from its origin along conductive surfaces until it reached the fuel pump. A lack of proper bonding at the pump left a gap over which a spark was produced when the potential difference grew great enough. The spark contained sufficient energy to cause ignition of the flammable mixture of air and fuel when the two reached the combustible limit. This combustion happened during flight because the mixture was too rich when the tanks were full or almost full on the ground. As fuel was used up, it was replaced by air until a combustible mixture was present. It was lucky, in one sense, that the limited amount of air restricted the amount of fuel that could burn in the closed tank.

2. The interconnection may fail entirely. High-pressure gas hoses are excellent examples. They have burst when inadvertently overloaded to pressures greater than those for which they were designed or which they could withstand in a deteriorated condition. In other cases, complete failures of hoses have caused them to whip violently, injuring personnel and damaging equipment within their range. Complete failures of interconnections can also produce the same effects that would result if the connections had never been made.

3. The interconnection may suffer a partial failure. Leakage is a frequently encountered example. It may occur in the line itself

or at the interface between a line and unit. If the line contains an extremely hazardous fluid, such as a highly toxic gas or extremely flammable liquid, even a very small leak may prove highly damaging or dangerous. Analysis must therefore consider the characteristics of the fluid and the effects of its loss. Some characteristics and effects to be considered are:

a. Flammability. The mechanism by which leakage takes place has great consequences on the effects produced. A spray from a pressurized system exposes minute particles of liquid to the oxygen in air, creating a highly combustible mixture. The energy required to ignite a spray is much less than that for a liquid in bulk form.

b. Toxicity. Leaks of some toxic agents are readily detectable by their odors or irritant properties, even when the amounts are small. When the fluid is extremely dangerous but is odorless and does not irritate, it is sometimes advisable to add an odorant to provide warnings of leaks. Leaks of odorless gases, such as carbon monoxide, nitrogen, or vaporized solvents, in enclosed spaces have resulted in the deaths of many persons involved with operations related to large missile systems because they were unaware that the oxygen level was less than that necessary for respiration. No deaths with these systems can be attributed to the highly toxic propellants that some of these missiles contained.

c. Odor. A material with a foul odor can irritate or sicken personnel, so they cannot perform required duties or perform them badly. The amount of gas which is offensive varies with numerous factors. However, even a substance that is pleasant at low concentrations is offensive when the concentration is high. Conversely, an offensive odor may not be a problem if the person's olfactory sense has become desensitized.

d. Corrosiveness. The fluid might be compatible with the line through which it normally flows, but leakage could expose other materials, and possibly personnel. Even so mild a fluid as water will cause corrosion of many ferrous materials.

e. Moisture and water. Leakage of moisture and water can cause high humidity, resulting in personnel discomfort, irritation, and the tendency to produce errors. Larger amounts in electrical connectors can cause short-circuiting and system failure.

f. Lubricity. Oils and other liquids cause surfaces to become slippery. Personnel unaware that a leak has covered a floor with a slippery coating may fall and injure themselves.

g. Contamination. Fluid lost may contaminate other materials, so their value is lost. An oil or solvent on food, insulation, or fabric would ruin its usefulness. Other liquids, especially those leaving residues, can coat parts so that they cannot carry out their intended functions.

h. Loss of matériel. The fluid may be in a line where it moves from one unit to a second unit to perform a specific function.

Flow Analysis

169

Loss of the fluid can cause the second unit to fail. For example, leakage between an oil tank and a diesel engine can deplete the system so that the engine fails.

i. Loss of pressure. When a line is designed to transfer energy, loss of fluid can degrade the system so that pressure cannot be maintained. Leakage can also reduce the amount of fluid to a level at which energy transfer cannot take place.

4. The interconnection may be inadequate. Flow would be restricted, sometimes with grave consequences. Electrical conductors that are too small will overheat. The temperature rise may be so great that the wire, insulation, or solder may melt. In extreme cases, the increase may cause ignition of flammable materials in close contact. Life of electrical equipment could be shortened.

Inadequacies can be due to design, deterioration, or improper operation. The piping in a cooling system may be too small to conduct away the heat generated during a thermal process. The piping may have originally been adequate, but buildup of scale or other contamination can reduce the size of the passage available for flow. Lastly, a valve left partially instead of fully open could also reduce flow.

Procedure The procedure for analyzing problems that may be generated by flow of fluids may be accomplished as follows:

- Review the fluid under consideration for inherent hazards, such as flammability or odor.

- Determine whether the fluid could affect the surroundings or other equipment with which it might come in contact. Determine whether any incompatibility would exist.

- Review the proximity and relationship between lines, containers, and equipment containing incompatible fluids. Establish that they have been separated adequately or that protection and means to isolate them have been provided. Ensure that hot lines and surfaces are separated or shielded from cold lines and surfaces. Determine whether the drip from a leak could hit a surface that could be damaged or otherwise become a hazard; for example, a fuel leak on an engine manifold.

- Establish the level of leakage that would constitute a problem and the allowable level. If only a small amount could produce grave effects, ensure that piping specifications stipulate maximum leakage permissible.

- Determine the type of connection best suited for minimizing leakage. Where advisable, conduct tests to ensure that leakage does not exceed established levels.

- Indicate requirements in engineering specifications and drawings.

Prototypes Prototypes are end products of hardware design and development. Successful operation of a prototype may lead to approval for full-scale production; failure may lead to problems and economic loss, especially if the failure results in a mishap or involves a hazard difficult or costly to eliminate. However, few products or systems are fault-free when their first items are produced; problems are expected. Therefore, prototypes are built before production begins on a massive scale in order to ensure that:

- The item performs satisfactorily and meets performance requirements.
- No unforeseen hazards, problems, or incompatibilities exist in the system. (See Fig. 7-9.)

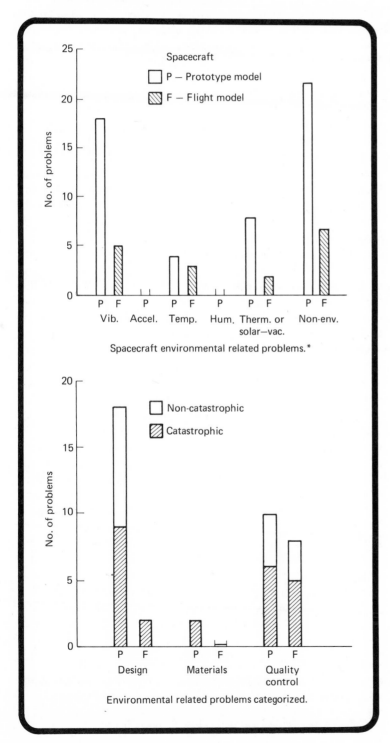

Fig. 7-9. Problems discovered: Prototype testing and actual flight. K. R. Mercy, *Environmental Test Contribution to Spacecraft Reliability,* (National Aeronautics and Space Administration: Goddard Space Flight Center, Greenbelt, Md., November 1967) NASA TN D-4181, p. 13.

171

- Production deficiencies apparent in this first item are detected and eliminated.

A prototype may be called by any of numerous names, such as first article, pilot model, or pilot plant. It differs from a mock-up (Chapter 8), which is a static representation of the prototype in size, configuration, and arrangement but which cannot be operated. It precedes production models, which are not as well instrumented. This use of instruments is to carry out the primary function of a prototype: acting as a test vehicle with its attendant telemetry to provide information on performance, operational characteristics, stresses, and effects. Information desired can be determined directly or indirectly in terms of a variable that measures a specific parameter; for example, temperature, vibration, voltage, or pressure. Each of these parameters can be measured by transducers indicating changes in a specific property, such as electrical resistance, or by changes in the effects that they generate.

Figures 7-10, 7-11, and 7-12 provide information on types of characteristics and applications of transducers. Testing may be accomplished on either the entire product or system or on subsystems, in the laboratory or in the field. It is generally more effective and economical to conduct laboratory tests of smaller units first. This procedure permits better control of affecting conditions, limits the complexity of the tests and the amount of test equipment required, permits easier analysis of problems and failures since there are fewer items being tested simultaneously, and avoids the presence of secondary effects that various subsystems might produce on each other. After subsystems are functioning properly, the complete product or system may be tested, first in the laboratory and then in the field. This procedure is to review whether the constituent assemblies have any deleterious effects on each other and whether they operate properly when interfaced and integrated.

In some instances, it may not be possible or practicable to test a complete prototype in the laboratory, and field testing is required. The Polaris missile illustrates how mission requirements make laboratory testing of the complete missile structure difficult. Flight operation of the Polaris begins when the missile is ejected from a pressurized launch tube in a submerged submarine. The pressure for ejection and from the water imposes an external compressive load on the missile. The external pressure descreases gradually during progress of the missile through the cold water until the surface is reached. External pressure is then atmospheric. Ignition of the first-stage motor shortly before the surface is reached causes an internal, expansive pressure and large amounts of heat.

The reversals of pressure and stresses and changes of temperature can be computed, but the difficulty lies in establishing the effects and damage that might occur to the propellant grain, motor case, bonding, and insulation. Actual conditions and effects are difficult to establish by tests other than subsurface launch of missiles or motors. Some of the effects possible include:

- Missile buckling during ejection. This type of failure could cause damage to internal components, possibly severe enough to cause misalignment and guidance problems.

- Loosening propellant grain in the case. Acceleration imposes

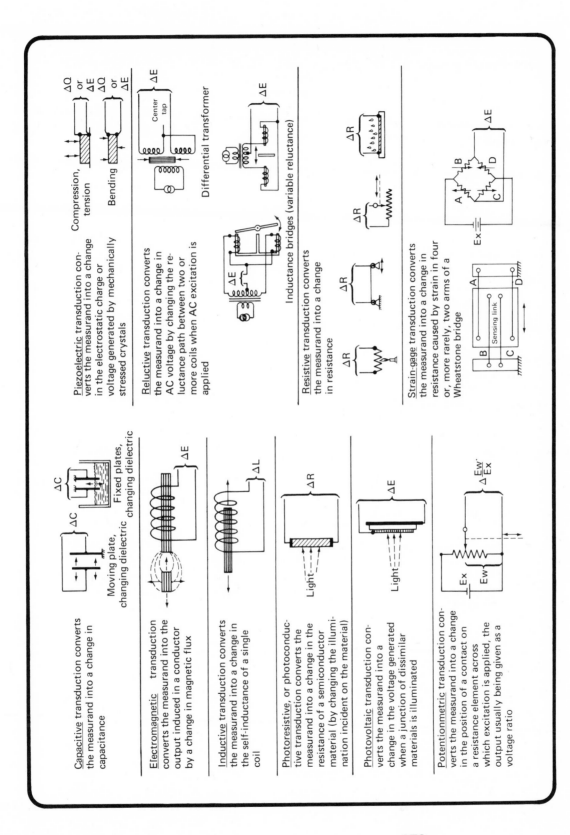

Fig. 7-10. Transducers for monitoring purposes. N. H. Norton, "Transducer Selection." *Space/Aeronautics*, October, 1962, pp. 51–53.

Capacitive transduction converts the measurand into a change in capacitance

ΔC

ΔC

Moving plate, changing dielectric

Fixed plates, changing dielectric

ΔE

Electromagnetic transduction converts the measurand into the output induced in a conductor by a change in magnetic flux

Inductive transduction converts the measurand into a change in the self-inductance of a single coil

ΔL

Photoresistive, or photoconductive transduction converts the measurand into a change in the resistance of a semiconductor material (by changing the illumination incident on the material)

Light

ΔR

Photovoltaic transduction converts the measurand into a change in the voltage generated when a junction of dissimilar materials is illuminated

Light

ΔE

Potentiometric transduction converts the measurand into a change in the position of a contact on a resistance element across which excitation is applied, the output usually being given as a voltage ratio

$\Delta \frac{E_w}{E_x}$

E_x

E_w

Piezoelectric transduction converts the measurand into a change in the electrostatic charge or voltage generated by mechanically stressed crystals

Compression, tension

ΔQ or ΔE

Bending

ΔQ or ΔE

ΔE

Center tap

Differential transformer

Reluctive transduction converts the measurand into a change in AC voltage by changing the reluctance path between two or more coils when AC excitation is applied

ΔE

Inductance bridges (variable reluctance)

Resistive transduction converts the measurand into a change in resistance

ΔR

ΔR

ΔR

Strain-gage transduction converts the measurand into a change in resistance caused by strain in four or, more rarely, two arms of a Wheatstone bridge

ΔE

A   B   C   D

Ex

A

B

Sensing link

C

D

173

FACTORS TO CONSIDER IN SELECTING TRANSDUCERS*

Factors that Depend on the Characteristics of the Expected Input Variable:

> Range (maximum and minimum values to be measured)
> Overload Protection
> Frequency Response
> > Transient Response
> > Resonant Frequency

Factors Affecting the Transducer Input/Output Relation:

> Accuracy
> Linearity
> Sensitivity
> Resolution
> Repeatability
> Friction
> Hysteresis/Backlash
> Threshold/Noise Level
> Stability
> > Zero Drift
> > Loss of Calibration with Time

Factors Relating to the System of Which the Transducer is a Part:

> Output Characteristics
> Size and Weight
> Power Requirements
> Accessories Needed
> Mounting Requirements
> Environment of Transducer Location
> Cross Talk
> Effect of Presence of Transducer on Measured Quantity
> Need for Corrections Dependent on Other Transducers

Factors Relating to Measurement Reliability:

> Ease and Speed of Calibrating and Testing
> Time Available for Calibration Prior to and/or During Use
> Duration of Mission
> Stability Against Drift of Zero Point and Proportionality Constant
> Vulnerability to Sudden Failure (Probability of proper performance for a given life time)
> Fail Safety (Will transducer failure represent system failure, or invalidate data from other transducers?)
> Failure Recognition (Will transducer failure be immediately apparent so that subsequent erroneous data can be rejected?)

Factors Relating to Procurement:

> Is Item Off-the-Shelf? Must development de done to make it operational?
> Price
> Availability and Delivery
> Previous Experience with the Vendor
> Availability of Calibration and Test Data from Manufacturer

*Source unknown.

Figure 7-11

TRANSDUCER APPLICATIONS IN AN AERODYNAMIC MISSILE TEST PROGRAM*

MEASUREMENT	TRANSDUCER TYPE	RANGE	ACCURACY	OUTPUT
Longitudinal acceleration	Linear accelerometer with undamped nat. freq. of 5 cps	±0.5 g	Combined friction, resolution, and hysteresis, 0.04 g	0–3 v dc to subcarrier oscillator
Lateral acceleration	Linear accelerometer with undamped nat. freq. of 6 cps	±1 g	Combined friction, resolution, and hysteresis, 0.1 g	0–3 v dc to subcarrier oscillator
Normal acceleration	Linear accelerometer with undamped nat. freq. of 10 cps max.	+3 to −6 g	Combined friction, resolution, and hysteresis, 0.1 g	0–3 v dc to subcarrier oscillator
Fin flutter (vibration)	Unbonded strain gage accelerometer	10 g; 20–2000 cps	Non-linearity and hysteresis combined, ±1% of full scale	12 mv full scale, open circuit, for 3 v excitation
Vibration at numerous points throughout the vehicle	Piezoelectric vibration transducers	0.1 to 400 g	±10% of stated calibration	5 mv/g
Acoustic noise at numerous places throughout the vehicle	Piezoelectric microphone	127 to 155 db, 37 to 12,000 cps	±10% of stated calibration	100 mv/psi open circuit sensitivity. AC output to cathode follower, to ac amplifier, to subcarrier oscillator.
Jet engine fuel flow rate	Turbine flowmeter	2 to 20 gpm	±0.5% of full scale flow rate	0–3 v dc proportional to flow rate and ac voltage with freq. proportional to flow rate
Indicated air speed	Differential pressure transducer	150 to 850 knots		0–3 v dc
Engine inlet control position	Rectilinear potentiometer	Mechanical travel = 12.750 inches	Linearity ±0.75% of full scale	0–3 v dc
Engine fuel pump inlet pressure	Potentiometer type pressure transducers (three)	0–20 psia; 0–30 psia; 0–40 psia; 0–50 psia	Linearity, ±1% of full scale	0–3 v dc
Engine fuel pump inlet pressure	Potentiometer type pressure transducer with Bourdon tube	0–100 psig	Linearity, ±1% of full scale	0–3 v dc
Engine fuel pump inlet pressure	Potentiometer type pressure transducer	0–250 psia	Linearity, ±1% of full scale	0–3 v dc
Elevator flutter (torsion and bending)	Strain gage, 4-arm bridge	10 to 150 cps	Limited by associated equipment	Millivolts
Engine RPM	Tachometer	0–11,500 RPM	Limited by readout equip.	Freq. and amplitude proportional to RPM

*Source unknown.

175

Figure 7-11 continued.

MEASUREMENT	TRANSDUCER TYPE	RANGE	ACCURACY	OUTPUT
Equipment compartment temperature	Semi-conductor resistance element with 30 sec. time constant	−65° to +300°F	±1% of full scale	0−3 v dc from bridge
Hydraulic fluid temperature	Semi-conductor resistance element with 3 sec. time constant	+150° to +300°F	±1% of full scale	0−3 v dc from bridge
Air temperature	Wire wound resistance element	+100° to +350°F	±1% of full scale	0−3 v dc from bridge
Fuel temperature	Semi-conductor resistance element with 3 sec. time constant	−50° to +250°F	±1% of full scale	0−3 v dc from bridge
Instrumentation rack temperature	Surface temp. transducer with semi-conductor resistance element. Time constant = 3 sec.	−50° to +250°F	±1% of full scale	0−3 v dc from bridge
Free stream air stagnation temp.	Probe with chromel-alumel thermocouple. Time constant = 1.5 seconds		Recovery factor of 98%	Millivolts dc to chopper-amplifier to subcarrier oscillator

Figure 7-11 continued.

a load on supports and bonds inside the case that is compounded by the effects of pressure reversals and temperature change.

- Bending of supports and separation devices. Stresses may produce bending so that stage separations cannot take place.
- Weakening of motor case. Reversal of pressure may weaken the motor case so that it fails even under normal internal pressure loads.

The principal function of a prototype is to act as a vehicle for testing and evaluating performance. This can be done through monitoring by suitable instruments, observation by personnel, or both. A missile or fully automated plant is monitored to provide information to a regulating device or computer that directs the functioning of the system, controlling adjustments and changes as necessary or desirable. Prototypes employ the same devices, possibly with added provisions for transmitting or recording the various data for later review. Where personnel are parts of the system, they are the monitors of various performance characteristics, assisted and supplemented by electronic and mechanical devices. Cooper ratings (Fig. 7-13) are one type of evaluation that cannot be accomplished by these devices. These ratings are usually supplemented by more detailed reports prepared by the pilot from notes or comments made during the flight.

Telemetry was initially adopted to warn the pilot of any dangerous condition not readily apparent to him. Since he was an extremely busy individual unable to monitor all the information provided, data was transmitted to ground stations where it was evaluated by experienced engineers. They warned the pilot of possible adverse conditions and impending problems.

Prototypes

As mentioned in Chapter 4, man is superb in his ability to monitor, evaluate, and analyze new and unique conditions and to correlate them

III Ab—ELECTRICAL SYSTEM FAILURES

REFER NO.	CONDITION, EVENT OR CAUSE	RELATIVE FREQUENCY	PREVENTIVE OR CORRECTIVE MEASURES	ANALYSES ORG. — STUDY NO.	REMARKS	ACTION TAKEN
1.	Battery failure	Chronic	There is only one battery in the missile for operational purposes. (A few are provided with instrumentation batteries.) It therefore constitutes a component through which a "single-point" failure could cause loss of a missile. If redundancy is impracticable, the battery must be an extremely high reliability item. It should be considered a critical item.	84.59 — Newell, FMEA; 11/11/67	Design Engineering to prepare specifications for battery which will ensure item of highest possible reliability is obtained for output required. Reliability Engineering to develop quality assurance test plan to ensure that manufacturer is maintaining high level. Advise manufacturer is maintaining high level.	Battery has been designated a critical item with need for high quality control and special handling. Test engineering advised of need for rigid quality control. Manufacturer advised of problem areas indicated by these trees and tables. Requested to report on measures being taken to minimize possibilities of failure.
1.1	Overheating	Remote	Use current limiters to ensure any possibility of excessive current drain over extended periods is avoided.	84.50 — Hochman RQM 87326; 7/21/68	Safe procedure for removal of battery from missile required. Should contain contingency provisions in case battery is defective. Design Engineering to prepare mission profile to determine required battery loads.	Measures to be taken by Design Engineering have been incorporated into design standards and into checklists for review personnel. See Standard No. XX-OO and checklist on Electrical Systems.
1.1.1	Excessive current drain		Ensure battery capacity is adequate to carry any load under all foreseeable conditions.			
1.1.2	High internal resistance					
1.2	Bursting	Random	Minimize any type of overheating which could cause gas or electrolyte expansions in case. Maintain battery within prescribed temperature limits. Procedures for assembly and before installation of battery should ensure relief valve operates properly.		Battery manufacturer to be requested to indicate battery temperature limits on the battery. Technical writers to insert in procedures warning and caution notes on assembly and installation of battery, on maintaining battery temperature within prescribed limits, and testing of relief valve. Manufacturer to be requested to indicate how he intends to maintain high quality level of cases and relief valves.	Manufacturer will fasten a plate indicating temperature limits and warning to avoid exceeding them. Instructions indicating criticality and need for tight control have been furnished quality assurance personnel. Warnings and caution notes on installation of battery have been included in maintenance procedures.
1.2.1	Overpressurization					
1.2.2	Plugged or faulty relief valve		Maintain close quality control of cases and relief valves.			
1.2.3	Defective manufacture of container					
1.2.4	Hydrogen produced by cell reversal pressurizes container or ignites		Preventing excessive drain will prevent cell reversal and generation of hydrogen gas.			
1.3	Lack or leakage of electrolyte	Chronic	Ensure cell container is not cracked before filling. Ensure reservoir is full. Handle with care to avoid container damage. Ensure fill caps are secure after filling. Avoid incompatibility of materials which could cause corrosion and lead to leakage. Ensure brazed joints in manifolds and other parts are leaktight. Use helium or dye leak tests to ensure overall tightness. Investigate machine methods of brazing, since present manual methods could result in wide variations and poor quality products.		Battery manufacturer to be requested to explain test methods he intends to use to ensure there is no leakage of electrolyte. Periodic audits should be carried out to ensure quality control is effective.	Manufacturer will use dye leak tests to ensure integrity of cases and electrolyte reservoir before filling.
1.3.1	Incompatibility and attack of seals, joints, diaphragms, and other components					
1.3.2	Deterioration of battery case with age					
1.3.3	Cracking: minor fault developed into a crack due to vibration or flight load					
1.3.4	Joints not leaktight					
1.4	Terminal or connection failure	Chronic	Inspect during installation to ensure connections are made properly. Ensure no physical load is on connection. Ensure connector halves are clean, contain no debris, corrosion, solder, cut wire, or dirt. Seal to prevent entrance of moisture, KOH, or other foreign material. Make connections tight to prevent loosening by vibration. Ensure pins are wired correctly by having individual pin assemblies checked visually, and the entire connector tested electrically. Inspect for bent pins prior to assembly. No undue force to be used to mate the halves of the connector.	Design analysis 81-XX, dated 5/12/68,analyzed necessary length and clamping required.	Design Engineering to ensure leads are long enough and clamps designed to avoid loads on connections. Manufacturing Engineering to establish that designed lengths are adequate. Technical writers to incorporate steps for inspection for cleanliness, bent pins, and deleterious materials in procedures. Procedures also to include warning and caution notes to make connections correctly, tight and sealed, and to avoid forcing of connector parts during assembly.	Lead lengths confirmed by Manufacturing as adequate. Warning and caution notes incorporated into manuals and checklists for operational procedures.
1.4.1	Connection improperly made					
1.4.2	Physical load causes separation					
1.4.3	Vibration causes separation					
1.4.4	Foreign matter in connector halves					
1.4.5	Moisture of KOH in connector					
1.4.6	Improper pin wiring					

Figure 7-12

COOPER PILOT RATING SYSTEM*

OPERATING CONDITIONS	ADJECTIVE RATING	NUMERICAL RATING	DESCRIPTION	PRIMARY MISSION ACCOMPLISHED	CAN BE LANDED
Normal operation	Satisfactory	1	Excellent, includes optimum	Yes	Yes
		2	Good, pleasant to fly	Yes	Yes
		3	Satisfactory, but with some mildly unpleasant characteristics.	Yes	Yes
Emergency operation	Unsatisfactory	4	Acceptable, but with unpleasant characteristics	Yes	Yes
		5	Unacceptable for normal operation.	Doubtful	Yes
		6	Acceptable for emergency condition only.	Doubtful	Yes
No operation	Unacceptable	7	Unacceptable even for emergency condition	No	Doubtful
		8	Unacceptable — dangerous	No	No
		9	Unacceptable — uncontrollable	No	No
	Catastrophic	10	Motions possibly violent enough to prevent pilot escape	No	No

*E.W. Vinje and D.P. Miller; Interpretation of Pilot Opinion by Application of Multiloop Models to a VTOL Flight Simulator Task; United Aircraft Corporation; Third Annual NASA-University Conference on Manual Control; NASA SP-144; March 1967.

Figure 7-13

with previous knowledge. This ability not is only beneficial in assessing any hazards or problems present during testing but also has frequently prevented loss of the prototype system or vehicle through immediate corrective action. Examples are common of an operator, pilot, or driver who has taken emergency measures, such as making quick adjustments or repairs, that have avoided destruction of the equipment.

Procedure Many aspects of analyzing a system for hazards through use of prototypes are similar to those used with mockups (Chapter 8). These steps include establishing the objectives to be achieved, evaluation of equipment and its arrangement, run-through of tasks, and review of designs and procedures through use of checklists. The following steps generally complement these. The test procedures can be categorized into those undertaken to obtain data transmitted or recorded and those to be accomplished by personnel.

Detailed Analyses

178

• Establish the limits of tests, in duration or in results to be achieved. It is generally desirable to undertake as few tests as possible at one time and to start on the smallest cohesive unit possible.

- Establish those parameters that are significant and are to be instrumented and monitored.

- Select the types of transducers best suited to sense those parameters selected. Capabilities, sensitivities, operating range, output characteristics, weight, and cost are factors to be considered.

- Select location at which sensors are to be placed. These locations should be selected with care to ensure that readings actually consist of meaningful data, represent existing conditions, and are not affected by unrelated stresses. For example, a transducer to determine air temperature should not be mounted on heat-producing equipment unless properly shielded. All transducers should be protected from possible damage in their selected locations.

- Select the means by which the signal from the transducer is to be transmitted to the readout device or recording instrument. This means will depend on the use to be made of the information: indicative signal, such as a warning; parameter level indicator; or recorded data to be analyzed at a later date, mathematically or statistically. The types of information to be recorded and the means should be established.

- Determine the participation of personnel in the tests as operators, directors, monitors, analysts, emergency crews, and other tasks. Delineate the duties that each person is to perform and ensure that they are knowledgeable and proficient in their accomplishment.

- Provide checklists for each operator and monitor for the tasks that each one will undertake, the functions and characteristics to be observed, the measurements to be taken, and the information to be noted. In some instances, both instrumental and personal monitoring might be required: An observer might monitor for cracks; a transducer could evaluate the stress under which it occurs. Have suitable forms and other material for note-taking and recording of data ready and available for use of personnel.

- Prepare sequences in which tests are to be accomplished. If a series is to be undertaken in which each step in the series is to begin only after successful accomplishment of the previous one, the indicators of successful accomplishment should be prescribed.

- Establish the critical parametric values that would indicate difficulties and prescribe actions to be taken should those occur. Indicate the conditions under which a test will be aborted. Ensure that each operator, monitor, and emergency crew member knows the warning signs and the actions that they are to undertake in such cases.

- Review hazards that might be encountered during or might result from the tests. Ensure that safeguards are provided to protect personnel and to minimize damage.

- Ensure that all transducers are properly installed, that all leads and connections are correct, and that each system is suitably calibrated.

- Begin tests only when the prototype to be tested, personnel conducting the test, and supporting functions are ready.*

- Abort tests as rapidly as possible and in accordance with prescribed procedures if any of the pre-established adverse conditions or events occurs.

- Evaluate the results of the tests to establish whether any hazards or safety problems exist, whether changes in design or procedures are necessary, or if additional safeguards should be provided.

Detailed Analyses

180

* In December 1960, the contractor in charge of activating a prototype ICBM test site elected to proceed with a flight test even though the hydraulic control on the missile elevator had failed. Rather than wait nine days for a replacement, he chose to make a temporary correction and to conduct the test. The temporary fix failed, resulting in a missile explosion, and loss of a $45-million missile test site.

Chapter 8

OPERATING SAFETY ANALYSES

In spite of his propensity for making errors and despite any desire to eliminate him from systems in which he can generate damage, man is still the most important single item in any system, no matter how complex. To minimize the errors in design, production, test, transportation, handling, maintenance, or operation and the injuries and damage they may cause, consideration and care given to the human element must be at least as intensive as that given to any other complex mechanism or subsystem. The logical means to do this is to designate the human being as a subsystem. This personnel subsystem can then be subjected to the same rigorous analysis, control, care, and protection as any other subsystem.

The actual definition of a personnel subsystem has been given as[*] "that major functional part of a system which, through effective implementation of its various elements, provides the human performance necessary to operate, maintain, and control the system in its intended environment." Personnel subsystem considerations are generally within the province of Human (Factors) engineering. In addition, considerations of personnel in environments that might be hazardous are the concern of Bioenvironmental (Life Support) engineering.

The involvement of the human being with a product or a system, the effects that each can have on the other, and the problems that the interrelationships between them can generate may be the concern of Human engineering, Bioenvironmental engineering, and Safety engineering. All three are interested in personnel well-being. Many of the types of analyses described in this chapter are therefore common to or may be used by all three disciplines.

Human Engineering

A control panel designed for operation by a single person can overwhelm his mental and physical capabilities if an overabundance of instruments must be monitored at any one time. Should the instruments be located in widely separated areas, much head turning would be necessary unless the operator had four eyes or was two-headed. Any other type of operator would either exhaust himself rapidly trying to perform an impossible task, make errors, or ignore some of the instruments, possibly leading to an accident. Human engineering attempts to design equipment that can be operated easily and rapidly and with a minimum of undue strain.[†] Safety is concerned with optimizing operating conditions so an accident will not result.

To obtain maximum effectiveness in any system, the best capabilities of men and machines must be integrated. Figure 4-5 lists some comparable abilities of both. The functions to be performed by personnel

[*] United States Air Force, *Handbook of Instructions for Aerospace Personnel Subsystem Designers,* AFSCM 80–3, (Andrews AFB, Maryland; Air Force Systems Command, 1963).

[†] Numerous excellent books and pamphlets have been written on the subject, but basically all contain similar data, oriented toward the system involved. The fundamental document for contractors to the Department of Defense is MIL-STD-1472, *Human Engineering Design Criteria for Military Systems, Equipment and Facilities.* An early, but still informative, pamphlet is *Human-Factors Engineering,* by J. D. Vandenberg and C. T. Goldsmith, available from *Machine Design,* which has reprinted a series of articles published originally in that magazine. An excellent text is: Albert Damon, H. W. Stoudt, and R. A. McFarland; *The Human Body in Equipment Design* (Cambridge, Mass.: Harvard University Press, 1966).

and hardware can be reviewed through suitable analyses. This review is necessary for three major reasons:

- The absolute necessity that man be considered in the system or for a specific task. Safety requirements for systems in which personnel must be present are generally more stringent than those for unmanned systems. For hazardous operations automatic systems and controls can sometimes replace the human element entirely.

- Since man is involved in and necessary to all systems to some degree, the functions that he should perform because of his capabilities must be determined and the possibilities of errors that can generate accidents minimized.

- The tasks providing the interfaces between man and machine must be developed, organized, and coordinated into an effective operating element.

After the functions of man and equipment, separate and interrelated, have been developed, the number and qualifications of personnel required can be determined. Human capacities must be considered over the work cycles during which they must perform (see Fig. 4-9), positions and tasks identified, and new performance requirements anticipated. Skill levels must be determined. Procedures must be written, analyzed, tested, and revised to ensure that the operators can carry out their functions without accident in consonance with the machines that they must operate and the missions that they must accomplish.

The entire personnel subsystem must be reviewed repeatedly all through the design, development, production, and operation of a system. This process continues until it has been verified that the system can be operated, maintained, and controlled without accident by the personnel who perform these duties. As the system develops, the adequacy of the original recommendations, designs, and procedures are reviewed continually. The evaluations cover all affecting factors: performance tasks, human engineering designs, life support, personnel levels, and procedures.

These evaluations can identify problem areas and deficiencies in the personnel subsystem where the effectiveness of the total system might be lessened. They can supply the feedback necessary for improvement of conditions and for elimination or prevention of hazards.

Life Support

Life Support engineering ensures that the environment in which a person exists will not be detrimental to his well-being. It therefore involves:

1. Analysis of the environment in which he must operate. (See Chapter 6.)

2. Determination of physiological and psychological effects on the body.

3. Provision of controls for any hazards. This step can be done by:

   a. Shielding personnel from the harmful factor; for example, providing shades against solar radiation or protection against winds.

b. Removing the undesirable factor, for example, using respiratory filters to remove dusts and smokes or providing absorbent or adsorbent materials to eliminate harmful or annoying gases.

c. Isolating any undesirable source of harmful material.

d. Isolating personnel in controlled environments that differ from the excluded natural environment; for example, using pressurized, heated cabins for high-altitude aircraft.

These actions are necessary because man can exist only within narrow biological limits.* He can survive without oxygen for a period no greater than three minutes, without water for three days, or without food for about six to eight weeks. Even within these periods, any lack of essentials will degrade his abilities and efficiency, affect his bodily functions, and at the least make him irritable. Excesses of oxygen or food over his normal intake requirements can also generate adverse effects.

The interrelationships between the physiological and psychological states of a person make consideration of mental well-being an equally important life support function. Anyone who must work under adverse environmental conditions is also subjected to psychological stresses. Excessive temperatures, noise, vibration, a cold current of air, or a strong reflection may irritate a person and reduce his efficiency. When environmental conditions approach or exceed dangerous levels, the person involved may suffer from anxieties that distract his attention from critical operations that he is programmed to perform.

Life Support engineering is also the province of those designers concerned with escape, rescue, and survival. Not only must a suitable environment be provided during normal operations but also during contingencies. If there is accident to an aircraft, a pilot may have to eject from the closed, protected environment of a cockpit into an extremely cold, rarefied atmosphere. Life Support engineers must ensure that a person who ejects is provided safeguards to survive against the cold, lack of oxygen, and impact of high velocity through the air. He must be furnished with a parachute to bring him safely to the earth's surface and with survival equipment once he lands there.

Human Engineering, Life Support engineering, and Safety engineering are therefore related areas; all involve personnel, their well-being, and optimization of their performance. In certain instances, the environmental conditions under which a man must operate can hamper his physical abilities. A person who must wear a gas mask cannot see as well, react as fast, breath as easily, or exert himself as long as he could when unencumbered in a normal atmosphere.

Hill indicates the results of tests in which five teams were assigned seven identical oil field service jobs to be accomplished on land in a dry, conventional environment, and then in 30 ft of water.† One comment by the investigators was that an abnormal number of errors was made

---

* Two outstanding works on life support are: E. M. Roth, *Compendium of Human Responses to the Aerospace Environment*, NASA Report CR-1205 (I–IV) (Albuquerque: New Mexico, Lovelace Foundation, 1968), 4 vols. and H. E. Price and B. J. Tabachnick, *A Descriptive Model for Determining Optimal Human Performance in Systems*, Vol. 3, NASA Report CR-878 (Chatsworth, Cal., Serendipity Associates, 1968).

† E. C. Hill, "Performing Identical Tasks in Air and Under Water," *Ocean Industry*, July 1968, pp. 62–64.

underwater even by highly experienced personnel. The increases in time required for task accomplishment varied with the task. Hammering was much more difficult because of water resistance. Other tasks such as drilling or ones involving small hand tools like screwdrivers and wrenches were affected little. Hardware specially designed for underwater maintenance required little more time for disassembly and assembly than on land, but it was also noted that the designs permitted the tasks to be done in less time than with conventional designs.

These tests were accomplished in water at 65 °F and depths of 30 ft. Efficiency drops rapidly with decrease in water temperature or increase in depth. During the rescue of men trapped in the submarine *Squalus* in 1939, the water temperature was 29 °F and working depth was approximately 240 ft. The divers were also hampered by their suits, air lines, and life lines. Simple tasks requiring a minute or two on land required 20 to 25 minutes or sometimes could not be accomplished at all. The divers' thoughts would begin to wander, their speech would become incoherent, and some would black out. A great improvement was made when helium was substituted for nitrogen in the gas mixture used for divers' breathing and pressurization.

The human being constitutes the most complex subsystem in any system because of his abilities and limitations. In addition, the number and variety of actions that a group of persons, either as individuals or as groups, can take in any situation generates a high probability that any existing deficiency in the system will sometimes be linked to and affected by personal factors that can generate an accident. The means by which human performance, problems, and contributions to accidents can be analyzed are presented in the following sections.

Link Analysis

Link analysis is a means of evaluating transmission of information by type (visual, auditory, tactile), rate, load, and adequacy. It indicates the operational relationship between two units, whether they are two men or a man and a piece of equipment. It is concerned with their positions, arrangements, and frequency of interchanges, but not with time. A man can be one of two or more units between which a link must be established, or he himself can constitute the link. He can be the link by physically carrying a message from one station to another, or he can establish the link by eye movement from one display instrument to a second.

A *link* is any connection between two elements; an *element* is a person, control, display, piece of equipment, or station. Link analysis attempts to reduce the lengths of the most important or most frequent links at the expense of those of less importance or frequency. Links are therefore rated according to their use-importance relationships. The use factor is indicated by the frequency of an action. Importance is an indicator of its criticality. Both can be assigned arbitrary numerical ratings to indicate relative values. The number of values is dependent on the number of actions that are under consideration and are selected to provide good comparisons. Scales can be 1 to 5 or 1 to 10, but the higher the number, the greater the frequency of occurrence or the criticality. The two ratings of each action are then added to give the use-importance value. Those actions with the highest ratings are the most critical and should be given the most careful attention. They should be arranged for ease of accomplishment to minimize the possibility of error.

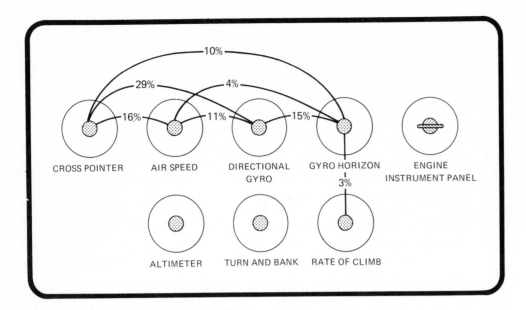

Fig. 8-1. Percentage of times pilots made eye movements between various cockpit instruments during blind-landing approaches using Instrument Landing Approach System. Values less than 2 per cent have been omitted. P. M. Fitts, R. E. Jones, and J. L. Milton "Eye Movements of Aircraft Pilots During Instrument Landing Approaches," *Aeronautical Engineering Review*, February 1950, p. 24.

A low rating would indicate an action that was infrequent, unimportant, or both.

Figure 8-1 indicates a link analysis of eye movements by pilots during aircraft instrument approaches to landings.* These scanning movements were recorded by a motion-picture camera and then compared against a set of standards prepared previously. In this case, only the frequencies of use are shown as percentages of the total number of movements. This frequency constitutes the use factor; all links are considered equally critical and important.

It can be seen that the most frequent link, between the directional gyro and cross pointer, required eye movement past an intervening instrument. In 10 per cent of the actions, two instruments had to be passed over during an eye shift. Such an analysis indicates where improvements could be made in instrument arrangements.

Older provides another application of link analysis, this time to an airborne radar control.† Initial and final designs are shown in Fig. 8-2. Link analysis was used here to minimize hand movements. When controls must be operated in a sequence, analysis of the various links can establish the best arrangement. Lines show the movements from control to control with the sequence of use. The original panel requires irregular, zigzag movements, whereas a more systematic pattern is established in the modified version.

Link Analysis Procedure   A link analysis is carried out as follows:

1. A drawing is prepared, indicating the locations of the elements to be studied. Where distances are important, the drawing should be to scale.

2. Links are drawn between the various stations between which communication will exist.

---

* P. M. Fitts, R. E. Jones, and J. L. Milton,"Eye Movements of Aircraft Pilots During Instrument Landing Approaches," *Aeronautical Engineering Review*, February 1950, p. 24.

† H. Older, "A Procedure for Representing Results of Human Engineering Studies," paper presented at the Human Engineering Conference, Naval Research Laboratory, Washington, D.C. (October 1953).

Operating Safety Analyses

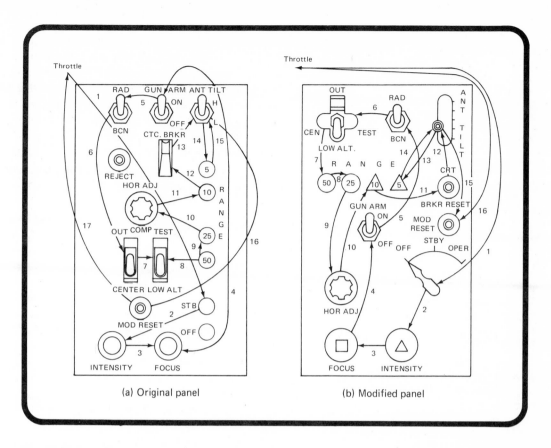

3. The frequency of each link is determined. This frequency may be obtained by counting the number of times that each task element in a procedure is to be accomplished and the number of times that the procedure is to be carried out.

4. The importance of each link is established according to its criticality. Criticality may be based on:

   a. Importance of the task to be accomplished

   b. Level of difficulty

   c. Need for speed and control by the performer

   d. Frequency with which each task must be accomplished

   e. Total time involved for its accomplishment during a complete series of tasks

5. A value is assigned to each link by multiplying frequency or total time times importance.

6. Elements are then arranged so that links with the highest use-importance values are the shortest in length. Consolidation of related elements may reduce motions that could be tiring, be interrupted or interfered with, or lead to errors. Training of personnel is easier than with designs in which motions are widely separated or haphazard. The need to "hunt" for an element in an emergency when normal sequences are disrupted is also reduced.

Fig. 8-2. Example of modification of hypothetical airborne radar-control panel. The numbered lines show normal sequence of movements. C. E. Cornell, "Minimizing Human Errors," *Space/Aeronautics,* March 1968, p. 79.

A common complaint is that failings of one system are often carried over into new designs. Military specifications frequently require that safety problems encountered in existing systems be analyzed for applicability

Critical Incident Technique

to a system being developed. Generally, however, analyses are limited to designs causing accidents or near accidents. Less attention is paid to those designs and conditions that may have been hazardous but to which accidents or near accidents were never attributed. Many of these near accidents were not recorded because there were no suitable reporting requirements or channels.

Such information and data can be valuable and beneficial. The qualitative information can provide much wider coverage of possible accident causes than actual accident causes alone. Use of all types of information generates a much larger and statistically better sample on which to base quantitative analyses.

The Critical Incident Technique is one means by which previously experienced difficulties can be determined by interviewing persons involved. It is based on collecting information on hazards, near misses, and unsafe conditions and practices from operationally experienced personnel. It can be used beneficially to investigate man-machine relationships in past or existing systems and to use the information learned during the development of new systems, or for the modification and improvement of those already in existence. The technique consists of interviewing personnel regarding involvements in accidents or near accidents; difficulties, errors, and mistakes in operations; and conditions that could cause mishaps. The surveys generally request the persons interviewed to include their own experiences and also experiences of other personnel whom they have actually observed. The person is asked to describe all near misses or critical mishaps that he can recall. As Tarrants states, "Studies have shown that people are more willing to talk about 'close calls' than about injurious accidents in which they were personally involved, the implication being that if no loss ensued, no blame for the accident would be forthcoming."*

In effect, the Critical Incident Technique accomplishes the same end result as an accident investigation: identification through personal involvement of a hazard that has or could result in injury or damage. It has been estimated that for every mishap there are at least 400 near misses. When the witnesses who observed a mishap or near miss, but were not participants, are added to those who were involved, an extremely large population is available from which information on accident causes can be derived.

Even isolated incidents reported by the technique can be investigated to determine whether corrective action is necessary or advantageous. However, when a large number of persons are interviewed regarding similar types of equipment or operations, similarities begin to appear in reports of hazards and near misses. Where these indicate deficiencies, difficulties, or other inadequacies, they can be accepted as indicators of areas in which improvements are necessary in the design of a product or system.

The Critical Incident Technique is not new. Fitts and Jones used it very effectively after World War II when they conducted interviews with Air Corps pilots on errors made in operating aircraft controls and in reading aircraft instruments.† Figure 8-3 indicates the classifications of

* W. E. Tarrants, "Utilizing the Critical Incident Technique As a Method For Identifying Potential Accident Causes," (Washington, D.C.: U.S. Department of Labor).

† P. M. Fitts and R. E. Jones, *Analysis of Factors Contributing to 460 "Pilot Error" Experiences in Operating Aircraft Controls,* Memorandum Report TSEAA-694-12 (Wright-Patterson Air Force Base, Ohio, July 1947).

CLASSIFICATION OF 460 ERRORS MADE BY PILOTS
IN OPERATING AIRCRAFT CONTROLS

		No. of Errors	Percent Errors
1.	SUBSTITUTION ERRORS: confusing one control with another, or failing to identify a control when it was needed		
a.	Using the wrong throttle quadrant control (confusing mixture, prop pitch, throttle, etc)	89	19
b.	Confusing flap and wheel controls	72	16
c.	Operating a control for the wrong engine (feathering button, ignition, mixture, prop pitch, throttle, etc.)	36	8
d.	Failing to identify the landing light switch or confusing it with some other control	11	2
e.	Confusing other controls (alarm bell, bomb-bay door, carburetor heat, cockpit heater, droppable gas tanks, emergency bomb release, engine heat, intercooler, oil bypass, oil coller. parking brake, pitot heat, radio tuning control, salvo switch, trim tab, wobble pump)	21	5
	TOTAL	229	50
2.	ADJUSTMENT ERRORS: operating a control too slowly or too rapidly, moving a switch to the wrong position, or following the wrong sequence in operating several controls		
a.	Turning fuel selector switch to the wrong tank	19	4
b.	Following wrong sequence in raising or lowering wheels	18	4
c.	Failing to obtain desired flap setting	17	4
d.	Adding power too suddenly without proper change in trim	9	2
e.	Failing to lock or unlock throttles properly	5	1
f.	Failing to roll in trim fast enough	4	1
g.	Failing to adjust other controls properly	11	2
	TOTAL	83	18
3.	FORGETTING ERRORS: failing to check, unlock, or use a control at the proper time		
a.	Taking off with flight controls locked (aileron, elevator, rudder, or all controls locked)	16	4
b.	Forgetting generator or magneto switch	14	3
c.	Forgetting to make proper engine or propeller control adjustments (mixture, prop pitch, etc.)	11	2
d.	Forgetting to lower, lock or check landing gear	7	2
e.	Taking off with wrong trim settings	6	1
f.	Taking off without removing pitot cover	4	1
g.	Forgetting to operate other controls (bomb-bay doors, bomb-rocket selector switch, coolant shutter, flaps, auxiliary fuel pump, fuel selector, hydraulic selector, lights, PDI switch, pitot heat, tail wheel lock)	25	5
	TOTAL	83	18

460 errors in control operation. Over 80 per cent of the errors reported can be considered as errors of design: design of the controls, their arrangements, and their locations.

Fitts and Jones also made numerous recommendations for changes that would reduce human error, improve controls, and increase system effectiveness.* These recommendations, many of which were incorporated in later aircraft and in human engineering standards, are quoted here to illustrate benefits that can be generated by this technique as a method of developing accident prevention measures:

Figure 8-3

Critical Incident Technique

* P. M. Fitts and R. E. Jones, *Psychological Aspects of Instrument Display*, Memorandum Report TSEAA-694-12A (Wright-Patterson Air Force Base, Ohio, October 1947).

	No. of Errors	Percent Errors
4. **REVERSAL ERRORS:** moving a control in a direction opposite to that necessary to produce a desired result		
a. Making reversed trim correction	8	2
b. Making reversed wing flap adjustment	6	1
c. Making reversed movement of an engine or propellor control (mixture, prop pitch, etc.)	6	1
d. Making reversed movement of some other control	7	2
TOTAL	27	6
5. **UNINTENTIONAL ACTIVATION:** inadvertently operating a control without being aware of it (Brakes, carburetor heat, cowl flaps, generator, ignition, ignition, inverter, landing gear, lights, master switch, pitot heat, radio supercharger)	24	5
6. **UNABLE TO REACH A CONTROL:** accident or near-accident resulting from "putting head in cockpit" to grasp a control, or inability to reach a control at all (Carburetor heat, fuel selector, hydraulic switch, landing gear, nose wheel crank, rudders)	14	3

Figure 8-3 continued.

1. More than half of all errors in operating cockpit controls can be attributed directly or indirectly to *lack of uniformity* in the location and mode of operation of controls.

2. *Substitution errors* can be reduced by: (1) uniform pattern arrangement of controls; (2) shape-coding of control knobs; (3) warning lights inside the appropriate feathering button; and (4) adequate separation of controls.

3. *Adjustment errors* can be reduced by: (1) automatic fuel flow control; (2) simplified one-step operation of wheels and flaps; (3) easily accessible and continuously operable trim controls; and (4) improved throttle locks.

4. *Forgetting errors* can be reduced by: (1) making it impossible to start the take-off run until all vital steps are completed; (2) uniform "off" positions for all switches; (3) more functional check lists; and (4) more effective warning systems.

5. *Reversal errors* can be eliminated almost entirely by adherence to uniform and "natural" directions of control movement.

6. *Unintentional activation of controls* can be remedied by application of existing anthropometric data on body size and use of a maximum reaching distance of 28 inches from the shoulder for all controls used during critical procedures.

Critical Incident Technique Procedure

Tarrants described the technique as carried out at one plant of the Westinghouse Company. The steps may be summarized as follows:[*]

- A group of employees with previous experience and involvement in manufacturing processes and equipment was selected. Each person included was listed according to various factors to produce

Operating Safety Analyses

* W. E. Tarrants, "Utilizing the Critical Incident Technique As a Method For Identifying Potential Accident Causes," (Washington, D.C.: U.S. Department of Labor).

as wide a range of experience as possible. Representatives were selected randomly from each factor group.

- The participants were interviewed and informed of the study and its objectives. They were given an opportunity to withdraw from participation.

- At the end of the interview the participant was given a copy of the statement on the study and its objectives and a list of typical incidents gathered at other plants. This procedure was to stimulate the recall process.

- Participants were asked to described any incidents that they could recall, whether or not they had resulted in injury or property damage. They were asked whether they recalled any incident similar to those that had occurred at other plants, as described on the list they had been provided.

- Questioning was carried on until human errors or unsafe conditions in any recalled incident could be described.

The 20 participants related 389 incidents of 117 different types. Over 50 per cent more potential accident causes were found by this method than had been identified from accident records. One participant estimated that almost 70 per cent of the problems reported occurred every day, indicating an almost constant exposure to danger.

Attempts have also been made to produce similar effective results in obtaining information through the use of questionnaires to be filled in by selected personnel. This method has proved to be unsatisfactory for a number of reasons. One fundamental problem was the need for extreme care in selecting and phrasing the questions. Too often, the person completing a questionnaire would give the questions interpretations neither considered nor intended by the person who prepared them. Any question should be avoided whose answer requires involved reasoning which is not immediately apparent to the reader.

Much information is also submitted to control and action agencies in the form of hazard or trouble reports. However, hazard or trouble reporting itself generates discrepancies that can be avoided through use of the Critical Incident Technique. Reports may require entries in narrative form or in checklist form or both. Personnel find it time-consuming and difficult to prepare a narrative. Even conscientious report writers tend to select the easiest and most rapid means of accomplishing them. Reports are therefore usually lacking in detail and precision that could indicate the source of the problem. Formats requiring checking off items can be done much more rapidly, but these too result in omissions of information that may be critical. In both types, entries may include information on the immediate or principal cause of an accident, but other contributory causes and factors may be neglected.

Figure 8-4 lists some findings by the Stanford Research Institute and cited by Geise on variations between written and verbal reports of incidents.* The findings substantiate the experience of data collecting and analyzing agencies. In some instances, entries on reports have been so markedly in error they are immediately recognizable. Corrective action is sometimes possible if the problem or data is critical. However,

* John Geise, W. W. Holler, *et al., Maintainability Engineering*, (Prepared by Martin-Marietta Corporation and Duke University for U.S. Army Materiel Command, 1965) p. 217 (AD630 131.)

VARIATION BETWEEN WRITTEN AND VERBAL REPORTS
OF INCIDENTS ON THE SAME MISSILE SYSTEM

TYPE OF CRITICAL INCIDENT	FREQUENCY OF INCIDENTS (PERCENTAGE)	
	AS NOTED IN REPORTS	AS GIVEN IN INTERVIEWS
Attributable to faulty design:	(1.9)	(21.7)
Faulty console design	1.0	6.3
Ground equipment "cumbersome"	0.0	5.6
Parts not accessible or special tools required	0.6	6.0
Safety hazards	0.3	3.8
Attributable to faulty construction:	(80.8)	(29.0)
Wiring errors	27.7	1.7
Parts errors (including fasteners, connectors, lugs, etc.)	49.3	23.4
Other construction errors	3.8	3.9
Attributable to faulty operation:	(17.3)	(49.3)
Faulty communications	4.4	17.8
Poor work-place arrangements	3.8	18.2
Missiles damaged by use of support equipment	2.5	2.8
Specific switching operations in error	5.3	2.4
Incidents based on "time pressures"	0.0	5.6
Other incidents (including faulty logistics)	1.3	2.5
Sum of percentages	100.0	100.0
Total number of incidents	318.	286.

Figure 8-4

the entries that are in error but not immediately recognizable are the ones generating analysis problems. The Critical Incident Technique tends to eliminate many of these.

Procedure (Task) Analysis

Chapter 4 indicated problems arising whenever personnel are involved with a system; it discussed human capabilities, causes of human error, and effects of various factors on performance. In order to minimize the errors, problems, and accidents that could take place, it has been found advisable to prepare procedures showing how tasks should be accomplished correctly. A procedure is a set of instructions for sequenced actions to accomplish a task such as conducting an operation, maintenance, repair, assembly, test, calibration, transportation, handling, emplacement, or removal. Procedure analysis is a review of the actions that must be performed, generally in relation to the mission tasks; the equipment that must be operated; and the environment in which personnel must exist. These procedures may change as the system progresses along any segment of its time profile, each in turn involving a series of actions to be accomplished in a programmed sequence to reach the desired mission goal. Analyses must ensure that the procedures are not only effective and efficient but also safe. Such analyses involve determination of the required tasks, exposures to hazards, criticality of each task and procedural step, equipment characteristics, and mental and physical demands.

Some tasks are inherently more hazardous than others and procedures for their accomplishment must be analyzed in detail. Welding is such an inherently hazardous task. The three most costly fires in dollar loss during the last 50 years in the United States were:

1. Ruin of the *S. S. Normandie* at its pier in New York in 1942, at a loss of $53,000,000. Sparks resulting from a welder cutting steel stanchions with an oxyacetylene torch ignited a pile of dry kapok life preservers. The fire spread. All the water poured on caused the ship to capsize.

2. Destruction of the General Motors plant at Livonia, Michigan, in 1953, at a cost of 3 lives and $45,000,000. Sparks from a welding operation undertaken to replace a steam line under the roof of the plant ignited rustproofing oil in a tank. The fire spread until almost all of the plant (1,500,000 sq ft) was destroyed.

3. Damage to the aircraft carrier *U.S.S. Constellation* at the Brooklyn Navy Yard in 1960, at the cost of 50 lives, 150 injured, and more than $40,000,000. The ship was being fitted out when a lift truck broke a plug on a gasoline tank. The gasoline flowed down a shaft to a lower deck where the vapors were ignited by the flame of a welder. The fire then spread.

The deaths of 53 men in a Titan II silo (see page 136) were also due to a welding accident.

A procedure analysis is sometimes designated by the activity to be analyzed. Some common examples are Test Safety Analysis, Operation Safety Analysis, Maintenance Safety Analysis, and Transportation Safety Analysis. Each analysis is performed to identify equipment, procedures, and operations that could be dangerous to personnel, hardware, and facilities during test or field activities. Test safety analyses conducted during development of a system are of three types: those to evaluate system component characteristics and especially those that are inherently hazardous; those necessary to establish component or system reliability; and those to prove the efficacy of the procedures generated for use of field personnel.

Personnel involved in field operations of a system may also conduct tests, but such tests are usually routine procedures on equipment whose hazards have already been established. Operations in this instance include not only procedures for accomplishment of the end mission of the system but also for maintenance and repair, check out, transportation and handling, and related activities. Operations analysis reviews these activities and the procedures prescribed for their accomplishment. Tests of these procedures are conducted to determine their effectiveness, completeness, accuracy, and safety. If these tests indicate that the procedures are acceptable, they may be adopted for publication in instruction manuals for field operators.

The chief differences between tests and operations analyses result from the fact that tests are generally more hazardous. To ensure that operations can be conducted under conditions that are the worst

Procedure (Task) Analysis

193

foreseeable and still have a margin of safety, environmental tests may exceed by far any actual adverse conditions. The uncertainties of component characteristics at the field test stage necessitate more rigid safety controls and contingency planning. In certain instances, the items are tested to establish when and under what conditions they will fail. Precautions must therefore be taken to minimize the effects of what might be considered a controlled accident.

By the time a system is operational, hazards have been evaluated and eliminated or controlled or safeguards have been provided to minimize adverse effects. Hazards that have not been eliminated can be identified for operations personnel through incorporation of limitations and warning and caution notes in instruction manuals, procedures, and checklists. Suitable monitoring, warning and protective devices and equipment can also be installed for operational use as solutions of problems encountered during test. In addition, tests are conducted by personnel who generally have had more intensive, higher level, and longer technical training and experience than operations personnel. This factor may help in reducing errors or in taking necessary actions during contingencies. The analyses must therefore consider the differences in these capabilities.

Failure to recognize the hazards involved during a test was considered as one of the causes of the accident in which three astronauts died in Apollo 204 at Cape Kennedy on 27 January 1967. The U.S. Senate hearings* on the accident brought forth the point again and again that the test conditions at the time of the accident were "extremely hazardous," but that the test was not recognized as being hazardous by either NASA or the contractor prior to the accident. Adequate safety precautions therefore were neither established nor observed for this test.

Some errors in accomplishing procedures may generate no problems; however, the same error at an inopportune moment can be catastrophic. The sinking of the submarine *Stickleback* off Oahu in June 1958 is a case in point. The *Stickleback* and the destroyer-escort *Silverstein* were simulating attacks and counterattacks on each other. The submarine made an attack and then dove to evade the *Silverstein's* counterattack. Soon after she submerged, the *Stickleback* lost power and uncontrollably rose to the surface in the path of the destroyer. The *Silverstein* rammed the submarine forward of the control room, where she began to fill. The 8 officers and 64 men left the *Stickleback* and boarded the destroyer. The submarine sank in 9,000 ft of water.

A Board of Inquiry established that a crew member had turned a rheostat in the wrong direction, so the submarine had lost its power at a critical instant. Loss of power and subsequent rise of the submarine to the surface at any other time would have generated no problem.

Some of the types of human errors generated by procedural problems have been listed in Fig. 4-4. These include problems with the procedures themselves, which may be lacking, incorrect, lengthy, awkward, poorly written, and hard to understand. There are numerous other factors involving relationships between personnel and equipment. Some of these can be determined by Link Analysis, described previously, in which various operational interrelationships are analyzed. Procedures can be written as the result of a Link Analysis or can be subjected to an

* "Hearings Before the Committee on Aeronautical and Space Sciences, United States Senate, 90th Congress." (Washington, D.C., U.S. Government Printing Office, 1967.)

evaluation by that method after they are prepared. Link Analysis explores the operation to determine the most efficient means of accomplishment. Procedures analysis, from the safety standpoint, explores all related matters that could degrade performance or cause injury by an accident even when the most efficient method is to be adopted. Some basic precepts of factors that must be considered in the development of procedures are indicated in Fig. 4-4; however, the writer who prepares the procedure and the analyst who reviews them must also realize that:

- Any equipment or procedures that can be utilized incorrectly will someday be employed the wrong way. The effects of such actions must therefore be investigated and preventive measures taken to eliminate possibilities of error and to minimize the effects if an error does occur.

- No matter how simple a procedure appears, it should be examined critically for possibilities of error and danger.

- Personnel tend to take shortcuts to avoid arduous, lengthy, uncomfortable, or unintelligible procedures. These shortcuts frequently are open to error, which can generate accidents. Equipment that is difficult to maintain will suffer from lack of maintenance.

- Most man-machine relationships involve procedural problems in the use of the equipment rather than in failures of the equipment itself.

- Personnel believe that they themselves are so knowledgeable, careful, and adept at the tasks involved that they will make no error, although other persons might. These personnel who are so assured of their own capabilities are the ones who must be especially protected.

- All procedures and each step within a procedure should be examined for necessity. All extraneous operations should be eliminated. Critical steps should be accented.

- Requirements for special training for personnel should be kept to a minimum. In addition, procedures analysis should assume that at certain times training may be lacking or faulty.

- Procedures requiring person-to-person communications should be kept to a minimum and be as simple as possible. Errors in communication or lack of communication are frequent sources of procedural failures that can cause accidents.

- Procedures involving interruptions will generate circumstances under which steps may be forgotten when the procedures are resumed. Such interruptions are especially prevalent in maintenance and repair where there are no instructions regarding the parts or tools required for carrying out the procedure. The need for obtaining the parts and tools after the procedure has begun will then cause interruptions.

The first step in making this type of analysis is ensuring that the procedure contains the following:

- A description of the equipment or system and a statement of the purpose of the operation

Making the Procedure Analysis

- A list of reference documents used in preparing the procedure
- A statement relative to the qualification of personnel
- Preparatory assembly, installation, and servicing instructions
- Operating instructions for the proper operation of the equipment or system including, where applicable, tables, charts of operating data, adjustments, warnings, and precautions
- Service instructions necessary for routine maintenance procedures, inspections, adjustments, cleaning, localizing trouble, repairing, and replacing defective parts
- A list of all test facilities, communications equipment, tools, instruments, and power requirements
- A list of warnings and precautions required to prevent injury to personnel or damage to equipment
- Requirements for a visual inspection if equipment is to be tested: determining that dimensional characteristics have been met, the presence of calibration stickers, and any apparent discrepancies
- Preparatory procedures necessary for the required operation, including environmental requirements, assembly or test equipment setup, and preliminary checks or tests
- Step-by-step instructions for performing the operation
- Instructions for recording data
- Instructions for stopping the operation and disassembling or disconnecting equipment
- Emergency shutdown and backout instructions
- Provisions for originator and approval signatures

In many instances, the first notes on a procedure are written by the designer of the equipment. He is generally the one who best knows the principles on which it was designed, the sequences of events taking place and their human inputs, the pitfalls to be avoided, and the dangers involved. He should then check the rough procedure against the mock-up, simulator, or prototype of the system being developed to ensure that he has included all necessary tasks and steps, that there are no impediments to their accomplishment, and that the procedure is the best that he considers possible.

Next to be involved are the technical writers and the Human Factors engineers. The first prepares the written material, using simple, proper, and clear language, adequate for the level of personnel expected to operate the equipment. A writer too may run through the procedure, preferably without the design engineer being present, to ensure that he understands what is to be done without outside help. If any task or step is not clear, he requests an explanation so he can rewrite the procedure until it is clear.

The Human Factors engineer conducts a similar review. He checks that the design of the equipment, the expected environment, the procedure, and any other affecting factors do not violate any good practices of Human engineering. The Human Factors engineer or the System Safety engineer, or both, may then undertake to identify the hazards that might be involved in each task of the procedure.

Special care should be exercised when the operation involves hazardous materials, especially such high-energy sources as explosives,

TASK	DANGER	EFFECT	CAUSE	CORRECTIVE OR PREVENTIVE MEASURES
Charge nitrogen pressure vessel	1. A loose hose may whip.	Personnel could be injured or equipment damaged.	Hose failure; connection failure; failure to tighten connection adequately	Tie down, chain or sandbag hose at close intervals. Personnel wear hard hats and face shields. Establish torque values for tightening connections. Warning and caution notes in procedures.
	2. Vessel bursts.	Fragmentation. Fragments may injure personnel or damage near by equipment.	Inadequate strength	Use high safety factor design. Provide warning against over-pressurizing system. Do not expose pressure vessel to heat. Incorporate relief and safety valves. Test vessel to ensure that it will carry required pressure.
	3. High-velocity gas escapes.	Gas may blow solid particles into eyes or against skin. Loss of gas may cause system to become inoperative due to lack of pressure.	Leak; hose failure; loosening fitting on pressurized system; crack	Procedures to provide warnings to depressurize system before attempting to disassemble connectors. Personnel to wear face shields.

Figure 8-5

propellants, flammable liquids, electrical power, compressed gases, radiation, or reactive chemicals. Each task item must be examined to determine the danger to personnel and equipment. Hazard causes and effects should be listed and corrective or preventive measures indicated. This process will often reveal safety problems that were not considered during preparation of the procedures or show need for additional safeguards or preventive measures. If a change is made in procedure, the change should be reviewed to determine whether it is the safest possible.

The exact format of the analysis and the table on which the data are recorded depends on the analyst and the purpose for which the information is prepared. Figure 8-5 indicates a format that can be utilized. Most of the headings are self-explanatory.

The outputs that can be generated from a proper analysis of procedures for a product or system include:

Outputs of Procedures Analysis

- Corrective or preventive measures that should be taken to minimize the possibilities that any error will result in either an emergency or an accident. The procedures for analysis of possible contingencies are described in the next section.
- Recommendations for changes or improvements in hardware or procedures to improve efficiency and safety.
- Development of warning and caution notes to be included in the most effective locations in the procedures.
- Requirements for special training of personnel who will carry out the procedures reviewed.

Procedure (Task) Analysis

197

• Recommendations for special equipment, such as personnel protective clothing, which would be required for the conduct of the operations to be undertaken.

Quantitative Analyses of Procedures

A number of methods have been proposed for evaluating numerically the probability of an accident being caused by a procedural error. One of these methods is THERP (Technique for Human Error Rate Prediction).* Briefly, the method can be described as follows:

1. The proposed procedure for the operation is prepared.

2. Each procedure is broken down into the simplest tasks possible.

3. Each task is then broken down further into segments. For example, the task of pressurizing a tank to a prescribed level from a high-pressure source is accomplished by:
   a. Opening the shutoff valve to the tank
   b. Opening the high-pressure regulator from the source
   c. Observing the pressure gauge downstream from the regulator until the prescribed level is reached in the tank
   d. Shutting off the high-pressure regulator
   e. Shutting the valve to the tank

4. Each segment is assigned a probability of success (reliability). Many of these have been established empirically. (A few values are indicated in Fig. 8-6.) Where alternatives of action are possible, suitable assignment of values is necessary.

5. The probability of successful accomplishment of each task is obtained by multiplying the probabilities for each segment. In certain instances, the task segments must be examined to decide whether they are dependent or independent events and to establish suitable mathematical relationships.

6. The probability of successful accomplishment of each procedure is obtained by multiplying the probabilities for each task.

At present the chief drawback to using this method is the accuracy of the probabilities for each segment. Almost all of these probabilities were derived from laboratory tests, and values may be low. This fact may be due to the desire of research personnel to show measurable differences between events, especially with the limited number of tests undertaken. In addition, not only will field conditions vary from those in the laboratory but field personnel will also have different capabilities than laboratory workers. Variations in temperature, vibration, noise, and stresses will also cause field results to differ from theoretical or test considerations. It should be emphasized here, however, that it is not the methodology that is at fault but the data employed. This objection may be eliminated gradually with usage and experience.

Contingency Analysis

On 23 May 1939, the American submarine *Squalus* sank in 240 ft of water off the New Hampshire coast during a trial dive. The main air-induction valves were open during submergence even though indicators

* A. D. Swain, *A Method for Performing Human Factors Reliability Analysis,* Report SCR-685 (Albuquerque, N. M., Sandia Corporation, 1963).

MEANS AND STANDARD DEVIATIONS OF RATINGS AND
RELIABILITY ESTIMATES FOR THE TASK ELEMENTS*

TASK ELEMENT	RATING MEAN	S.D.	RELIABILITY ESTIMATE	TASK ELEMENT	RATING MEAN	S.D.	RELIABILITY ESTIMATE
Read technical instructions	8.3	2.2	0.9918	Remove initiator simulator	4.1	1.9	0.9983
Read time (Brush Recorder)	8.2	2.1	0.9921	Install protective cover (friction fit)	4.1	2.2	0.9983
Read electrical or flow meter	7.0	2.8	0.9945	Read time (watch)	4.1	2.1	0.9983
Inspect for loose bolts and clamps	6.4	1.9	0.9955	Verify switch position	4.1	1.9	0.9983
Position multiple position electrical switch	6.3	2.4	0.9957	Inspect for lock wire	4.1	2.1	0.9983
Mark position of component	6.2	2.1	0.9958	Close hand valves	4.0	2.6	0.9983
Install lockwire	6.0	2.3	0.9961	Install drain tube	4.0	2.1	0.9983
Inspect for bellows distortion	6.0	2.7	0.9961	Install torque wrench adapter	3.9	1.7	0.9984
Install Marman clamp	6.0	1.8	0.9961	Open hand valves	3.8	2.6	0.9985
Install gasket	6.0	2.1	0.9962	Position two position electrical switch	3.8	1.5	0.9985
Inspect for rust and corrosion	5.9	2.1	0.9963	Spray leak detector	3.7	2.0	0.9986
Install "O" ring	5.7	2.2	0.9965	Verify component removed or installed	3.5	2.4	0.9988
Record reading	5.7	2.3	0.9966	Remove nuts, plugs, and bolts	3.5	1.7	0.9988
Inspect for dents, cracks, and scratches	5.6	2.4	0.9967	Install pressure cap	3.4	1.6	0.9988
Read pressure gauge	5.4	2.2	0.9969	Remove protective closure (friction fit)	3.2	1.6	0.9990
Inspect for frayed shielding	5.4	2.3	0.9969	Remove torque wrench adapter	3.0	1.6	0.9991
Inspect for QC seals	5.3	2.6	0.9970	Remove reducing adapter	3.0	1.7	0.9991
Tighten nuts, bolts, and plugs	5.3	2.6	0.9970	Remove Marman clamp	3.0	1.7	0.9991
Apply gasket cement	5.3	2.3	0.9971	Remove pressure cap	2.8	1.8	0.9992
Connect electrical cable (threaded)	5.2	2.2	0.9972	Loosen nuts, bolts, and plugs	2.8	1.3	0.9992
Inspect for air bubbles (leak check)	5.0	2.2	0.9974	Remove union	2.7	1.4	0.9993
Install reducing adapter	4.9	1.6	0.9975	Remove lockwire	2.7	1.5	0.9993
Install initiator simulator	4.9	2.5	0.9975	Remove drain tube	2.6	1.4	0.9993
Connect flexible hose	4.9	2.4	0.9975	Verify light illuminated or extinguished	2.2	1.6	0.9996
Position "zero in" knob	4.8	1.6	0.9976	Install funnel or hose in can	2.0	0.8	0.9997
Lubricate bolt or plug	4.7	1.6	0.9979	Remove funnel from oil can	1.9	1.4	0.9997
Position hand valves	4.6	1.6	0.9979				
Install nuts, plugs, and bolts	4.6	1.7	0.9979				
Install union	4.5	1.8	0.9979				
Lubricate "O" ring	4.5	2.5	0.9979				
Rotate gearbox train	4.4	2.0	0.9980				
Fill sump with oil	4.3	1.6	0.9981				
Disconnect flexible hose	4.2	2.0	0.9982				
Lubricate torque wrench adapter	4.2	2.2	0.9982				

Figure 8-6

in the submarine showed them closed. Twenty-six of the 59 men aboard died by drowning almost immediately. The submarine was equipped with Momsen lungs for emergency escape, but their use was inadvisable except as a last resort because of the water depth and temperature. Because prescribed procedures were followed, the submarine's predicament was known in a few hours; rescue personnel, hardware, and vessels were in action on the site within 24 hours; and the other 33 men were rescued 16 hr after that. A diving bell developed by the U.S. Navy for such rescue purposes was used.

On 1 June 1939, the bow of the British submarine *Thetis* sank to the bottom of the Irish Sea in 130 ft of water when two forward compartments flooded during a trial dive. Eighteen feet of the 275-ft craft were above water. Although the regular crew consisted of 53 men, 103 persons were aboard. These included technicians, officials, observers, and two waiters hired to feed the crowd. Seven men used escape apparatus, but only four reached the surface. The British had declined to build or buy rescue diving bells. Other rescue attempts were unsuccessful due to lack of equipment. Ninety-six men died of suffocation, principally from overcrowding, which reduced available survival time. It was the worst submarine disaster up to that time.

A *contingency* is an emergency or potential emergency situation arising from the occurrence of an unprogrammed event, unavoidable natural phenomenon, or human error. The severity of any contingency depends on the magnitude of the affecting condition and the ability of the system to withstand it, the configuration at the time of occurrence, available reaction time, and the capability of the operator or equipment to take corrective action. A contingency analysis must consider all of these factors. It involves review of actions that must be taken at any point in time and the sequencing of such actions until a safe condition is achieved. Contingencies can be due to:

- Malfunctions or failures of equipment
- Hazards generated by other equipment or personnel
- Climatic conditions, such as rain, hail, snow, dust, high winds, lightning, or floods
- Environmental stresses, such as heat, cold, humidity, high pressure, low pressure, or vibration

As long as a hazard exists, there is also a possibility that loss of control will occur. The time and exact circumstances are uncertain. The only thing certain is that actions during the first few seconds after control over the hazard is lost may determine whether control can be reestablished, and damage or injury avoided, or whether an accident will develop. To ensure that an accident does not occur in such situations, emergency and backout procedures must be prepared long before the system is put into operation. When an emergency arises, time may not be available to react properly if it is simultaneously necessary to determine what is wrong, the best corrective action, and then to carry out the action decided on. A person required to accomplish all of these things within the extremely short span of time available will probably be overwhelmed and unsuccessful in meeting the requirements of the situation. Even the most controlled individual is under a stress when a critical or emergency situation occurs unexpectedly. His ability to react calmly and suitably is degraded. His best chance of successfully rectifying the crisis is through use of previously developed and tested procedures.

These procedures may be the result of a contingency analysis of each critical operation where control of a hazard could be lost or of a test/operations procedure analysis. Analysis may determine that a person cannot react fast enough to overcome certain adverse situations. The system and its operation then have to be altered to reduce the reaction time necessary in event of a failure, or automatic monitoring and activating devices have to be provided for rapid corrective or suppressive action. These devices may bring the hazard back under control again, extend the reaction time operating personnel can have to take corrective action, or provide means of containing possible damage. One example is a fire-suppression system using automatic sprinklers. Sprinklers operate automatically if a fire occurs. They may put out the fire entirely or inhibit it against spreading. Fire-fighting personnel can then control and extinguish it completely.

Where more time for reaction is available, the analysis should determine the various effects that could result from a malfunction or failure, whether containment can be effected by the operator, or whether it is necessary to evacuate the premises. The containment procedures should be simple and easy to enact. If special controls, equipment, or tools are required, they should be prescribed or designed. Generally, more than one procedure will usually be necessary, each one to cover a specific set of possible conditions. In any case, these procedures should be written so that they are easy to understand, with no ambiguity, complexity, or lack of clarity that would delay the operator in understanding or carrying them out.

Personnel actions to be taken in emergencies must include consideration of the fact that reaction times are generally longer than those during test or practice. It is therefore necessary to ensure that proposed actions can be accomplished within the allowable response times. Some factors affecting reaction times are:

Response Times

- Normal work load. An operator with a work load near the limit of his capacity may be overwhelmed in a contingency situation. This is especially true when the contingency requires the operator to take over the functions of automatic equipment.

- Abnormal environments. Environments such as extreme cold can slow muscular and mental activities, while extreme heat can cause rapid fatigue, leading eventually to slowdown.

- Fatigue. This factor is more likely in demanding situations, rather than in normal situations. Performance will be adversely affected because a person tires rapidly under strain.

- Stress. Stresses can cause inappropriate reactions generating errors and producing further degradation of the emergency. These errors may cause confusion and require additional corrective action, both of which require increased time to bring the situation back to normal.

- Nonessential information. Such information intrudes in an emergency and detracts from the ability of the operator to evaluate the situation. Any indicator or arrangement that will attract atten-

Contingency Analysis

201

tion to the essential sources of information will reduce time to respond.

- Instructions that are lengthy, complicated, or lacking in clarity. As a result, there is delay, confusion, and sometimes error. Procedures for contingencies must be at least as simple, clear, and short as those for normal operations.

- Training. Lack of previous instruction in procedures to be followed in emergencies or lack of practice under simulated conditions will also reduce the ability of personnel to respond rapidly and without error.

Another aspect of response time analysis involves study of the interval that may be available for rescue or survival. This interval depends on how long personnel can remain in the existing environment during an emergency. In this case, an emergency is considered to exist from the time a situation arises from which injury can result until the persons are situated where they are safe.

One report postulates that when a large number of emergencies for which survival times, approximate or definite, are charted against probabilities of survival, a family of curves can be developed depending on the specific hazard.* These curves will have the general form:

$$F = e^{-f(t)}$$

where F = the fraction of cases having survival times exceeding a specified time t

$f(t)$ = a function of time

The form of the curve was derived from data taken from accidents in which submarines were lost. The study was attempting to determine how long crews involved in space flight emergencies could survive threats to their lives. The results are shown in Fig. 8-7 for the seven threats considered. The average curve approximates the general function just described with a Weibull curve of the form:

$$F = e^{-At^\alpha}$$

where the constants $A = 0.219$ and $\alpha = 0.5$. The average curve is shown by the dotted line. The authors indicate that a closer fit to empirical data would be:

$$F = 0.3e^{-Bt} = 0.7e^{-Ct}$$

where the first term applies to death by drowning and the second to asphyxia. Due to the lack of data, determination of values for the constants for these curves was not possible. It should also be pointed out that values used in at least one case are questionable. The *Thetis* (discussed earlier in this chapter) carried personnel (103) who numbered almost twice the normal complement (53). The survival time was therefore reduced by at least that ratio.

Certain causes of death can be calculated by determining how long it would take in an emergency for a specific environmental condition

Operating Safety Analyses

* S. H. Dole, *et al., Contingency Planning for Space-Flight Emergencies*, Memorandum RM-5200-NASA (Santa Monica, Calif., RAND Corporation, 1967).

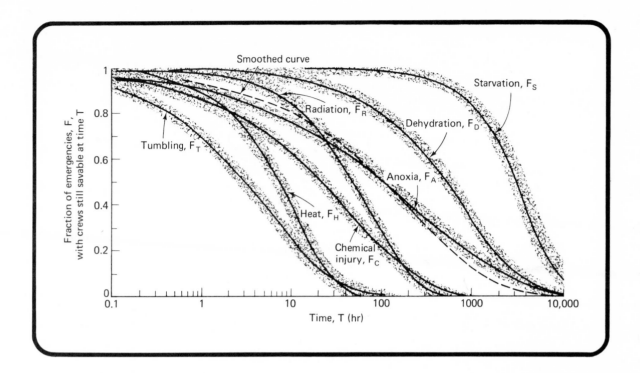

Fig. 8-7. Survival times associated with each of seven major threats to life. S. H. Dole, et al; *Contingency Planning for Space-Flight Emergencies,* Memorandum RM-5200-NASA (Santa Monica, Calif., RAND Corporation, January 1967) p. 48.

to reach a harmful level. Figure 8-8 indicates normal, luxury, and discomfort levels of some conditions. The discomfort level is the point at which the body begins to object physiologically to its environment. As conditions worsen, they may finally reach a lethal level, the exact amount varying for each person and the existence of other stresses that may or may not have reached points of discomfort.

When a contingency arises in a manned system, the first consideration must be given to safeguarding the well-being of personnel and, secondly, to conserving the equipment. Wherever possible, effort should be made to prevent the loss of either, and, in most cases, saving the system may save the personnel. In any circumstances, analysis of measures for the safety of personnel must consider and evaluate:

Contingency Analysis Procedure

- **Normal Procedures.** The time at which the system is most vulnerable must be determined, and the effects of malfunctions and failures, personnel error, climatic conditions, or environmental stresses must be evaluated. For example, each type of error, of omission or commission, which could generate a contingency, should be reviewed.

- **Detection Methods.** The means by which the malfunction, error, condition, or stress can be detected should be indicated. In some instances, an operator will realize that he has committed an error or that a malfunction has occurred without need for detectors. In other cases, the adverse condition may be difficult to detect without the assistance of suitable devices before complete loss of control of the hazard occurs.

- **Location and Extent of Problems.** Elimination of guesswork on the part of the operator is necessary to ensure proper evalua-

Contingency Analysis

203

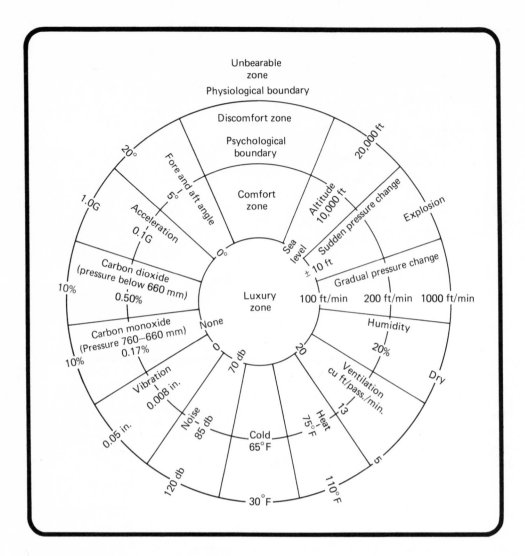

Fig. 8-8. Zones of luxury, comfort, and discomfort for thirteen variables commonly encountered in flight. R. A. McFarland, *Human Factors in Air Transportation* (New York: McGraw-Hill Book Company, 1953), p. 705.

tion of the situation. This can be done only by providing him with sufficient information on the location and extent of the problem.

• **Corrective Actions.** Optimum actions to be taken to effect recoveries, minimize or contain damage, and to eliminate or reduce injuries must be determined long before the system is operated. Wherever possible, system design should permit recovery from a contingency without exposing personnel to danger. Means of carrying out these corrective actions must also be evaluated. The necessity for provision of automatic or semi-automatic equipment, where reaction times are extremely critical, must be reviewed. Equipment to be used for recovery, suppression, or containment must be adequate for the conditions and reaction times involved.

• **Points-of-No-Return.** In some cases, the measures provided may be inadequate for the contingency, and the situation will worsen. A state may then be reached at which attempts to correct the situation should be abandoned and efforts redirected to safeguarding personnel. In certain emergencies, efforts must be diverted from saving the system to preventing the adverse condition from affecting other systems. The time at which these transfers of effort should be made must be delineated carefully before operations begin. Persons involved in an emergency who arrive at such a point-of-no-return generally have little time to evaluate conditions carefully or to review all possible actions to determine which is optimum. They may then wait too long in heroic attempts to save the equipment and endanger their lives unduly. On the other hand, since they are generally in a state of shock, they may abandon the system prematurely and make no attempt to take corrective action long before they are endangered. To ensure that personnel realize exactly when they are in danger and when they should abandon the equipment, instructions* must be provided as to where the point-of-no-return lies. Procedures must indicate the point at which control of a hazard can be considered lost and any attempt abandoned to save the system, equipment, or vehicle. This is the point at which a person should eject from an aircraft, abandon ship, or stop fire-fighting at the position he occupies.

- **Safety Zones and Evacuation Routes.** A contingency analysis must also determine locations in which personnel will be safe during an emergency. Protective structures can be provided beforehand to house personnel if there is a likelihood that damaging effects can occur so rapidly that reaction time will be lacking, damage can be so extensive that the area could not be evacuated, or the number of personnel who could be affected is such that some would be injured. In other instances, it may be necessary to evacuate personnel from an unsafe structure or vehicle to a safe area or from an unsafe area to a safe structure. Routes to be taken should be determined and analyzed beforehand. The routes must be adequate for the number of personnel who must be evacuated and for the time that would be available.

Every contingency analysis encompasses a specific period of time. The length of this period and the intervals at which conditions change so that corrective actions must be modified are dependent on the criticality of the operation. Manned space flights were analyzed for contingencies that could occur at intervals separated by extremely short spaces of time. These were listed sequentially. During an operation, this list was followed by a ground-based flight director. If a foreseeable contingency occurred at any time, he could immediately instruct the personnel in the space vehicle on actions to be taken. Unfortunately, the extent of the period analyzed for Apollo operations did not include the interval during which a disastrous fire caused the deaths of three astronauts.

Problems that could arise in manned space flight (Figs. 8-9 and 8-10) have been investigated by another method of analysis.† This method begins by choosing the emergency condition to be investigated. Possible causes and other pertinent information that could have a bear-

---

* The Navy has been investigating the possibility of developing a device which will inform pilots of stricken aircraft when their planes should be abandoned.

† *Manned Space Flight Program Risk Analysis,* prepared for the Office of Manned Space Flight, NASA (Washington, D.C., General Electric Company, 1967).

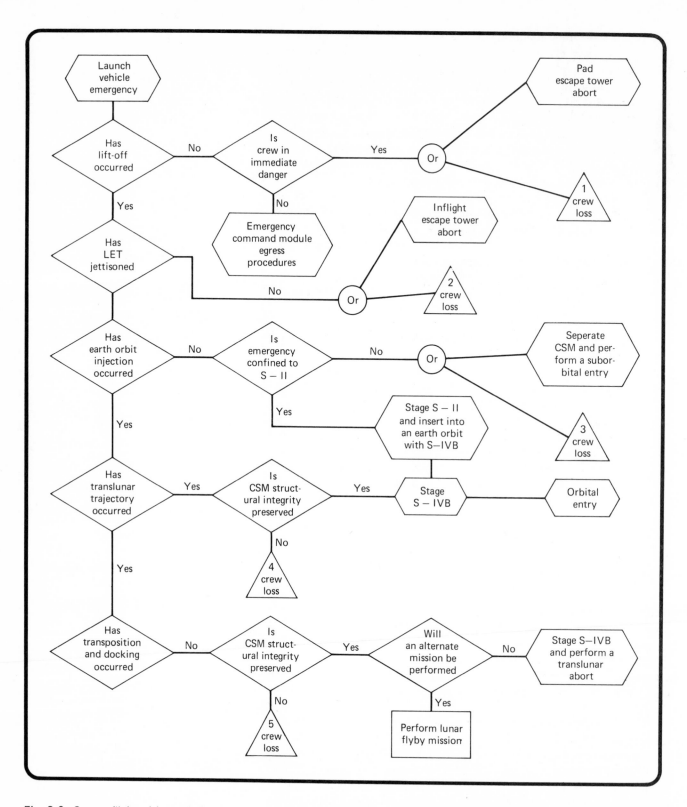

Fig. 8-9. Space flight risk analysis—Launch vehicle emergency.

ing on the situation are then indicated. The outcome of any potentially adverse condition or action is listed. A specific condition or action is categorized into one of two outcomes: Whether it does occur ("Yes") or does not occur ("No"). The next condition or action reviewed depends on whether the outcome was "Yes" or "No." As many conditions, events, and contingencies are investigated as the analyst can think of.

206

STAGE/MODULE SUBSYSTEM	EQUIPMENT/ FUNCTION	FUNCTIONAL DESCRIPTION	FAILURE ACTION SEQUENCE	
			ORIGINATED	LED TO
S—1C	Thrust vectoring	Provides flight control forces necessary to control the thrust vectors of the four outboard F—1 engines.	Hydraulic loss of thrust vectoring by leak, seizing, erroneous signal	Loss of thrust vectoring capability
	Fuel pressure	After engine starting sequence has begun, fuel tank pressure is obtained from four high-pressure helium cylinders located in the fuel tank.	Failure of pressure switch to actuate	Premature loss of helium vented over board leading to engine shutdown
	F—1 engines	Five liquid-propellant (RP—1 and LOX) rocket engines, four of which are gimbal-mounted (outboard) and one of which is fixed (centered).	(a) Loss of one engine thrust (b) Explosion of an engine	(a) Loss of total stage thrust (b) Vehicle loss
	Fluid power	Supplies pressurized hydraulic fluid (fuel) to the servo-actuators.	Failure of check valve to remain closed	Loss of ground supplied fluid into the engine turbo pump and then into the fuel tank
	Retro rocket	Helps to decelerate S—1C to provide necessary rate of separation.	Motor case rupture	Structural failure of vehicle
	LOX delivery	Supplies liquid oxygen to F—1 engines.	Major leak	Loss of LOX into structural area and engine shutdown

Figure 8-10

The table provides information on the equipment or function that could effect any of the entries on the accompanying diagram. Major failure modes are presented. There is no one-to-one relationship between the table and the diagram: A malfunction is considered possible any time that the equipment is in operation. The narrative summary contains evaluations of the information on the diagram and in the table. Recommendations for accident prevention and damage containment, other considerations that aspects to be investigated, and possible complications are included.

This method is less well organized or intensive as other methods discussed previously. Although probabilities could be applied to specific occurrences and malfunctions, the nature of the events shown on the chart does not lend itself to mathematical analysis. The method therefore finds its best application in qualitative studies. It can be employed effectively in contingency analyses for development of backout or emergency procedures. In such cases, the emergency or other possible unforeseen condition are listed chronologically. "Yes-No" alternatives are then added in branches to each condition, and the branches are extended until specific, ultimate end points are reached. These points

Contingency Analysis

could be when the operation had been aborted, had returned to a normal operational mode, had achieved a fail-safe status, had allowed personnel to escape, or had required rescue efforts.

Analysis Results   A proper contingency analysis can generate a variety of useful outputs:

- Changes in operating procedures and equipment. Certain procedures and equipment may be suitable and adequate for normal operations but undesirable and insufficient in any contingency situation. In some instances, they may even tend to increase personnel errors, which could generate emergencies.

- Emergency and backout procedures. These are instructions for actions to be taken immediately after it is determined that a contingency exists. This may be the most critical time in any such condition, since rapid action may overcome existing problems; delay could permit them to worsen.

- Containment and suppression procedures and equipment. If the contingency develops to a point where initial emergency and backout procedures are inadequate, more stringent corrective actions will be required. These actions are expressed in containment and suppression procedures and in provision of specialized equipment for the purpose.

- Escape and evacuation procedures and equipment. Progress of an emergency may reach a state in which the situation is considered irremediable. These analyses establish procedures to allow personnel to make safe escapes and to provide adequate equipment for the purpose. An example of aircraft ditching procedure, developed after a contingency analysis was made, and later incorporated in an operative manual, is indicated in Fig. 8-11. (See also Chapter 10.)

- Rescue procedures and equipment. These are required for situations in which personnel involved in an accident must be removed by outsiders because of their own inabilities to do so without assistance. (See also Chapter 10.)

The lack of suitable emergency procedures and equipment can be disastrous. On 7 May 1966, a fertilizer plant worker in Raga, Michigan, descended into an 18-ft cistern to finish work that he had started on the previous day on a water-control device. The device was located approximately 6 ft below ground level. Soon after, another man working on the surface saw that he was in trouble and shouted for help. A worker ran out of the plant and jumped into the cistern to help. He and the man he wanted to rescue died. A second plant worker did the same. He too died. A passerby who heard fire sirens ran over to help, broke away from the plant manager who attempted to restrain him, and jumped into the cistern. He too died. Firemen arrived soon after. The chief donned a gas mask, tied a rope around his body and descended. He too died. The coroner later stated that the five men had been killed by hydrogen sulfide gas, which had accumulated from an unknown source. The gas mask provided no protection against hydrogen sulfide. Adequate emergency procedures to rescue a man in trouble and proper respiratory protective equipment would have saved at least four lives, possibly five.

DITCHING CHART

CREW MEMBER	DUTIES BEFORE IMPACT	POSITION	DUTIES AFTER IMPACT	EQUIPMENT	EXIT
Pilot	1 Use call position to warn crew to "prepare for ditching in - - - - - - - - minutes." 2 Give six short rings on alarm bell and phone call light. 3 Have transponder master switch positioned to emergency. 4 Have copilot get position report from radar-navigator and transmit it to any station able to receive or in the blind. 5 Have copilot instruct crew to open emergency exits and jettison loose equipment. 6 Open and secure side window. 7 Check hand-hold opening. 8 Remove flak suit, parachute harness, and flying boots. 9 Put on exposure suit (if time permits), life vest, gloves, and flak helmet. (if able to brace head and neck.) 10 Have emergency keyer turned on. 11 Salvo bomb bay tanks. NOTE: Do not salvo bomb bay tanks if empty, as they will aid buoyancy of aircraft. 12 Fasten safety belt and shoulder harness; lock intertia reel. 13 Lower seat and push aft, feet on rudder pedals. 14 Give "station for ditching, impact in - - - - - - - - - - - seconds", on call position. 15 Give "ready for impact", on call position, and one long ring on alarm bell and phone call light. 16 Feather inboard propellers approximately five seconds before impact. 17 Instruct engineer to turn off main tank valve switches, move mixture levers to fuel cutoff and turn off battery switch.	1 In seat, lowered and pushed aft. 2 Feet on rudder pedals knees flexed.	1 See that crew is clear. 2 Supervise removal of any injured crew member. 3 Exit through side window. 4 Inflate life vest when outside. 5 Release and inflate left life raft and supervise securing emergency equipment and life rafts. NOTE: Guide raft over leading edge of wing to escape ragged edges of flaps and to keep raft drifting into the wing and not away from the aircraft. Pilot should ascertain that cord is cut after crew members have boarded raft, to prevent loss of raft when aircraft sinks. 6 Ascertain that assigned crew members are accounted for. 7 Take position in left raft and assume command. 8 Proceed away from aircraft and have rafts tied together with ropes provided.	1 One-man raft 2 Parachute 3 Life vest 4 Exposure suit 5 Flashlight	Side window

Fig. 8-11. Contingency Procedure. Air Force Technical Order IC-137(V)B-1, 10 March 1968.

209

Mockups Mockups are another important means by which possible product or system hazards can be determined and evaluated. A mockup is a three-dimensional replica of a proposed item of equipment, hardware, vehicle, or structure. Its configuration represents the intended real-world item. It is a visual aid to permit early review and analysis for:

- Necessary man-machine relationships
- Possibilities of physical interference between pieces of equipment, personnel, or both
- Work-flow patterns
- Personnel traffic
- Determination of characteristics that may endanger personnel
- Location and accessibility of exits for normal and emergency use
- Separation or isolation of incompatible materials, operations, and equipment
- Location and availability of emergency equipment
- Compartmentalization for work separation or hazard and damage isolation
- Maximum effective utilization of available space

Mockups are generally built early in the development of a product or system and updated as changes are made for improvement or new arrangements are to be tried. The earliest mockup may be on a small scale; after the design is more fully developed, a full-sized model may be constructed. A proposed change can be evaluated in a mockup before the actual change is made in design to ensure that it causes no degradation of safety or effectiveness.

Numerous examples can be cited of hazards and deficiencies that were determined through mockup analysis:

- Air-to-ground missiles being developed for launch from the bomb bay of an aircraft appeared to be dimensionally adequate. However, when full-sized missile mockups were loaded into a mockup of the bomb bay, it was found that the missile tail fins interfered with each other. To avoid possibilities of mutual damage, the tail assembly was redimensioned.
- Use of a mockup of an aircraft cockpit revealed that instruments necessary for aircraft flight could not be seen by the pilot because of interference of the control column and wheel.
- Personnel were killed when they removed respiratory protective equipment to enter tanks filled with inert gases. The manholes were adequate for normal activities but not for a situation such as that in Fig. 8-12 where added equipment had to be worn. The men were overcome when they entered the tanks after removing the backpacks and masks temporarily, intending to put them on later.
- Protuberances that personnel might hit in the event of a hard landing or crash were discovered through use of a helicopter mockup. The lower portion of Fig. 8-12 illustrates a possible problem, which could be very real and dangerous in an emergency although not apparent during normal operations. In an emergency there may be interference not only from the pedals and wheel

Failure to consider personal equipment.

Normal opening

Required opening

Emergency escape hindered by obstructions at knee and foot

but also from gear shift lever, the door and window handles, and the badly positioned door posts.

Mockups are fundamental tools for the Human Factors engineers, tied closely to the data on human dimensions and capabilities. Figure 8-13a is an example of data used by Human Factors engineers for the design of system equipment. Similar data would provide the basis for design of access space to confined spaces such as those shown in Fig. 8-13b. Assurance that designs are correct and that there is no unforeseen interference can be established only through mockups or, much later, prototypes. Correction of designs that have reached the prototype state are extremely costly; use of mockups is much more economical and efficient.

Tabulated data on human factors must be applied judiciously to ensure that they satisfy foreseeable requirements. The dimensions shown in Fig. 8-13b are adequate for normal activities but not for a situation such as that shown in the upper part of Fig. 8-12.

Irvine cites an extraordinarily inept design that probably could have been detected easily if a mockup had been constructed and tried:*

Fig. 8-12. Problems apparent through use of mockups. A. Damon, H. W. Stoudt, and R. A. McFarland, *The Human Body in Equipment Design*, (Cambridge, Mass.: Harvard University Press, 1966), p. 37.

---

* W. L. Irvine, *Systems Safety*, Ballistics Systems Division, Norton AFB, Calif; paper presented at the University of Southern California System Safety Program Management Course (November 1964).

MINIMAL TWO-HAND ACCESS OPENINGS WITHOUT VISUAL ACCESS

Reaching with both hands to depth of 6 to 19.25 inches:

Light clothing:	Width:	8″ or the depth of reach *
	Height:	5″
Arctic clothing:	Width:	6″ plus 3/4 the depth of reach
	Height:	7″

Reaching full arm's length (to shoulders) with both arms:

Width:	19.5″
Height:	5″

Inserting box grasped by handles on the front:

1 2″ clearance around box, assuming adequate clearance around handles

Inserting box with hands on the sides:

Light clothing:	Width:	Box plus 4.5″
	‡Height:	5″ or 0.5″ around box *
Arctic clothing:	Width:	Box plus 7″
	‡Height:	8.5″ or 0.5″ around box *

* Whichever is larger.

‡ If hands curl around bottom, allow an extra 1.5″ for light clothing, 3″ for arctic clothing.

MINIMAL ONE-HAND ACCESS OPENINGS WITHOUT VISUAL ACCESS

	Height	Width
Empty hand, to wrist:		
Bare hand, rolled:	3.75″ sq or dia	
Bare hand, flat:	2.25″ x 4.0″ or 4.0″ dia	
Glove or mitten:	4.0″ x 6.0″ or 6.0″ dia	
Arctic mitten:	5.0″ x 6.5″ or 6.5″ dia	
Clenched hand, to wrist:		
Bare hand:	3.5″ x 5.0″ or 5.0″ dia	
Glove or mitten:	4.5″ x 6.0″ or 6.0″ dia	
Arctic mitten:	7.0″ x 8.5″ or 8.5″ dia	
Hand plus 1″ dia object, to wrist:		
Bare hand:	3.75″ sq or dia	
Gloved or mitten:	6.0″ sq or dia	
Arctic mitten:	7.0″ sq or dia	
Hand plus object over 1″ in dia, to wrist:		
Bare hand:	1.75″ clearance around object	
Glove or mitten:	2.5″ clearance around object	
Arctic mitten:	3.5″ clearance around object	
Arm to elbow:		
Light clothing:	4.0″ x 4.5″ or 4.5″ dia	
Arctic clothing:	7.0″ sq or dia	
With object:	Clearances as above	
Arm to shoulder:		
Light clothing:	5.0″ sq or dia	
Arctic clothing:	8.5″ sq or dia	
With object:	Clearances as above	

MINIMAL FINGER ACCESS TO FIRST JOINT

Push button access:	Bare hand:	1.25″ dia
	Gloved hand:	1.5″ dia
Two finger twist access:	Bare hand:	object plus 2.0″ dia
	Gloved hand:	object plus 2.5″ dia

Fig. 8-13a. Arm and hand access dimensions. MIL-STD-1472 *Human Engineering Design Criteria for Military Systems, Equipment and Facilities,* (Washington, D.C.: Department of Defense, 15 May 1970), p. 138.

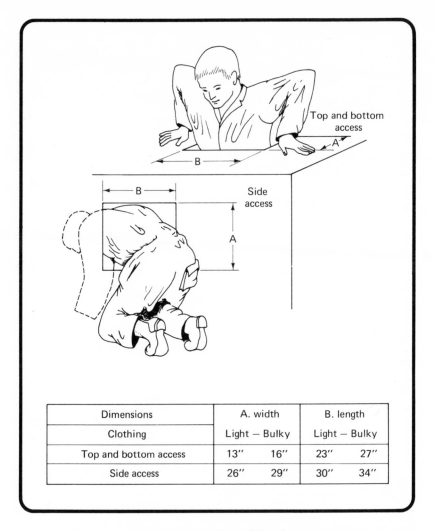

Dimensions	A. width		B. length	
Clothing	Light — Bulky		Light — Bulky	
Top and bottom access	13"	16"	23"	27"
Side access	26"	29"	30"	34"

Fig. 8-13b. Whole body access opening. *Ibid.,* p. 114.

The real classic of all the design deficiencies which have come to our attention was a combination safety shower and eyewash constructed at a northern missile site. In order to operate the eyewash, it was necessary for a man, who might already be blinded by acid, to put his head in the eyewash bowl and then turn the water valve on with his right foot. The only problem was that the foot-operated valve was about four feet to his rear and higher than his waist. As an additional feature, if a man did happen to hit the valve, he got a full shower from overhead as well as getting his eyes washed out. However, the whole problem became academic in winter because the whole system froze up.

Figure 8-14 indicates another use for mockups. Requirements for visibility from vehicles have often been stipulated in specifications. Plots are made on graphs indicating the limiting angles of any window frames as viewed from the operator's eye position. Unfortunately, because people differ physically, some configurations of cockpit construction can produce "blind spots" even when window areas are large. The lower portion of Fig. 8-14 reflects this situation in the statement: ". . . safety is determined not only by total solid angle of visibility, but by locations of solid angles of visibility with respect to possible (driving) hazards." Blind spots can be noted easily when mockups are used. Although derived from an operable vehicle, the upper portion of Fig.

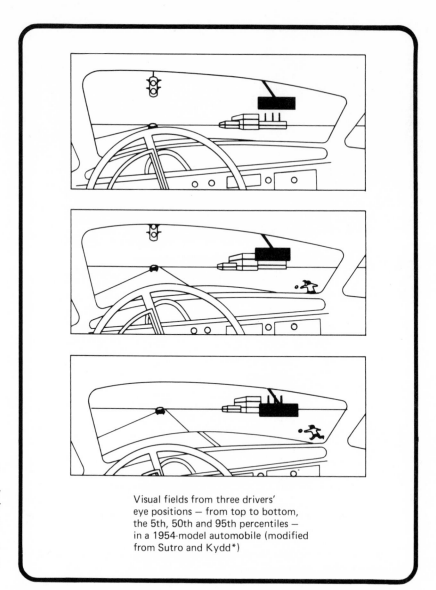

Visual fields from three drivers'
eye positions — from top to bottom,
the 5th, 50th and 95th percentiles —
in a 1954-model automobile (modified
from Sutro and Kydd*)

Fig. 8-14. Use of models and prototypes to establish adequacy of visibility.
* P. J. Sutro and G. H. Kydd, *Human Visual Capacities as a Basis for the Safer Design of Vehicles,* CAA Project No. 53–209, (Washington D.C.: Civil Aeronautics Administration, 1955).
† N. Wood, "Man vs Car: Where Safety Research Stops," *Machine Design,* 4 January 1968, p. 47.

8-14 illustrates how visual fields can be established through use of mockups and how blind spots can be noted. The lower figure describes how the fields can be measured.

Mockup Analysis Procedure

The procedure for use of mockups differs somewhat in each case, depending on the purpose, but generally may be performed in accordance with the following steps. Suitable adjustments may be made for specific purposes.

- Establish the purpose for the mockup or analysis to be made.
- Construct the mockup. Construction should be done initially with the most economical materials suitable for the purpose, such as cardboard or thin plywood. Construction, material, or weight need not duplicate actual items (except where these affect the analysis) but should be of similar size, configuration, and arrangement. Where the exact locations of units are not established definitely, they should be made in modules or other forms to permit easy relocations. Displays such as dials or screens,

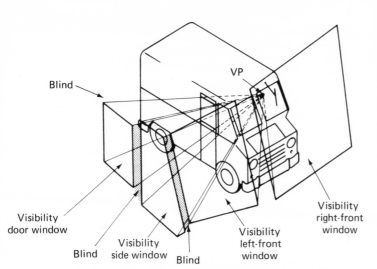

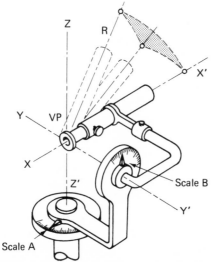

Modified transit (right) is used to determine line-of-sight boundaries of windows, windshields and mirrors from fixed viewing point, or eye position, within specific eye-range contour. By recording elevation and azimuth area of visibility (windows, mirrors), data is acquired to define the solid angle of vision through each window or mirror in vehicle from given VP.

By plotting a number of eye locations (relocating the VP of instrument), data is collected which is defined within each eye-range contour region. Solid angles of driver visibility are then identified quantitatively (as shown). Obviously, vehicle safety is determined not only by total solid angle of visibility, but by location of solid angles of visibility with regard to possible driving hazards.

Measuring Visibility from Vehicle Windows[†]

Figure 8-14 continued.

access openings, and controls may be shown by painted outlines, cutouts, or other replicas. Preference should be given to devices that can be moved easily to establish optimal locations by trial and error.

- Prepare a detailed checklist of items to be reviewed, relationships to be established, dimensions to be measured, and other criteria to be met.

- Make an initial study of the mockup for any interference problem,

Mockups

for possible difficulties in use of equipment and controls or in viewing displays, for adequacies of interfaces, and to make sure that criteria such as viewing angles and access spaces are met.

- Make suitable entries against checklist items to ensure that all aspects of the review have been accomplished. Note any deficiencies or recommendations for improvement in detail.

- Have similar reviews made by other persons, preferably of different height and weight. Note their comments.

- Run through any programmed procedures that will be undertaken by the ultimate users. Note any difficulties. An initial Link Analysis can be accomplished at this point. The initial run-through may be made in informal attire, but subsequent trials should be done in whatever special clothing the operators will wear.

- Run through contingency procedures slowly to evaluate each step for possibilities of errors. Repeat this process as rapidly as possible to establish whether any arrangements could cause delays in action, such as evacuations, use of emergency equipment, or rescue. Time to accomplish the procedure should be determined to ensure that it is within the limits permissible by the type of contingency. Here again, the procedures should be repeated, using the various types of garments to be worn by an operator.

- Repeat the process with any updated mockups as design and manufacture of units proceeds.

Limitations   Mockups are not as sophisticated as simulators, being static, non-operating devices. In their early stages, mockups may involve a form of play-acting that depends on the imagination of the analyst as he mentally visualizes various relationships. This necessity for imagination decreases as the hardware becomes more and more realistic, until prototype or production equipment replaces the nonoperable replicas.

Mockups are employed for evaluations of hardware and their interfaces with personnel or other hardware. Occasionally they may be used to evaluate environmental stress problems, such as whether vibration will cause adjacent items of hardware to hit each other. Their capabilities to produce environmental stresses for test, training, or evaluations is generally inferior to those of simulators. Examples of uses in which they may be entirely adequate are evaluations of adequacy of lighting or ensuring that glare does not affect an operator.

Benefits of mockups in accident prevention are principally those relating to arrangements of systems and equipment, to interfaces, to clearances, and to the hazards that inadequacies would generate.

Simulation   The benefits derived through simulation have generated a rapid increase in such methods in the past few years, especially for safety or related areas of interest. Simulation can begin early in development of a system by mathematical modeling (see Chapter 5) and computer techniques. However, the simulation methods discussed here include those three-dimensional models that physically represent, in whole or in part, actual or proposed hardware.

The complexities and sizes of three-dimensional simulators can vary tremendously. Fire tests have been conducted using 4-in. hollow cubes with openings cut in them to represent windows. Flammable materials were inserted and ignited, then subjected to various wind conditions to establish flame shapes and growth. At the other end of the scale, large buildings that were to be demolished were instrumented and burned to simulate real fires on which fire-fighting procedures, materials, and equipment could be tested. Building-size simulators also include those used for environment analysis and those containing large aircraft and other matériel and personnel.

Some of the earliest simulators employed for safety purposes were probably those dummies that were substituted for human beings during hazardous tests. Cocking lost his life by jumping from a balloon when he tested a new type of parachute that he had designed. Now tests of new parachutes and similar escape equipment are made with dummies until a fair degree of confidence is achieved in the capabilities and reliabilities of the devices. Dummies are also employed to simulate the motions, impacts, and injuries to which human being would be exposed during tests of automobile and aircraft crashes. These tests may also be used to evaluate the efficacy of restraining devices and crashworthiness designs. Comparisons between results from such simulations and actual effects of accidents indicate that the dummies originally employed for many of these tests were inadequate and tended to give erroneous results. More sophisticated ones therefore had to be developed to represent more truly human actions and reactions and the effects produced on human bodies. Other types of simulators can be categorized according to their uses and benefits. Some of these types include:

- Simulators for testing effects of climatic stresses on equipment, personnel, and procedures. Tests under simulated environmental conditions can be conducted on either prototype or operational equipment or components to determine problem areas and actual effects that might be generated by environments. Operational limitations of such equipment can be established in this way. The simulators are chambers in which the items to be tested are enclosed and the test environments, which represent real-world natural or induced conditions, are generated. One of the early uses for simulation of this type was for testing effects of extreme cold. Chambers for the purpose could be cooled to −100°F, even though natural terrestrial temperatures had never dropped to that level. Materials were tested for property changes to establish those characteristics that could be adversely affected. Equipment and personnel were tested to determine whether they could operate in natural environments found in frigid areas.

- Training of operators by use of simulators can be accomplished at costs far less than use of expensive operational equipment. Simulators can be used to increase operator proficiency in procedures occurring rarely during actual operations but may possibly be required, such as during an emergency, or to increase proficiency in programmed operations for which training cannot be provided in any other way. A pilot can be trained to operate a jet by practicing in a simulator at a cost much lower than that required for actual operation of an aircraft. In addition, an aircraft is not tied up for this purpose, nor is it subjected to the possibility

Simulation

217

of damage if the pilot makes an error. In one eight-year period, 14 commercial airliners were lost in training accidents.* It has been said that many airline pilots live through their entire careers as pilots without being subjected to a flight emergency that could lead to a catastrophe. However, they must be proficient in the procedures to be undertaken if such an emergency should occur. This capability can be acquired most effectively, efficiently, and economically by means of simulators.

Different types of simulation can often be employed for similar purposes. For example, four techniques have been employed to simulate weightlessness or reduced gravity to determine the effects that might be generated and to practice procedures to be undertaken in space or on the moon:

1. Keplerian trajectories, in which an aircraft was flown in a vertical parabolic curve. The centifugal force at the top of the curve opposed and nullified the gravitational force, producing a weightless and reduced-gravity condition. This condition lasted only a few seconds, limiting the durations of tests and activities that could be undertaken.

2. Gimbal suspension systems, in which a person was placed in a supporting device that was free to rotate freely about three axes. His weight was carried by the suspension system so that efforts to move required only the energy that would be necessary at reduced gravity. The equipment restrained the person from moving as freely as he should, limiting tests and operations that could be conducted.

3. Air-bearing devices, which also suspended a person to reduce the effects of his weight. Magnets held the lines to a steel overhead plate but compressed air forced through the center of each magnet and between the magnet and plate prevented clamping. The entire mechanism was therefore free to move forward, backward, and sideways. The remaining structure and harness counteracted the man's weight and permitted movement in certain directions. In other direction, movements were restrained.

4. Neutral-buoyancy water immersion, where the weight of the person was exactly the same as the water in which he was immersed and displaced. This was the most successful method. The person was completely unrestrained as he would be in outer space. This technique was first employed to establish the adequacy of procedures and devices for accomplishing tasks exactly as they were to be carried out during extravehicular activities of Gemini flights. After returning from a flight during which he completed in space the tasks he had practiced under simulated conditions, the astronaut made comparisons between use of the simulator and actual conditions.† Evaluations indicated that

* "New Training Concepts Studied for 747." *Aviation Week and Space Technology,* 20 November 1967, p. 161.

† O. F. Trout, G. P. Beasley, and D. L. Jacobs, *Simulation of Gemini Extravehicular Tasks by Neutral-Buoyancy Techniques,* NASA TN D-5235 (Washington, D. C., NASA Manned Space Flight Center, 1969).

the fidelity of simulation to actual experience was good, and the technique had much value. Water immersion techniques used for other series of tests to establish feasibility of programmed and contingency procedures in restricted spaces are described by Loats and Bruchey.*

The Society of Automotive Engineers issued the results of a survey on simulators employed in the aerospace industry in 1964.† Although most of these simulators were listed as tools for research, design, and development, the greatest number consisted of types that could be employed for training purposes. Figure 8-15 indicates how one type of simulator operates.

Training by simulation has one major benefit for safety: shattering the learning curve. Statistics of accident rates plotted against the time that a system has been in use show that the rate is always highest when operators have to learn the new system by operating it. During this time, the operator is not only required to acquire new knowledge, techniques, and habits but also to learn to disregard much he had previously known and done. This transition stage is the most dangerous period for the operator and is the one during which use of simulators can be most rewarding. Errors during training by simulator would not be catastrophic, as could similar errors during real-life operations.

Simulation has other advantages:

- Personnel can be tested in simulators to establish whether their performance meets a specified level. In some states, police have begun using simulators to test driving abilities. These tests establish whether the ability of a person to drive has been impaired by alcohol. The simulators can provide specific situations to generate reactions by the person being tested and then record actual results. Any abnormalities or impairment of abilities can be established and become a matter of record.

- Variations in designs can be made in simulators to determine whether they are adequate and which design is most effective for solution of a specific problem or set of problems. Integration of different units into one system can determine which arrangement would be the most efficient and effective. Prototype units can be tested in this way under simulated conditions to establish their capacities and reliabilities.

- Simulators can also act as time compressors. Sequences of events normally taking long periods can be shortened by omitting repetitions. Specific sequences can be started at selected points without the necessity of proceeding through an entire routine from its beginning. Training or testing a pilot in making an approach or landing can be accomplished without need for takeoffs, climbs, cruises, or letdowns.

---

* H. L. Loats, Jr., and W. J. Bruchey, *A Study of the Performance of an Astronaut during Ingress and Egress Maneuvers thru Airlock and Passageways*, NASA CR-971 (Rand-allstown, Md, Environmental Research Associates, 1968).

† *A Survey Report of Simulators Used as Tools for Research, Design and Development*, S. A. E. Aerospace Information Report AIR 779 (New York City, Society of Automotive Engineers, 1964).

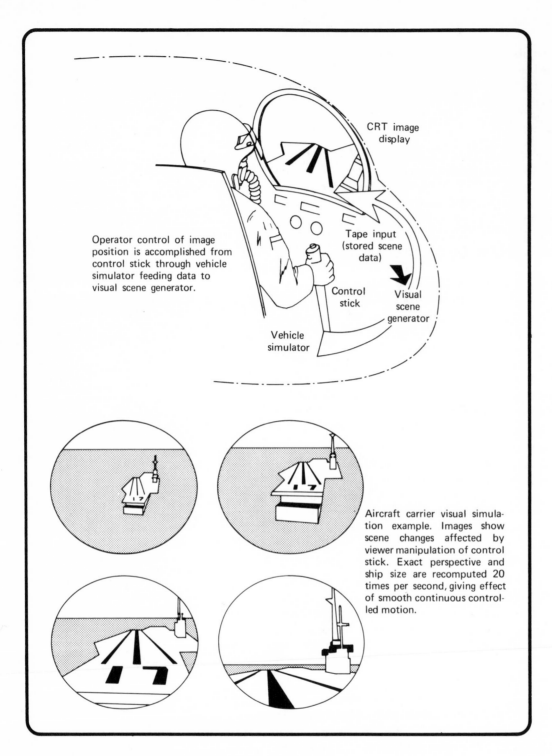

CRT image display

Operator control of image position is accomplished from control stick through vehicle simulator feeding data to visual scene generator.

Tape input (stored scene data)

Control stick

Visual scene generator

Vehicle simulator

Aircraft carrier visual simulation example. Images show scene changes affected by viewer manipulation of control stick. Exact perspective and ship size are recomputed 20 times per second, giving effect of smooth continuous controlled motion.

Fig. 8-15. Computer simulated flight trainer. "Computer Simulates Visual Flight," *EDN*, April 1968, p. 42.

Simulation Procedure   The procedures for simulation vary greatly, depending on its purpose and complexity. The following steps indicate in broad terms how simulations may be employed for safety purposes. Simple simulators will not require all these steps.

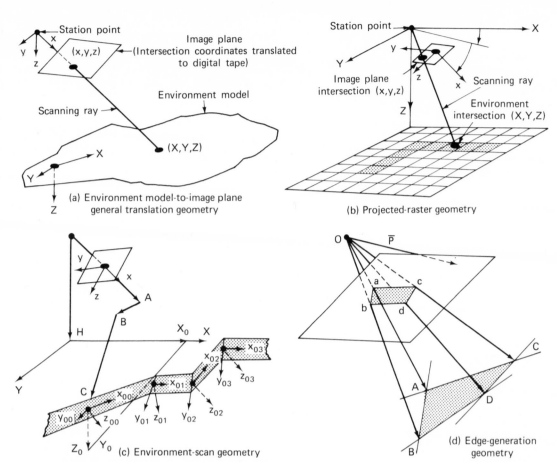

(a) Environment model-to-image plane general translation geometry

(b) Projected-raster geometry

(c) Environment-scan geometry

(d) Edge-generation geometry

Visual simulation image based on formulation environment numerical model. Perspective equations are defined by relation of environment (X,Y,Z) and image plane (x,y,z). As shown in (a), each ray from observer's eye (station point) passes through image plane to intersect environment. Numerical data, describing environment texture, are stored in computer. Visual scene generating computer solves perspective equations and defines color of each environment point projected onto the image plane. Projected-raster technique, shown in (b), generates ground-and-sky-plane perspective scenes. Environment-scan system (c) is employed to generate images of more complex environments. Edge-generation geometry (d) establishes three-dimensional images of objects with six degrees of freedom.

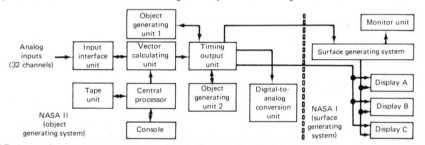

NASA-GE electronic scene generator system block diagram. The NASA 11 subsystem generates the three-dimensional objects, which may be located anywhere on the infinite, textured planar surfaces generated by the NASA 1 subsystem. NASA 11 system generates up to 40 objects in high-resolution color with 10 MHz video, 614 lines and 1000 color shades.

Computer-generated perspective images are projected on a display to impart real-time motion to objects and vehicles in space. The operator manipulates the controls as he would in a real craft, relative to points in the view shown in the display, such as ground terrain, an aircraft carrier, or other moving objects. Three image-generating techniques: (1) projected-raster, (2) environment-scan, and (3) edge-generation, develop textured pattern surfaces, objects on the surface and three-dimensional objects. All are viewed on the color display. Scenes can be controlled with six-degrees-of-freedom, with three view capability. For example, vehicle A can be seen from vehicle B, B from A, or A and B from a third point. A wide selection of scenes to be simulated is stored on punched paper tapes. These scenes include airport landing strips, aircraft carrier decks, space vehicle docking, and aircraft dogfights. The display system was built by General Electric Electronics Laboratory for NASA Manned Spacecraft Center, Houston, Texas.

Figure 8-15 continued.

- The operation or problem to be analyzed is selected.

- The critical factors affecting or relating to the operation or problem are established. A descriptive model may then be prepared to indicate the various factors and interrelationships required to produce the desired effects. Inputs required from real life are then evaluated.

- The types of representation or reproduction that can suitably simulate the desired effects are determined. The similarity of these selections to real-life conditions must be as close as possible, within the constraints of cost, size, weight, and complexity.

- Selections are made of equipment, such as analogue or digital computers; type of simulations, such as physical, psychological, or physiological; and man-machine interfaces, such as displays, controls, and other outputs and inputs.

- Real-life inputs are obtained or prepared and furnished as inputs to computers as the bases for simulation. Other required parametric data and adjustments are incorporated, and the entire system is integrated.

- Necessary adjustments are made, and the system is tested to determine its fidelity to real-life situations.

- If simulation is inadequate, the entire process is reviewed to ensure that the model, method of simulation, and input data are sufficient and correct.

- When simulation appears to be adequate, identical tests or operations using the simulator and real-life equipment are conducted. Any possible differences are determined. Necessary adjustments are made or simulated results evaluated in terms of these differences.

- Intended tests, operations, analyses, or studies within the established and determined limitations and differences are conducted.

- Simulator data are updated as additional information from real-life situations, conditions, and operations are obtained.

Limitations Simulation is a means to study an end result or how it can be generated or affected, but it is not an end result in itself, like a prototype. Failure to include all pertinent factors in a simulation may produce results different from those that would be generated in a real-world situation. On the other hand, in some instances, inclusion of all factors may make the simulation process so complex and costly it becomes impracticable. Judicious compromises must therefore be made where necessary to employ simulators for evaluation of factors actually needed. Results must be interpreted in terms of limitations imposed by the compromises.

A simulator for contingency training has one major drawback: The person undergoing training expects the contingency and is alert for it, although he may not know exactly when it will take place. In a real-world situation, a contingency is wholly unexpected; so much so that it may cause a shock to the operators, possibly impairing their performance.

Similarly, the effect of time compression means that to accomplish an operation in a simulator requires much less time than an actual flight. The person using the simulator is therefore less fatigued and less liable to make errors.

In flight simulation, films are prepared by flying a photo plane over the landing, takeoff, or cruise path to be programmed into the computer of the simulator. By special photography and computer techniques, deviations can be shown if the pilot using the simulator veers from the normal flight path. However, the deviations that can be shown are limited; wide ones are impossible.

The chief problem for accident analysis is that outputs depend on inputs. It frequently happens that accidents are caused by factors never considered, incompatibilities or combinations that were unknown prior to the mishap, or events or conditions with such low probabilities that they were not programmed into the simulator. Simulators may therefore be valuable tools but only within limits.

chapter 9

QUANTITATIVE SAFETY ANALYSES

It was pointed out in Chapter 5 that quantitative safety analyses could be relativistic or probabilistic. Relativistic methods were discussed in the same section. Probabilistic methods have been touched upon in Failure Modes and Effects analysis, Critical Component analysis, and in quantification of human error under Procedure Analysis. These methods have sometimes proved inadequate where complex designs and affecting factors involve conditional probabilities and long sequences and affecting factors involve conditional probabilities and long sequences of events. Methods using Boolean logic are therefore being employed more and more in safety analysis. (The basics of Boolean algebra and some applications are indicated in Fig. 9-1.) Some of these methods, such as network logic analysis, were evolved for use in other disciplines and for other applications but can be fruitful as a means of determining and evaluating problems that could generate hazards in products and systems. Other methods, such as Fault Tree Analysis, were developed primarily for safety studies. Network logic analysis, Fault Tree Analysis, and the safety trees described in Chapter 5 are all logic techniques. Network analysis, from which the Fault Tree method was derived, was used to determine the probability of inadvertent activation of the Poseidon fleet ballistic missile; Fault Tree Analysis was similarly used for the Minuteman Intercontinental Ballistic Missile.

In spite of the objections often raised (see page 249), probability estimates of safety levels are being increasingly used by government agencies in providing targets for system designers. In the past, some of the levels have been chosen rather arbitrarily, being adjusted values derived from operational data of doubtful value. It is expected that usage may improve correlation between theory and practice.

Dependable numerical safety data and levels can be usefully applied in:

1. Determinations of probabilities of failure or of inadvertent operation of products and subsystems through network logic analysis. Applications to safety involving electrical systems are pointed out later in greater detail. Little use has been made of logic analysis, using network theory, of mechanical systems, especially for safety purposes. However, the developing symbology for hydraulic and pneumatic systems will permit logic analyses of such equipment. Logic analysis has already been applied to fluidic systems, themselves in a state of development. Analogies have often been made between hydraulic and electrical systems, and comparable analogies can be made between electronic and fluidic circuits. Logic analysis can also provide an extremely useful means by which effects of various failure modes and design inadequacies can be determined in hydraulic and pneumatic systems when suitable constraints are applied to modulating and multiposition components.

2. Evaluations of attrition rates on which system and product replacement planning are predicated. The attrition rate is based on expected losses that are due to accidents (for military equipment during peacetime) and therefore are dependent on the accident rate. Design deficiencies constitute a portion of all accident causes, and can be approximated; design safety levels and attrition rates can therefore be correlated. If the stipulated

BOOLEAN LOGIC AND ITS APPLICATIONS

Boolean algebra was developed originally for the study of symbolic logic. Its rules and expressions in mathematical symbols permit complicated propositions to be clarified and simplified. Boolean algebra is especially useful where conditions can be expressed in no more than two values, such as yes or no, true or false, on or off, up or down, go or no-go. It has found wide application in areas other than symbolic logic. For example, it is used extensively in the design of computers and other electromechanical assemblies incorporating large numbers of on-off (switching) circuits. Other uses are in probability analysis, studies involving decision making, and more recently, in safety and fluidics. The chief difference between the various disciplines in their employment of Boolean algebra is in notation and symbology. Since the information in this section presents basic elements only, expressions most commonly found in safety analyses will be used.

A <u>set</u> is a group of objects having at least one characteristic in common. The set may be a collection of objects, conditions, events, symbols, ideas, or mathematical relationships. The unity of a set can be expressed by the number 1, and an empty set, which contains none of these, by 0. The numerals 1 and 0 are not quantitative values: $1 + 1$ does not equal 2. They are merely symbols. There are no values between the two as there are in probability calculations. Set relationships are sometimes illustrated by Venn diagrams. The following rectangle represents a set of elements that have an undefined common characteristic. In addition, a subset has the characteristic A. All other elements in the set do not have the A-characteristic and are considered being "not-A," designated by $\bar{A}$. $\bar{A}$ is the <u>complement</u> of A, and vice versa. It can be seen that the total of A and $\bar{A}$ is the complete set, expressed mathematically by $A + \bar{A} = 1$, where the left side of the equation is the <u>union</u> of A and $\bar{A}$. The + sign is read "OR", and may be designated in mathematical expressions by other symbols, such as U.

The second diagram illustrates the concept of <u>disjoint</u>, or <u>mutually exclusive</u>, sets. The elements of one subset are not included in the others, and therefore are not interrelated (other than being in the same set). In this case, however, because A, B, and C contain all the elements in the overall set, they are said to be mutually exclusive and <u>exhaustive</u>: $A + B + C = 1$.

The third diagram indicates that some elements of A also have B characteristics. These are indicated by AB, $A \cdot B$ or $A \cap B$, called the <u>intersection</u> of A and B. The intersection contains all the elements with the characteristics of both A <u>and</u> B. When all elements with the characteristic A are counted, those in AB will also be counted. The remaining diagrams in the row illustrate some of the relationships between union, intersection, and complement. Numerous other relationships that can be employed in mathematical expressions have been developed, some of them having been designed as <u>laws</u>. These are listed below, with some explanations on their meaning in Boolean logic.

RELATIONSHIP	LAW	EXPLANATION
$A \cdot 1 = A$	Full and Empty Sets	The only portion within 1 that is both 1 <u>and</u> A is that within A itself.
$A \cdot 0 = 0$		An impossible condition; if it is within the set, it cannot be outside the set.
$A + 0 = A$		The element in a subset plus anything outside the set will have only the characteristics of the subset.
$A + 1 = 1$		The whole, expressed by 1, cannot be exceeded.
$\bar{\bar{A}} = A$	Involution Law	The complement of the complement is the item itself.
$A \cdot \bar{A} = 0$	Complementary Relations	An impossibility; a condition cannot be both A <u>and</u> $\bar{A}$ at the same time.
$A + \bar{A} = 1$		Those elements with a specific characteristic and those without it constitute the total set.
$A \cdot A = A$	Idempotent Laws	An identity.
$A + A = A$		Also an identity.
$A \cdot B = B \cdot A$	Commutative Laws	The elements having both characteristics have them no matter the order in which expressed.

Figure 9-1

RELATIONSHIP	LAW	EXPLANATION
A + B = B + A		The total of those elements having the characteristic A or B will be the same no matter the order in which they are expressed.
A(B·C) = (A·B)C	Associative Laws	The elements having all the characteristics A, B and C will have them no matter the order in which expressed.
A + (B + C) = (A + B) + C		The total of all the elements in any subsets will be the same no matter the order in which expressed.
A(B + C) = (A·B) + (A·C)	Distributive Laws	The union of one subset with two others can also be expressed as the union of their intersections.
A + (B·C) = (A + B)·(A + C)		The union of one subset with the intersection of two others can also be expressed by the intersection of the unions of the common subset with the other two.
A(A + B) = A	Absorption Laws	A(A + B) = AA + AB = A + AB since AA = A; A + AB = A(1 + B) = A since B is included in 1.
A + (A·B) = A		A + (A·B) = A + AB $\doteq$ A(1 + B) = A.
$\overline{A·B} = \overline{A} + \overline{B}$	Dualization (de Morgan's) Laws	The complement of an intersection is the union of the individual complements.
$\overline{A + B} = \overline{A}·\overline{B}$		The complement of the union is the intersection of the complements.

Other useful identities are frequently used for simplification of complex Boolean equations. Four of these are:

Identity	Derivation
A + $\overline{A}$B = A + B	Using the Distributive Law: (A + $\overline{A}$) · (A + B) = A + B
A·($\overline{A}$ + B) = AB	Using the Distributive Law: A · $\overline{A}$ + AB = AB
(A + B)($\overline{A}$ + C) · (A + C) = AC + BC	Expanding the last two terms: (A + B) (A$\overline{A}$ + AC + $\overline{A}$C + CC); CC = C, A$\overline{A}$ = 0, AC + $\overline{A}$C = C(A + $\overline{A}$) = C(1) = C, and C + C = C; ∴ remainder is (A + B)C, or AC + BC.
AB + $\overline{A}$C + BC = AB + $\overline{A}$C	This can be simplified by adding a term such as A + $\overline{A}$. The left-hand side then becomes: AB + $\overline{A}$C + BC(A + $\overline{A}$) = AB (1 + C) + $\overline{A}$C(1 + B) = AB + $\overline{A}$C.

With the development of Boolean logic for electronic systems, the concept of gates or connectives was introduced. The symbols for these, a few of which are shown and explained below, are used in logic diagrams to indicate the interrelationships in circuits. These circuits employ numerous bi-stable, or two-state, devices, that can be considered open or closed, off or on. These are known as switching functions, and the mathematics is called switching algebra or network logic.

The truth tables shown on the right are means to indicate when a specific state will exist as an output when any combination of inputs is present. As shown here, the symbol 1 indicates that an input or output is or will be present; the 0 indicates that it is not or will not be present. Each of the truth tables shown is for a two-input gate. Gates with more inputs are more common, differing only in complexity.

Figure 9-1 continued.

Quantitative Safety Analyses

safety level for a design cannot be met, an attrition rate higher than planned must be expected.

3. Comparisons that can be made of two or more choices of designs, equipment or components, courses of action, or man-machine relationships. Probabilities of success or accident, even though not entirely accurate, can be indicative of differences between available selections. Expression in this way of comparative values can do much to determine whether investment of additional funds to improve safety is justified.

4. The probabilities in risk determination (see Chapter 4), on which the entire insurance industry is founded. Here it can be pointed

GATE (CONNECTIVE)	SYMBOL	EXPLANATION	TRUTH TABLE	

OR

Symbol: A + B (OR gate), inputs A and B

The OR connective indicates that when one or more of the inputs or governing conditions is present, the statement will be true or an output will result. Conversely, the statement will be false if, and only if, none of the governing conditions is present.

A + B		OR	
0	0	0	(False)
0	1	1	(True)
1	0	1	(True)
1	1	1	(True)

AND

Symbol: A · B (AND gate), inputs A and B

The AND connective indicates that all of the governing conditions or inputs must be present for a statement to be true. If one of the conditions or inputs is missing, the statement is false.

A · B		AND	
0	0	0	(False)
0	1	0	(False)
1	0	0	(False)
1	1	1	(True)

NOR

Symbol: A + B (NOR gate), inputs A and B

The NOR connective may be considered a "not OR" state. It indicates that when one or more of the inputs is present, the statement will be false or no output will result. When none of the inputs, neither A nor B, is present, an output will result.

A + B		NOR	
0	0	1	(True)
0	1	0	(False)
1	0	0	(False)
1	1	0	(False)

NAND

Symbol: A · B (NAND gate), inputs A and B

The NAND connective indicates that when all of the inputs or governing conditions or inputs are not present, the statement will be true or there will be an output. When all of the inputs or governing conditions are present, the statement will be false or there will be no output.

A	B	NAND	
0	0	1	(True)
0	1	1	(True)
1	0	1	(True)
1	1	0	(False)

out that methods of hazard analysis presented in this book are as applicable to risk determination for insurance purposes as they are for accident prevention.

Figure 9-1 continued.

Network Logic Analysis

Network analysis by application of Boolean logic techniques has been employed for many years in the design and evaluation of complex electrical and electronic circuitry. Its use is increasing as systems grow more complex, as the consequences of failures increase, as familiarity with its methodology grows, and as new applications are found. It has not only been employed to determine how safety of a system can be affected by failures of components in a circuit but also whether the circuit can generate damaging outputs or failure modes. It can therefore be used for interface analysis. It can be employed to establish the possible modes in which a damaging event could occur in electrical or electronic subsystems. It can provide the means to establish the quantitative safety level of a system. The principles involved also formed the basis for the Fault Tree method, described in the next section, which it sometimes complements at certain levels of analysis.

In network analysis, system operation is described in terms of interacting electronic circuits and mechanical devices, which open or close to permit flow of energy from one point to another. These circuit devices are then represented by logic elements. A logic equation can be developed to express the condition (on or off, open or closed, successful or failed) of each element required to produce an output event.

Network Logic Analysis

229

The equations can be simplified to eliminate redundant expressions and to highlight signal flow paths.

In logic analysis each network element is identified by a symbol (see Fig. 9-1.) Starting with the end event, a Boolean equation is written expressing the conditions that could cause it to occur. The equation represents each element involved in causing or permitting such an event and the input and output conditions to that element.

The expression for each element, in addition to describing its inputs and outputs, must include a term indicating that it will operate properly. For example, an output may be generated from a relay if, and only if, three inputs take place simultaneously *and* the relay itself operates properly. Specific symbols may be designated to distinguish between inputs to an element and its operation. In the example used later, parentheses and brackets indicate inputs and outputs; a symbol not enclosed represents the operation of the element itself. The same symbols can also designate the *probability* that the operation being considered will take place.

A separate equation is written for each gate. These equations are then combined in chains of events leading to investigation of the ultimate event. This produces one set of equations representing the series of elements and conditions that can cause that ultimate event. These equations are often very complex initially, especially when all are incorporated into a single master equation. However, it is frequently possible to apply reduction techniques to simplify them by eliminating logical redundancies. This consists of the use of the Boolean identities and relationships in Fig. 9-1. For example, a logic chain, which consists of $AB \cdot AC \cdot BD(AB + \overline{AC})$, can first be expanded to $AB \cdot AC \cdot BD \cdot AB + AB \cdot AC \cdot BD \cdot \overline{AC}$. One redundant AB in the first group can be eliminated, leaving $AB \cdot AC \cdot BD$. Also, since $AC \cdot \overline{AC} = 0$ (AC cannot be both on and off at the same time), the second term can be eliminated entirely. The final expression is therefore $AB \cdot AC \cdot BD$.

The final equation indicates those factors whose condition will affect operation of the system to produce the end event being investigated. The state of a connective, either on or off, which will produce this end event will be shown by the mathematical symbol. This state will point up the failure mode which will have an adverse effect on the system. Parallel or redundant paths are shown as sums, whereas series (nonredundant paths) are shown as products, either as an individual event or in a bracketed sum of events. A failure of any item in a series will prevent an output through that path. It should be noted here that a failure does not indicate in many cases that the device is open (which may be its normal, designed mode) but that it does not operate as required.

Systems that are designed so they will *not* operate until specific events occur involve the concept of *blocking elements*. Blocking elements are those components, assemblies, or designs that in normal modes will contribute to the safety of the system. A blocking element could consist of a device that must be activated or inactivated for the system to operate. The method to accomplish activation could be an action by a person or the result of a mechanical or electrical process. Electrical interlocks are blocking elements. Mechanical devices as blocking elements are common to ordnance systems. Safe-and-arm devices are examples. For an explosion to occur, the blocks provided by the safe-and-arm must first be removed. The acceleration of a missile or shell may remove a block to permit a timer or timed rotating device to achieve a state permitting the next step in the arming or activation train. This procedure ensures that the missile is distant enough from the launcher or the shell from the gun so that any early burst will not cause injury or damage to the operators. Knowledge of the safe distance and velocity permits determination of the time interval for safety.

Another group of blocking devices are pressure sensitive. A baroswitch operates with change of atmospheric pressure. A block may be removed when pressure drops to a preset level, as in a surface-to-air missile; increases to a specific level, as in a bomb; or both. Both types may be incorporated in a warhead, which must first pass through decreasing air pressure to its set level and then through an increasing air pressure phase. Other types of pressure switches include those requiring a specific depth of water to operate. Depth charges are examples of ordnance utilizing this type of device.

A blocking element such as those described may then be connected to a device installed in a circuit to prevent passage of current unless the prescribed condition is satisfied. When it is, the device, such as a relay, will change its state to an unsafe, *operable* mode.

When counting blocking elements, only those series elements that actually perform blocking functions should be included. In systems with interacting elements, certain elements that supposedly act as blocks may be bypassed along other paths and will not serve as independent blocks. Where two or more parallel paths exist, the effective number of blocks is the number in the shortest path. This is the smallest *number* of elements that must be changed from a safe to an unsafe state. It should be pointed out, however, that the number of blocking elements in each of two or more paths is not the only criterion on which to establish whether one path is safer than another. One path may have only two blocking elements, but their failure probabilities may be far less than those in paths with more blocks. The first arrangement would then have a lesser probability of a mishap.

The number of blocking elements present in a system is governed by the configuration at any specific time. Logic analysis can therefore be employed to establish when a system with numerous blocking elements that must be removed to operate becomes unsafe. After analysis indicates which and how many blocks exist, a program can be developed that will show when each one is removed as an operation progresses through a program. Indicators can be provided to show when only a specific number of blocks remain or when the system is enabled to operate.

For example, the procedures and concepts just indicated can now be applied to an analysis of a missile destruct system. Each of the large test or practice missiles fired on ranges are provided with a destruct system for flight safety. If a missile flight is unsuccessful, so it appears that it will violate establish range safety limits, the range safety officer can terminate the flight by activating the destruct system. An analysis must establish not only that this step can occur as programmed but also that it will not occur inadvertently. Such premature operation could cause injury and damage if it happened on or close to the ground and could cause loss of the missile in flight. The system must therefore be analyzed for two conditions: inadvertent activation and activation when required in flight.

The missile is destroyed by initiating explosive charges on the

Network Logic Analysis

forward dome of the rocket motor case or cases. These linear charges produce large eccentric openings in the case from which gases from the burning propellants are vented. As a result, there is a zero net thrust on the missile and missile tumbling, which prevents it from impacting outside range limits.

There are two ways by which the flight can be terminated: *command* destruct and *automatic* destruct. Command destruct is at the discretion of the Range Safety Officer when he observes an unsafe flight condition, such as an obviously erratic flight, possibility of flight outside of the established impact limit line, or loss of flight tracking data. Destruct is directed by means of a coded signal transmitted from the ground. The missile receives, demodulates, and decodes the signal, and a direct current destruct signal voltage is applied to the destruct initiation units. Tumbling due to loss of control, premature separation, or vehicle breakup causes automatic destruct. This autodestruct may also be initiated by such conditions as loss of electrical power combined with high acceleration (over 1.5 g).

Figure 9-2 is the functional block diagram; and Fig. 9-3, the logic diagram for a missile destruct system. The OR and AND symbols indicate the relationships between the inputs and outputs, but any proper analysis must also study the failure modes of each component to determine

Fig. 9-2. Simplified Functional Destruct System Diagram.

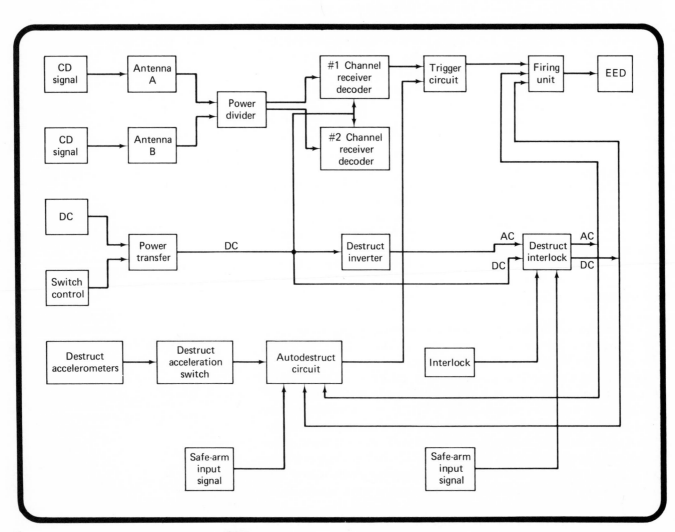

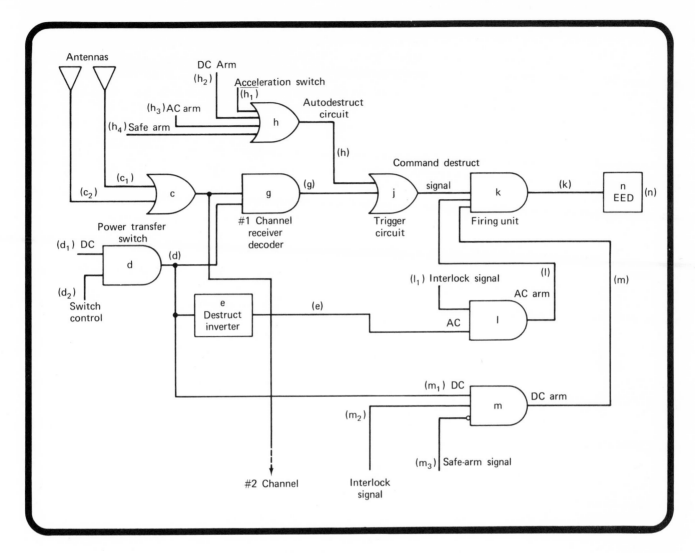

Fig. 9-3. Simplified Destruct System Logic Diagram.

all the problems that could occur. Relays can mulfunction in five ways: fail open, fail shorted, intermittent operation, sticking, and arcing. Intermittent operation may cause outputs to produce pulses similar to those activating code-operated devices. The intermittent pulses from the relay may inadvertently generate the proper code to trigger other blocking elements prematurely. The safety of the system would then be compromised.

Logic diagrams are developed from wiring diagrams (not shown here) which, in turn, are developed from functional block diagrams. Generally, two firing units for initiating the explosion are provided for each location where destruct action is to occur. Because these are redundant and similar, logic analysis of one is sufficient to indicate whether the design is adequate for established criteria, whether inadequacies exist, and where precautionary measures should be incorporated. Some of these measures include separation of circuits and protection of critical components and wiring. Two independent destruct channels are generally provided, including separate power supplies, electronic control circuits, and ordnance initiation devices. Design is such that no single component failure can prevent proper operation.

At least two blocks are maintained prior to launch, when premature

Network Logic Analysis

233

ignition would be hazardous to personnel, equipment, and facilities. Both must fail in order to generate a dangerous situation. The destruct system can be armed only by a control signal from an accelerometer, which indicates that the missile has been launched. The number of active circuits is minimized as long as the missile is on the pad to prevent any cross talk that could induce voltages in the destruct system. External power from the launch facility is supplied only to the radio frequency link checks prior to launch. Other circuits are without power until switch-over to battery power immediately prior to launch. This satisfies a requirement for minimum probability of premature operation before lift-off.

The first part of the analysis is undertaken to determine:

(1) the sequences of events leading to normal, programmed activation;

(2) blocking elements that must be removed for normal operation and that safeguard the system against unscheduled activation; and

(3) how those blocking elements can be bypassed or removed.

For this last determination, the failure modes of all elements of the system must be studied. It must establish whether the failure mode will be fail-safe and, in this case, permit destruct system operation, or degrade its operation. Since each failure mode is dependent on the individual characteristics of the component used, it is impossible to illustrate this last example here except in generalities.

The following symbols and equations describe logically the conditions under which the destruct system will work properly during flight. In the equations, letters within parentheses indicate inputs and outputs; those without parentheses represent the units or components themselves.

$$(n) = n(k) \qquad\qquad (k) = (j)(l)(m)k$$

The output of n (ignition) will occur if n operates properly and there is a signal from k.

An output from k will occur if there are inputs from j, l *and* m, and k works properly.

$$(j) = [(h) + (g)]j \qquad\qquad (l) = (l_1)(e)l$$
$$(m) = (d)(m_2)(m_3)m \qquad (h) = (h_1 + h_2 + h_3 + h_4)h$$
$$(d) = (d_1)(d_2)d = (m_1) \qquad (g) = (c)(d)g$$
$$(c) = [(c_1) + (c_2)]c \qquad (e) = (d)e$$

Substituting:

$$(n) = n(j)(l)(m)k$$
$$= n[(h_1 + h_2 + h_3 + h_4)h + (c)(d)g]$$
$$\quad j(l_1)(d)el(d_1)(d_2)d(m_2)(m_3)mk$$
$$= n\{(h_1 + h_2 + h_3 + h_4)h + [(c_1) + (c_2)]c(d_1)(d_2)dg\}j(l_1)$$
$$\quad (d_1)(d_2)del(d_1)(d_2)d(m_2)(m_3)mk$$

Here $(d_1)(d_2)d$ occurs twice outside the brackets and can be reduced to a single expression. The same term inside the brackets can also be dropped, leaving:

$$(n) = n\{(h_1 + h_2 + h_3 + h_4)h + [(c_1) + (c_2)]cg\}$$
$$j(l_1)(d_1)(d_2)del(m_2)(m_3)mk$$

Progressive elimination of the blocks by a switching program will alter this expression and reduce, step by step, the number of blocks in effect at any time. Finally, only the operation of the trigger circuit will remain, with only a signal from either autodestruct or command destruct required for ignition. At this point, j, k and n will have essentially been unblocked and vulnerable to an input signal. Once the signal is provided through the trigger circuit, ignition will occur.

The last equation shows 12 independent factors outside the bracketed expression, which constitutes a 13th. Failure of any one of these will cause a failure of (n), so the destruct system will not operate. The two major terms inside the brackets indicate that both the auto-destruct aspects *and* the command destruct must fail for total loss from lack of an initiating signal. Failure of any one of the factors outside of the brackets is common to both the autodestruct and command destruct and will render the system inoperative.

The reliability of the destruct system depends principally on the reliabilities of the 13 independent factors. (Connections and wiring are not considered.) In these cases, designs should attempt to ensure fail-safe conditions; that is, that the system will operate if an element fails.

To determine whether inadvertent activation can take place, each blocking element must be examined. In this case, the expression *failure mode* is not proper, and the examination must be conducted with a view to damage that could result from any unprogrammed event. For example, n represents the electroexplosive device (EED). Its manufacturer might indicate that its reliability is 0.995 and that the probability of its not working (failure) is 0.005. Failure in this sense will not result in inadvertent activation. The EED can be activated itself by static electricity or high temperature. The other blocking elements would be ineffective in such a case. (A complete, rigorous analysis must determine the effects of similar factors on each of the blocks.)

In addition, the analysis must consider what the effects might be of spurious inputs. The equation (n) = n(k) states that the EED will activate with an output signal from k (assuming n works properly). However, in case of a short circuit or inductive coupling in the line from k to n (the electromagnetic radiation hazard), k will be bypassed. The need for protection is apparent. This is the reason that connectors to EEDs should not contain any pins or connections for other circuits that will be activated and the reason for shielding against electromagnetic radiation.

The second part of the analysis is to establish the possibility of failure of the system at a time when it should operate. The previous equation indicated 13 blocking elements, the failure of any one of which could result in system failure. However, to determine the overall probability of failure, all individual failures and combinations must be computed. Use of the complements of reliability (failures) provides an easier means.

Each symbol in the equation indicates the condition that could contribute to a system failure. The NOT symbol (dash over the letter) is used in this case, therefore assuming that *any* mode of failure will contribute to the ignition failure.

Starting from the right side of Fig. 9-3:

$$(\bar{n}) = \bar{n} + (\bar{k})$$

The EED, n, will not operate if the EED itself fails or if no signal is received from the firing unit, k.

$$(\bar{k}) = \bar{k} + (\bar{j}) + (\bar{l}) + (\bar{m})$$

There will be no output from the firing unit, k, if the unit itself fails or if there is no input from either the trigger circuit, AC arm or DC arm units.

$$(\bar{j}) = \bar{j} + (\bar{g})(\bar{h})$$

There will be no output from the trigger circuit if the trigger circuit element itself fails, or if both the No. 1 channel Receiver Decoder *and* Autodestruct Circuit Unit fail.

$$(\bar{g}) = \bar{g} + (\bar{c}) + (\bar{d}) = \bar{g} + \bar{c} + (\bar{c}_1)(\bar{c}_2) + \bar{d} + (\bar{d}_1) + (\bar{d}_2)$$
$$(\bar{h}) = \bar{h} + (\bar{h}_1)(\bar{h}_2)(\bar{h}_3)(\bar{h}_4)$$
$$(\bar{l}) = \bar{l} + (\bar{e}) + (\bar{l}_1) = \bar{l} + (\bar{l}_1) + \bar{e} + \bar{d} + (\bar{d}_1) + (\bar{d}_2)$$
$$(\bar{m}) = \bar{m} + (\bar{m}_2) + (\bar{m}_3) + (\bar{d})$$
$$= \bar{m} + (\bar{m}_2) + (\bar{m}_3) + \bar{d} + (\bar{d}_1) + (\bar{d}_2)$$

Then:

$$(\bar{n}) = \bar{n} + \bar{k} + \bar{j} + [\bar{g} + \bar{c} + (\bar{c}_1)(\bar{c}_2) + \bar{d} + (\bar{d}_1) + (\bar{d}_2)]$$
$$[\bar{h} + (\bar{h}_1)(\bar{h}_2)(\bar{h}_3)(\bar{h}_4)] + \bar{l} + (\bar{l}_1) + \bar{e} + \bar{d} + (\bar{d}_1) + (\bar{d}_2)$$
$$+ \bar{m} + (\bar{m}_2) + (\bar{m}_3) + \bar{d} + (\bar{d}_1) + (\bar{d}_2)$$

All the identities of $\bar{d}$, $(\bar{d}_1)$ and $(\bar{d}_2)$ except one can be eliminated. The final equation will therefore be:

$$(\bar{n}) = \bar{n} + \bar{k} + \bar{j} + [\bar{g} + \bar{c} + (\bar{c}_1)(\bar{c}_2)][\bar{h} + (\bar{h}_1)(\bar{h}_2)(\bar{h}_3)(\bar{h}_4)]$$
$$+ \bar{l} + (\bar{l}_1) + \bar{e} + \bar{m} + (\bar{m}_2) + (\bar{m}_3) + \bar{d} + (\bar{d}_1) + (\bar{d}_2)$$

Insertion of probabilities for each of these factors will generate the probability of failure of the destruct system.

The benefits that can be derived from analysis of a system by this logic method include:

- Determination of the components and interconnections that must be safeguarded or separated to ensure that blocking elements are not bypassed.
- Evaluations of locations where single point failures are possible.
- Determination of places where greatest benefits can be derived from use of high reliability components.
- Identification of points at which connections should be made if monitor or test systems are to be incorporated

Quantitative Safety Analyses

Quantitative analyses can be made by inserting a probability value for each factor in a Boolean equation, as indicated above. However, care must be taken to ensure that the value actually represents the mathematical expression and all affecting states. For example, if an expression is based on a relay failing to open, the probability value must correspond, and not include all modes of relay failure. Quantitative analyses made in this way can establish:

- Probability of success or failure of an entire network or system.

- Probability of failure of each blocking element. Since the number of blocking elements will be established by the analysis, the overall safety level of the system analyzed can be determined.

- Where improvements in design can best be made to benefit the safety of the system.

It was mentioned earlier that the number of applications of logic analysis to electrical and electronic systems is increasing. Some of these applications with safety implications include:

- Investigation of the possibilities of inadvertent activation of ordnance devices or solid-propellant motors by electrical or electromechanical means. Analyses of safeguards against accidental detonations of nuclear weapons were early applications of this method.

- Failure analysis of such devices as fuel quantity indicators, malfunction detection systems, submarine hatch closure monitoring systems, and warning systems.

- Investigation of interlocks to ensure: orderly operation of timed or load-sensitive devices that must be activated sequentially, de-energization of electrical equipment if access panels or doors are opened, and the interrelationships of blocking elements to prevent occurrences of adverse events.

- Analysis of electrical connectors to determine effects that could be generated if: one-half of a connector were wired incorrectly; one or more pins were bent and touched other pins or the connector shell; one or more pins were missing; moisture, debris, solder particles, or pieces of cut wire short-circuited all or various combinations of pins; or circuits were grounded due to a damaged connector. Connectors have been sources of concern in almost every aerospace system because of the problems they have generated. This method of analysis could therefore permit concentrated effort on the most critical items. If bending of a specific pin could generate a highly damaging condition, action could be taken, such as increasing the pin diameter, to prevent bending. Where short-circuiting between two pins could also create a problem, the pins could be separated by other pins, guards, or use of two connectors instead of one.

- Design and analysis of electronic and electromechanical systems for aircraft (see Chapter 10), which use logic techniques such as majority voting, median selection, TRISAFE (Triple Redundancy Incorporating Self-Adaptive Failure Exclusion), and self-organizing concept.

- Determination of fail-safe designs that will produce minimal damage in event of a malfunction of electrical equipment.

Fault Tree Analysis

Fault Tree Analysis was developed by Bell Telephone Laboratories in 1962 at the request of the Air Force for use with the Minuteman ICBM system. Bell personnel, longtime users of Boolean logic methods for communications equipment, adapted its principles to create the method. Engineers and mathematicians of the Boeing Company devoted much effort to develop its procedures further and became its foremost proponents. Most of the information contained in this section is therefore taken from documents published by the Boeing Company or presented by its personnel at technical meetings.

Fault Tree Analysis is an excellent method (within its limitations) for studying the factors that could cause an undesirable event (fault, primary hazard, or catastrophe) to occur. The Bell Telephone Laboratories study was undertaken to determine those combinations of events and circumstances that could cause specific catastrophes, one of which was the unauthorized launch of a Minuteman missile. Reliability analysis methods in use at that time did not lend themselves well to determination of possibilities and probabilities of occurrence of these events because of the complex interrelationships of matériel, personnel, and environmental factors. Fault Tree Analysis finds its best application in such complex situations because of the systematic way that the various factors can be presented. It is, in effect, a model to which probability data can be applied in logical sequences.

Broadly, the method may be described as follows:

1. The undesirable event, or fault, whose possibility or probability is to be determined is selected. This event may be inadvertent or unauthorized launch of a missile, failure of an aircraft in flight, ignition of an ordnance device, injury to personnel, or any similar mishap.

2. System requirements, function, design, environment, and other factors are reviewed to determine conditions, events, and failures that could contribute to an occurrence of the undesired event.

3. A tree is prepared by diagraming contributory events and failures systematically to show their relation to each other and to the undesirable event being investigated. The process begins with the events that could directly cause the undesirable event (first level). As the procedure goes back step-by-step, combinations of events and failures that could bring about the end result are added. The diagrams so prepared are called *fault trees*.

4. The circumstances under which each of the events in the fault tree could occur are determined. Each component of the subsystem capable of producing an event is examined and how its failure would contribute to a mishap determined. Other conditions or personnel actions that could have adverse effects are also included.

5. Suitable mathematical expressions representing the fault tree entries are developed using Boolean algebra. When more than one event on a chart can contribute to the same effect, the chart and the Boolean expression indicate whether the input events must all act in combination (AND relationship) to produce the effect, or whether they may act singly (OR relationship). The mathematical expression of the AND/OR relationships for the tree is then simplified as much as possible.

6. The probability of failure of each component or of the occurrence of each condition or listed event is determined. These probabilities may be from failure rates obtained by past experience; vendors' test data; comparison with similar equipment, events, or conditions; or experimental data obtained specifically for the system.

7. These probabilities are then entered into the simplified Boolean expressions. The probability of occurrence of the undesirable event being investigated is then determined by calculation.

8. Other fallouts from use of the trees can be: determination of the most critical and probable sequence of events that could produce the undesirable event, identification of the most important affecting factors, single-point failure possibilities, and discovery of any sensitive elements whose improvement could reduce the possibility or probability of a mishap.

Certain assumptions and stipulations must be made concerning the characteristics of the components, conditions, actions, and events:

1. Components, subsystems, and similar items can have only two conditional modes; they can either operate successfully or fail. No operation is partially successful.

2. Basic failures are independent of each other.

3. Each item has a constant failure rate that conforms to an exponential distribution.

The first two stipulations are necessary if Boolean logic is to be applied. In actual systems, partial failures may occur so that the system may operate to a limited degree at other than a successful or failed condition. However, the stipulation of total success or failure generally constitutes use of worst-case conditions.

The success in predicting the probability of any specific occurrence depends on how accurately the system is represented in a fault tree, the detail into which the tree enters, and validities of the mathematical expressions and probabilities employed. Interrelationships between inputs must be scrutinized carefully and provided for in the Boolean expressions if the sequences of time in which they must occur are important. For example, an AND relationship may exist when order or length of time of occurrence of the contributing input matters. Input X must occur before input Y for the event being considered to occur; or X must occur for a certain number of seconds before Y. If one input must occur before the other, the limiting condition is entered on the tree diagram as an inhibit gate, which represents AND.

The Fault Tree diagram is an excellent means of presenting relationships between events; however, the amount of information that can be included is limited. It is therefore necessary that additional information be provided to supplement that on the diagram. In many cases, this is not done. The Fault Tree then provides only a diagram indicating the interrelationships of cause and effect factors. For a quantitative analysis, especially a complex one or one with great detail or with numerous levels or factors, a computer is generally necessary to calculate the probability of any top-level event or the most critical sequence of events.

The following example utilizes diagrams and a modified description

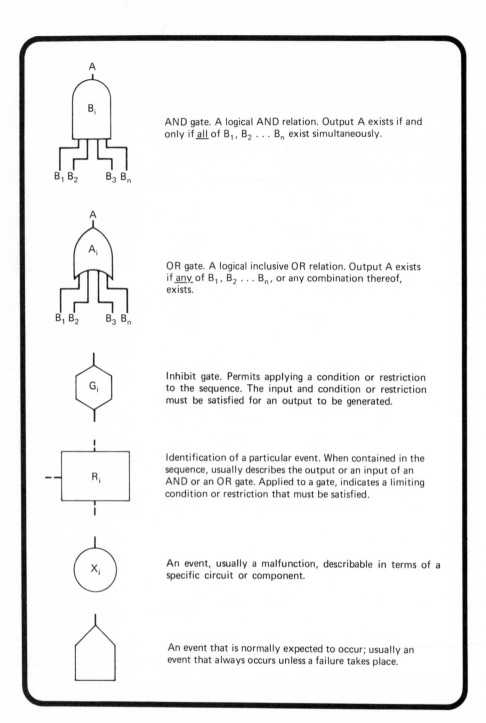

AND gate. A logical AND relation. Output A exists if and only if all of B_1, B_2 . . . B_n exist simultaneously.

OR gate. A logical inclusive OR relation. Output A exists if any of B_1, B_2 . . . B_n, or any combination thereof, exists.

Inhibit gate. Permits applying a condition or restriction to the sequence. The input and condition or restriction must be satisfied for an output to be generated.

Identification of a particular event. When contained in the sequence, usually describes the output or an input of an AND or an OR gate. Applied to a gate, indicates a limiting condition or restriction that must be satisfied.

An event, usually a malfunction, describable in terms of a specific circuit or component.

An event that is normally expected to occur; usually an event that always occurs unless a failure takes place.

Fig. 9-4. Fault tree symbols. (Letters are identification frequently used in math models.)

of the procedure presented by Haasl.* The expressions generally used to prepare Fault Trees are shown in Fig. 9-4. In this example, the event to be analyzed is the possibility of overheating of the wire shown in the upper portion of Fig. 9-5. The system is designed to activate and operate the motor whenever the switch is closed by an external control system. When the switch is closed, power is applied to the relay coil through the time contacts, closing the relay contacts and applying power through the fuse to the motor. By opening the switch, power is removed from the relay coil, opening the relay contacts and cutting off power from the

Quantitative Safety Analyses

* David Haasl, "Advanced Concepts in Fault Tree Analysis," paper presented at the System Safety Symposium, Seattle, Wash. (1965).

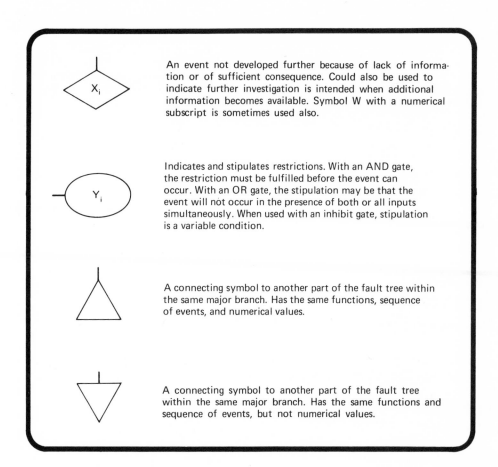

An event not developed further because of lack of information or of sufficient consequence. Could also be used to indicate further investigation is intended when additional information becomes available. Symbol W with a numerical subscript is sometimes used also.

Indicates and stipulates restrictions. With an AND gate, the restriction must be fulfilled before the event can occur. With an OR gate, the stipulation may be that the event will not occur in the presence of both or all inputs simultaneously. When used with an inhibit gate, stipulation is a variable condition.

A connecting symbol to another part of the fault tree within the same major branch. Has the same functions, sequence of events, and numerical values.

A connecting symbol to another part of the fault tree within the same major branch. Has the same functions and sequence of events, but not numerical values.

Figure 9-4 continued.

motor. The timer and fuse are safety devices. The timer contacts open and remove power from the relay coil if the switch fails to open after a preset interval. The fuse opens and de-energizes the circuit if the motor shorts while the relay contacts are closed. The critical fault to be analyzed is that wire *AB* may overheat.

The overheating may be due to two basic causes: *overcurrent in system wiring* and *power being applied to the system for an extended time*. The Fault Tree is started by showing on the lower diagram these two factors as a first level of events. An AND gate is necessary since both events must occur for an overheated wire to result. On the left side of the tree, it can be seen that an overcurrent will occur if the fuse does not open and the motor fails shorted. It should be noted here that this is a specific failure mode for the motor. Since the two events must occur to have an overcurrent, they are connected by an AND gate. The fuse will not operate if an oversized one has been installed or if the correct size one fails. This interrelationship necessitates use of an OR gate.

The same reasoning is applied to development of the lower level events in the other branches of the tree. The events represented by circles are basic faults that can generally be quantitatively verified either from records of past experience or from laboratory test. Those events that are difficult to verify are indicated by diamonds. All the events indicated by the branch under the A enclosed in the triangle at the right side of the diagram are to be repeated at the location shown by the second A at the lower left. The same is true for the events branching from the B in the triangle. (This duplication will be simplified mathematically by reduction of the Boolean equations.)

Fault Tree Analysis

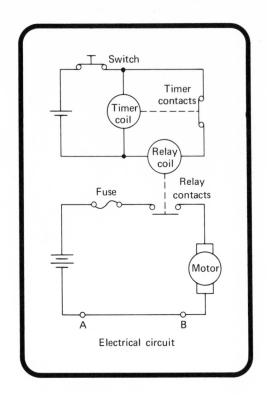

Fig. 9-5a. Fault tree example. Electrical circuit.

The events marked primary failures indicate those events that do not depend on the occurrence of other events. A secondary failure is one generated as the result of a contributory failure. Here again, some of these secondary or contributory failures may appear elsewhere on the overall tree, to be removed mathematically during the simplification process. In this way, simplification eliminates the duplication of numerical probabilities that would distort the end value.

The Boolean expressions for the logic trees in Fig. 9.5 are:

$$\text{Top} = B_1 \qquad G_1 = A_3 \cdot Y_1 \qquad B_3 = A_1 \cdot X_5$$
$$B_1 = B_2 \cdot A_4 \qquad A_3 = X_3 + B_4 \qquad B_4 = A_6 \cdot A_7$$
$$B_2 = A_1 \cdot A_2 \qquad A_4 = A_5 + B_4 \qquad A_6 = X_7 + X_8$$
$$A_1 = X_1 + X_2 \qquad A_5 = G_2 + X_6 \qquad A_7 = X_9 + X_{10}$$
$$A_2 = G_1 \cdot X_4 \qquad G_2 = B_3 \cdot Y_2$$

NO.	PART	FAILURE OR CONDITION	MTBF (HRS)*	PROBABILITY SUCCESS	FAILURE
X_1	Fuse	Oversized fuse installed	0.40×10^6	0.9975	0.0025
X_2	Fuse	Fails to blow	0.20×10^5	0.9512	0.0488
X_3	Relay	Fails closed	0.30×10^5	0.9675	0.0325
X_4	Motor	Fails shorted	0.40×10^5	0.9753	0.0247
X_5	Motor	Fails shorted	0.40×10^5	0.9753	0.0247
X_6	Relay	Contact failure	0.30×10^5	0.9975	0.0325
X_7	Timer Coil	Fails open	0.25×10^5	0.9608	0.0392
X_8	Timer Coil	Fails closed	0.25×10^5	0.9608	0.0392
X_9	Switch	Fails closed	0.35×10^5	0.9719	0.0281
X_{10}	External control	Fails to release switch	0.60×10^5	0.9836	0.0164
Y_1	Motor	Fails shorted	0.40×10^5	0.9753	0.0247
Y_2	Relay	Contacts fused	0.30×10^5	0.9675	0.0325

* Assigned, not actual, values. Duration for all operations: 1,000 hr.

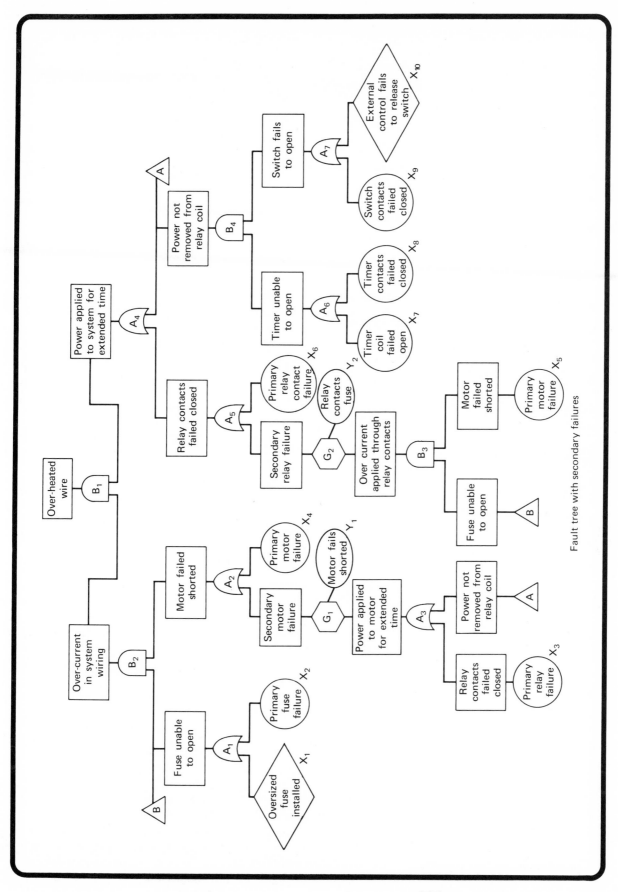

Fault tree with secondary failures

Fig. 9-5b. Fault tree.

$$B_1 = B_2A_4 = A_1A_2A_4 = (X_1 + X_2)A_2A_4 = (X_1 + X_2)(G_1X_4)A_4$$

And continuing the substitutions:

$$B_1 = (X_1 + X_2)Y_1X_4[X_3 + (X_7 + X_8)(X_9 + X_{10})]$$
$$[(X_1 + X_2)X_5Y_2 + X_6 + (X_7 + X_8)(X_9 + X_{10})]$$

From the table and trees, the following relationships are apparent:

$$X_4 = X_5 = Y_1 \text{ and } X_3 = Y_2 = X_6$$

Then:

$$Y_1X_4 = X_4 \text{ and } X_4X_5 \text{ (inside the bracket)} = X_4$$
$$\text{(Idempotent Law)}$$

The first $(X_1 + X_2)$ times $(X_1 + X_2)$ inside the bracket = $(X_1 + X_2)$ for the same reason. Therefore $(X_1 + X_2)$ inside the bracket can be replaced by unity (1). Replace X_6 and Y_2 by X_3; therefore $X_3 + X_3 = X_3$. The equation can then be rewritten with these substitutions:

$$B_1 = (X_1 + X_2)X_4[X_3 + (X_7 + X_8)(X_9 + X_{10})]$$
$$[X_3 + (X_7 + X_8)(X_9 + X_{10})]$$

The two bracketed expressions are the same, therefore one can be eliminated:

$$B_1 = (X_1 + X_2)X_4[X_3 + (X_7 + X_8)(X_9 + X_{10})]$$

Substituting the values in the table for probability of failure:

$$B_1 = (.0025 + .0488)(.0247)$$
$$[.0325 + (.0392 + .0392)(.0281 + .0164)]$$
$$= (.0513)(.0247)(.0360) = 4.57 \times 10^{-5}$$

The final Boolean expression can be redrawn for an equivalent tree (Figure 9-6). In actual practice the duration of each operation during which the fault condition could occur may differ. In such cases, they may be obtained through use of a method such as Time Sequencing (Chapter 6). Each sequence which can produce the top event can also be listed. Insertion of probability values can then be used to determine which sequence is most likely to occur.

It may be noted that in the process of simplification redundant events and secondary failures which are the same as primary failures have been eliminated. The resultant expression and tree indicates only primary failures.

Limitations

Fault Tree Analysis can be employed to better advantage if its limitations are understood. Some of these limits have already been indicated under the assumptions and stipulations for making the analyses, such as the fact that each event must be described in terms of only two possible conditions and no more.

One of the principal limitations of Fault Tree Analysis is its inadequacy at levels lower than the "black box" in electronic systems. To

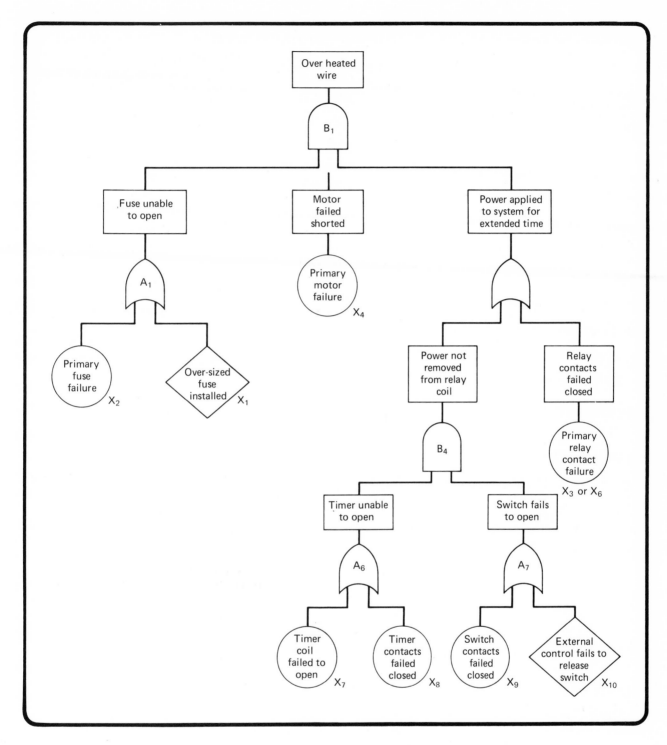

Fig. 9-6. Simplified fault tree.

make such analyses, other methods, such as network logic analysis, should be used.

When a logic tree is used for a quantitative analysis, care is required in the description of each event to be sure it can be fitted with a suitable probability. (This is no problem with network logic analysis, in which each gate or symbol is a firm statement without variation and without opportunity for misinterpretation.) Each factor that will have a quantitative value must be expressed in terms permitting assignment of a probability. The expression must have a subject, verb, and descriptor.

Fault Tree Analysis

245

For example, Relay 3Z045 Fails Closed. In this case, the word "Closed" is the descriptor and connotes a specific mode. If the expression had been Relay 3Z045 Fails, the connotation is that *any* mode in which it fails will contribute to the adverse event being evaluated.

When used for qualitative analyses, the Fault Trees may resemble the safety consideration trees in Chapter 5. The safety consideration trees are simpler, thus reducing the need for training to prepare the trees and improving the ease with which managerial personnel and personnel of other disciplines can understand them. These simplified trees are easier to draw than are Fault Trees, especially where there are a great many levels of events. This simplification may be accomplished because the top levels are generally all OR relationships; AND connectives are more common at the part level. The OR symbols are omitted with the understanding that this is the existing relationship; AND symbols are used only where such relationships are present. Where Fault Trees indicate restrictions and stipulations on inhibit gates, the consideration trees show them as AND conditions.

The interrelationship between the safety consideration trees and the tables, studies, and narratives make that method more effective for an overall safety program than use of Fault Trees alone. Fault Tree Analysis may be regarded as one type of detailed study that may be employed to complement the broader approach of the safety consideration trees.

Logic and Decision Making

Quantification of personnel error was pointed out in Chapter 8 as a simple function of human reliability. Sometimes the interrelationships between man, machine, and operation involve more complex situations to which logic analysis can be applied.

The application of logic analysis to personnel-equipment operations has been presented in NAVWEPS OD 18413A,* based on work done by others. The method in this case is applied to decisions that must be made during use of alternate types of collision avoidance systems.

The problem consists of evaluating the probability of error that could result when either of two types of avoidance systems is used. One type is predicated on manual calculations; the other employs a computer. The basic conditions, events, and sequences are shown in Fig. 9-7, with a list of symbols used. It can be seen that these symbols differ substantially from those used for network logic analysis or other previously decribed logic system. More detailed illustrations are provided in Fig. 9-8 of the traditional, manual method of analyzing the need for a change of course to avoid a collision and of the proposed computer-assisted method.

The traditional, manual method of avoiding a ship collision necessitates that a target be identified and quick determination made as to whether it could be on a collision course with the ship on which the calculations are being made. The courses of the two ships are plotted to determine if a threat of collision exists. If the ship is to maneuver to avoid a collision, a new safe course is plotted manually. The results indicate the new speed and course to be taken. A replot of the other

* *Human Factors Design Standards for the Fleet Ballistic Missile Weapon System*, NAVWEPS OD 18413A, (Washington: D.C., Special Projects Office, 1963).

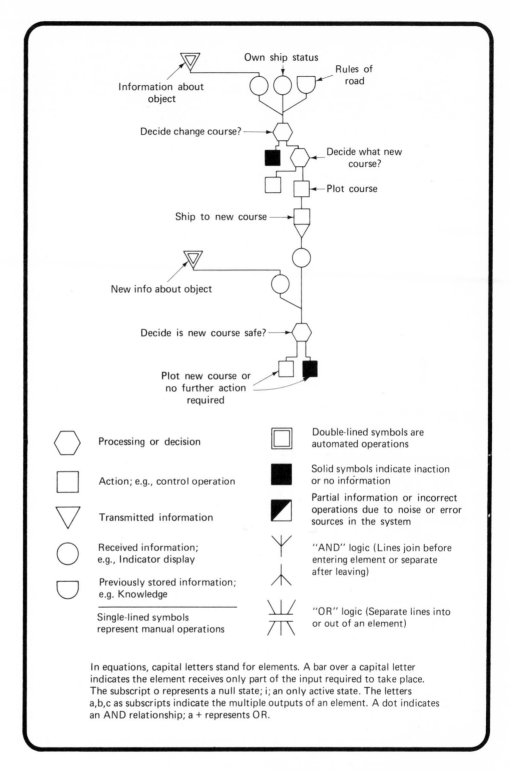

Own ship status

Rules of
road

Information about
object

Decide change course?

Decide what new
course?

Plot course

Ship to new course

New info about object

Decide is new course safe?

Plot new course or
no further action
required

⬡ Processing or decision

□ Action; e.g., control operation

▽ Transmitted information

◯ Received information;
e.g., Indicator display

◡ Previously stored information;
e.g. Knowledge

Single-lined symbols
represent manual operations

▣ Double-lined symbols are
automated operations

■ Solid symbols indicate inaction
or no information

◪ Partial information or incorrect
operations due to noise or error
sources in the system

Y "AND" logic (Lines join before
entering element or separate
after leaving)

⅄ "OR" logic (Separate lines into
or out of an element)

In equations, capital letters stand for elements. A bar over a capital letter
indicates the element receives only part of the input required to take place.
The subscript o represents a null state; i; an only active state. The letters
a,b,c as subscripts indicate the multiple outputs of an element. A dot indicates
an AND relationship; a + represents OR.

ship's course is then made to determine whether the collision threat has been eliminated.

Use of the computer also requires recognition and identification of the threatening vessel. Data on both ships is entered into the computer, which evaluates the threat. When a collision course is indicated, a display and alarm alerts the watch officer who chooses a change of course or speed and enters the data into the computer. The computer evaluates the proposed action and indicates whether a collision course

Fig. 9-7. Basic collision avoidance system. Department of the Navy, *Human Factors Design Standards for Fleet Ballistic Missile Weapon System;* (Washington, D.C.: Director, Special Projects, U.S. Navy, 1963) OD 18413A, p. 55.

Logic And Decision Making

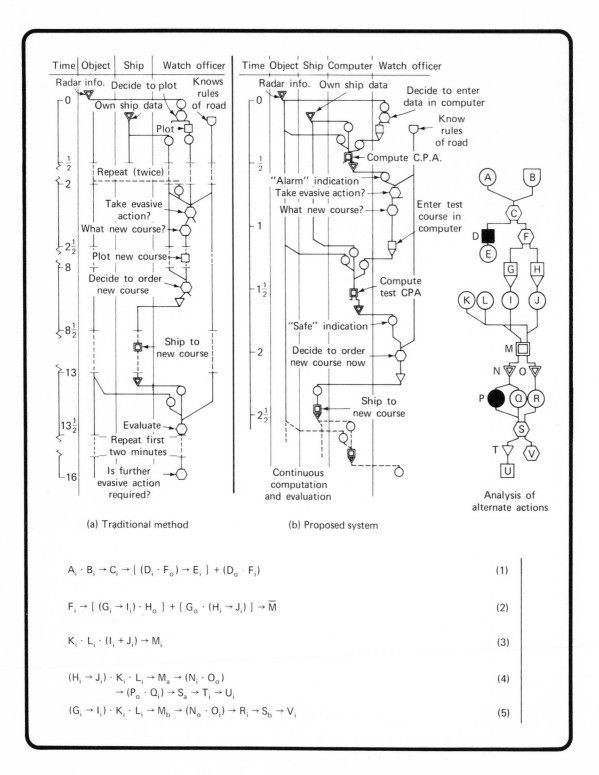

(a) Traditional method (b) Proposed system

$$A_i \cdot B_i \rightarrow C_i \rightarrow [\ (D_i \cdot F_o) \rightarrow E_i\ ] + (D_o \cdot F_i) \qquad (1)$$

$$F_i \rightarrow [\ (G_i \rightarrow I_i) \cdot H_o\ ] + [\ G_o \cdot (H_i \rightarrow J_i)\ ] \rightarrow \overline{M} \qquad (2)$$

$$K_i \cdot L_i \cdot (I_i + J_i) \rightarrow M_i \qquad (3)$$

$$(H_i \rightarrow J_i) \cdot K_i \cdot L_i \rightarrow M_a \rightarrow (N_i \cdot O_o)$$
$$\rightarrow (P_o \cdot Q_i) \rightarrow S_a \rightarrow T_i \rightarrow U_i \qquad (4)$$

$$(G_i \rightarrow I_i) \cdot K_i \cdot L_i \rightarrow M_b \rightarrow (N_o \cdot O_i) \rightarrow R_i \rightarrow S_b \rightarrow V_i \qquad (5)$$

Fig. 9-8. Detail analysis of alternate collision avoidance systems. Ibid, p. 56.

Quantitative Safety Analyses

248

will be avoided. If the threat is eliminated, the watch officer orders the changes he had proposed. The time required for calculation is a fraction of that required for the manual method.

Figure 9-8 indicates the logic diagram and related equations applying to one set of decisions that could be made by the watch officer. Insertion of suitable probability values in the equations permits determination of the overall probability of a successful avoidance. In this case the logic analysis begins when the watch officer makes a decision on the choice (F) of a new course. If he chooses one (G) of two alternatives, radar data (K) on the other ship and data (L) on his own ship are entered into the computer. Should the determination be that another collision course would result, the computer would display this (R). The watch officer must choose another course and speed by two new decisions (S and V). Should course H with inputs K and L be chosen and determined to be safe, the computer will process this at N. Q will be the computer's indication that a safe condition will result from the chosen action, while P, which would have indicated the proposed course as unsafe, is inactive. The watch officer makes his decision (S) and orders a change in course (T).

It is apparent that a similar procedure for analysis of decision making by a man-machine combination can also be applied to problems of aircraft collision avoidance, which this example resembles closely. Use of symbology similar to that for network logic analysis would reduce the need for learning two systems of notation.

Objections to Quantitative Analyses

Many safety analysts object to making quantitative analyses, even though they may employ the same methods, Fault Tree Analysis or network logic analysis, for qualitative purposes. Objections generally include the following problems:

1. Lack of dependable probability data for initiating and contributory events, especially for human error, produces numerical results that also are not dependable.

2. Much effort is frequently diverted to proving theoretically that a product or system meets a stipulated level when the effort could be better applied to eliminating, minimizing, and controlling hazards. The tendency to reduce the safety effort once it is shown, justifiably or not, that the stipulated level has been met negates the prime objective of a safety program—that is, making the product or system as safe as possible.

3. Most calculations for reliability analysis and prediction of safety levels are predicated on the exponential function because of the ease with which it can be applied. This method depends only on knowledge of the supposedly constant failure rate and time. However, in most cases the exponential function is not truly representative of actual conditions. A constant failure rate exists when there is a very large number of similar components that fail from random causes at approximately equal intervals and then are replaced. For this reason, use of the exponential function was initially with electrical and electronic equipment, which approximated these requirements. The exponential function was also applied erroneously to items whose numbers did not provide a constant failure rate, either because there were comparatively few random failures or because, as frequently happened, no replacement occurred.

Lives of such items are often described better by other distributions, with substantially different values for probabilities of survival of failure. For example, a group of mechanical components described by a normal distribution function has a mean or expected life of 200 hr. Fifty per cent of the group will fail at or before that time, and 50 per cent afterwards. The probability of survival (reliability) of any one in a group

COMPARISON OF RELIABILITY ESTIMATE,
EXPONENTIAL VERSUS NORMAL DISTRIBUTIONS

Probability of Survival (Reliability)

t	Incorrect (Based on Exponential with $\lambda = 1/2000$)	Correct (Based on Normal with $\mu = 2000$, $\sigma = 200$)
500	0.779	1
1,000	0.607	1
1,500	0.472	0.994
2,000	0.368	0.500
2,500	0.287	0.006
3,000	0.223	0
4,000	0.135	0

Figure 9-9

COMPARISON OF RELIABILITY ESTIMATE
EXPONENTIAL VERSUS WEIBULL AND GAMMA DISTRIBUTIONS*

Probability of Survival (Reliability)

t/μ	Incorrect (Based on Exponential)	Correct (Based on Weibull)	Correct (Based on Gamma)
0.1	0.905	0.922	0.996
0.2	0.819	0.968	0.977
0.3	0.741	0.950	0.937
0.5	0.607	0.646	0.809
1.0	0.368	0.451	0.423
2.0	0.135	0.043	0.062
3.0	0.050	0.0008	0.006

*For source see footnote to text

Figure 9-10

of similar items will therefore be 50 per cent. On the other hand, according to the exponential distribution, an item having a mean time to failure of 200 hr and is operated for that length of time will have an expected reliability of only 36.8 per cent.

Lynch provides a comparison of reliabilities (Figs. 9-9 and 9-10) predicted by both the exponential and other distribution functions.* In Fig. 9-9, the mean time between failures for the exponential distribution and the mean life for the normal distribution are both 2,000 hr. Values for the normal distribution are also based on a standard deviation of 200 hr. It can be noted that, in some cases, the normal value for reliability is higher and, in other cases, lower than the exponential for the same period of time.

* W. N. Lynch, C. B. Clark, and B. Epstein; *Advanced Vehicle Guidance Systems Reliability Investigation,* ASD-TDR-62-359 (Menlo Park, California; Stanford Research Institute; Report prepared for Aeronautical Systems Division, Air Force Systems Command; July 1962), p. 49.

chapter 10

SAFETY
ACHIEVEMENT

The end result of a proper hazard analysis is the determination of methods for the elimination or reduction of conditions that could cause damage or injury. The various methods can be arranged in a rough order of preference (Fig. 10-1). In general, safety of the system will be improved the higher the method is in the order. Each listing is predicated on the condition that the equipment or device necessary for each type of control is equally efficient and reliable. Furthermore, mission requirements or practicability of certain modes of accomplishment may preclude adoption of a safer method on the list. The necessity to evaluate and establish these facts constitutes the fundamental reason for the conduct of tradeoff studies.

Elimination

Hazards can sometimes be avoided by good designs or procedures. A very common example of hazard avoidance is good housekeeping. Tripping over misplaced objects, slipping on oily or wet surfaces, spontaneous ignition of trash or oily rags, or accidental ignition of other combustibles can all be eliminated simply by keeping facilities clean and orderly. There are numerous other examples that can be cited, some of which include:

- Using nonflammable instead of combustible materials. This procedure has been followed with flight-suit materials, hydraulic fluids, solvents, and electrical insulation.
- Using pneumatic or hydraulic, instead of electric, systems where there is a possibility of fire or excessive heating. Fluidic control systems, developed only recently, have already been applied for these reasons.
- Using hybrid propulsion systems, which have a solid fuel and liquid oxidizer and so eliminate the possibility of combustion and explosion as long as the two are separated. They also eliminate the possibility of uncontrolled combustion due to cracks, voids, or other separations in the solid propellant.
- Rounding edges and corners on equipment to prevent cutting and injuring personnel.
- Using different sizes and types of critical electrical connectors on similar adjacent lines where cross-connections could generate damage.
- Eliminating leaks by using continuous lines instead of lines with connectors. In many cases, this result can be achieved most economically by welding. Where a failure would be extremely critical and damaging, lines can sometimes be manufactured in one piece.
- Eliminating vibration, shock, rail separations, and derailments by using welded and ground joints on railroad lines.
- Avoiding automobile accidents at highway intersections and railroad crossings through use of grade separations.
- Eliminating protuberances, such as handles, ornaments, and similar devices in vehicles, which could cause injury after a sudden stop.

SAFETY MEASURES

ACCIDENT PREVENTION

1. Hazard elimination

2. Hazard level limitation
    a. Intrinsic safety
    b. Limit-level sensing control
    c. Continuous monitor and automatic control

3. Lockouts, lockins, and interlocks
    a. Isolation
    b. Lockouts and lockins
    c. Interlocks

4. Fail-safe designs
    a. Fail-passive
    b. Fail-active
    c. Fail-operational

5. Failure minimization
    a. Monitoring
    b. Warning
    c. Safety factors and margins
    d. Failure rate reduction
        • Derating
        • Timed replacements
        • Screening
        • Redundancy

6. Backout and recovery
    a. Normal sequence restoration
    b. Aborting entire operation
    c. Inactivating only malfunctioning equipment
        • Automatic
        • Manual

DAMAGE MINIMIZATION AND CONTROL

1. Isolation
    a. Distance
    b. Energy absorption
    c. Deflection
    d. Containment
        • Hazard
        • Operation
        • Personnel
        • Matériel
        • Critical equipment

2. Personal protective equipment
    a. Programmed dangerous operation
    b. Investigations and corrections
    c. Emergencies

3. Minor loss acceptance

4. Escape and survival
    a. Point-of-no-return warning
    b. Crashworthiness designs
    c. Escape and survival equipment
    d. Escape and survival procedures

5. Rescue
    a. Procedures
    b. Equipment

Figure 10-1

253

Hazard Level Limitation

In certain instances, the hazard itself cannot be eliminated or it may not be practicable to do so. However, the level of hazard that could create damage can be limited. This principle is illustrated in Fig. 10-2. Defective electric drills powered by 110-v alternating current have caused fatalities. Some alternatives are shown. The hand bit is safest of all, eliminating the hazard completely, but its low effectiveness as a tool makes it an undesirable substitute in most instances. By using compressed air the pneumatic drill involves a much lesser hazard than 110-v power. However, only industrial plants and repair shops generally have compressors.

Figure 10-2. The drill problem.

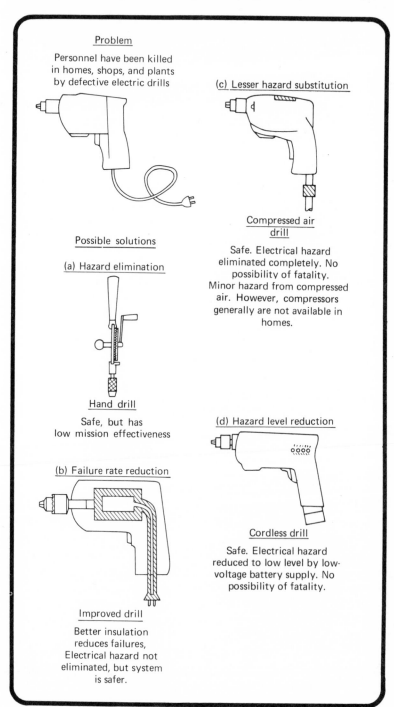

Problem

Personnel have been killed in homes, shops, and plants by defective electric drills

(c) Lesser hazard substitution

Compressed air drill

Safe. Electrical hazard eliminated completely. No possibility of fatality. Minor hazard from compressed air. However, compressors generally are not available in homes.

Possible solutions

(a) Hazard elimination

Hand drill

Safe, but has low mission effectiveness

(d) Hazard level reduction

(b) Failure rate reduction

Cordless drill

Safe. Electrical hazard reduced to low level by low-voltage battery supply. No possibility of fatality.

Improved drill

Better insulation reduces failures, Electrical hazard not eliminated, but system is safer.

A better designed drill reduces the probability of a failure that could cause a fatal shock but does not eliminate the hazard or reduce its level. The cordless battery drill is safe, convenient, and effective. The battery provides low voltage and limited amperage power, which eliminates the hazard of a fatality from electrical shock. However, as long as electrical power is present, it is conceivable that a condition could exist in which a slight tingling shock could occur. Such systems are considered to be intrinsically safe.

There are numerous other circumstances in which hazard levels can be limited successfully. Low-voltage circuitry can also be used in homes to avoid fatal shocks. Safety valves, relief valves, and other devices keep pressurized systems below levels that could be dangerous. Since failures do occur even with devices that restrict hazard levels, the maximum hazard level possible under any condition is sometimes limited. For example, safety valves on boilers are fairly reliable, but the boiler may have a defect, so it may fail at a pressure less than the safety valve setting. Building codes therefore frequently limit the steam boiler pressure that can be utilized in densely populated areas unless a trained attendant is always present and boilers are inspected periodically by certified personnel.

Testing of pressure vessels is generally done with water or other liquid and not with gas to limit hazard levels. The rupture of a vessel containing pressurized gas can generate a shock wave and damage similar to that caused by a high explosive. A liquid will not expand the way a gas will when pressure is released. Pressure release of liquid in a vessel that ruptures is therefore much less hazardous than if gas were employed. No shock wave will be created after rupture.

Limitations on hazard level may necessitate employment of suitable automatic relief or monitor and relief equipment. The safety valve just mentioned is an example of a relief device that can be used to prevent the hazard from reaching a level where it could endanger the pressure vessel under foreseeable conditions. These devices function automatically to maintain pressures within prescribed limits. In electrical systems, grounds may be used to relieve discharges on condensers or other components where high voltages injurious to personnel might accumulate.

Monitors can be used for detecting specific hazards and for activating suitable control equipment to maintain a predetermined safe level. (See the more detailed discussion on monitors on page 262.) They can continuously evaluate atmospheres that might be toxic, flammable, or explosive, or in which unsafe levels of radiation, temperature, pressure, vibration, or structural stress could exist. This monitoring equipment must be capable of detecting a hazardous condition at a level low enough to ensure that action can be taken before it reaches or exceeds the prescribed limit. Such monitors can activate controls that will reduce the hazard level or shut down the operating equipment when the preset limits are exceeded. Where a situation could develop very rapidly into a dangerous one with serious consequences, the same monitoring device can automatically activate suitable countermeasure equipment.

Such systems require that designers or safety engineers determine which hazards could be present, the level at which each hazard would constitute a danger, and limitations that should be prescribed. For example, a fuel gas, such as methane, is dangerous and will burn when its concentration in air is within its flammable limits. It is common practice to ensure that concentration of such a fuel gas outside its usual container or in a combustion chamber never exceeds 20 per cent of the lower flammable limit. If the 20 per cent point is exceeded, a blower could be activated to force in air to reduce the flammable gas concentration; another inert gas could be introduced; or a fire suppressant could be injected.

Other methods by which hazard levels are limited include:

- Use of low-voltage electrical systems or of solid-state devices and assemblies in locations where flammable or explosive gases might be present. The power requirements of such devices are far below the level required for ignition of a combustible mixture.
- Mixed gas atmospheres instead of oxygen alone in space cabins to limit the ease with which flammable materials ignite and burn.
- Addition of diluents to air where explosive dusts are present to minimize the possibility of an explosion.
- Pressure systems with automatic relief provisions to maintain pressure within a safe level.
- Use of accumulators or ullage in highly pressurized liquid systems to maintain the pressure within prescribed limits.
- Use of accumulators to limit the magnitude of water hammer that could occur due to sudden stoppage of a moving liquid.
- Governors to regulate the speed of rotating or moving equipment.

Lockouts, Lockins, and Interlocks

These methods and devices include some of the most common safety measures in use. Figure 10-3 lists only a few, but these devices and measures may be considered indicators of types that can be employed. They are predicated on two basic principles, or a combination of the two: (1) isolating a hazard once it has been recognized; and (2) preventing incompatible events from occurring, from occurring at the wrong time, or from occurring in the wrong sequence.

Isolation

Isolation involves separation employed either as an accident prevention measure or to minimize damage that could result should an accident occur. In this section, uses of isolation for accident prevention are discussed. Here again, there are a variety of means by which isolation can provide benefits.

1. Isolation can separate incompatible materials or conditions that together would constitute a hazard. Fire requires the presence of a fuel, oxidizer, and ignition source. Isolation of any one of these from the others will eliminate any possibility of fire. Some highly flammable liquids are "blanketed" in their containers with nitrogen or other inert gas to isolate them from contact with oxygen in air. Similarly, a fire involving a fuel and air can be suppressed by covering the fuel with a foam or film that prevents further contact between the two. Other common examples of isolation include:

   a. Use of thermal insulation to prevent transfer of heat from

LOCKOUT, LOCKIN AND INTERLOCK
DEVICES AND MEASURES

1. Lock on automobile engine ignition system and steering column.

2. Guards to prevent personnel contacting moving machinery or parts.

3. Fenced enclosures or vaults for high voltage transformers to keep out personnel who might be electrocuted.

4. Interlocks to deactivate hazardous electrical equipment when panels or drawers are opened or removed for replacement, maintenance or repair.

5. Limit stops to restrict travel of mechanical parts.

6. Safe-and-arm devices in explosive trains.

7. Safety wiring and other locking devices on nuts and bolts.

8. Locks securing switch levers to prevent activation of electrical circuits or equipment on which work is being accomplished.

9. Interlocks on devices which must be operated in specific sequences.

10. Shields to keep out foreign objects which might jam critical controls, such as those in aircraft.

11. Lockout to prevent pumping of highly flammable liquid into a tank or tank car unless the system is adequately grounded.

12. Shielding on reactors and similar nuclear devices to contain emission of harmful radiation.

13. Blocks to prevent movement of automobiles jacked up for repairs.

14. Guards or lockwires to prevent critical switches against inadvertent activation.

15. Parking blocks in automobile transmissions to prevent car movement.

16. Storing subbituminous and similar grade coal, which is subject to spontaneous ignition, under water.

17. Storing oily rags away from air in covered metal containers, until they can be disposed of.

Figure 10-3

a thermal source to materials or components that could be damaged or adversely affected

b. Use of vibration and noise isolators

c. Potting of electrical connectors and other equipment to prevent entrance of moisture and other deleterious materials that could degrade the system

d. Use of "explosion-proof" or encapsulated electrical equipment in hazardous atmospheres

e. Keeping corrosive gases and liquids from incompatible metals and other materials

2. Isolation is also employed to limit the effects of controlled energy release. Tests of explosives and electroexplosive devices may require their activation or determination of limits beyond which they will activate. A small amount of explosive to be tested can be placed in a suitable box or vault that absorbs or contains the energy of the explosion if one should occur. The test conductor activates the equipment from a safe distance or location. Sensitive explosive devices are generally transported and handled in small quantities in containers which isolate them from outside sources of energy, which could cause their activation, and that will withstand the force of an inadvertent explosion.

3. Certain materials are harmful to personnel at all times unless isolated when used. Radioactive materials are in this category. If they are to constitute part of a scheduled process, protection

Lockouts, Lockins, and Interlocks

must be provided. Examples of vital protection include shielding persons from light generated by a welding arc, having workers in paint-spraying booths or sand-blasting rooms wear protective equipment, and using gas masks, air packs, or oxygen generators in toxic atmospheres.

4. An operational activity that generates a problem can be isolated from personnel who can be injured and equipment that can be damaged. An engine producing great amounts of vibration, noise, and heat can be isolated through use of suitable vibration mounts or shields, noise suppressors, and thermal shields and sinks.

5. Machine guards are widely used to isolate hazards in industrial plants. These guards are fixed over rotating parts, sharp edges, hot surfaces, and electrical devices to prevent a person from coming in contact with the dangerous object. Security fences around electrical substations are similar. In such instances, the isolator is fixed. In other cases, such as railroad crossing guards, they are removable when conditions are safe, thereby constituting an interlock.

Lockouts and Lockins

Lockouts and lockins constitute more positive means of isolation than merely separating a hazardous device or operation from personnel who could be injured or equipment that could be damaged. The difference between a lockout and lockin is, of course, relative. A lockout prevents an event from occurring or prevents someone, some object, force, or factor from entering a dangerous zone. A lockin is provided to maintain an event or condition or to keep someone, some object, force, or factor from leaving a safe restricted zone. Locking a switch on an open circuit to prevent it being energized is a lockout; a similar lock on a live circuit to prevent current being shut off is a lockin.

Men have been killed when equipment they had de-energized to repair was inadvertently activated by other personnel. These accidents have happened with both electrical and mechanical equipment. Workers repairing electrical circuits that they had opened were shocked fatally when the system was energized by someone who did not realize that the work was being done. A repairman working inside a vat that contained rotating mixers was killed when someone mistakenly started the equipment. These accidents could have been avoided if the switch opening the circuit had been secured in place with a lock to which only the person conducting the repairs or his immediate supervisor had the key or combination.

This type of safeguard can be used to lock out motion that could be dangerous. The doors to a weapons bay on an aircraft were held open by compressed air. An airman working on the system inadvertently released the pressure himself by loosening a fitting while standing between the doors. The doors caught and crushed him. The accident resulted from other factors (failure to follow prescribed procedures, including precautions against working on systems under pressure), but blocking open the doors so that motion was locked out would have prevented him from being crushed.

Safety Achievement

Blocking to lock equipment in position is frequently used. A very common example is the use of blocks of wood, steel, or stone, placed under a raised car to permit work on its underside. The blocks are more secure than some jacks, which may fail or from which the car may fall. Similarly, blocks of wood or rocks are used against car tires to prevent the car from rolling when it is raised so that a wheel can be replaced.

Other types of blocks used as lockouts or lockins for automobiles include the PARK position in automatic shifts, which prevents motion as long as the rear wheels are on the ground, and the keyed ignition, which prevents the steering wheel being turned unless the key is in the proper position. Here again, a sequence of operations that must be followed constitutes an interlock.

Interlocks are provided to ensure that event A does not occur at the following times:

Interlocks

1. Inadvertently. In such cases, for event A to occur a preliminary, intentional action, B, is needed; for example, lifting the cover that protects a critical switch, permitting it to be thrown.

2. While condition C exists. An interlock may be placed on an access door or panel to equipment where a high voltage exists. If adjustments must be made and the door or panel is opened, the circuit is opened so that the unsafe condition no longer exists. Guard gates at a railroad crossing are a combination of isolator, lockout, and interlock. They isolate the railroad tracks and passing train, keep other vehicles and pedestrians from the tracks when a train is imminent, and open to permit traffic to pass when there is no danger.

3. Before event D. Such interlocks are desirable where the sequence of operations is important or necessary, and a wrong sequence could cause a mishap. Lack of an interlock caused damage and failure of a missile tank for a cryogenic liquid. Two buttons on a console controlled the operations for filling the tank but had to be operated in a specific sequence. The first opened a vent so that the pressure generated by the pump and by the evaporating liquid could be relieved before the tank was overstressed; the second started the pump. In this case, pumping was started without opening the vent valve; pressure built up; and the tank was damaged. Redesign involved providing an interlock that would permit tank filling only if the vent valve was opened first. Manufacturers provide numerous types of pushbutton switching arrangements with many variations that can provide interlocks. Analyses of operating procedures and of the consequences resulting from a switching error will indicate the type of switch to be used.

Not all accidents result from equipment failures, but failures do produce a high percentage. Since failures will occur, fail-safe arrangements are another means to prevent disabling of a system or to prevent a catastrophe involving major damage to equipment, injury to personnel, or degraded operation. Fail-safe design ensures that occurrence of a failure will leave the system unaffected or convert it to a state in which no injury or damage can result. In some instances, this action may cause inactivation of the system. In any case, the fundamental principle is

Fail-Safe Designs

Fail-Safe Designs

259

that a fail-safe system will first protect personnel; second, prevent damage to equipment; and last, prevent loss of function or degraded operation.* Fail-safe designs can be categorized into three types:

1. *Fail-passive* arrangements reduce the system to its lowest energy level. The system will not operate until corrective action is taken, but no further damage will result from the hazard causing the inactivation. Circuit breakers and fuses for protection of electrical circuits are fail-passive devices. The circuit breaker or fuse opens when the system is overloaded or a short circuit occurs; the system is de-energized and safe.

2. *Fail-active* design maintains an energized condition that keeps the system in a safe mode until corrective or overriding action occurs or that activates an alternate system to eliminate the possibility of an accident. Examples of such arrangements are:

   a. A monitor system that activates a visual indicator if a failure or adverse condition occurs in a critical monitoring operation or that incorporates features by which a malfunction in the warning system itself is indicated by a continuous, blinking, different color, or auxiliary light. In this way, there would be a very high degree of certainty that the monitoring and warning systems are operative.

   b. An air-to-air missile has a self-destruct system or flight termination system that causes its destruction should it fail to hit a target or to impact within a specific time after launch.

3. *Fail-operational* arrangements allow system functions to continue safely until corrective action is possible. This type of design is the most preferable since, unlike the other two types, there is no loss of function. The American Society of Mechanical Engineers requires fail-safe orientation and installation of feedwater valves for boilers. Water must flow first under, rather than over, the valve disk. Detachment of the disk from the valve stem will still permit it to be raised by the pressure of the incoming water. Continued flow keeps the boiler functioning normally and keeps it from being depleted of water. If flow had been over the disk, its detachment would have forced it into the closed position, shutting off further flow of water into the boiler. In the past, such occurrences have resulted in lack of water, increased steam pressure, and violent boiler ruptures.

4. Other examples of fail-safe devices include:
   a. Air brakes on railroad trains and large trucks
   b. Deadman throttles on locomotives
   c. Automatic blocks on railroads
   d. Control rods on nuclear reactors, which drop automatically into place to reduce the reaction rate if it exceeds a preset limit
   e. Self-sealing breakaway fuel-line connections
   f. Automobile headlight covers that open and expose the lights in event of a malfunction

* Recently, a new requirement for fail-safe systems has been generated: protection against damage to the environment. This requirement comes after protection of personnel and precedes prevention of damage to equipment.

g. Safety tires for automobiles

h. Automobile turn indicators that glow steadily instead of remaining dark or blinking in case of failure

Much railway equipment is designed on fail-safe principles. A great deal of such equipment design is predicated on the principle that gravity is the only force that can be depended on in an emergency. As a result, semaphores, switch signals, and the lights to which they are connected are weighted devices. In event of failure, a heavy arm drops and the warning signal is activated.

The same principle is employed in the design of retractable aircraft landing gear. Should the pressure system that raises and lowers the gear fail, the wheels will drop and lock in the landing position.

It should be pointed out here that the term "fail-safe" is sometimes employed incorrectly for redundant arrangements. Redundancy, which is discussed later in this chapter, means replication of components, assemblies, or systems. If one of these items fails, a second or third is available to keep the system functioning. However, should all of these items fail, the entire system will fail, possibly causing an accident. With a fail-safe system that operates properly, no accident will occur.

On 18 January 1969, a three-engine airliner crashed into the ocean off Los Angeles, killing the passengers and crew. The Federal Aviation Agency (FAA) indicated that the accident may have been due to loss of electrical power. Although each engine drove a generator, one generator had been inoperative before takeoff. Just before the crash the pilot reported a fire in a second engine and probably shut it down, and with it, its generator. As a result, the third and last generator was overloaded and failed.

It should also be recognized that the fail-safe arrangement itself may fail or may not operate rapidly enough. A fuse in an electric circuit may not blow fast enough to prevent damage to the system. In extremely critical systems, therefore, it may be necessary to provide redundant fail-safe devices. Very large boilers are so equipped.

Failure Minimization

Most accidents result from failures of operating systems or failures of personnel at unforeseen or unexpected times; these accidents involve conditions for which fail-safe designs cannot be or have not been provided. On the other hand, the process may be so critical that even a fail-safe arrangement is less preferable than a system that will fail only rarely. Nevertheless, to ensure that hardware or personnel failures that could cause accidents have been minimized, four principal methods are employed:

1. Parameter monitoring. A specific parameter, such as temperature, vibration, pressure, or radiation, is kept under surveillance to ensure that it is within specified limits and to determine when it exhibits an abnormal characteristic. Corrective action can then be taken to prevent failure.

2. Warnings. Most types of warnings are means by which personnel are apprised of hazards, equipment problems, or other noteworthy conditions, so they will not make incorrect decisions that could cause accidents.

3. Safety factors and margins. Under this concept, components are designed with strengths greater than those normally required to allow for variations in both strengths and stresses, unforeseen transients, material degradation, and other random factors.

4. Failure rate reduction. This is the principle on which reliability engineering is predicated. By this means, unmanned systems can be designed to complete their missions successfully. Where humans are present, failure rate reduction is necessary to minimize contingencies that could devolve into accidents.

Monitoring

Monitoring devices can be incorporated into a product or system to check that conditions do not reach dangerous levels or states and to ensure that no contingency exists or is imminent. Greater benefits can be derived if contingencies are prevented rather than having to be overcome. The principles, however, are equally applicable to both types of situations.

Monitors can be employed to indicate:

- Whether or not a specific condition exists
- Whether the system is ready for operation or is operating satisfactorily as programmed
- If the required input is being provided
- If the output is being generated
- If the limit is being met or exceeded
- Whether the measured parameter is abnormal.

In addition, a monitoring system is of no value unless it includes provision for application of suitable corrective action when necessary. In some instances, it may consists simply of conveying information to an operator, considered to constitute part of the system, who then accomplishes any tasks. The actions in the overall process involve four principal steps, whether the system consists wholly of hardware, wholly of personnel, or of hardware and personnel:

1. Detection. A monitor must be capable of sensing the specific parameter for which it has been selected in spite of all other environmental stresses that could be expected to exist during system operation, programmed or emergency. (Figures 7-10, 7-11, and 7-12 contain information on transducers that may be employed for monitoring purposes.) For toxic gases, a detector may be capable of measuring extremely small concentrations of toxicants in a laboratory. In an operating vehicle, vibration, temperature variations, moisture, electrical interference, or other environmental stresses may degrade performance or cause complete failure. The sensing function may be accomplished continuously, continually but intermittently, or intermittently at the desire of an operator. It must be able to sense and provide readings for only those parameters for which it has been selected, without being affected by extraneous or similar conditions. It must be capable of detecting a hazard at a level low enough to permit corrective action before an emergency condition arises. The input element of the monitoring device should be

located to sense any hazardous condition that could exist for the selected parameter. Frequently, poor locations negate the value of any monitor. Fire detectors in homes are sometimes placed in living rooms, when the fires generally originate in kitchens or closets where furnaces or hot-water heaters are located.

2. Measurement. The parameter that a monitoring device senses may be one in which only one of two bi-stable conditions can exist; that is, a device is either on or off. The monitor may also determine additional information, such as the existing level of a parameter being monitored continuously or when a predetermined level is exceeded. The second type of monitor requires comparison of existing and predetermined levels. Methods for such monitoring vary from extremely simple ones to others quite complex. A simple method is to mark a display, such as a dial, with the predetermined limit; an indicator then points out the existing level. An operator observes and compares the existing level and the limit to determine whether there is an abnormality. One style of automobile gauge to monitor radiator water temperature is of this type. In the second type of automobile gauge, a light goes on to warn the operator only when the water temperature exceeds a preset level.

3. Interpretation. An operator must understand clearly the meanings of any readings provided by the monitoring devices. He must know whether a normal situation exists, whether an unusual condition is impending, or whether corrective action must be taken. Displays and signals should employ means by which personnel are provided information with the least ambiguity, minimum possibility of misinterpretation, and minimal necessity for additional information. Monitors should provide timely and easily recognizable displays and signals. Indicators and signals within a specific system are frequently standardized for this reason. Readouts may be displayed continuously, when preset limits are exceeded, or on demand. At the same time, personnel must be trained and be knowledgeable of the exact meanings of any output generated by a monitor or warning device. The combination of information from the monitor plus previous training is required to produce a decision on a subsequent course of action. If either one of these is lacking or inadequate, a suitable decision may not be possible within the time available or may necessitate delay until the deficiency is eliminated.

4. Response. When a monitor indicates a normal situation, no response other than continuation of a program is necessary. When corrective action is required, the more time available to interpret information, reach a decision, and respond, the more likely that the decision and response will be proper and effective. For this reason, wherever possible the monitor should indicate as early as possible the approach of an adverse condition. In some instances, the level at which a monitor will indicate existence of a problem can be set far from the actual danger level. For example, air contains approximately 21 per cent oxygen; the danger level for respiration is 16 per cent. A monitor could indicate when the level of oxygen in an enclosed space drops below 20 per cent. The atmosphere at this point is still breathable, but the deficiency indicates the existence of a

situation that should be investigated. When the system is such that any response must be made by a person, analysis of the procedure should ensure that time to respond will be adequate to take corrective action under foreseeable circumstances. Occasionally, the attention of a person who should be aware of an unusual condition is focused elsewhere than on a visual indicator. In those instances in which a failure to take timely action could prove disastrous, auxiliary aural alerting or warning devices may be used. Where a serious, critical, or catastrophic condition would result if corrective action were not taken very rapidly, a monitor should be interlocked to activate automatically hazard suppression or damage containment devices. Monitoring and warning devices must be analyzed as critically as the system in which they are to be incorporated. In 1939, the submarine *Squalus* sank in 240 ft of water because of false readings on the monitor panel. The air-induction valves were open when the indicators showed them to be closed. Critical monitor and warning circuits should be analyzed by the same logic analysis methods used for other electrical and electronic networks to ensure maximum effectiveness for safety.

There are other features that should be considered during the design of monitoring (and of warning) devices:

- Monitors must perform their functions at the highest practicable reliability levels. In extremely critical applications, they must be designed to indicate any failures of their own circuits or, if advisable, to permit periodic, quick checks of these circuits.

- They must be accurate, quick-acting, and easy to maintain, to calibrate, and to check. Procedures to test and calibrate the devices must be provided.

- Failure of monitoring equipment or circuits must not produce damaging effects on the system itself or other hazardous conditions.

- Where system failure could cause loss of the power that is necessary for monitoring and warning functions, monitors should have independent and reliable power sources and circuits.

- The energy level for monitoring must be lower than that which will constitute, contribute, or activate a hazard to the system being monitored.

- Circuitry within the monitoring equipment must not provide a path that could cause degradation or failure of the system during operation. Monitor circuit and devices should not generate RF energy or other noise in other system circuits.

- Power for monitoring should not be routed through devices where it could change a safe condition, remove a blocking element, or cause inadvertent activation.

Signature Analysis. Highly sophisticated methods of monitoring have been developed to permit determining incipient failures in their very early stages. One such technique is known as *signature analysis*. It is predicated on the concept that any operating system will have particular patterns of noise, vibration, heat, pressure, and electromagnetic energy during normal operation and will have distorted patterns when abnormalities exist.

Each of these factors can be recorded graphically. This recording is first done during normal operation of the system, when a reference pattern, or *signature*, is established. Any change in this signature may then indicate the beginning of a condition that could produce a failure. Experience in the laboratory or in the field will establish the meanings of variations in the measured parameters in specific types of equipment.

Figure 10-4 indicates the signature that might be generated by a piece of equipment under various conditions, including those where damage and catastrophic failure have occurred. Use of signature analysis, however, is to prevent equipment from reaching such a state by detection and correction long before failure would occur. Figure 10-5a (right) indicates signatures for three types of bearing malfunctions. These malfunctions may be due to such causes as fatigue, overload, externally induced vibration, corrosion, or lack of lubrication. Because of background vibration, signatures are generally not as clear or regular as those shown. Figure 10-5b presents the results of an actual test. The upper portion of Fig. 10-5b shows a normal bearing in good condition; the lower is a signature when the outer race has two dents.

Signature analysis with its amplification and recording techniques can provide warnings that problems are beginning long before they can be detected by other means. It constitutes an excellent method of pinpointing defects in operating equipment long before a failure, and perhaps an accident, occurs. Continuous surveillance of test results can determine the reasons for and the rate at which signature changes and degradation of the equipment are taking place. Maintenance and repair activities can then be programmed for accomplishment of corrective action at the most suitable time.

SOAP. Signature analysis is an indirect method of monitoring the physical condition of a piece of equipment through its operational characteristics. It is not unique in this respect; many indirect methods

Fig. 10-4. Hypothetical signature analysis. F. J. Lavoie, "Signature Analysis: Product Early Warning System," *Machine Design*, 23 January 1969, pp. 150–155.

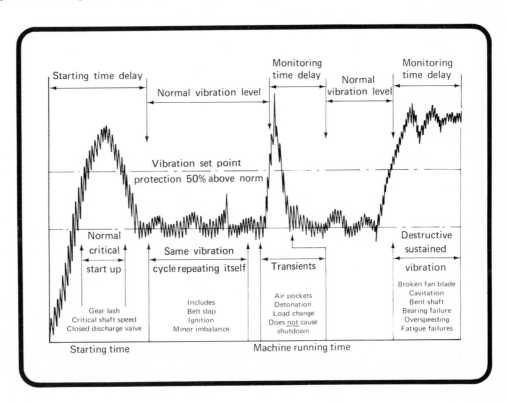

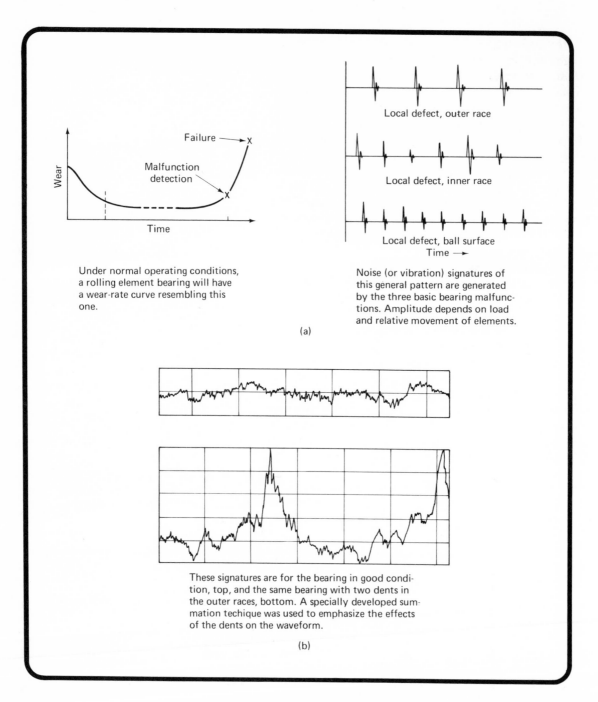

Under normal operating conditions, a rolling element bearing will have a wear-rate curve resembling this one.

Noise (or vibration) signatures of this general pattern are generated by the three basic bearing malfunctions. Amplitude depends on load and relative movement of elements.

Local defect, outer race

Local defect, inner race

Local defect, ball surface

(a)

These signatures are for the bearing in good condition, top, and the same bearing with two dents in the outer races, bottom. A specially developed summation techique was used to emphasize the effects of the dents on the waveform.

(b)

Fig. 10-5. Signature Analysis for Bearings. F. J. Lavoie, "Signature Analysis: Product Early Warning System," *Machine Design,* 23 January 1969, pp. 150–155.

Safety Achievement

are used for the same purpose when direct measurement of a specific parameter is impractical. SOAP (Spectrometric Oil Analysis Program) is another indirect method in use. As the title implies, oil is subjected to a spectrometric analysis; in this case, to determine the presence of minute amounts of aluminum, iron, copper, chromium, nickel, and other metals. The oil is taken from the supply in a mechanical system, such as an engine, in which it has been used as the lubricant.

Oils supplied to aircraft engines contain no metals, either in free form or as particulate matter. Any particles that analysis of used oil determines to be present must be the result of abrasion caused by friction between moving parts. These particles are suspended in the oil and can be detected spectrographically accurately in concentrations as low as two to three parts per million. The metals of which the particles are composed are readily and reliably identifiable since they have not undergone chemical change. The components from which they have been torn can therefore be identified, indicating where wear is taking place.

In addition, the rate of abrasion can be established through quantitative analysis. These rates can be compared with predetermined standards or threshold limits. Analyses are generally made for metals characteristic of those parts whose failures would cause engine failure. Any abrasion rate exceeding the pre-established limits can be interpreted as an indicator of a problem area where a failure may eventually occur in the absence of corrective action.

Monitoring by SOAP allows early detection of incipient failures long before they will occur. Thus, it is similar to signature analysis. Results can be employed to determine what corrective action is necessary. Sometimes the action should be immediate. For example, an aircraft should be grounded until correction is accomplished. Sometimes wear has taken place, but no immediate danger is involved and operations may continue under surveillance; sometimes wear is minimal. In addition to minimizing failure that could result in accidents, SOAP permits better programming of maintenance, reducing the necessity for emergency work.

SOAP has other uses. Analyses may indicate that certain alloys or metals are much more susceptible to erosion than they should be. In accident investigation it is frequently important to know that certain parts did *not* fail and cause the accident. This can sometimes be done by analysis of the lubricating oil.

Other Applications of Monitors. A few of the many other applications of monitoring may be mentioned here:

- Temperature and radiation monitors for nuclear reactors
- Odorants to indicate leakage of gases or high temperatures of metals, insulations, or other materials
- Gas monitors to determine the presence of toxic or flammable substances
- Infrared detectors to indicate the presence of hot-spots or of flames
- Smoke detectors to determine emissions of pollutants from stacks
- Liquid-level indicators that warn when the fluid reaches a preset limit
- Governors that activate warning signals or lights or take corrective action automatically when a predetermined speed is exceeded

The Buddy System. Personnel may also be employed as monitors to ensure the safety of persons who undertake hazardous operations. This is accomplished by means of the *buddy system*. The buddy system has been employed for many years by the Boy Scouts, Girl Scouts, and similar organizations for such hazardous activities as swimming.

Two methods have been employed. In the first, two persons who constitute a buddy pair are subject to the same hazard at the same time. Each must ensure the well-being of the other, monitoring his activities, providing assistance when required, or summoning aid when needed. Power company personnel who must work on live electrical systems employ this type of mutual aid system.

In the second type of buddy system, only one person of the pair is exposed to the hazard. The other acts as a lifeguard, with the sole duty of protecting and assisting the person in danger should the need arise. A common example in industrial work is the task during which a man must enter a tank to accomplish any cleaning or repair. A buddy is stationed outside to monitor the activities of the man in the tank and to ensure his well-being. He provides warnings on any adverse conditions that he may note, assists his buddy in need, and calls for aid when he feels it is required.

The outside man in this type of buddy system should have no duty except that of monitoring the man in danger. He might be authorized to perform such minor activities as passing tools when required. However, under no circumstances should he have to leave his station to obtain such tools. This prohibition against leaving includes performing any errand for the man being monitored, even at his own request. A means of communicating with other personnel for either supplies or assistance should be devised and instituted.

Procedures for operations involving the buddy system must indicate exactly what each person must do and the hazards that must be monitored. Supervisors must ensure that participating personnel in the buddy pair or persons who may be called on for assistance are aware of their duties, the hazards involved, the actions to take in the event a contingency arises, and know how to use rescue equipment.

Although they are not designated as part of the buddy system, there are other personnel who may be employed to monitor hazardous conditions. Wing walkers for taxiing aircraft are in this category. They monitor the route an aircraft must follow for obstructions or other hazards. When there appears to be inadequate clearance between the aircraft and a structure or other aircraft, danger to other personnel, or possibility of collision with another vehicle, the wing walker warns the person at the controls.

Warnings   A mishap due to a hazard that cannot be eliminated can frequently be avoided by focusing attention on the existence of the hazard and the need for care. Identification is a method of accident prevention involving relationships between personnel and hardware. In almost all instances, the intent of identification is to attract or focus the attention of an operator or other person on the item that constitutes or could generate the hazard. There are numerous examples of its use, and also of its misuse, since identification is often employed to point out the hazard instead of eliminating or minimizing it through improved design.

Every method of identifying and notifying personnel that a hazard exists requires communication. All of men's senses are used for this purpose. In the following list, the methods of warning personnel are presented in order of the frequency with which the particular senses are used for communication. The examples that are cited to point out how each sense has been used for warning constitute only a few of the many current applications.

Visual. Vision is the principal means by which hazards are identified to personnel. There are more variations of visual methods than there are when other senses are involved. These variations include:

1. Illumination. A location where a hazard exists is lighted more brightly than surrounding, less hazardous areas, as a means of

focusing attention. In some instances, these also provide a benefit in any security effort. For example, a power substation may be spotlighted brightly at night to prevent entrance of persons who might attempt to steal equipment, but the spotlight also indicates that there is danger. Other locations are often illuminated more brightly than surrounding areas because accidents have occurred there or in similar locations. These locations include highway intersections, entrance and exit ramps on expressways, stairways, fixed ladders, and obstacles. In many places in the United States, traffic deaths at previously dark intersections decreased dramatically after lighting was installed.

2. Discrimination. A structure, piece of equipment, or fixed object that could be impacted by a moving vehicle is painted a bright, distinctive color or in alternating light and dark colors. This method of attracting attention to the danger should be used only when the object cannot be relocated so that it no longer constitutes a hazard.

   A very common example of the use of discrimination in aircraft, electrical, missile, boiler plant, and other systems is color coding. Lines carrying high-pressure, high-temperature, toxic, corrosive, flammable, or otherwise dangerous fluids are color coded to indicate the hazards involved. Compressed gas cylinders are color coded for the same reason. Color coding is also employed to identify gasoline containing tetraethyl lead; a red dye is added. Accumulations of dye at connections and joints in a fuel system using such gasoline help to indicate where a leak may exist. Desiccants to keep equipment and materials dry in containers where they may be adversely affected by humidity are sometimes selected to turn color when saturated with moisture. This indicator warns that the dessicants are no longer providing protection.

3. Procedural notes. Warning and caution notes are inserted in maintenance and operations procedures, manuals, and checklists to alert personnel of hazards, possibilities of errors, special care or actions that must be taken, or protective devices, clothing, or tools that must be utilized. In any procedure, those steps in which a malfunction or error will produce a reaction that could cause system degradation, personnel injury, or death should be preceded by a precaution. One method is indicated in MIL-M-5474*:

NOTE: An essential highlight for an operating procedure, condition, or arrangement required for clarity and emphasis.

CAUTION

An emphatic notice requiring correct operating or maintenance procedures or practices to prevent damage to or destruction of equipment, and warning against improper procedures and practices. A major caution warns against a procedure, condition, or practice which may destroy the effectiveness of the equipment (mission).

---

*Technical Manuals, Preparation of; MIL-M-5474, (Washington, D. C., Bureau of Naval Weapons, January 1962), p. 9.

WARNING

A more emphatic notice requiring correct operating or maintenance procedures and practices and ensuring safe conditions, to prevent personal injury or loss of life.

4. Labeling. Warnings are painted on or attached to equipment in which a hazard is present or whose operation constitutes a hazard. "NO STEP" markings are painted on structural elements or other surfaces, such as unsupported aircraft or missile areas and hydraulic or pneumatic lines, that could be damaged by stresses generated by a person's weight. Special markings warn of the need to use jacking points; point out high voltage, phase, and frequency hazards in electrical and electronic equipment; give load, speed, pressure and temperature limitations; indicate low head room; or designate the pipes, hoses, and tubing that carry hazardous materials. The last warning generally complements color coding.

5. Signs. The commonest of these are fixed types such as road signs to point out curves, intersections, narrow bridges, dips, slippery roads, and other hazards. In this country, these signs are in English, are distinctively shaped, or both. Many countries where there are large numbers of foreign visitors are now attempting to employ symbols that can be understood by persons unfamiliar with the language.

   Equipment consoles frequently have electrically activated signs to indicate when a hazard exists or when a specific action should be taken. Some of the more expensive cars now contain devices that warn the driver to check his gauges when there is less than a quarter of a tank of gasoline remaining, when his seat belt is not fastened, or when his emergency brake has not been released.

6. Signal lights. Colored lights constitute a very common method of identifying hazards and preventing accidents. Fixed or flashing lights may be employed. In either case, the colors and their intended meanings generally are:

   a. Red—Existing danger, emergency, malfunction, failure, error, stop

   b. Yellow—Impending danger, marginal condition, caution, proceed slowly

   c. Green—Satisfactory conditions, proceed, ready, function, activated properly, parameter within limits

   d. White—System available, operation in progress

   Flashing lights are employed to attract attention and to indicate urgency. When headlights on locomotives were made to oscillate they became much more effective as warning devices to automobile drivers at railroad crossings. The swinging or flashing red lights at such locations are also effective devices. Flashing lights on aircraft attract attention so that collisions will be avoided. The fixed wing-tip and tail lights are coded to indicate which side of the aircraft is being observed and which aircraft has the right of way.

   Fixed lights will also attract attention, but to a lesser extent. Long-distance bus operators found their accident rates decreased when they left on the headlights on their vehicles during daylight. Another type of fixed-light signal is the reflector. They are used as warning devices on bicycles, road shoulders, barriers, and as lane markers. They require no source of power of their own and are cheap and effective.

7. Flags and streamers. These have a long history, especially as signaling devices by ships to indicate such hazards as operations with explosives or the presence of sickness aboard. Railroads use a type of mechanical flag in their semaphore signals. There are even more common usages. A red streamer to attract attention marks the end of a long load protruding over the tail of a vehicle. Red streamers are tied to safety pins on aircraft rocket launchers, ejection seats, and similar items as mnemonic devices. Flags are also attached to wires, ropes, or cables to ensure that personnel do not fail to see them and hence avoid them. Flagmen at construction sites use flags to warn motorists whether or not it is safe to proceed. Another type of flag is the tag on a switch or circuit breaker to indicate that the system has been inactivated for repairs, or other reasons, and should not be changed. Tags are attached to components that should not be used except after special precautions are first taken or because they have malfunctioned.

8. Hand signals. These are generally a series of motions to pass instructions, warnings, and other information from one person to another. The signals are sometimes the same for more than one purpose. For example, a man giving signals to a pilot for the parking of a plane may use the same signal to have him stop during a normal operation that a wing walker would use in an emergency to warn him to stop because of an obstruction.

Auditory. In some situations, visual warnings may not be suitable. Personnel who must be warned sometimes are so occupied with other tasks that they fail to note visual signals even when close to them. Persons may also move about, often into positions from which they cannot see a visual warning. Although a bright, visual signal can be seen over a greater distance, an auditory signal may be more effective within its smaller range. Sirens are excellent examples.

Auditory signals can also be employed to focus attention on visual displays that will provide additional and more detailed information on the condition constituting a problem. Or auditory signals can be coded to indicate the type of emergency that exists and the procedure that should be followed.

MIL-STD-1472 states that auditory displays should be employed when:*

- The information that is to be processed is short, simple, and transitory, requiring immediate or time-based response.

- The common mode of visual display is restricted by overburdening; ambient light variability or limitation; operator mobility; degradation of vision by reason of vibration, high G-forces, hypoxia, or other environmental considerations; or anticipated operator inattention.

Italic Failure Minimization

* *Human Engineering Design Criteria for Military Systems, Equipment and Facilities*, MIL-STD-1472 (Washington, D.C.: Department of Defense, 15 May 1970) p. 43.

- The critically of transmission response makes supplementary or redundant transmission desirable.
- It is desirable to warn, alert, or cue the operator to subsequent additional response.
- Custom or usage has created anticipation of auditory displays.
- Voice communication is necessary or desirable.

Besides the auditory signal methods already mentioned, other usages are common. Buzzers, bells, or other alarms on timing devices indicate when a specific period has passed or that the time has arrived to take the next step in a sequence. Some compressed air packs that provide respiratory protection for limited periods contain alarms that sound when the pressure level in the pack decreases to a predetermined level or after a preset time has passed. Alarms indicate when power to an aircraft engine is reduced below a specific level or that aircraft wheels have not been lowered for landing.

Olfactile. Odors can be detected only when certain types of gas affect a small area (approximately one-inch square) in the nasal cavity. Some gases have no odor. Other gas odors are extremely strong so that even small amounts may sicken the person affected. The body has the ability to desensitize itself against odors fairly rapidly. This ability is an advantage in one way: Odors generally constitute little problem after the person has become desensitized to their presence. In addition, the ability to detect odors varies considerably with individuals and their habits. These factors reduce the advantages that odorants have for warning purposes, except for short periods and in an environment where desensitization has not already occurred. However, odorants are employed successfully as a warning medium, and other usages have been proposed. Examples include:

1. Addition of an odorant to highly flammable and explosive gases that have no odor of their own and that are burned in homes and shops. Natural gas from which sulfur compounds have been removed has no odor since methane and ethane, its two chief constituents, are odorless. Fires and explosions from ignitions of accumulations of these gases are common. To reduce the number of such occurrences, an extremely small amount of a gas, such as a mercaptan compound, with a strong odor is mixed with the natural gas. The amount added is such that any leaking gas would be readily detectable even when the concentration of flammable gas is far below the amount at which it will ignite.

2. Overheating of equipment can sometimes be detected by the odors produced. This odor is generally due to the volatilization of substances with fairly low vaporization temperatures. Some lubricating oils are of this type so that surfaces that overheat because of friction can be detected readily. This principle was formerly employed with bearing boxes on railroad car wheels. A material was added that vaporized if a bearing became too hot, pinpointing the problem to any crewman making an inspection during a stop.

3. The presence of fires can be detected by the odors of gas produced from combustion. Different materials, such as wood and rubber, have characteristic odors that can indicate the type of

substance burning. It has been proposed that insulation on electrical wires and cabling located where they cannot be seen contain a material that will give off a strong odor if the insulation overheats and a fire starts or is imminent.

Tactile. The chief means of providing warnings through the sense of feeling is vibration. It warns that the motion involved in an operation is not as smooth as it should be. A rotating shaft or bearing beginning to wear may indicate this danger by the vibrations it produces. Rough running of a gasoline engine may also be due to a worn part, poor timing, low-grade fuel, or lubrication failure. The magnitude of the vibrations indicates the severity of the problem.

Vibration as a medium to provide warnings is employed on streets and highways in a number of ways. Raised lane markers cause a car hitting or passing over them to vibrate. A driver who dozes off may be awakened. Such markers may indicate that the car is too close to a shoulder or to a center divider or that it is crossing into another lane. Rough, corrugated road surfaces were sometimes placed before safety zones for bus and streetcar stops located in the middle of streets. A car hitting the corrugations would vibrate strongly, warning the driver of the danger. Pedals on aircraft with electric or hydraulic flight controls are generally equipped with "feel" systems or pedal shakers to apprise the pilot of aerodynamic conditions.

Another method of providing warning through feeling is temperature sensing. A maintenance man can frequently determine whether a piece of equipment is operating improperly by feeling it with the palm of his hand. If the temperature is abnormally high, the equipment may have to be shut down to determine and rectify the cause of overheating. An increase in temperature of an air-conditioned space may warn of problems with the equipment, under-capacity for normal requirements, or abnormal loads.

Taste. This sense is probably the least important as a warning mechanism. In some instances, taste can be utilized to determine whether a food, drink, or other material taken into the mouth is dangerous or contains a dangerous contaminant. Caution should be exercised when taste indicates the material is acid, bitter, excessively salty, or unusual in any other way.

Incorporating safety factors into equipment design to minimize failures during use was one of the earliest methods of accident prevention. Theoretically, if an item was to withstand a prescribed stress, making it strong enough to withstand three, four, or five times that stress would reduce the number of failures and accidents; that is, a structure or container that had a safety factor of 4 would fail half as frequently as one that had a safety factor of 2. However, in practice, this has not been the case. Inadequacies in using the safety factor therefore led to another concept: *margin of safety*.

A safety factor can be expressed as the ratio of strength to stress. Initially, strength was the nominal ultimate strength of the part: the value at which it would fail completely. A similar ratio was also employed based on yield strength to give a *yield factor of safety*. However, it was found that the ultimate and yield strengths of a specific material were not constant but would vary. For example, a large lot of steel rods may

**Safety Factors
and
Safety Margins**

Failure Minimization

273

be required in which each rod will withstand a stress of 10,000 lb per sq in (psi). However, differences will occur in the composition of the material involved, in manufacturing and assembly processes, in handling, in environment, or in usage. As a result, some of the rods will fail at less than 10,000 psi; others, at greater stresses; and the remainder, at the stipulated strength. The occurrence of failures at various stresses may be indicated by distribution curves such as the Normal or Weibull.

With a Normal distribution, the strengths may be indicated by curves similar to those shown in Fig. 10-6a. Curves A and B both have the same nominal, or mean, value. (See Fig. 10-7 for explanations of terms.) However, the distribution of values is narrower in B than in A and has a smaller standard deviation. This fact may be due to better workmanship and manufacturing processes, closer control of material

Fig. 10-6. Relationships between stress and strength.

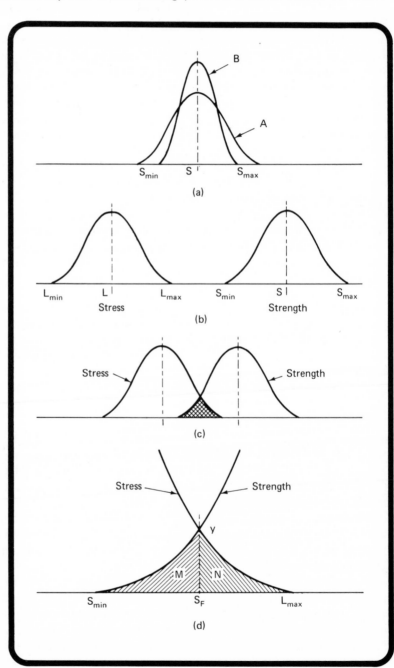

PROBABILITIES AND STATISTICS

Probabilities.   The outcome of any trial regarding occurrence of a specific event or result can have two possibilities and no more: that the specific event will occur (success) and that it will not occur (failure). In any series of trials, S successes and F failures will result from a total of $S + F$ possibilities. A probability is the ratio of number of successes or failures to the total number of possibilities. When the ways in which these can occur are equally likely and mutually exclusive, probabilities can be determined by:

$P_S = S/(S + F)$ = Probability of success;

and

$P_F = F/(S + F)$ = Probability of failure.

Any probability can be expressed as a common fraction or as a decimal within the limits 0 and 1. Decimals are in more common use, especially for computer processing. The value 1 indicates that the selected event is certain to occur; there is no possibility of failure. A zero probability indicates that the event is certain not to happen, a complete impossibility·by which failure must occur. Since the only possible events are either success or failure, it follows that $P_S + P_F = 1$.

Probability Distributions.   The probability derived through theoretical considerations and without actual trial is called an *a priori* probability. On the other hand, a probability determined by repeated trials is an empirical, statistical, or *a posteriori* probability. Empirical probabilities have an important place in statistical analyses, reliability studies, insurance, and in almost every science. Mendel's Law was derived from his empirical study of sweet peas and later substantiated by theory. Experimental probabilities follow the same rules as those for *a priori* probabilities. However, it must be noted that the value of an experimental probability is dependent on the total number of trials. When the ratio of chosen events to the total number of trials approaches a constant, that constant may be considered the probability of the chosen event, if the total number of trials was large.

Plotting the number of occurrences of any variable in a series of trials against the numerical values that result will produce clusterings called frequency distributions. Frequency distributions can be predicated on either discrete or continuous measurements. A discrete distribution, called a histogram, is made up of results that can fall only in specific, predetermined classes such as 0, 1, 2, 3, 4,..... In such cases, the variable can change only by set increments. Any characteristic that has a measured value between 0.501 and 1.500 would be in the 1 class; 1.501 and 2.500, in the 2 class; and so on. A continuous distribution is one in which a variable can have any value within an interval. It permits any reading, such as 1.25, 1.37, 3.2, or 4.05, to be indicated. If the number of classes is great enough, a discrete distribution will approach the continuous distribution as a limiting condition.

The total area in a histogan is equal to the width of each class times the frequency of its occurrence. It can also be shown that the same holds true for a continuous distribution. The total area in either case is based on all trials that were made, the total of which can be considered unity. The area involved in a histogram class, or under any portion of a continuous curve, when related to the total number of trials indicates the ratio of times that those values occurred. They can therefore be used to indicate probabilities.

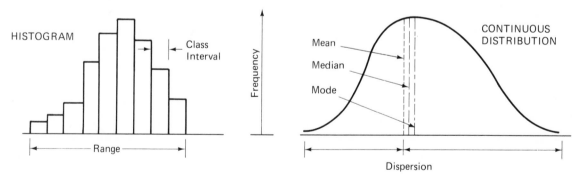

Some of the most common distributions are described below:

Binomial: One of the most important discrete distributions. It results from a series of Bernoulli trials in which there are only two possible, exclusive outcomes; the probability of either outcome (p or q) is always the same; and each trial is independent of all others. The distribution is one in which the frequencies of occurrence are proportional to the successive terms of the binomial expansion of $(p + q)^n$

Figure 10-7

Poisson: Use of the binomial distribution is extremely difficult when n is large or p or q is small. It is then often advantageous to approximate the probability of occurrence by use of the Poisson. If finds good application where the product of n and either p or q ($n \cdot p$ or $n \cdot q$) is 5 or less. The probability of an event x occurring in n independent trials is: $f(x) = (np)^x e^{-np}/x!$, where p is the probability of success, a constant. This distribution has wide application, especially in games of chance and reliability.

Exponential: A special case of the Poisson, typifying "chance" or random occurrences over a period of time. Chance occurrences are few in number compared to the large fraction of events that do not take place. The rate of occurrence, such as failures, is a constant. This distribution is the most common one used in reliability analyses but is slowly being replaced because it has been employed too frequently where it does not apply. The distribution function that expresses the probability that an item will survive to the end of operational time, t, is: $R(t) = e^{-\lambda t}$, where λ is the failure rate. Since time is generally known, the failure rate is the only parameter required for solution of this equation. The use of the single variable parameter is the principal reason that this distribution is used so frequently, although the results are not completely accurate.

Normal (Gaussian): This is the most important distribution in probability or statistics. It represents the case of the continuous variable that is the limiting condition of the discrete, binomial probability function.

Log-Normal: This distribution is useful in representing the condition in which several independent factors influence the outcome of an event in accordance with the value of each factor. It often provides a good fit for failures resulting from accelerated life testing of semiconductors and similar items. It is more difficult to use than the Normal distribution.

Gamma: This distribution is useful for analogue computer approximations of the Normal and exponential distributions. It is a continuous function that indicates times to failure of various failure modes.

Weibull: This is an empirical distribution developed to eliminate discrepancies of the exponential when the failure rate determined by observation is not constant. It actually represents a series of curves, each governed by parameters that define the shape and dispersion of the curve applicable to the test results. It is finding wider and wider use as experience indicates more accurate results in predictions of behaviour of components and assemblies are achieved than with other distributions.

Related Definitions Used in Probabilities and Statistics

Arithmetic Mean—The numerical average value of the trials that have taken place
Median— The value in a series at which one half of the items are the same or larger, and the other half are the same or smaller
Mode—The value around which the values concentrate. It is the maximum frequency in a distribution.
Limits — The minimum and maximum values of a series
Range — The difference between the limits
Dispersion — The extent to which values spread on either side of a mean, median or mode
Deviation — The amount by which each value in a series differs from the mean or median
Average deviation—Sometimes called *mean deviation*. It is obtained by adding each deviation from the mean, regardless of sign, and dividing the total by the number of items.
Standard deviation — Is obtained by squaring each deviation, adding the values, and taking the square root of the total. The symbol σ, sigma, is used to indicate standard deviation. Probabilities or percentages are frequently expressed by *sigma limits* for the Normal distributions. The areas included under the curve are

LIMITS	AREA (percentage of total under curve)
1σ (-1σ to $+1\sigma$)	0.6826
2σ (-2σ to $+2\sigma$)	0.9544
3σ (-3σ to $+3\sigma$)	0.9974

Figure 10-7 continued.

Safety Achievement

differences and quality of final products, or more care in handling and assembly. The curves indicate:

- Although the mean strength (S) may be the nominal value prescribed, actual strength will vary from a minimum (S_{min}) to a maximum (S_{max}).

- The strength values on either side of the mean vary with the control exercised in producing and handling the part and with differences in material. A better indicator than either the nominal value or mean alone would therefore involve use of the standard deviation.

- The actual strengths of 50 per cent of the items are the mean strength or less. Any load causing a stress equal to or slightly higher than the mean strength will cause 50 per cent of the parts to fail.

Imposed stresses (L) may also vary, although there may be an entirely different type of distribution. Both distributions, for stress and strength, may be presented on one diagram similar to that in Fig. 10-6b. In this illustration there is no overlap of curves: Theoretically there should be no failures. Actually, since the tails of a normal curve extend to infinity, the possibility of failure is always present. Generally, however, a 3-sigma limit is used so that maximum and minimum values can be cited. In addition, whether or not there are failures will depend on the confidence levels of these curves. A low confidence level means that probabilities still exist of occurrences of either higher stresses or lower strengths than those shown. Safety factors based on the curves in this figure may be expressed in a number of ways:

1. As the ratio of nominal strength to nominal stress:

$$\text{S.F.} = \frac{\text{Nominal Strength}}{\text{Nominal Stress}} = \frac{S}{L}$$

2. As the ratio of the strength and stress at any specified standard deviation (σ) from the mean:

$$\text{S.F.} = \frac{S - k_s \sigma_s}{L + k_L \sigma_L}$$

where k is any real number, generally 1, 2, or 3. The same or different values for k may be used for strength and stress.

3. As the ratio of the minimum probable strength (S_{min}) to the maximum probable stress (L_{max}):

$$\text{S.F.} = \frac{\text{Minimum Strength}}{\text{Maximum Stress}} = \frac{S_{min}}{L_{max}}$$

The applicable specification or code should stipulate clearly which values are to be used. It is becoming more common to consider safety factors as the ratio of minimum strength to maximum stress. In such cases, yield and ultimate safety factors may therefore be as low as 1.00 or 1.25.

When the minimum strength exceeds the maximum stress, as with a safety factor of 1.25, a margin of safety exists. Here again there are variations in expression. In some cases, the difference is stated in terms of the stress or strength, such as pounds per square inch. In others, it is expressed as a ratio:

1. Safety Margin = Safety Factor − 1.
   The safety factor may be determined by any of the means indicated above.

2. Safety Margin = $\dfrac{\text{Minimum Strength} - \text{Maximum Stress}}{\text{Maximum Stress}}$

   $$= \frac{S_{min} - L_{max}}{L_{max}}$$

In this case, the safety margin is related to maximum stress.

Failure Minimization

277

3. Safety Margin $= \dfrac{\text{Minimum Strength} - \text{Maximum Stress}}{\text{Minimum Strength}}$

$$= \frac{S_{min} - L_{max}}{S_{min}}$$

In this case, the safety margin is related to minimum strength. The safety margin will be lower than that of (2) when there is no overlap of distribution curves but will be higher when overlap exists.

The easiest way to determine probabilities of failure where there is an overlap of strength and stress is from plots of the curves themselves. Curves developed from either empirical or theoretical data require knowledge of mean or nominal values and actual or permitted standard deviations. At the point of intersection, stress will equal strength. The value can then be read on the horizontal axis. The shaded areas M and N in Fig. 10-6d represent where stress exceeds strength.

Area M is the left tail of the strength distribution, between the limits S_{min} and S_F. Area N is the right tail of the stress distribution, between the limits S_F and L_{max}. Both areas can be calculated from the means, standard deviations, and limits. The total of $M + N$ is the probability of failure.

When the strength and stress distributions overlap, definite and easily distinguishable probabilities of failure exist between the minimum strength and maximum stress. This fact is shown in the area common to both curves. In this case, a number of steps can be taken to eliminate or reduce possibilities of failure:

- Increase the nominal or mean strength of the part with better properties. This method will make no change in the distributions.

- Reduce the nominal stress that will be imposed on the part by increasing the size of the area stressed by the total load. This method too will not change the distribution.

- Reduce the variations from the mean or nominal strength by closer control of manufacturing processes, material, workmanship, assembly, and handling. The mean strength will not be changed but the deviation will be decreased.

- Reduce the variations from the mean unit stress by more rigid controls of loads that could be imposed on the part. This reduction will not change the mean unit stress itself but will decrease the standard deviation.

- Use any combination of methods indicated above.

The possibilities and probabilities of failure will be reduced by any of these methods. However, the first two methods will require or result in an increase in the safety factor computed as the ratio of nominal (or mean) strength to nominal (or mean) unit stress. The next two methods will not require or cause a change in this safety factor.

Failure Rate Reduction Operating components will not last forever. Actions therefore should be taken to limit failures while the system is operating, the rates of failure, and shutdowns of the system from component failures. Methods by which these can be accomplished include use of:

- Components with life expectancies much longer than their usages would normally require (*derating*)
- Timed replacements
- Screening
- Redundant arrangements of two or more similar components or subassemblies, only one of which is required for operation of the system
- Redundant arrangements of two or more components or subassemblies that may or may not be similar. One operates and the other is in a standby mode until the first fails, then the second is activated.

Reliability is the discipline principally involved with the problems of failures and failure rate reduction. The basic concepts are indicated in Figure 5-3. Like many other disciplines, there is an overlap between reliability and safety. In this case, the overlap results from the fact that failure of a part or system is the principal cause of accidents, incidents, and near misses. (Only certain highlights of reliability are touched here, to show applications to safety. For more details, a good text on reliability should be consulted.)

Derating. Manufacturers are constantly working to produce components with longer lives. Parts are rated by their manufacturers for failure, which will occur under specific conditions and stresses. Reducing the stresses under which components must operate will reduce their failure rates and increase their reliabilities. One of the stresses affecting the lives of electronic equipment is temperature. Failures increase with operating temperature; reducing the temperature prolongs their lives.* In one form of derating, therefore, cooling is provided even when the components operate at their normal capacities.

Derating can also be accomplished through use of components whose capacity is much greater than that actually required. Another means is by load sharing in redundant systems. In these designs, parallel redundant circuits are designed so that each one can carry the entire load. However, since each carries only part of the load during normal operations, each is utilizing only a portion of its total capacity. Such load reduction generally results in lowered failure rates.

Figure 10-8 illustrates variations of failure rates with various conditions. The nominal failure rates, shown by the ratio of operating to rated voltage, indicate how often malfunctions may be expected under conditions of operation recommended by the manufacturer for normal, economical use.

Timed Replacements. To maintain a constant failure rate, components must be replaced before they wear out. In addition, some operations are so critical that it is necessary to keep failures to an absolute minimum. This task may be done by monitoring the components and replacing them before they reach the period at which wear-out failures

---

* The reduction in failure rate that results from derating is generally far less than can be obtained through redundancy, as is shown later. The chief advantages of low-failure-rate components over redundant arrangements are lower overall cost, less maintenance, and lower weight. The last factor may be critical in missiles, space vehicles, and aircraft.

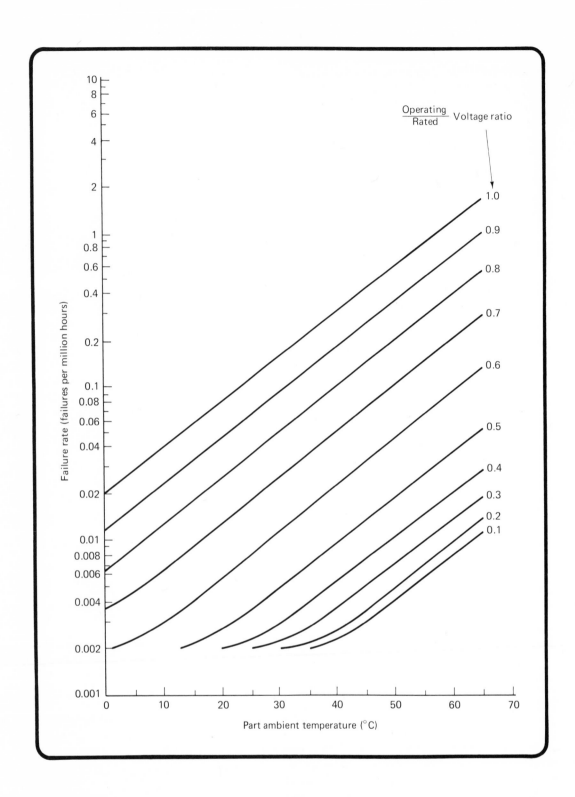

Fig. 10-8. Failure rates (in failures per 10^6 hours) for MIL-C-19978, polystyrene capacitors. Department of Defense, Military Standardization Handbook 217A, *Reliability Stress and Failure Rate Data for Electronic Equipment,* Washington, D.C., 1 December 1965, p. 7.6–70.

begin. Replacement too soon is wasteful and imposes an unnecessary maintenance and supply work load. In addition, excessive use of new units can increase burn-in failures.

There are two means by which timed replacements can be made effectively and efficiently. One method combines data obtained from controlled laboratory tests of similar components or assemblies with operational surveillance. The laboratory tests will indicate the time interval after which wear-out failures can be expected to begin. Replace-

280

ments can then be programmed at intervals shorter than these. This is the premise on which maintainability programs are generally based.

The second means of determining the optimum time to make replacements is by noting component *degradation* or the *drift* in operational systems. This procedure is based on the fact that most components, especially electronic and electrical units, deteriorate gradually; hence, components are replaced before they fail at critical times. A large group of new components in a system is tested for a specific characteristic, such as current flow through a tube under a specific voltage, which must be maintained within specific limits. The results of the tests are plotted in a frequency distribution. At specified time intervals, the same lot of components is tested again to determine whether degradation has occurred and, if so, how much. The change in value of the characteristic is the *drift*.

The lengths of time that it will take until the components will no longer perform their functions adequately can then be determined. Replacement of the entire lot can be made at the most opportune time, either after a time period calculated from the drift rate, or when the tests show that degradation has reached a predetermined level.

Screening. The curves in Fig. 10-5 indicate that one means of reducing failures is to reduce the dispersion of strengths through close control of component quality. The components with inferior strengths that will not permit them to meet imposed stresses or will cause them to fail at time intervals shorter than those that are allowable for the system are rejected. These are the components that produce burn-in failures. Screening employs methods similar to those for quality control but with one important difference: Quality control is undertaken to determine and eliminate those components that are defective at the time of inspection. Screening for reliability purposes means eliminating those components that pass the operating tests for specific parameters but with indications that they will fail within an unacceptable time. Reliability and quality control activities can be combined by setting suitable limits. One limit can be prescribed for extremely high-reliability items; a second, for less critical applications; and a third, as a minimum or failure level.

The technique for screening a population of components may be accomplished in four steps:

- The parameters whose limits are not to be exceeded are selected.
- The limits for each parameter are established. When system requirements are known, the limits can be based on conditions under which the components must operate.
- The components are inspected and tested to determine how well they meet prescribed parameter limitations.
- Those items having any characteristic value outside a specified limit are rejected.

In the first method of reliability screening, the dispersion of strengths over the entire range of values can be maintained so that the limits are symmetrical about the mean but are as narrow as practicable. The lower limit is constrained to the highest possible level so that the margin of safety becomes a maximum. The upper limit is therefore constrained similarly. This type of control is necessary for a device such as a diaphragm, which must not fail at pressures less than a specific level but must rupture at another, higher level. Similarly, electronic components whose lower and upper limits must be controlled to prevent wide fluctuations in output are also in this category.

In most cases, the upper limit need not be controlled; extremely high strength values merely indicate extremely high abilities to withstand imposed stresses. In such cases, the curve becomes skewed to the left, generally producing a truncated shape rather than one which gradually appoaches a lower limit. The acceptable limit may be expressed as a percentage of the nominal value of the parameter being measured. This nominal value is the mean of a normal curve that would be produced if all values, even those less than the lower limit, were included.

The third type of screening is accomplished by operating the component or assembly over a period during which burn-in failures may be expected to occur. If we refer to the bathtub curve in Fig. 5-3, this step consists of eliminating those items that would fail during the interval before the constant failure rate portion of the curve begins. Screening is predicated on the fact that defects in manufacturing or assembly may become apparent immediately or soon after operation begins. These substandard components can then be eliminated so that the remainder of the original components will have a higher average reliability (and lower failure rate) than the entire number tested.

Burn-in screening is accomplished on a 100 percent basis: Each item of the group is tested. Unfortunately, as a result, the method is extremely time-consuming and costly. Its use is therefore limited to components and assemblies whose criticality can justify the added effort or to short-duration burn-in tests. Furthermore, there is no assurance that any item tested in this way will not fail as soon as the system into which it is incorporated begins operation. Another problem is the effect that testing has had on the component or assembly. For this reason, some devices, such as large rocket engines, are subjected to burn-in tests, torn down and inspected for adverse effects, and then reassembled.

The procedure for conducting a burn-in test requires that the stresses to which the components are to be subjected and the criteria that they must meet are first established. The levels of stress and their durations are determined and specified. These levels are selected to ensure that substandard items that would fail under conditions of proposed system operation will become apparent but that no damage is done to satisfactory components. The tests are then conducted, the various parameters metered, and the results recorded. Where necessary, visual inspections are made immediately after the tests are completed. Those components failing to meet the established criteria are then replaced.

The last method of screening is accelerated-life testing. This method is employed principally to shorten the lengths of time necessary to determine the periods over which long-lived components will last. It involves subjecting the items tested to much higher stresses than those to which they would be subjected under programmed operations. It may be considered the reverse of derating.

Accelerated-life testing is subject to a number of weaknesses, the principal one being that there may be a change in the mode of failure. An increase in temperature may cause soldered connections to melt and fail where such failures would not occur at normal operating temperatures. The processes by which the components wear out may be altered, producing a condition in which many more wear-out failures would be generated than usually would occur. There may also be difficulty in determining the true relationship between the relative increases in stress and failure rate. An exponential increase in stress may produce only a linear increase in failure rate. On the other hand, some types of stress may not be time dependent so that increasing stress levels may not accelerate the effects. The method therefore requires that the parameters be selected that are suitable for accelerated testing.

Three types of accelerated-life testing are used. The basic type is constant-stress testing in which groups of components are stressed at levels that are constant for each group. The number of components in each group is large enough to make the test statistically indicative. The results are then plotted and analyzed. Where justified, extensions of values for predictions can be made. The other two types are step-testing and progressive-stress testing. In step-testing, the components are subjected to increasingly higher levels of stress, remaining at each level for a specific duration of time. The progressive-type test consists of starting different groups at different stress levels and then increasing them constantly at the same, regular rate.

Accelerated-life testing differs from the previous methods of screening principally because it is a means of testing groups of components by destruction of a sample. It therefore cannot be employed as a 100 percent method of screening. To a limited extent, accelerated testing could be adapted to certain types of burn-in screening.

To increase reliability by reducing the possibility that one failure may make a system inoperative, redundant arrangements are used. Two general types are employed: parallel redundant designs and switching. These may be categorized further as nondecision and decision.

Redundancy

1. Parallel redundant components perform the same function at the same time. This type of redundancy is generally applied to equipment requiring continuous operation within a specific time period. (Parallel circuits are not necessarily redundant, therefore the correct terminology is *parallel redundance* or *replication*.) The outputs of both or all parallel redundant items are not required for the system to operate successfully. In the most common designs involving replication, there are generally only two components, assemblies, or subsystems in parallel, each of which could carry the entire load.

   The simplest form of redundancy is the replication of single components in parallel circuits *A* and *B*. An output will result if *A*, *B*, or both *A* and *B* operate. Since reliability is a probability, the reliability of the system is expressed by:

$$R_{system} = R_A + R_B - R_A R_B$$

   This can be expressed in another way. The system will fail only if *A* and *B* both fail. The reliability can then be expressed as the complement of the probability of dual failure:

$$R_{system} = 1 - (1 - R_A)(1 - R_B)$$

   Exploding bridgewire (EBW) devices for activation of large or critical ordnance devices require that capacitors in the system be grounded to prevent accumulations of electrical charges that could activate the system. Generally, two grounds are required on the premise that although one is adequate and the probability of its failing is low, redundancy reduces the probability of complete failure to an extremely low value. If the reliability of each ground connection is taken as 0.95, the reliability of both would be:

$$R_{system} = 1 - (0.05)(0.05) = 1 - 0.0025 = 0.9975.$$

When three parallel configurations are involved, the system may operate when one, two, or all three of the circuits operate. The three circuits may be load-sharing when all operate, so they are derated and have longer lives.

However, if one circuit does fail, the others have the capacity to assume the entire load until replacements can be made. Here again, the commonest design is to ensure successful operation with only one operating unit. The reliability of a triple redundant system in which one good circuit permits the system to operate can be determined through use of the complement of the probability of failure:

$$R_{system} = 1 - (1 - R_A)(1 - R_B)(1 - R_C)$$

The reliability of a triple redundant system in which at least two circuits must be operative for the system to work can be determined through use of binomial probabilities. If the reliability of each component is R_c, the probability of at least two working is:
$P(\text{at least two working}) = P(\text{two working}) + P(\text{three working})$

$$R_{system} = 3R_c^2(1 - R_c) + R_c^3$$

If the redundant components have different reliabilities, the equation would have to be modified suitably.

Use of circuits involving more than triple redundancy is rare. The increase in reliability resulting from more than three circuits is offset by the increased probabilities of loss of the more numerous components and by the increased weight. One notable exception is the Boeing 747 airliner, which has four redundant hydraulic flight control systems.

2. Series Redundancy. Redundant arrangements can also be employed to prevent an action that could be damaging if it occurred prematurely. These preventive actions, or blocking elements, are generally arranged in series. All of the elements must be converted from a safe to an unsafe configuration before the system can be activated. An example of a redundant arrangement of this type involves the three blocking elements in a nuclear weapon. Three devices in series, each operated from a different source and parameter, must be activated before the device can be energized. The probability that all three blocking elements will fail to operate as designed is extremely low. Actually, there are generally more than three blocking elements in effect. The subject is discussed more fully under network logic analysis in Chapter 9.

3. Decision Redundancy. The development of hydraulically powered flight control systems for jet aircraft has placed more dependence on automatic controls. Safety therefore has become

dependent on assurance that this highly critical equipment is operable even if a specific component fails. Redundancy is the basic means for assurance. To ensure that a single malfunction will not cause system failure, logic techniques are employed for design and analysis of electronic and nonelectronic equipment. However, the miniaturization that has permitted electronic redundancy with substantially little increase in weight is usually not practical with mechanical systems. Weight is the critical constraint that frequently determines the suitability of a redundant design. Decision techniques are being used increasingly for electronic systems. These include:*

1. Majority vote. Critical units operate on three input signals from parallel redundant systems. When one of the signals differs from the other two, the unit being operated accepts the two similar signals as being correct. The probability of having two failures at the same time is remote but possible. Should this occur or the voter decision unit fail, an error will result. Methods have been suggested by which even this problem can be minimized by additional replication.†

   When only one voter is present, the probability of successful operation (P) is:

   $$P = q[p^3 + 3p^2(1 - p)]$$

   where q = probability of the voter working correctly

   p^3 = probability all three logic units work

   $3p^2(1 - p)$ = probability two logic units work and one fails

   The equation can therefore be simplified to:

   $$P = qp^2(3 - 2p)$$

2. Median select. The mid-value of three signal outputs is selected in this arrangement. Variations in the average are comparatively small when all three channels provide outputs. However, system design still permits discrimination and acceptance of the middle signal. This acceptance also occurs if one or two channels fail, even if failures occur in opposite directions. This method has been applied to a greater extent than the others mentioned here for control of high-speed aircraft. It is already in production, whereas the others are still in the laboratory and test stages.

3. TRISAFE (Triple Redundancy Incorporating Self-Adaptive Failure Exclusion). Three amplifiers are connected at a common output point from which feedback gain is provided. If one channel fails, gain in one of the other amplifiers varies

* F. R. Taylor, *Impact of Reliability Requirements on Flight Control Development*, (Wright-Patterson AFB, Ohio; Air Force Flight Dynamics Laboratory, March 1967). (AD 648 563)

† M. Longden, L. J. Page, and R. A. Scantlebury; "An Assessment of the Value of Triplicated Redundancy, in Digital Systems; *Microelectronics and Reliability*; (Oxford, England, Pergamon Press, 1966.) pp. 39–55.

to compensate while the third continues to operate normally. The system will function unless all three signals to a voting point fail.

4. Self-Organizing Concept (SOC). This method involves selection of an alternate signal path in event of a failure. It is analogous to the capabilities of the nervous system in carrying out its functions. A detection unit determines when a failure has occurred and selects a new signal path until output is correct.

4. Standby systems. Another method of increasing system reliability is to have inoperative or idling standby units that take over if an operational unit fails. Failure detection and switchover devices are necessary to activate the standby unit at the proper time. The inoperative or idling redundant unit wears out much more slowly than the operating unit and requires much less frequent replacement. In some instances, one unit can provide standby capacity for four or five units that operate continuously.

Activation of the standby unit may be manual, automatic, or both. A common example of the manual method is the braking system on an automobile: If the hydraulic foot brake system should fail, a hand brake is available. In this case, the human operator is the detecting and activating agency. In other systems, the failure can be detected and indicated by suitable instruments so that the operator can activate the standby system if he desires. In fully automatic systems, detection and activation are interlocked so that failure of the operating unit immediately initiates action of the standby equipment.

Electrical power supply systems may be designed for manual, semiautomatic, or automatic operation of standby units. Hospitals that are normally dependent on commercial power frequently have an alternate backup source to furnish power for operating rooms, incubators, and intensive care units. Diesel generators may back up commercial power supplies, batteries back up diesels, or both. If the primary source fails, the diesel may be started manually or automatically; the criticality of the effects produced by power loss is the determining factor.

The method does have disadvantages. Both the failure detecting and switching devices have reliabilities less than 100 per cent and may fail. In addition, the standby unit itself may not operate properly. Like parallel redundant systems, standby arrangements increase cost, weight, volume, complexity, and maintenance.

Standby systems with detection and switching devices may not only suffer from failures of these units but also from their erroneous activation. In other words, the operating unit may not fail, but the detector may, and thereby send a signal that causes switching to occur. Or the switch may operate spontaneously. In most cases, premature operation of the standby unit may not cause failure of the entire system or any other damaging effect. However, all possibilities should be investigated to determine whether premature activation can generate a mishap.

The fact that detection and switching devices, and the standby units themselves, are subject to failure limits the reliability attainable by this method to a definite maximum. Beyond this limit, system reliability decreases. Thus, the application of switching redundancy is confined to comparatively small units.

A failure, error, or other adverse condition may develop eventually into a mishap. The situation at this point is abnormal and extremely dangerous but has not as yet generated any injury or damage. It is a critical point: With suitable corrective action an accident can be avoided; failure to act or action that is incorrect or inadequate can permit the situation to deteriorate into a mishap. This interim period extends from the time that the abnormality begins to the time that either normality is recovered or a full-scale mishap develops. If recovery takes place, the incident can then be considered a near miss. Actions that should be taken in such a situation must be established by a contingency analysis for each particular operation. In general, these actions can be divided into:

1. Normal sequence restoration. Conduct of certain operations in wrong sequences may subsequently lead to a failure and mishap. However, there may be an interval during which the situation can be corrected without damage. A change may be made directly to the correct step in the sequence, or the procedure may go back to the beginning of the sequence or to another predetermined step from which a new start can be made.

2. Aborting the entire operation. Each operation has a point at which the sequence can be halted without injury to personnel. Sometimes a halt can also be called without damage to equipment, although this is secondary to safeguarding lives. A missing bolt, leaking oil line, inoperative device detected before the operation begins might cause an abort whose only adverse effect might be delay. Abort after the operation begins could have effects of varying magnitudes.

3. Inactivating only malfunctioning equipment. This step can be accomplished when the problem occurs with the following items:

   a. Those that are nonessential to the overall operation at any time

   b. Those that can be spared because of redundancy

   c. Those that have already fulfilled their functions in the overall operation and are no longer required

   d. Those for which temporary substitution can be made

4. Suppressing the hazard. When a hazard becomes apparent or exceeds a specific limit, it can sometimes be removed or suppressed. Spillage of a large amount of gasoline could produce a flammable mixture and a fire. The possibility of an accident is eliminated by flushing away the gasoline and recreating a normal atmosphere. Such actions may be either automatic or manual, depending on the type of monitoring and control equipment available.

Backout and Recovery

As long as a hazard exists, there is the possibility, no matter how improbable, that an accident will occur. There is no way of knowing when it will take place. Dangers of accidents are greatest when the system or its components are being tested during development. Through

Damage Minimization and Containment

experience and knowledge personnel learn what improvements can be made by correction of designs and replacement of undependable items. Tests are carried out by highly trained operators, who are working in protected environments and who are alert to the possibility that failures at that stage are highly likely. When the developed system becomes operational, the operational personnel may be less skilled, knowledgeable, protected, or capable of meeting emergencies. Designers must therefore assume that in the hands of the ultimate user accidents will occur if any hazard exists, and precautions must be taken to minimize and contain any damage or possibility of injury.

The need for assuming worst-case conditions for design of a system has already been mentioned. The same assumption must be made for accidents and their effects. One form of the so-called "Murphy's Law" states that an accident will occur at the worst possible time and place. People have an unhappy propensity for following "Murphy's Law" in ways that were never considered by system designers. It is therefore necessary that designers explore, to the fullest all means to minimize injury and contain damage. Unfortunately, considerations of cost or mission requirements may make it impractical to incorporate safeguards for complete protection. However, some of the protective methods that can be applied are explained in the following paragraphs.

Isolation

Isolation has been indicated as an accident prevention measure. It is also employed frequently as a method of reducing damage that can be generated by violent release of energy as a result of an accident.

One of the commonest methods is locating the site of a possible accident far from personnel, matériel, or structures. Explosives safety quantity—distance criteria are predicated on this principle. In this way, standards are set for the amounts of explosive that can be located or stored at specific distances from other critical items or inhabited areas or structures. Explosives that detonate accidentally will not initiate explosions of other explosives, cause damage to buildings or other structures, or cause personnel injury.

Energy-absorbing mechanisms isolate personnel and sensitive equipment from the effects of impact. Bumpers and padded interiors reduce injuries to occupants of automobiles involved in accidents. Foams, excelsior, and similar materials in containers protect items that would otherwise be damaged if the container were dropped or jarred in any way. Pertinent facts regarding energy-absorption processes are illustrated in Fig. 10-9.

Most of the protective features involved in the term *crashworthiness* are actually predicated on the principle of absorption of energy. Shoulder straps, seat belts, and other harnesses restrain and isolate an occupant of a vehicle so that he will not impact nearby objects or surfaces or be thrown about and injured. A pilot who may have to eject from a high-speed aircraft is provided with a shield or capsule that isolates and protects him from the air through which he will be propelled.

Another type of isolation may be provided by deflectors. Barricades between explosives and inhabited or other critical buildings are doubly effective since they absorb the energy of an explosion and deflect the remainder upward where it will do no harm.

Fig. 10-9. From "New Ways to Soften Shock," by A. Coppa in *Machine Design,* 28 March 1968, p. 133.

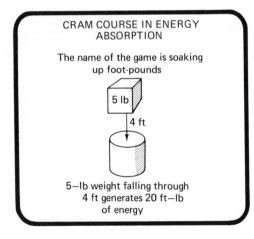

CRAM COURSE IN ENERGY ABSORPTION

The name of the game is soaking up foot-pounds

5 lb

4 ft

5—lb weight falling through 4 ft generates 20 ft—lb of energy

Containment processes are other common means of isolation for damage control:

- Hazards generated by a mishap can be contained; for example, limiting the spread of fire resulting from an accident, using fire-breaks to restrict a forest fire, and spraying water around a magnesium fire to prevent ignition of nearby flammables or damage from the intense heat.
- An operation may become uncontrolled as the result of an accident, but damage and injury can be avoided by limiting the effects. A tire may blow on a racing car, so it spins out of control in the vicinity of spectators. Suitable barriers could confine the vehicle to the limits of the track so that no spectator is injured.
- Personnel themselves can be provided protection. This point has been made before under crashworthiness and under control of operations. In some systems, certain areas or structures can be designated as "safety zones" where personnel will be safe from the hazards generated by an accident.
- Matériel can be protected by methods similar to those for personnel. Containers of metal, plastic, or other impermeable or impenetrable substances are effective in minimizing damage to materials if a mishap occurs. Waterproof boxes or containers will prevent contents from damage by water present as the result of an accidental leak or a flood.
- Critical equipment can be protected in the same way. An electric motor whose operation may be required in an emergency, such as a flood, can be hermetically sealed, so it will run even when under water.

A few other examples of isolation can be cited:

- Compartmentation of ships to limit flooding after a collision in which the hull is holed
- Fire walls and fire doors on buildings to prevent spread of fire
- Cutting off fuel or oxidizer in a fire
- Containment spheres around nuclear reactors to prevent dispersion and spread of radioactive material in the event of an accident
- Use of sealants in such containers as tanks and tires to prevent loss of fluid due to accidental holing

Containment

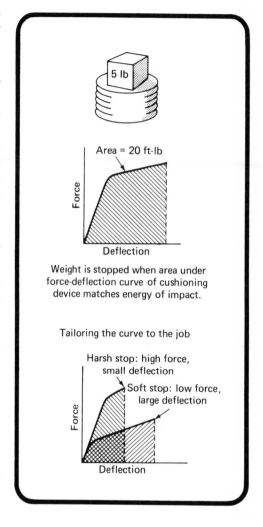

Weight is stopped when area under force-deflection curve of cushioning device matches energy of impact.

Tailoring the curve to the job

Figure 10-9 continued.

Use of personal protective equipment is another means by which protection from hazards can be achieved through isolation. The user is provided with a limited, controlled environment different in at least one respect from the ambient environment. The difference is the isolation from the hazard.

Personal protective equipment here connotes those garments or devices that a person would wear for protection against a hazard. They may vary from a complete space suit with oxygen equipment that an astronaut would wear to a simple set of ear plugs. In the first case, the astronaut is isolated from all space hazards; in the second, the user is isolated from noise and the adverse effects that noise could generate.

Personal Protective Equipment

Isolation

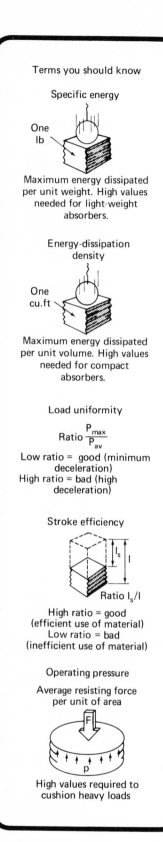

Terms you should know

Specific energy

One
lb

Maximum energy dissipated
per unit weight. High values
needed for light-weight
absorbers.

Energy-dissipation
density

One
cu.ft

Maximum energy dissipated
per unit volume. High values
needed for compact
absorbers.

Load uniformity

Ratio $\dfrac{P_{max}}{P_{av}}$

Low ratio = good (minimum
deceleration)
High ratio = bad (high
deceleration)

Stroke efficiency

Ratio l_s/l

High ratio = good
(efficient use of material)
Low ratio = bad
(inefficient use of material)

Operating pressure

Average resisting force
per unit of area

High values required to
cushion heavy loads

Figure 10-9 continued.

290

Personal protective equipment may be required to safeguard personnel against harmful environments that cannot be eliminated during necessary operations or that result from mishaps. The equipment must be adequate to protect its user under the worst possible foreseeable conditions. Conditions may change so equipment that is suitable for one set of circumstances may not be suitable for another. For example, a gas mask usable against chlorine and similar gases would not provide protection against the presence of carbon monoxide or hydrogen sulfide or against the absence of air. In these cases, an air pack or oxygen generator is necessary.

Needs for personal protective equipment can be divided into three broad categories:

1. Scheduled hazardous operation. Operations may have to be conducted in environments that could be as damaging as if an accident had occurred, because the hazard cannot be eliminated. Spray painting in an enclosed space is an example. Another example is connecting and disconnecting lines and equipment during transfers of liquid propellants from a tank truck to a rocket or missile. The liquid might be highly toxic, corrosive, or at a cryogenic temperature. Connectors are generally designed to prevent liquid escaping when the connection is broken after filling is completed. However, a small amount frequently drips or sprays out. Unless personnel performing the operation wear protective equipment, they may be injured.

   Protective equipment is frequently provided for numerous other operations, to be worn while the operation is being conducted. However, the use of personal protective equipment as a substitute for good design, hazard elimination or control, or safe operating procedures should be avoided. An example is requiring a man to wear respiratory protective equipment for operations conducted in a tank or other closely confined space. This procedure is much less desirable and less safe than ventilating the space so that a normal, breathable atmosphere exists and monitoring it to ensure that it remains breathable.

2. Investigations and corrections. Detection equipment may indicate or personnel may suspect that an environment is dangerous. It may then be necessary for someone to enter the area, determine the source of the contamination or other dangerous condition, and take corrective action. In some instances, the hazardous material may be known, such as during neutralization or decontamination of a leak or spill of a toxic, corrosive, or flammable liquid. At other times, the exact natures of the contaminants or their concentrations may be unknown or uncertain. Personal protective equipment for this purpose must be capable of providing protection against a wider range of hazards than for a known hazard.

3. Emergencies. An emergency generates the severest conditions and requirements for usage, design, and capabilities of protective equipment. The first few minutes after a contingency becomes imminent or occurs may be critical. Reaction time to suppress or reestablish control of the hazard or to minimize damage or injury is therefore extremely important. Emergency equipment must permit quick response. It must be easy to don and simple to use, especially by personnel under the stress of

an emergency. It must be highly reliable and effective against a broad variety of hazards. It must not degrade the mobility or performance of the user unduly nor constitute a hazard itself.

Emergency equipment can also be categorized into items needed for:

- Crashworthiness. Examples: helmets, hard hats, safety goggles, seat belts, shoulder harness, padding and other shock isolators.
- Escape, egress, and survival. Examples: ejection seats, parachutes, ladders, slides, gas masks, small compressed-air respiratory protective equipment, and life rafts.
- Prevention and containment. Examples: asbestos or aluminized suits for thermal protection, rubber suits for corrosive or toxic material protection, respiratory protective equipment, body armor, and fire blankets.
- Countermeasures and rescue. Examples: heat shields, respiratory protective equipment, resuscitators, and first aid equipment.

System designers must ensure that equipment designed or selected for personnel protection is suitable for the hazardous conditions that might be encountered. As emergency equipment, it should be considered only as a backup, as a redundant arrangement to be employed only in case more preferable methods of accident prevention or damage and injury control cannot be employed. However, when personal protective equipment is necessary, it had better work as intended or the user will be exposed to a second mishap having a much higher probability of being fatal. Analyses of designs, hazards involved, procedures for use, and safeguards to prevent impairment of their performance must be even more stringent than for systems and equipment for normal mission purposes. The designs must be extraordinarily foolproof, since the possibilities of ever-present human error are increased because of the stress to which all personnel are subjected during emergencies.

Designs and tests of protective equipment should ensure to the greatest degree practicable that:

- It will not deteriorate rapidly in storage or in the presence of the hazard against which it is supposed to provide protection.
- Protective coverings will not become brittle or crack because of the flexing action in normal movement, deleterious materials, temperature extremes, sunlight or other radiation.
- It is easy to clean and decontaminate.
- Clothing to protect against toxic or corrosive gases or liquids is impermeable.
- Coverings that might be exposed to fire are noncombustible or self-extinguishing.
- Facilities for storage of emergency equipment are located as close as practicable to the point where its use might be required. It must not be so close that the condition generating the emergency will affect the equipment or prevent reaching it for use. Storage units should be easily accessible and marked for quick identification, and locations should be identified in operating procedures.
- Instructions are provided on proper methods of fitting, testing, and maintaining protective equipment.

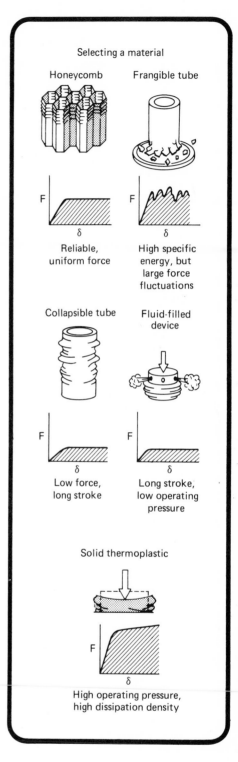

Figure 10-9 continued.

Minor Loss Acceptance This technique involves utilization of the basic principle on which insurance is predicated: acceptance of a small loss to ensure that a large one does not occur. A few examples of how this principle has been applied to the design of equipment include:

1. The freeze plug in the cooling system of an automobile engine. Should the water in the cylinder block freeze completely, its expansion will force the plug out rather than crack the block.

2. The fusible plug in a boiler. The plug will not be kept cool if it is exposed by the water level dropping below a predetermined level. The heat will not be conducted away; the temperature of the plug will rise; and it will melt. The opening that it creates permits the steam to escape, reduces the pressure in the boiler, and eliminates the possibility of a boiler explosion.

3. Providing oil and gas furnaces with blowout panels that give way if overpressurization should result from delayed ignition of accumulations of fuel vapors and gases. This feature prevents or reduces damage to furnace walls, boiler tubes, and other critical parts of the equipment and structure. Similar use of blowout panels or frangible walls is made in explosives-processing plants, where an explosion would otherwise destroy a structure completely.

4. Collapsible steering columns now being installed on automobiles. Formerly, drivers were killed or severely injured in collisions when their chests hit the steering columns. With the new designs, the columns collapse under a load so that only slight injury will result from that contact.

5. Frangible signposts that are being used more and more on highways. If directional control of an automobile is lost and the post is hit, the possibility of injury to people and damage to the automobile is minimized.

6. Shear pins on couplings of motor-driven equipment. If an overload occurs, the torque causes shearing of the pin, preventing damage to the driving or driven shaft or burnout of the motor.

7. Blowout plugs that are often provided on solid-propellant motors. If an overpressure occurs because of uncontrolled combustion, the plugs give way. Pressure is reduced so that the motor does not explode, and combustion stops.

Escape and Survival Deterioration of a contingency may continue until a point is reached after which it is necessary to abandon or sacrifice system equipment, vehicles, hardware, or structures to avoid injury to personnel. It was pointed out under contingency analysis (in Chapter 8) that this point is a point-of-no-return. Effort has been made to recover from the emergency, to suppress the hazard and any damage that could result, to restore normal conditions, or to isolate adverse effects. If these efforts are unsuccessful, it may be necessary to abandon ship, bail out, eject, or, in some other way, leave the danger area. For such situations, escape and survival equipment are literally vital: Lives depend on them.

A distinction should be made here between equipment for escape and that for survival. An example is a jet pilot's emergency equipment.

His ejection seat helps him to escape from the aircraft; other devices safeguard him in and against his new environment. A shield or capsule protects him against air blast, since the pressure of the air through which he will be traveling initially at extremely high velocity would be similar to that from a high-explosive shock wave. A parachute is then required, so he can survive falling from the height at which he finds himself. In some instances, a temporary supply of oxygen and insulation against the cold may be required. If the flight is over the ocean or other very large body of water where a landing might take place after a parachute descent, an inflatable life raft is necessary. This raft would have to include rations and water to permit survival for an extended period until he is found. Similar provisions would have to be made if flights were over arctic or jungle areas.

The importance of escape and survival equipment cannot be over-stressed for those situations in which they are necessary. However, in many instances, undue reliance is placed on their possible use, resulting in lack of suitable emphasis on controlling accident causes. Escape and survival equipment should be considered and employed only in cases of last resort. To avoid occurrence of last-resort situations, engineers must do their utmost to eliminate or minimize those conditions that could result in loss of control of hazards and in accidents. Systems equipment design should maximize use of safety devices and procedures to avoid the necessity for use of escape and survival equipment. It is recognized, however, that there are numerous cases in which hazards cannot be eliminated entirely, that accidents will occur, and that escape and survival equipment must be provided.

In some instances, escape may be a fairly easy process; under only slightly different conditions, escape may be impossible. The discussion of helicopter accidents in Chapter 6 indicated that in most accidents the helicopter had a tendency to flip onto its right side. If the right side was the only one having a door through which passengers could leave the vehicle, escape would generally be impossible. A similar problem that existed (until corrected by use of a more secure latching device) was slamming of the sliding door. In this case, forward impact caused the door to slide shut, trapping the passengers when it jammed.

The same type of situation applies to other types of vehicles, such as automobiles and passenger aircraft. Collision of an automobile may cause its doors to jam. The occupant may then have to be rescued. If he is badly injured and bleeding or a fire occurs when escape is blocked, the results would be fatal. Commercial aircraft, for this reason, are generally provided with multiple exists to permit evacuation of passengers within a specified time even when a number of escape routes are blocked.

The designs and devices to permit escape after a collision are another aspect of crashworthiness mentioned under isolation of damage in this chapter. Crashworthiness is a three part-concept:

- Protect a person by isolating him, generally against impact and other energy effects and hazards, such as fire.

- Permit him to escape from the vehicle and to reach safety from any hazards resulting from the crash.

- Permit rescue operations if he cannot escape by his own efforts (see following section).

Designs for the crashworthiness escape aspects therefore include such items as escape doors and panels, nonjamming doors, slide chutes, knockout windows, and breakaway sections. This last method involves designing a vehicle such as an aircraft so that on impact it will break apart at specific locations to provide large openings for the exiting of personnel.

It is evident that escape and survival devices to be incorporated into a system must be considered critical items. They must be analyzed and tested intensively to ensure that they meet their intended purposes with low probabilities of failure. Such equipment and the environment for which each one is designed are subject to hazards, as was the basic operative system, with one major difference: Control of a hazard has been lost and the danger level is much higher.

Failure of a piece of escape or survival equipment may be worse than if no equipment at all had been supplied. In some instances, such items themselves have injured the users because of their poor design or manufacture. Failure or inadequacy when a crisis occurs produces a traumatic shock over and above that which the mishap to the system produced. In addition, the time lost in establishing that the equipment did not work or worked improperly, in determining an alternative course of action, and then taking that action under stress reduces the chances of successful accomplishment.

Alternative courses of action may be possible in some instances and not in others. Some actions may be possible up to a specific point in time, after which they are not. The pilot of an aircraft whose single engine fails may elect to attempt a landing rather than use his parachute. He has the alternative to a certain point: the altitude below which he cannot use the chute. On the other hand, when he elects to parachute, he is committed to a single, unchangeable course of action. If the parachute fails, he will almost certainly be killed.

The need for escape and survival equipment and procedures must be established by contingency analysis. Once this task is done, the equipment to be employed must be selected carefully. It must be analyzed to ensure that it will fulfill all foreseeable needs and that procedures for its use are available and adequate. The equipment should be studied in detail through Failure Modes and Effects Analysis, logic trees, or other methods. A test program must be developed to ensure that the items will work under expected conditions, that they will satisfy established requirements, and that procedures are adequate. Tests should also be conducted under worst-case conditions to determine whether the equipment can be operated and the procedures followed by someone partially incapacitated.

Very often, escape and survival equipment furnished for emergencies is suitable for that purpose, but failure to maintain it properly allows it to deteriorate so that it will not work as it should. Procedures must therefore be established for both proper use and maintenance, with replacements to be made when necessary.

Rescue Procedures and Equipment

In any emergency the possibility will exist that the person (or persons) involved may not be able to escape under his own resources. Provisions must be made for rescue by other personnel if the need should arise. Rescues may be attempted by:

- Persons familiar with the system and its associated equipment and with their operation, hazards, and emergency devices.

- Personnel familiar with the hazards in general but not with the specific equipment. A city fireman may be well-trained in fire-fighting but may lack training in rescue of personnel from burning aircraft.

- Untrained personnel, unfamiliar with the system or the hazards involved, but who want to help.

Because these last two categories of personnel can (and do) provide vital assistance, it is advisable to mark any emergency devices so that volunteers can determine how and where to assist the persons to be rescued. Suitable markings and the presence of available devices may mean the difference between a successful and unsuccessful rescue attempt. Latches on the outside of aircraft to release cockpit canopies are examples. Their existence may permit rescue by all these categories of personnel if they are marked. If the latches are not marked, only personnel familiar with aircraft or those latches may be able to operate them.

Such devices must be foolproof in an emergency, require little physical effort to operate, and be easy to operate when only a few words of instruction are provided. The instructions should be marked so that they are easy to recognize and easy to understand by a person under stress.

The time to develop suitable rescue devices and procedures and to study the adequacies of those proposed is early in the design stage, when contingency analyses should be made. The results of these analyses may determine whether changes in equipment or procedures are required or whether other protective or rescue devices are necessary. The necessity, indicated in the previous section, that escape and survival equipment be subjected to rigid analyses because of their criticality is even more applicable to rescue devices. If an escape device fails, the user may be injured or killed. Should rescue equipment fail, both the rescuer and the person he is attempting to assist may be killed.

Rescue equipment may be specifically designed for a system, may be general-purpose items usable for a wide a category of emergencies, or may be improvised from items built for other purposes. An example of the first category is the emergency canopy release for an aircraft. The crash truck on an airfield is an example of the second. The use of helicopters for rescue of people from burning aircraft exemplifies the third category. The helicopter was not made specifically for the purpose, but it was found that the downdraft from its rotor blades would blow the flames in a direction that would permit the escape of persons in the aircraft. The downdraft also provides a path along which rescuers could pass.

Organizations that use systems containing rescue devices and equipment should develop preaccident plans. These are necessary even though the plans may never be put into actual practice. Training must be undertaken to ensure that operators and rescue personnel understand and are proficient in carrying out rescue procedures. Simulated emergencies will also help increase proficiency. Investigations of many serious accidents frequently reveal that personnel died because of lack of proficiency in the use of rescue equipment and devices or because of failure to follow established procedures.

chapter 11

MANU-
FACTURING,
MAINTENANCE,
AND TRANS-
PORTATION

Next to design inadequacies and deficiencies, the principal causes of equipment and system failures and accidents are errors made during manufacturing and maintenance. Beau states:*

> Practically all people engaged in Quality/Reliability work and Field Engineering are painfully aware of the effect of workmanship defects which escape into the field. This awareness is acquired by daily contact with unhappy customers, analysis of failed hardware, troubleshooting and, in general, answering mountains of correspondence brought into being because of this problem.

He also points out:*

> Three facts of life are with us continually, and are stated as follows:
> 1. All factory mechanics will certainly make mistakes resulting in poor workmanship some of the time.
> 2. All inspectors will certainly make mistakes and pass (accept) bad work some of the time.
> 3. It is a certainty that some material will progress to higher levels of assembly or be delivered to the customer with unknown and undetected defects which might cause trouble.

These statements regarding manufacturing apply also to maintenance. Certain steps in manufacturing, such as welding or assembly of equipment, also take place during maintenance. However, such procedures involve problems that the other does not. Manufacturing normally has no problem with equipment that warped, fouled, or weakened during operation. A piece of equipment would not contain gas under pressure or be energized electrically during manufacture, whereas this danger might exist during maintenance.

In both manufacturing and maintenance (and in other logistic operations such as transportation, handling, and installation), the effects of negligence or error may cause degradation of the system or product so that failures are frequent and accidents common. The resultant reductions in safety level will depend on such factors as: the level of workmanship, quality control, the allowance that the designer permitted for human and environmental effects on the hardware, the actual environment encountered, and safeguards provided.

Manufacturing

Many accidents due to equipment failures can be traced back to defects generated during manufacture because of poor workmanship, design changes to reduce production costs or difficulties, or both. Loss of at least one multimillion-dollar aircraft was attributed to manufacture of a control rod that failed in flight. In the original design the rod had been a one piece, but to permit more economical manufacture it was made up in two pieces joined by a weld, which later failed.

This accident indicates the necessity for careful consideration of any proposed changes. These changes should not be made unilaterally but only after careful consideration and study with designers and reliability engineers. In the past, uncoordinated changes have caused degradation of entire systems and resulted in accidents. This has been a particular problem with items produced by subcontractors and vendors. In many instances, these suppliers have made such changes, which they believed

* J. F. Beau, *"Management of the Human Element in the Physics of Failure,"* paper presented at the 3rd Annual Symposium on the Physics of Failure in Electronics, Chicago, Illinois (29 September 1964); p. 8.

improved the product, without informing the customer to whom they were supplying the items. They could not tell that the "improvements" actually cause increased failures because of the ways in which the products were used. *No* changes in design, material, or manufacturing method should be permitted unless formal approval is granted after study of the factors involved.

In checking out some of the equipment during site activation of intercontinental ballistic missile facilities, field service personnel encountered problems in making electrical and electronic circuits operate properly. They would then make cross-connections so that the system would work during acceptance tests. Most of these "klujes" were left in place without being reported or being reviewed to determine whether any safeguards, such as blocking elements or interlocks, had been bypassed or any hazards introduced. These cross-connections might have activated circuits inadvertently or caused failure of critical equipment through overloads or short circuits.

Meister made the following comment regarding workmanship:*

> In sheer number, production and installation errors cause a very significant part of the equipment failures reported. Shapero (1960) made a survey of several major missile systems and reported that the percentage of equipment failures caused by human error (what we call 'human-initiated failures') ranged from 20% to 53% of the total failures reported. My own estimates tend to be somewhat more conservative. Of the 1425 failures referred to earlier (from an Atlas missile testing site) only 256 or about 22% of them were determined to be human-initiated. Of course, these failures were reported from a field test environment, in which the largest proportion of human-initiated failures would have been screened out by inspection prior to accepting the equipment for test. When a system is in production but before it is completed and sent to the field for testing, as much as 80% of all items reported as failed are caused by human error in the production process.

Critical Items

Certain components and assemblies are critical from a safety standpoint and must be given special care and attention. Generally these will fall into four categories:

- Materials and components that are extremely hazardous themselves: explosive and pyrotechnic devices, toxic substances, or radioactive materials
- Items that in combination are hazardous, such as certain solvents and alkali metals, hydrocarbons, and liquid oxygen, or dissimilar metals in contact with each other
- Safety devices, such as interlocks, safe-and-arms, destruct systems, or ejection seats.
- Single-point failure items whose loss or malfunction could cause an accident.

In some instances, critical items to be subjected to special tests or inspection are designated by the customer. MIL-I-6870 lists all the parts of an aircraft that are to be subjected to nondestructive tests for defects.† The last part of the listing includes "All items peculiar to the weapon

---

* David Meister, *Applications of Human Reliability to the Production Process* (Canoga Park, Calif., Bunker-Ramo Corporation), p. 33.

† *Inspection Requirements, Nondestructive, for Aircraft Materials and Parts*, MIL-I-6870 (Wright-Patterson AFB, Ohio, Aeronautical Systems Division, 1965)

system, the failure of which would affect the safety of flight." This stipulation evidently includes any metallic part whose failure could generate an accident; an extremely broad category. According to this specification, each unit manufactured of every item on this list is to be inspected.

Criticality may have been determined during FMECA or other analysis or be known from past experience. As indicated in Fig. 5-6, even components that do not appear significant to those who are not cognizant of the overall effects, such as touching plates in a missile battery could cause the loss of the missile as surely as a more spectacular motor explosion.

It can be seen that most of the components in a complex system could be classed as critical unless other safeguards are provided. The designer and reliability engineer should know whether any component, assembly, measurement, or process is critical, and they must inform the responsible quality control organization of any such items. Generally, this information on criticality is stipulated on drawings accepted for production. The problem, however, is that there is a tendency to minimize the number of critical items indicated. A judicious compromise must be reached between imposing an excessive number on quality control personnel, whose work load might be increased to the point where they would be overloaded and their effectiveness lost, and citing as many critical items as possible.

Inspection and testing of every individual component, subassembly, assembly, and subsystem in a complex system for each important parameter is prohibitive economically. Where testing must be done to verify the quality of production, a test plan must be developed and followed that will produce the greatest beneficial effect within the limits of available funds. This test plan requires knowledge of the criticality of each item, the best tests to indicate the hazardous failure mode that could generate a safety problem, and the points in time when tests should be made for maximal effectivity. It is uneconomical to permit a defective unit to be incorporated in a larger assembly and then have to tear down the assembly when the defect is found. Tests must therefore be carried out early enough to permit elimination of defective items before unnecessary work is done but not often enough to impose an unbearable work load and cost. Many defects cannot be detected by visual inspection after they are incorporated in larger assemblies. Others may be damaged in a subsequent operation. The operation may then be regarded as critical, and tests may be made after the operation is accomplished.

Quality Control

The quality control organization is responsible for ensuring a high-quality output is produced by the manufacturing and maintenance processes. It is also concerned with inspecting and testing of all materials, parts, and assemblies received from suppliers. A contractor is responsible for the product that he furnishes a customer; this responsibility includes all the items that he obtains from subcontractors and vendors.

The quality control effort may be divided into various phases: receipt of supplies to be processed, workmanship during the process, inspection of completed components, and inspection and testing of assemblies. Initial assurance that the items furnished by suppliers meet prescribed requirements can be undertaken at either the suppliers' plants, the receiving plant, or both. Generally, responsible suppliers will make their own inspections and tests to ensure that their products meet stipulated parameters. Records are maintained in the event that questions later arise concerning the quality of a specific shipment. Data may indicate that a lot has an undesirable and possibly dangerous characteristic. The close control and detailed records that automobile manufacturers maintain are to preclude claims in case of an accident and to establish the extent of a problem that becomes apparent in the field. For critical items, the contractor being provided the supplies may have his own quality assurance personnel conduct or observe inspections and tests in the supplier's plant. In such cases, title to the product passes immediately afterwards. The contractor may conduct reinspections in his own plant.

Inspections and tests during and immediately after processing and assembly must be carried out at those locations and times where the most effective results can be produced. In addition, it is necessary to establish whether inspections and tests should be done by sampling or on all items (100 per cent). For some items, such as electroexplosive devices, a 100 per cent test is impossible except for specific parameters; in others, it is impracticable and uneconomical to do so. Sampling programs that are judicious compromises must then be established. Critical items may require 100 per cent inspections and tests.

Chapter 10 indicated that inspections and tests are necessary to reveal those items that fail to meet prescribed limits and also to control those items that have not failed but that test parameters indicate will probably fail soon. The third reason was also pointed out in Chapter 10 in the discussion of safety factors and margins: Inadequate or loose quality control will result in wide dispersion of strength values and greater possibilities of failure than with tight control. The value of good quality control cannot be overemphasized.

Maintaining strict control over the components themselves must be supplemented by similar actions on the assemblies in which they are utilized. One of the commonest examples of system degradation during manufacture and assembly is connection failures in electrical, mechanical, and structural systems. At one time, it was considered that failures of complex systems were due principally to failures of components. It has now been shown that most failures actually occur because of the weak connections made to these components. In electrical systems a wire or cable may break because of flexing, crimping, or cutting during manufacture or installation. Connections may separate because of poor soldering, failure to remove corrosion products, failure to provide or connect electrical bonds or grounds, or lack of locking devices. In mechanical systems, fittings on pneumatic or hydraulic lines may not be tightened adequately; lack of cleanliness may cause clogging of orifices and other critical flow openings; welds may fail; or hoses may be damaged so that they fail under pressure, or separate from couplings, and whip. In the early Mercury flights the astronauts found that the capsules contained gum wrappers, cigarette butts, and miscellaneous contaminants that floated about during weightlessness and interfered with their vision and operations. These items had been left there during the manufacture and assembly of the capsules.

Stress Concentrators. Stress concentrators cause failures of mechanical and structural parts at loads far below those for which they were designed. The effects on the strengths of some of these parts are indicated in the charts in Fig. 11-1. Stress concentrators may be produced by manufacturing processes that fail to produce smooth surfaces,

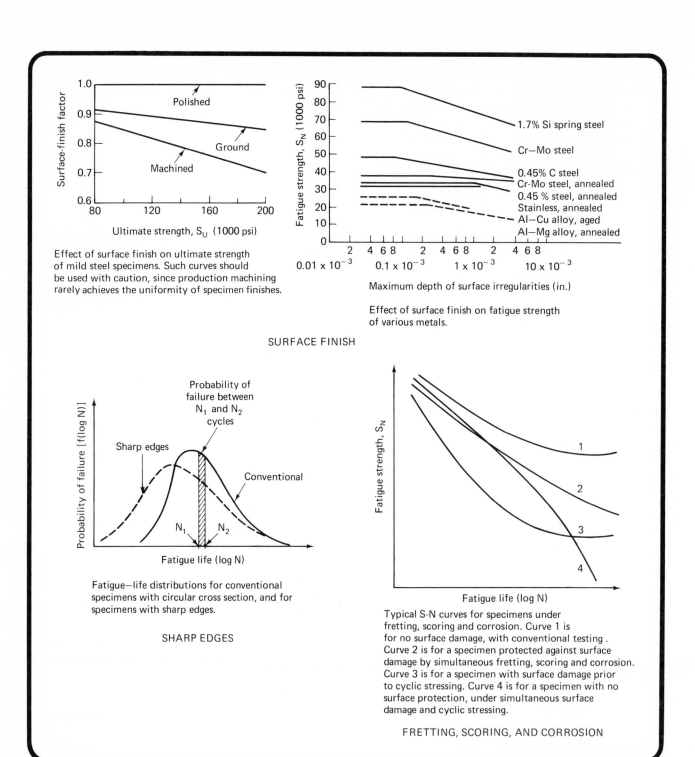

Effect of surface finish on ultimate strength of mild steel specimens. Such curves should be used with caution, since production machining rarely achieves the uniformity of specimen finishes.

Effect of surface finish on fatigue strength of various metals.

SURFACE FINISH

Fatigue—life distributions for conventional specimens with circular cross section, and for specimens with sharp edges.

SHARP EDGES

Typical S-N curves for specimens under fretting, scoring and corrosion. Curve 1 is for no surface damage, with conventional testing. Curve 2 is for a specimen protected against surface damage by simultaneous fretting, scoring and corrosion. Curve 3 is for a specimen with surface damage prior to cyclic stressing. Curve 4 is for a specimen with no surface protection, under simultaneous surface damage and cyclic stressing.

FRETTING, SCORING, AND CORROSION

Fig. 11-1. Effects of manufacturing, maintainance and other types of damage on strength. R. E. Little, "How to Prevent Fatigue Failure," *Machine Design,* 6 July 1967, pp. 133–137.

fillets on inside corners, or rounded edges on outside corners. Scratches, gouges, tool marks, and similar damage reduce the strength of parts or generate regions where corrosion can start. Such locations are the principal points at which fatigue cracking and failure of stressed parts will begin.

Critical Processes

Some manufacturing processes have been found to be particularly damaging to equipment, chiefly in the joining and connecting of parts. Welding is a notorious offender.

- The intense heat in welding processes melts the metals to be joined, frequently changing the metal's characteristics. In some metals, it may be due to changes in heat treatment, resulting in loss of desirable properties that may have been developed through annealing, tempering, or other processes. Certain metals are affected more severely. The melting of cast iron causes segregation of carbon in the zones on the outer edges of the weld, making these regions extremely brittle and liable to failure from shock or vibration.

- Because of the high conductivities of metals, materials remote from the welding zone may be damaged. Soldered connections may melt, sealants may flow into undesirable areas or leave gaps, or insulation may be damaged.

- Hot spatter, dripping weld metal (slag), and sparks may burn nearby materials or damage surfaces that they hit. These hot particles may not only ruin the appearance of the material but also weaken metal by producing regions of high-stress concentration.

- Poor welds will not provide the structural strength required. Some of the defects that may occur in welding are listed in Fig. 11-2. Incomplete fusion or penetration, undercutting, cracks, or indentation can result in early failure of the part or structure. Porous welds in containers may permit leakage of fluids.

- Failure to clean a weld may leave debris, residues, and other deleterious materials that induce or take part in corrosion reactions.

Soldering is less hazardous to personnel and hardware because the much lower level of heat employed constitutes a lesser danger. However, it too can generate problems, both in joining comparatively large metal surfaces and in smaller efforts, such as fastening a wire to a terminal. The quality of the joint is governed by the temperature of the parts to be joined, composition and temperature of the solder, and surface condition of the parts to be soldered. In hand soldering, a "cold joint" may result if the heat applied is not adequate to cause adherence of the solder. The joint may fail under vibration when the assembly is put into operation. Failure to remove surface films or other contamination will also produce weak joints. Excess amounts of solder could bridge small gaps to other unprotected conductors, thus causing short circuits during operation. Loose beads of solder from excess usage can lodge between connector pins or between a pin and the case to cause a short circuit when the system is activated.

Microelectronic systems often fail from another cause: either poor encapsulation or poor potting. Encapsulation has three principal functions: to provide support for the components; to insulate any conductors, which would otherwise be exposed; and to eliminate corrosion, contamination, and other adverse environmental effects. In poorly controlled processes, encapsulation is incomplete, so the adverse effects that were to be precluded can and do occur. If encapsulant temperature and process time are poorly controlled, the encapsulant material will not cure properly and will not provide adequate support for the components. Lack of rigidity of the assembly will allow it to be damaged by the shock and vibration to which it is generally subjected during transportation, handling, installation, and operation.

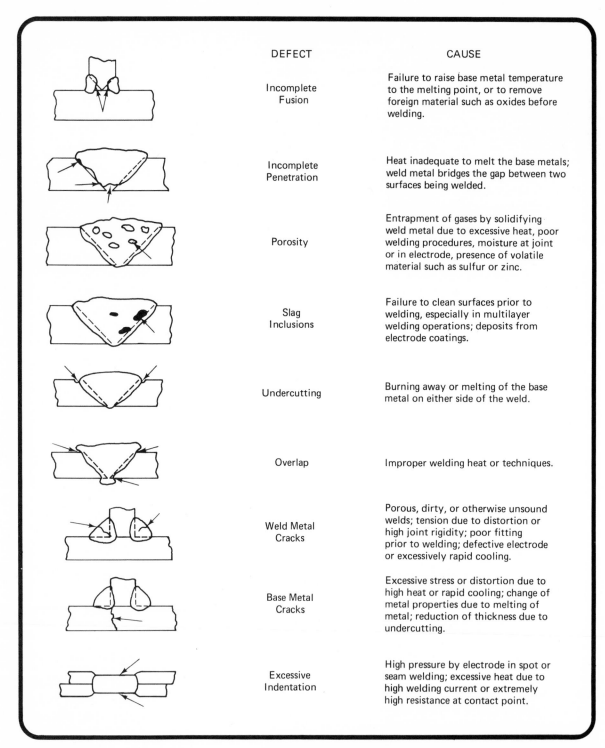

DEFECT	CAUSE
Incomplete Fusion	Failure to raise base metal temperature to the melting point, or to remove foreign material such as oxides before welding.
Incomplete Penetration	Heat inadequate to melt the base metals; weld metal bridges the gap between two surfaces being welded.
Porosity	Entrapment of gases by solidifying weld metal due to excessive heat, poor welding procedures, moisture at joint or in electrode, presence of volatile material such as sulfur or zinc.
Slag Inclusions	Failure to clean surfaces prior to welding, especially in multilayer welding operations; deposits from electrode coatings.
Undercutting	Burning away or melting of the base metal on either side of the weld.
Overlap	Improper welding heat or techniques.
Weld Metal Cracks	Porous, dirty, or otherwise unsound welds; tension due to distortion or high joint rigidity; poor fitting prior to welding; defective electrode or excessively rapid cooling.
Base Metal Cracks	Excessive stress or distortion due to high heat or rapid cooling; change of metal properties due to melting of metal; reduction of thickness due to undercutting.
Excessive Indentation	High pressure by electrode in spot or seam welding; excessive heat due to high welding current or extremely high resistance at contact point.

Fig. 11-2. Some types of welding defects.

Manufacturing, Maintenance, and Transportation

Failure to ensure that the assembly is completely filled with potting compound will also result in of lack of support; in addition, conductors may be exposed to moisture, dirt, and debris that could cause short-circuiting. The encapsulant must therefore fill the spaces between all parts, with no voids that would result in conductor exposure.

Pressure and temperature during encapsulation are the two principal process conditions that must be carefully controlled. Excess pressures can cause breakage of leads or result in material being forced inside components, such as potentiometers, which will then not function.

Excessive temperatures can cause damage to heat-sensitive components or cause changes to electrical resistance or other parameters. Improper cure of the encapsulant because of excessive heat could cause the filler to dry out and crack, exposing the components underneath.

Poor encapsulation can result from other causes. Most of these problems and their cures are indicated in Fig. 11-3.

Potting is another process that, if inadequately done, can generate numerous problems in electrical and electronic systems. A very common one is that gaps in potting may permit moisture to enter the part and cause short-circuiting or corrosion. A prime example was the umbilical connector on the line between a bomber and the large missile that it carried under its wing. At takeoff, climb, and at altitude there was no problem. However, when the aircraft descended, air, with the moisture

Fig. 11-3. Troubleshooting embedded assemblies. "The Proof of the Potting: Selection, Design, Testing," *Electronic Design,* 1 February 1968, p. 78.

TROUBLESHOOTING EMBEDDED ASSEMBLIES*

APPEARANCE	PROBABLE CAUSE	CORRECTIVE ACTION
Surface exhibits fine cracks, ripples or roughness	Cure too hot Too large a mass (primarily high-exothermic systems)	Reduce oven temperature in 10°C stages Pour casting in stages, allow first to gel before pouring second
Resin appears burned, especially in center	Cure too hot—mass of high-exothermic resin too large	Reduce cure temperature, reduce mass of resin, or use external cooling with room-temperature cure systems
Resin releases from components at edges, corners, terminals	Contamination of surfaces with oil, grease mold-release agent, skin oil Nonbondable surfaces Oxidized metal surfaces (resin bonds to oxide which releases from metal)	Grease component before casting, handle with gloves Replace or prime surfaces Abrade or chemically clean surface just prior to casting or use primers
Casting warps or distorts from mold shape	Cure temperature too hot Insufficient resin Poor design Excessive shrinkage	Reduce cure temperature, keep mold-temperature uniform Allow larger sprue volume or recap casting Keep resin wall thickness uniform, add ribs Use more filler. In extreme cases, pack mold with porous filler, impregnate with resin
Resin remains liquid or very soft and sticky	Cure temperature too low Cure time too short Mix ratio incorrect Insufficient mixing Separate parts not mixed Contamination	Increase oven temperature Extend cure time Check mixing process, adjust equipment Mix thoroughly; color, if the resin is pigmented, should be uniform Stir separate system constituents before blending Keeps parts, mold and resin clean
Casting appears normal at room temperature but becomes liquid or tacky at high temperatures (resin not completely cross-linked)	Mix ratio incorrect Excess mold release Moisture Contamination Incompatible insulation	Same as above Use release agents sparingly Dry component thoroughly before casting Check resin area for oils, dirt, greases, waxes Check component for plasticized films, such as vinyl or acetate, thermoplastics that liquefy at operating temperatures of component, tar or waxes. Dissect unit while hot and replace questionable insulation, with compatible material

Casting opens; liquid oozes out of fissure or around terminals, lugs	Moisture	Dry component thoroughly. Paper or fiber parts are prime suspects
	Incompatible insulation	Same as above
Surface rough or spotted	Rough mold surface	Clean or polish mold
	Excess mold release	Use thin release, such as Garan 225 (Ram Chemical Co., Gardena, Calif)
Exterior of casting has soft or sticky areas, possibly with voids	Excess mold release	Use release agents sparingly, dilute with solvent
	Dirty mold	Clean after use
Bubbles or holes in surface	Rough mold surface	Polish surface
	Leaky molds (air enters during vacuum cycle)	Seal molds, polish joints, replace gaskets, and release vacuum slowly
	Poor mold design, horizontal "shelf" areas trap air	Redesign mold, taper "shelves" for air exit
Bubbles, voids or "dry" areas in casting, low corona-starting voltage	Insufficient resin	Provide for a "head" of resin over component to allow for escaping air.
	Insufficient vacuum	Evacuate resin and part prior to casting and pour under vacuum. Apply power vacuum or extend time, try pressure after vacuum
	Resin cured before air escaped	Use slower curing system or lower temperatures
	Resin too thick	Heat component, mold, and resin to reduce viscosity, or use thinner resin
	Poor component design	Modify component layout
All or part of mold difficult to remove	Undercuts in mold	Remove undercuts and repolish mold
	Insufficient mold release	Reapply release agent
	Mold not "broken in"	Reapply release agent before each casting, use mold several times
	Rough mold surface	Polish surface
	Permanent-type release agent worn or abraded	Reapply or regrind Teflon-type coatings
Fissures develop during cure, cooling, or subsequent thermal shock	Resin not cured	Increase cure time
	Sticking	Resin damaged during mold removal. Recast
	Wrong resin	Flexible or filled resins should be considered
	Oven too hot	Check oven temperature
	Gel temperature too high	Use lowest possible temperature to minimize stresses
	Poor component or mold design	Design so that resin thickness is uniform around component, (1/16 in. minimum). Fillet sharp internal corners with heaviliy filled resin before casting, reinforce crack areas with glass cloth or glass-reinforced tape

Figure 11-3 continued.

it contained, entered the connector. The extremely cold metal surfaces of the connector caused condensation of the moisture and short-circuiting.

Numerous other examples exist of deficiencies and damage that can be generated during system production. A few may be mentioned briefly:

1. Manufacturing of electrical or electromechanical items

   a. Leads severed, broken, or pulled from components accidentally

   b. Connector pins bent, broken, missing, or improperly soldered to the wires

c. Insulation cut, torn, or abraded so conductors exposed

d. Glass tubes cracked, ruining hermetic seals

e. Insulation melted by soldering or welding

f. Diodes, transistors, and other delicate semiconductors damaged by currents generated in improperly grounded welding or soldering equipment

g. Failure to clamp wire bundles or cables properly

2. Manufacturing of mechanical items

a. Loose or overstressed parts

b. Inadequate thread engagement

c. Unidirectional components installed backwards

d. Failure to install lock washers, safety wires, and similar devices to prevent loosening or loss of connectors.

e. Failure to install critical parts, such as heat shields, bonds, or grounds.

f. Inadequate clearances of parts so they bind

g. Scratching, gouging, or denting of metal surfaces

h. Failure to install seals, gaskets, or "O" rings properly

i. Failure to avoid system contamination

Maintenance

Maintenance safety problems can be separated into three general categories:

1. Hazards that can lead to injury or damage during accomplishment of maintenance itself

2. Injuries or damage in accidents resulting from failure to carry out required maintenance

3. Injuries or damage in accidents resulting from improper maintenance

To establish hazards and effects that might exist or be generated during maintenance and to consider accident prevention measures and other safeguards, an analysis should be undertaken. The analysis is a procedures analysis. The methodology indicated in Chapter 8 may be employed for problems in the first and third categories in the preceding list. Problems in the second category will lessen reliability and increase failures due to higher wear-out rates.

On the other hand, proper maintenance can improve reliability to a level better than that which exists when equipment leaves the production plant. The components that fail during the burn-in period can be replaced so that the period of constant failure rate, the basis on which reliability engineers made their analyses, is reached. Components especially susceptible to failure induced by vibration or shock generated during transportation are eliminated.

Many of the processes employed during maintenance are similar to those during production, and the resulting safety problems are similar. In addition, field processes used as substitutes for plant production processes may introduce other safety problems. Maintenance itself can be separated into five phases:

- Initial inspection after receipt or prior to incorporation into the system ensures that the hardware to be used has been produced in accordance with drawings and specifications and is adequate for its intended purpose.

- Routine or programmed maintenance encompasses those services necessary to continue the proper functioning of equipment that is already operating as it should. Such services include oiling, greasing, adjustments of controls for maximum efficiency, replacing hydraulic fluid lost from a system, or replacing water evaporated from battery electrolyte.

- Checkout includes testing of the equipment to ensure that specific operating parameters or required outputs are within prescribed limits.

- Repair includes fixing and continued use of defective or damaged components.

- Replacement involves substitution of an operable item for one that is not economically repairable under existing conditions. (Some items may be replaced in the field where repair is not practicable but may be repaired at depots or factories.)

Personnel actions during each of these phases generally account for any conditions that could later result in accidents.

- Initial inspection. Opening sealed, moistureproof packages may destroy the environmental protection that had been provided. Metal parts may then corrode. Contamination from fingers or from airborne pollutants can also produce corrosion. Pulling plastic coverings from packages can generate static electricity adequate to initiate electroexplosive devices or to change characteristics of semiconductors.

- Routine maintenance. Failure to replace covers permits the entrance of moisture, debris, and other contaminants that can cause short-circuiting of electrical equipment, jamming of moving parts, or corrosion of both. Leaving tools in vulnerable locations can damage rotating equipment, jam moving parts, or prevent motion of critical controls. Failure to clean filters may cause clogging of fluid systems. Inadequate protection during refilling of hydraulic or lubricant lines may permit contamination of the system.

- Checkout. Equipment being installed into test fixtures may be damaged structurally if jammed because of improper alignment. Electrical connectors may have pins bent in the same way so a short circuit occurs either during test or during operation. Unless separation of connectors is done properly, wires may be pulled from the pins to which they were connected, producing open circuits. Testing itself may generate damage through applications of transient stresses, such as high current surges, or through shocks in hydraulic or pneumatic systems. Vibrating or shock of equipment during tests may cause degradation of vulnerable parts or their connections.

- Repair. The damaged part may be repaired while it is still in place in the equipment where it is used, or it may be removed and repaired in a shop. Generally, repair is handcraft work rather than machine production. Neither is it as thoroughly done as depot- or factory-renovated equipment. The end result may therefore be less desirable than replacement, but it may be necessary as an expedient when a replacement is not available. A major problem with repairs is that the person accomplishing the task may change the original design or system parameters to make the equipment work. Failure to clean parts properly may result in system contamination and later malfunctioning of other components. Welding of items in place may cause overheating of nearby components, which damages them. In any case, welding may change characteristics of metals or of electrical components.

- Replacement. Faulty diagnoses of failures may cause replacement of good parts with new ones, which may then fail during their burn-in periods. Other replacement problems include failure to use proper or designated parts, failure to make connections or to make them correctly, failure to provide environmental protection after assembly by sealing or potting, and failure to make suitable adjustment of operating parameters.

Failure to maintain equipment or to accomplish maintenance properly is one of the most frequent causes of accidents. There are countless ways in which maintenance can be done incorrectly, generally through improper use of prescribed procedures and checklists. This problem can be minimized by:

- Firm and close supervision to ensure that maintenance personnel realize the necessity for strict adherence to procedures and checklists and the consequences of unauthorized omissions, deviations, or additions.

- Critical quality control through inspections and check outs of equipment to ensure that maintenance has been done properly; that equipment operates properly within prescribed parameters; that there have been no omissions, deviations, or additions; and that there is no impairment of system quality, reliability, and safety.

- The Two-Man Concept (Chapter 4), which requires accomplishment of tasks involving nuclear devices by two or more knowledgeable personnel who can ensure that the tasks have been done properly. This same procedure can be applied to critical nonnuclear devices and systems. Some gas companies have a second maintenance man check the work a first man has done to ensure it has been done correctly.

Shock and vibration constitute the chief problems during transportation of components and assemblies, but other, less common hazards can be equally damaging. Effects on electrical and electronic equipment from shock and vibration include:

Transportation

- Permanent deformations to structures, frames, coils, pointers, and tube plates and grids

- Fractures and breakage of soldered joints, metal parts at stress concentrations, glass components, leads and connections, and cable clamps

- Misalignment of contacts
- Abrasion or cutting of insulation
- Changes in electrical characteristics of parts

Such damage has resulted from transporting expensive and critical items, even when handled in special packages, for missile and space systems. More common, commercial items frequently suffer more. Improvements in packaging techniques and in carrier equipment have been beneficial, but errors in packaging or extraordinary conditions encountered in transit still cause damage. Other problems include changes in environmental conditions, either alone or in the presence of vibration or shock:

- For example, a large ballistic missile was sealed completely to prevent contamination during delivery. It was flown from the high-altitude plant where it was manufactured to a sea-level base. The difference between the ambient sea-level pressure and the sealed internal pressure in the missile tanks imposed a high external load that caused collapse of the tanks.

- Figure 11-4 indicates the effects on failure rates of relays when they were shipped by commercial freight. The chart shows that interruption of tests caused increases in failures, which were

Fig. 11-4. Effect of interruption on relay failure. G. Chernowitz et al; *Electromechanical Component Reliability*, (Ridgefield, N.J.: American Power Jet Company; May 1963) (AD 422 327)

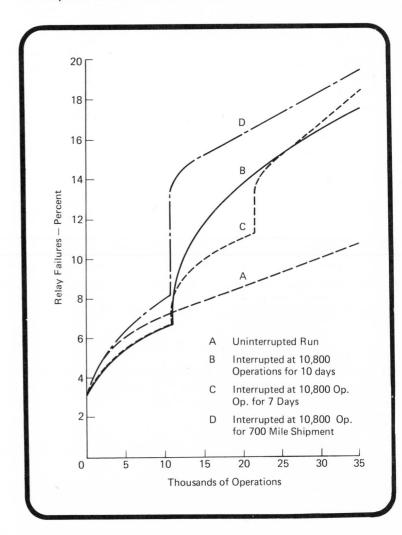

A   Uninterrupted Run

B   Interrupted at 10,800 Operations for 10 days

C   Interrupted at 10,800 Op. Op. for 7 Days

D   Interrupted at 10,800 Op. for 700 Mile Shipment

compounded by transportation stresses. One explanation was that there was probably a buildup of contaminants and of brittle corrosion products, which flaked or broke off because of the vibration and shock encountered in transit.

- Parameter shifts in the characteristics of resistors occurred because of static electricity generated during air transportation. Vibratory motion of the devices in the plastic bags in which each had been carefully packaged produced the static charges.

- Failures of containers because of impacts have resulted in release of toxic, flammable, or corrosive fluids. Some failures have been so massive that entire communities have been endangered and had to be evacuated until the danger was eliminated. In other instances, personnel have been killed or injured. (See Fig. 1-1.)

- Exposure to moisture because of changes in humidity or temperature, or both, has caused condensation and damage due to corrosion. Hygroscopic materials have absorbed moisture and swelled until they were unusable. Evaluation of material properties and of possible exposures during transportation and storage may indicate need for desiccants, protective wrappings, or sealed containers.

All regulatory agencies responsible for safeguarding the public against injury and damage which could result from the transportation of hazardous materials or devices have suitable requirements to minimize the possibilities and effects of accidents. A user of any means of transportation must ensure that any item he ships by common carrier, Department of Defense means, or over public roads is packaged, marked, and conveyed as prescribed. The determination of hazards that could be present during transit and the safeguards that will best meet regulatory requirements and the specific characteristics of the items being shipped must be established by analysis.

This chapter has indicated some examples of how errors during manufacture, maintenance, and transportation can cause damage even to a well-designed system. On the other hand, designers can do much to eliminate problems and to forestall situations in which damage can result:

Relations with Design

- Using metal instead of glass electronic tubes or using solid-state devices to reduce the possibility of damage.

- Including safety requirements on detail production drawings, indicating safeguards to be taken.

- Noting requirements for marking "NO STEP" on locations where the concentrated weight of a person may damage a susceptible member.

- Designing removable and replaceable panels to provide easy access to internal units during production and maintenance assembly and to reduce errors from inaccessibility. Easy access will also reduce the possibility that maintenance personnel will fail to accomplish all necessary tasks.

- Eliminating inadequately supported units, especially on cantilevers, that will deflect, deform, and break easily during transportation and handling.

- Designing containers to minimize the effects of vibration and impact during transportation and to protect critical or easily damaged items.

- Minimizing the need for special tools to reduce the possibility that maintenance will not be accomplished when the tools are not available or that damage will result if substitutes are used.

- Making designs with maximum possible clearances and tolerances to reduce the criticality and need for extremely fine adjustment during manufacture and maintenance and to minimize the possibility that transportation or handling stresses will make the system inoperative.

It must be repeated here that design, manufacture, maintenance, transportation, and all other operations of a system are interrelated processes. Each one bears a share in ensuring that the system operates as it should, is not damaged, and that no condition is generated that could result in an accident to others.

Relations with Safety Organizations

Generally, industrial safety personnel have been concerned with preventing injury to company workers and preventing damage to company property. Avoidance of damage to matériel during processing or transportation has been left to personnel responsible for conduct of those activities. It has become evident that when the scope of safety activities is broadened to include avoidance of damage, as well as prevention of injury, a problem arises as to who is responsible for such efforts within an industrial plant. Both industrial safety and System (or Product) Safety organizations have interests in minimizing damage and loss; but where the responsibilities lie for conduct of the necessary programs must, and can, be established only by top management itself.

An example of this possible problem may be cited here. A company manufactures a system involving metal parts that must be heat-treated. In the past, the production manager has been responsible for ensuring that heat treatment is carried out properly and no damage to the parts occurs. However, is the industrial safety division responsible for ensuring that protective devices are provided on the ovens so that they will not overheat and possibly cause a fire? Or is the System Safety department responsible for ensuring that protective devices are provided on the ovens so that they will not overheat and damage the parts going into the system? If the part fails in use, an accident might result to the customer's personnel, causing injury to them or damage to the customer's equipment and property. The production manager may not be aware of the safety problems that could result from use of improperly manufactured components. Here again, it may be a requirement for the System or Product Safety personnel to keep the production organizations informed on possible hazards to and from parts, matériel, and processes.

In such cases, the integrated effort that forms the basis of any effective safety program will be beneficial. However, integration of such efforts requires definite assignments of responsibilities.

Manufacturing, Maintenance, and Transportation

312

chapter 12

OPERATIONS

A system is designed, manufactured, and maintained to accomplish a specific mission. It has certain characteristics and limitations within which it will function properly, which must be observed, and which must not be exceeded if accidents are to be avoided. The consequences of any deficiency in design, material, or personnel are more immediate in this phase of a system's life cycle than in any other phase, since it is the operator who most frequently suffers from any mishaps. Designers and manufacturing personnel are remote from operations of a product and so are not endangered by their own errors. They can generally understand and realize the effects of an accident only as they themselves are operators of automobiles, production equipment, household appliances, lawn mowers, boats, and a multitude of other items. But it is as operators or as innocent bystanders affected by other operators that they may be injured.

The need for safe designs and safety analyses, as discussed in previous chapters, are all undertaken with the user in mind. Hazards to the operator (or bystander) must be eliminated, minimized, or controlled. However, a completely safe system or operation is rare. It is therefore necessary that the operator conduct himself within the designed and prescribed limits. He has specific responsibilities that he cannot disregard without increasing the probability and severity of injury.

It is impossible to indicate in one chapter all the precautionary measures that should be employed for the innumerable types of operations. Certain general rules can be applied to most systems and situations. These rules are presented briefly in the following sections, with amplifications and examples to stress specific points.

Management and Supervision

Without a doubt, the most important factor in accident prevention during operations is management supervision. This supervision may involve a plant, program, or system manager, a commanding officer, a superintendent, or a foreman. Ultimate responsibility for safety is theirs, although it is also frequently and truly said that safety is everyone's responsibility. Unfortunately, many people have a tendency to ignore or forget their duties. The manager or supervisor must ensure that such ignoring or forgetting does not happen if accidents are to be avoided. Lack of firm direction and control can lead to disastrous results that could otherwise be avoided.

The safety effort for any operation requires that supervisory and technical tasks be as integrated as those indicated in Chapter 3 for development of a new system. Some of the means by which a manager responsible for any operation can ensure that he has an effective safety program are to:

1. Establish in writing and disseminate specific and firm safety policies for his organization.

2. Direct the participation of all his subordinate organization heads in the safety effort, with specific responsibilities assigned to each.

3. Establish a safety element, which reports directly to him, to be sure that the safety program is carried out properly and effectively. Other duties of this element should include those in Fig. 3-3, as they apply to operational systems.

4. Check that safety training is carried out on a continuing basis for supervisors and workers, especially those newly employed or transferred. No supervisor should assume that any new subordinate has received adequate safety training but should check each individual's capabilities.

5. Check that every reported hazard and every accident is investigated. He should be apprised immediately of any serious injury, fatality, or dangerous condition.

6. Establish a program to monitor and audit operational activities for their safety aspects. Whenever possible, he should occasionally conduct such audits himself. If not, he should review audit reports made by others.

7. Establish a safety review board to evaluate, discuss, and take action on safety problems. The board should review mishap records and reports, hazard and failure reports, and safety studies and analyses to establish that improvements are being made where necessary or desirable. Whenever possible, a manager should act as chairman of the board or delegate the duty to a subordinate high-level manager to act in his place.

8. Above all, *maintain an active effective interest in the safety effort.*

Other procedures that each manager must follow for the safety of any product, system, operation, or program for which he is responsible include the following:

1. Any activity or system should be operated within the mission limitations and requirements under which it was designed. Figure 1-1 illustrates the effects of such nonobservance for railroads. A major cause for railroad accidents has been the use of trains with heavier loads moving at greater speeds than those loads and speeds for which the tracks and roadbeds were built originally. Another example has been the Atlas F ICBM system. This missile was designed to be placed in an underground silo where it would remain until it was to be raised to the surface and launched. It was later decided to ensure that the system and its crews were operationally ready by exercising them. The missiles were loaded with propellants and raised to the launch position, then lowered and unloaded. This was done repeatedly. The system lacked safety provisions that should have been available if exercising the system had been considered part of the original mission. Within two years, four missiles and their silos were destroyed by explosions during such exercises.

2. On receipt of equipment for a system or operation, a review should be made to ensure that all desirable safety requirements, devices, and procedures have been incorporated or provided. Any deviations from procedures considered safe or any obvious safety deficiencies should be corrected before the system or equipment is accepted. The review should ensure that the existence of any possible hazard has actually been avoided or eliminated to the greatest degree practicable. (The detailed list of hazards in the Appendix can be employed for this purpose.) Appropriate safeguards should have been established for any hazard that could not be eliminated.

3. All operating procedures should minimize the possibility of a mishap as a result of the existence of a hazard; the hazards should be identified and personnel warned by the most noticeable means appropriate.

4. Measures should be taken to contain and minimize the effects of any error or mishap. The methods indicated in Chapter 10 can be employed beneficially for this purpose, adapted to the specific purpose that the cognizant manager has in mind.

5. Detailed emergency procedures should be prepared to specify actions to be taken when a failure or dangerous condition occurs. These procedures should include preestablished warning signals or alarms, safe areas and evacuations routes, communications to notify support activities (such as the fire-fighting unit), and availability and use of protective clothing and rescue equipment. These procedures should be familiar to all personnel participating in system activities. As far as practicable, designs should permit corrective action for recovery from an emergency to be taken from outside the danger area.

6. Access to equipment components during maintenance, repair, or adjustment should not expose personnel to such hazards as electrical charge, moving parts, radiation, extremes of heat, chemical burns, cutting edges, or sharp points.

7. Hazardous operations and materials are isolated to the greatest degree practicable from other activities and personnel and from incompatible materials.

Personnel Each manager must ensure that personnel are neither endangered by the system, equipment, or operation nor that they themselves constitute dangers.

1. Undue exposure of personnel to physiological, psychological, or physical stresses should be avoided. No person should be required to perform duties involving operations under conditions that are unsafe due to lack of suitable protective equipment, adequate design, or prudent operating instructions.

2. No person should be required to perform an operation that could result in injury to other personnel who might be present in the same area because of incompatibilities of their tasks.

3. Only qualified personnel should be permitted to undertake hazardous duties or operations and to handle, service, transport, maintain, repair, or operate any vehicle, its components or associated equipment.

4. Programs should be instituted to qualify and certify personnel for their duties. Certification programs should include training and testing on safety subjects such as:
   a. Hazards involved in the operations for which they are being certified.
   b. Practices and procedures required to safeguard themselves and other personnel. Responsibilities and duties involved in buddy system operations should be explained.
   c. Necessity and procedures to report to their supervisor or safety officer any malfunction of equipment or safety device or any unsafe practice.

Operations

d. Remedial actions to be taken during any contingency.

c. Color coding and other means of identification of wiring, piping, and equipment; meanings of warning and other emergency signals; and other hazard identifications and markings.

5. Supervisory personnel should ensure that all persons under their control are currently qualified before they permit them to participate in activities that might be hazardous.

6. Any individual whose behavior or emotional instability presents a potential hazard should not be permitted to participate in any hazardous duties or operations.

7. No person should be allowed alone in a hazardous location, such as a storage tank, unless his location and condition are closely monitored. Where the buddy system is required, procedures should be stated clearly: whether the two persons involved may both enter the same hazardous area, where each one must ensure the well-being of the other, or whether one will enter and the other remain outside the hazardous area with no other duty but to safeguard the well-being of the exposed person. The buddy system should be specified and employed for operations that:

a. Require personal protective equipment whose failure could result in serious injury or death

b. May require mutual assistance in an emergency

c. Would require outside assistance for escape or rescue

8. Supervisors should ensure that personnel are physically and medically qualified to perform their duties. When there is any doubt regarding whether the limitations of a person might be exceeded, especially when a hazardous operation is involved, medical advice should be requested.

Operations

Each operation considered hazardous should be conducted strictly in accordance with those procedures and checklists included in approved publications or approved by authorized agencies, using only designated equipment. Managers should specify operations that are considered hazardous and that require surveillance by appropriate safety or supervisory personnel. For example, welding other than as an industrial operation carried out automatically or semiautomatically is in this category.

1. Supervisors should ensure that hazardous operations are conducted only in designated areas and monitored for compliance with established safety criteria.

2. Managers should establish policies and guidance on controls to limit access to areas in which hazardous operations are to be conducted. Only essential personnel should be permitted within the hazard area during a specific operation.

3. All personnel and organizations concerned or affected by a hazardous operation should be notified before the operation is begun.

4. Areas prescribed as hazardous should be posted conspicuously with appropriate warnings and, where advisable, controlled by

guards. The number of personnel permitted should be posted conspicuously at each entrance. Operations should not be conducted if the posted number is exceeded; operations should be halted if necessary.

5. Personnel permitted to remain at one time in a hazardous area or structure should be kept within the number that could be evacuated safely in an emergency or supplied with necessary protective equipment to safeguard them throughout the emergency.

6. Escape routes, exits, and stairways should be clearly marked, with provisions for emergency lighting. Evacuation procedures should be posted conspicuously and periodically tested by drills to ensure that personnel are proficient in their accomplishment.

7. Where certain winds or meteorological conditions could endanger personnel or inhabited areas if an accident should occur during an operation, such operations should be forbidden as long as those winds or conditions exist.

8. Open flames or unprotected electrical equipment should not be permitted in areas where flammable or explosive materials are present. Welding or flame-cutting operations should be permitted only in areas and at times approved by the responsible supervisor or safety officer and in accordance with prescribed limitations.

Personal Protective Equipment

The needs and uses for personal protective equipment are described in Chapter 10. There are specific operations, programmed or emergency, during which this equipment is required to prevent injury. Here again, supervisors must ensure that certain rules are observed:

1. Approved protective equipment and devices suitable for specific hazards that might be encountered during the operations should be available and employed. No supervisor should permit an operation to be conducted unless such equipment and devices are in proper working order and used as stipulated.

2. Only protective and rescue equipment approved for the purpose by responsible agencies should be used. Managers should ensure that procedures are available for the supply, maintenance, and operation of such equipment, and that all personnel are proficient in their upkeep and operation.

3. The locations of first aid, emergency, and personal protective equipment must be easily accessible and readily distinguishable. Equipment should be stored as close as practicable to the possible point of use. Operating procedures should identify the equipment stored and its location. Inspections should be made periodically to make sure that stipulated items are present.

4. No person should enter a hazardous environment without prescribed protective equipment, use poorly fitted or defective equipment, remove the equipment while in the hazardous environment, or remain in the hazard area if the protective equipment is damaged or torn.

5. All persons must be familiar with the capabilities, limitations, and proper methods of fitting, testing, using, and caring for protective equipment. Managers should ensure that courses of instruction

are provided to familiarize personnel with equipment, especially new types. Supervisors should schedule practice sessions or have training units conduct sessions to maintain user proficiency.

6. Devices should be available to detect, warn, and protect against an impending or existing dangerous condition. Such equipment should be used to evaluate atmospheres that might be toxic, flammable, or explosive, or in which excessive levels of radiation, heat, pressure, noise, or other hazard might exist, and to apprise personnel of the status of such conditions or when control of the hazard is lost. Equipment provided should be adequate for detecting the hazard under conditions other than normal for the operating environment.

7. Detection and warning equipment should be maintained in a state in which operations and readings are dependable and accurate. To do this, they should be tested and calibrated periodically.

8. Detection and warning equipment should be installed, maintained, adjusted, or repaired only by personnel trained and assigned for the purpose.

9. Operating procedures should specify actions that personnel should take when a warning signal is heard. Shutdown procedures should be indicated where necessary. Managers should designate protective structures and safe areas to which personnel should move in time of danger or when a warning signal indicating danger is heard. Managers should also prescribe and ensure that exercises are conducted to maintain proficiency in these procedures. If these procedures are not already available, they can be developed as shown in Chapter 8.

Hazard Analyses

Hazard analyses can be conducted prior to or during operations, using most of the same techniques as indicated during the design and development phases. In certain instances, analyses of existing products or systems are much easier than when concepts and drawings must be used.

Such analyses are beneficial even when they have been made previously during design and development. Although designers attempt to analyze problems that may arise during operation, their talents may be inadequate in several respects. Both designers and operators may be highly competent in their own fields, but their technical abilities may differ. Their orientations may differ too; the designer strives to meet contractual requirements regarding performance, whereas the operator may be more interested in ease of operation and safety.

It is common practice, especially with military systems, to increase the scope of operations beyond that for which the equipment was originally designed. The problems with railroads and Atlas F missiles have already been mentioned as examples. The operating unit must ensure by analysis that the modified system will safely accomplish the new mission.

It frequently happens that analyses are not made until after failures have occurred. These analyses may have been undertaken as parts of accident investigations or merely because a troublesome problem arose. For example, during low-altitude firepower demonstrations, Sidewinder missiles launched at flares failed to home on the targets. Investigation revealed that firings occurred on days in which there had been much rain; rain clouds were still in the vicinity; and the humidity was extremely high. The Sidewinder had been designed for high-altitude work where little moisture is present to affect its infrared homing device. At low altitudes, moisture absorbed much infrared radiation, reducing the range of the missile's homing equipment. The pilots failed to realize this fact and launched at their usual firing distances, which, at low altitude and in the presence of much moisture, were actually out of range.

Analyses by operating units can do much to prevent repetition of design deficiencies. Information derived by field personnel is extremely valuable in establishing safety standards and good engineering practices. A lucrative source of such information is an effective hazard reporting and investigation system. Not only should this scheme be employed for correction of immediate problems, but it should also be part of a feed-back system to designers. Persons who submit field hazard reports are generally closest to any problems and are the first to recognize them.

Acceptance inspections and tests are another common and valuable source of system hazards. An effective method of conducting inspections is through use of checklists. As mentioned earlier, checklists can be prepared from standards, specifications, codes, regulatory requirements, and good engineering practices.

Industrial Safety

Most of the material presented in this chapter can be employed as effectively for industrial safety as for system or product safety. It is evident that the only difference between these activities is in the assignment of responsibilities. An industrial safety unit is responsible for the well-being of the company's employees and for preventing accidental damage and loss of its equipment and property. The system or product safety unit bears the same responsibility on behalf of the company's customers.

APPENDIX

HAZARD REVIEW CHECKLIST*

Hazard	Occurrence	Possible Cause	Possible Effects
ACCELERATION	Any mass that undergoes a change in velocity or direction	Acceleration: • Vehicle, body, or fluid being set into motion or increasing speed • Any falling body or dropped object • Vehicle on downgrade • Uncontrolled loss of altitude or height • Impact by another body • Force applied against an unrestrained body • Turbulence: clear air, thunderstorm, thermal, terrain • Sudden violent maneuver • Sudden valve opening in a pressure system Deceleration: • Vehicle, body, or fluid being stopped or decreasing speed • Impact against another body, structure, or terrain • Sudden closing of a valve in a fluid system with high velocity flow • Friction or resistance to body motion Failure to accelerate or decelerate: • Inadequate or loss of motive power • Excessive friction or drag • Failure of an unlatching or restraining mechanism to release • Loss, failure, or inadequate braking capability	Injury to personnel. A person may be: • Hit by an object set in motion by a sudden change in velocity • Thrown against a hard surface during sudden deceleration • Thrown backward during sudden forward acceleration • Thrown against an aircraft cabin ceiling in a sudden drop or maneuver Overloading and deformation of structural members Seating or unseating of spring loaded valves, electrical contacts Shorting of closely spaced electrical parts Deflection of piping Bending of bimetallic strips, thus changing instrument readings and calibration Pressure surges in liquid systems (water hammer) Loss of fluid pressure (cavitation) Sloshing and entrapment of liquids Deflection and bottoming of shock isolated parts and springs

*Extended from a similar list prepared by the author for the U.S. Air Force.

Hazard	Occurrence	Possible Cause	Possible Effects
CONTAMINATION	Any system or equipment: • Open to entry or dirt, dust, or other contaminants • In presence of contaminants • In which contaminants can be formed • Which generates contaminants or pollutants • Which discharges wastes	Poor quality control Polymerization Microbial and fungal growth Inadequate protection from contaminants Leakage or spillage of petroleum or its products, solvents, or other deleterious materials Wash water from oil and chemical process or storage tanks Filtration system overload or failure Solvent residues Inadequate solvent for cleaning Tropical environment Salt environment Oxide scale (corrosion) Metal particles Airborne dirt or other contaminants Silica sand Lapping compound Process residues Organic fibers Plastic and elastomer fragments Misalignment or poor fitting of parts, permitting leakages Discharge from industrial processes or plants Internal combustion engine exhaust Exhaust from furnaces and boiler plants	Deterioration of fluids; breakdown or alteration of fluids by direct chemical reaction; particle surface catalysis; formation of sludge; emulsification with water Increased friction and binding between sliding surfaces Degradation of performance Clogging and blocking of lines, valves, regulators, filters, nozzles, orifices Increased corrosion Scoring and abrading of closely fitted moving surfaces Ignition of flammable contaminants compressed in air or other oxidizer Erosion of lines and equipment by large particles in fluids Cracking or breaking of lines or equipment by impact of high velocity fragments Electrical leakage through degraded insulation Penetration of resilient materials Reduction in lubricity Interference in seating of valves Altered direction of flow Spring contraction prevented by large particles between coils Contamination of potable liquids Destruction of vegetation and marine life

Hazard	Occurrence	Possible Cause	Possible Effects
			Deterioration of organic material creates odors
			Loss of function, equipment, facilities and land
CHEMICAL REACTION	Fuels, oxidizers, or monopropellants	Temperature of compound raised to point where reaction begins	Explosion Nonexplosive exothermic reaction
	Explosives		Material degradation
	Organic materials	Presence of suitable catalyst	Toxic gas production
		Shock (impact)	Corrosion fraction production
	Epoxy compounds	Electric current	Swelling of organic materials
	Process chemicals	Chemical combination involving oxidants such as:	Increased reactivity of combustibles
	Cleaning compounds	• Oxygen or ozone	• Easier ignition
	Welding oxygen	• Halogens or halogen compounds	• High flammability of materials that are normally of low flammability
	Oxygen for respiratory protective equipment	• Oxidizing acids and their salts; nitrates, chlorates, perchlorates, hyperchlorites, chromates	• Possible violent or explosive reactions
	Laboratory chemicals	• Higher valence compounds of mercury, lead, selenium, and thallium	• Corrosion Formation of explosive gels between some fuels and strong oxidizers
		Replacement of a chemical radical by a more active one: fluorine and water, sodium and water, nitric acid and water	Deterioration of rubber, plastics, or other organic materials Violent spraying of corrosive material
CORROSION	Materials susceptible to moisture or airborne salts	Incompatibility of materials designed into a system	Material degradation Changes in physical and chemical properties
	Metals that react with air	Leakage of corrosive or reactive substances	Reduction in strength Surface roughness
	Any system with reactive chemicals.	Exposure to unforeseen environment	Binding of moving surfaces, nuts, and other parts
		Damaged protective surfaces	
		Electrolytic action (dissimilar metals)	Contamination of the system
			Loss in resiliency of springs
		Stray electrical currents	

Hazard	Occurrence	Possible Cause	Possible Effects
		Gases released from industrial processes	
		Acids resulting from combustion	
		Flooding or immersion	
		Condensation of atmospheric moisture	
		Vibration and fatigue	
		Salt atmosphere	
		Acids created by atmospheric lightning	
		Smog	
ELECTRICAL	Any "live" electrical circuit powered by: • Power generators driven by: •• Fossil-fueled boiler plants •• Water power •• Nuclear power •• Internal-combustion engine •• Propellant gas-driven turbines •• Solar power-driven turbines • Batteries • Thermoelectric power • Fuel cells Lightning Static electricity Solar cells Thermocouple effect	Accidental contact with live circuit through: • Erroneous connection • Faulty connector or connection • Touching bare conductor • Cutting through insulation • Inadequate insulation • Deteriorated insulation • Defective electrical tool or appliance Lightning strike Short circuit caused by: • Erroneous connection • Faulty connector or connection • Live wires touching • Dirt, contamination, or moisture • Corrosion • Excessive solder or loose particles • Pieces of cut wire • Bent pins Improper wiring Improper mating of connectors, due to worn keyways or poor alignment devices Inadequate or deteriorated insulation	Shock: • Electrocution • Clamping • Involuntary reactions • Interference with performance Burns to skin Thermal effects on materials and equipment: • Burnout of equipment • Melting of soldered connections • Ignition of combustibles • Increased operating temperatures • Softening and melting of plastics • Cutouts opening, deactivating equipment • Circuit breakers and fuses opening, deactivating circuits Electrical system failure, making: • Entire system inoperative • Necessary equipment unavailable • Release of holding devices • Interruption of communications • Detection and

Hazard	Occurrence	Possible Cause	Possible Effects
		Breakdown of dielectric Stray currents from: • Lightning strikes • Static electricity discharge • Inductive or capacitive coupling • Misapplied test equipment power • Cross-connections • Electrostatic discharge • Electrolytic action Power source failure caused by: • Failure of basic energy converter • Lack of fail-safe design • Lack of backup equipment • Power surges causing fuse opening or circuit breaker activation • System overloading • Short-circuiting Electromagnetic radiation caused by: • Radar equipment operation • Communication equipment operation • Nuclear detonation • Sparking and arcing from: •• Opening of switches, relays, and circuit breakers •• Coronas •• Short circuit over a gaseous gap •• Electric arc welding •• Lack of bonding or grounding	warning devices inactivated Inadvertent activation of systems or devices: • Firing of ordnance devices • Untimely electrical equipment starts • Endangering personnel working on circuits or equipment supposedly inoperative Discharges in air may cause: • Ignition of combustibles • Surface damage to metals and other materials • Buildup and welding of contacts Radiation effects: • Electrical noise and cross talk • Interference with electronic equipment operation • Saturation of electronic circuits • Heating of metal parts by induction and eddy currents

Hazard	Occurrence	Possible Cause	Possible Effects
EXPLOSION	Ordnance or munitions systems Any fuel system High-pressure equipment Cryogenic liquid system Highly reactive materials Compression Monopropellants Bridgewires	Activation of: • Explosives • Propellants in containers or cases • Combustible gases in confined spaces • Fine dusts and powders • Combustible gases or liquids: •• In high concentrations •• In presence of strong oxidizers •• At high temperatures Activation of confined solid propellants that are: • Cracked, defective, contain voids, improperly bonded, at excessive temperature, have excess oxidizer or burning catalyst Afterburning of confined combustion products Delayed combustion in a firing chamber Hot soaking of solid propellants Overpressurization of boilers, accumulators, or other pressure vessels Failure of compression device such as an engine or compressor cylinder Warming closed cryogenic or other system containing highly volatile fluid Fuel, lubricant, or solvent in contact with a strong oxidizer	Rupture of pressurized container Blast, causing: • Overpressures (impulse energy) • Collapse of nearby containers • Damage to structures and equipment • Propagation of other explosions Fragmentation, causing: • Holes in nearby containers, vehicles, and equipment • Impact of pieces against personnel, equipment, and structures • Ingestion of fragments by jet engines, oil coolers, and similar units Dispersion of burning, hot, combustible material

Hazard	Occurrence	Possible Cause	Possible Effects
		Defective solid-propellant motor case	
		Ignition of hydrogen from battery or fuel cell charging.	
		Contact between water or moisture with water-sensitive materials such as molten sodium, potassium or lithium; concentrated acids or alkalies; or similar substances, especially in containers or other restricted volume	
FIRE	All normally combustible materials: • Fuels •• Propellants: liquid, solid, or gel. •• Engine use: diesel oil, gasoline, JP & RP fuels. •• Engine start: ethylene oxide, TEA, TEB •• Heating: methane, ethane, kerosene, fuel oil •• Auxiliary power unit: hydrazine, monomethyl hydrazine •• Coal, wood • Solvents and cleaning agents • Lubricants • Welding gases • Paints and varnishes • Hydraulic fluids • Wood products • Elastomers (seals and gaskets) • Furnishings and upholstery • Plastics • Clothing	Combustible mixture with initiating source such as: • Open flame: •• Welding processes and flame cutting •• Matches, smoking •• Gas heaters •• Fired-process equipment and furnaces •• Nearby fires • Sparks: •• Electrical equipment •• Static discharges •• Lightning •• Mechanical (hot solid particles) •• Chemical (carbon particles in exhausts) • Combustible mixture heated to autoignition temperature by: •• External heat sources: ••• Electrical heaters or hot plates ••• High-wattage electronic equipment	Heat and high temperature effects Loss of oxygen Production of toxic gases and smoke Production of corrosive materials Destruction of matériel and resources Burns to personnel Explosions Equipment rendered inoperative Carbonization and contamination of matériel

Hazard	Occurrence	Possible Cause	Possible Effects
	• Vegetation • Refuse and trash • Other organic materials Normally low-combustible materials in presence of strong oxidizers or high temperatures: • Solvents (methylene chloride, trichloroethylene) • Lubricants • Hydraulic fluids Normally nonflammable metals in finely powdered form: • Aluminum • Magnesium • Titanium • Iron Afterburning of products of combustion of engine operations or incomplete combustion of organic materials Hydrogen from charging of batteries and fuel cells	••• Boilers, radiators, steam lines and equipment ••• Exhaust stacks and manifolds ••• Hot process equipment ••• Friction (mechanical, aerodynamic) •• Inadequate dissipation of chemical reaction heat (spontaneous ignition): ••• Oily rags ••• Sawdust, excelsior ••• Subbituminous coal, lignite, peat ••• Powdered plastics • Adiabatic compression of flammable gas mixture • Hypergolic mixtures • Pyrophoric reactions with air • Reactions with water-sensitive materials • Radiation from a nuclear detonation • Flash oxidation from meteorite penetration	
HEAT AND TEMPERATURE High Temperature	Any fuel-consuming process Other exothermic chemical process Electrical equipment Solar energy Nuclear energy Biological or physiological processes	Fire or explosion Other exothermic chemical reaction Heat engine operation Nuclear reaction Electrical resistance losses Inductive heating Aerodynamic or other vehicular friction	Ignition of combustibles Initiation of other reactions Increased reactivity Melting of metals and thermoplastics Charring of organic materials Reduced strength of metals and other materials Distortion and warping of parts Weakening of soldered seams

Hazard	Occurrence	Possible Cause	Possible Effects
	Moving parts	Friction between moving parts	Increased evaporation rate of liquids (fuels, lubricants, toxic liquids)
		Internal friction due to repeated bending or other work processes such as repeated impacts	
			Expansion causing binding or loosening of parts
		Gas compression	
		Exposure to sun or artificial light	Increased gas diffusion
			Reduced relative humidity
		Inadequate heat dissipation capacity	Increased absolute humidity
			Breakdown of chemical compounds
		Hot spots due to coolant fluid being blocked	Burns to personnel
			Reduced personnel efficiency
		Cooling system failure	Heat cramps, strokes, and exhaustion
		Welding, soldering, brazing, or metal cutting	Peeling of finishes, blistering of paint
		Proximity to operations involving large amounts of heat (radiation, convection, conduction)	Decreased viscosity of lubricants
			Increased electrical resistance
		Immersion in hot fluid	Changes in other electrical characteristics
		Lack of insulation from thermal sources	Softening of insulation and sealants
			Opening or closing of electrical contacts due to expansion
		Hot climate or weather	
		Human or animal heat output	
		Organic decay processes	
		Capacitive heating	Premature operation of thermally activated time-delay devices
		Peltier effect	
Low Temperature	Any heat-removal process	Cold climate or weather	Freezing of liquids
	Refrigerating or cryogenic systems	Endothermic reactions	Icing of operating equipment
		Exposure to heat sink	Condensation of moisture and other vapors
	Polar, high-altitude, or winter conditions	Mechanical cooling processes	
		Gas expansion	
		Joule-Thomson effect	Reduced reaction rate
	Deep water, especially in winter	Rapid evaporation	Frostbite or cryogenic burns
		Immersion in cold fluid	Reduced viscosity
		Inadequate heat supply	Gelling of lubricants
	Dark positions in space	Heat loss by radiation, conduction, or convection	Increased brittleness of metals

Hazard	Occurrence	Possible Cause	Possible Effects
		Solid-propellant cold soaking.	Loss of flexibility of organic materials
			Contraction effects, especially opening of cracks in metal
			Propellant cracking Delayed ignition in furnaces and combustion chambers
			Combustion instability in engines Changes in electrical characteristics Jamming or loosening of moving parts due to contraction
			Delayed operation of thermally activated time-delay devices
Temperature Variations	Any system or part that gains or loses heat	Diurnal heating and cooling Gain or loss of heat due to radiation, conduction, or convection	Cycling fatigue of metals Pressure changes in confined gases and liquids
		Stopping and starting of heat engines and other powered equipment	Dimensional changes, especially in metals
			Variations in stresses
IMPACT AND SHOCK	Any part or piece of equipment hit by or hitting another mass Any object hit by a shock wave	Handling and transportation damage Blast Mechanical interference Falling body Loss of control or poor guidance of a moving vehicle Inadequate or no brakes on moving vehicle Lack or failure of restraining device	Loss of control of a vehicle Vehicle damage or destruction Personnel injury Damage to other vehicles, structures, or equipment Rupture of fuel tanks and lines Breakage of cables, ropes, chains, pins Fracture of brittle materials

Hazard	Occurrence	Possible Cause	Possible Effects
		Inadequate or no shock-absorbent materials or devices	Detonation of sensitive high explosives
			Opening of normally closed contacts
		Stopping prevented by wet, icy, oily, excessively smooth surface	Closing of normally open controls, valves, contacts
		Quick-acting pneumatically or hydraulically actuated devices	Short circuit caused when closely spaced electrical parts contact each other
			Displacement of parts, hitting personnel or damaging equipment
		Detonating devices Hydraulic shock (water hammer) Heavy equipment vibrations Rotating part hitting fixed surface	Opening or closing of hinged parts Damage to metering equipment
LEAKAGE	Any vessel or conductor containing or immersed in a fluid	Cracks caused by structural failure	Release of toxic, radioactive, or flammable material
		Hole torn by impact Porosity or other weld defect	Loss of system fluids Early fuel exhaustion Loss of system pressure
		Inadequately fitted or tightened parts	Loss of lubricants Contamination or degradation of materials
		Fittings loosened by vibration	Slipperyness of surfaces Short-circuiting of electrical circuits and equipment
		Contact surfaces inadequately finished	
		Wrong type of gasket or seal	Corrosion of metals Displacement of air or other gas by liquid
		Permeable material Corroded metals or metal gaskets	
		Hose holes caused by kinking, wear, or deterioration	
		Worn parts Excessive fluid pressure Cuts in seals, gaskets, hoses	

Hazard	Occurrence	Possible Cause	Possible Effects
		Poorly designed connections	
		Dirt or other solid contaminants between mating surfaces	
		Overfilling of containers	
		Erroneously opened drain or connection	
		Expansion of liquid over open top of container	
		Tilting or upset of open or vented container	
MOISTURE High Humidity	Any environment in proximity to bodies of water or in which moisture is generated or used	Naturally high atmospheric humidity	Corrosion
		Wet climate or weather	Electrical short-circuiting
		Proximity to bodies of water	Personnel discomfort
		Moisture producing processes	Contamination
		Respiration	Leaching of solid-propellant ingredients.
		Inflow of underground water	Clouding of viewing surfaces
		Large amounts of vegetation	Icing of equipment and aerodynamic surfaces
		Personnel perspiring in inadequately ventilated enclosure, equipment, or impermeable coverings	Violent reactions, explosions, or fire with water-sensitive materials
		Rain, snow, hail, ice, or dew	Swelling of water-absorbent materials
		Flooding and immersion	Degradation of fuels
		Leakage	Warping and sticking of wood doors, drawers, and similar objects
		Temperature decrease without removal of moisture	
		Airconditioner or dehumidifier malfunction	
		Condensation on cold surfaces	
		Presence of humidifying equipment	
		Contact with materials that hold moisture	

Hazard	Occurrence	Possible Cause	Possible Effects
Low Humidity	Dry climate or proximity to drying process	Hot, dry weather	Organic materials easily ignited
		Frigid weather	
		Temperature increase without addition of moisture	Rapid combustion
			Static electricity easily generated
			Dehydration and debilitation of personnel
		Use of refrigerating equipment	
		Operation of dehumidifying equipment	Drying of mucous membranes
			Dehydration and cracking of organic materials
		Presence of moisture absorbent or adsorbent	
			Rapid cooling of moist surfaces
			Reduction in strength of wood products
POWER SOURCE FAILURE	Internal-combustion engines	Fuel exhaustion	Complete inactivation of power-dependent systems
		Oxidizer exhaustion	
		Blockage of fuel or oxidizer to reaction chamber	
	Rocket engines		Failure during flight of airborne systems
	Electric generators		
	Batteries and fuel cells	Blockage of steam, gas, or water used to drive turbines	Guidance failure of moving vehicle
	Nuclear power sources		
	Gas generators		Lack of propulsion during critical period
		Lack or failure of ignition source for chemical reaction	
			Inability to activate other systems
		Interference with reaction	Failure of life support systems
		Excessive wear of power equipment	
			Failure of safety monitoring and warning systems
		Mechanical damage to power equipment	
			Failure of emergency or rescue systems
		Poor adjustment of critical device	
		Failure at interface between power source and circuit or load	
		Excessive load	
		Failure of prime mover for generator	
		Loss of electrolyte for battery or fuel cell	

Hazard	Occurrence	Possible Cause	Possible Effects
		Open circuit	
		Failure of cooling system	
		Failure of lubricating system	
		Excessive speed due to lack of control	
		Lack of backup system	
PRESSURE High Pressure	Hydraulic systems Pneumatic systems Cryogenic systems Pressurized containers Boilers Compressors Engine cylinders Deep underwater environment	Overpressurization Connection to system with excessively high pressure	Container ruptured or crushed Blast Fragments of ruptured container blown about
		Excessively high combustion rate in combustion chamber with restricted exhaust passage	Unsecured container propelled by escaping gas
		No pressure relief valve or vent Faulty pressure relief valve or vent	Eye or skin damage due to blowing dirt or other solid particles
		Heating gases in closed containers	Whipping about of hoses Increase in chemical reaction rate Increase in burning rate
		Heating fluids with high vapor pressures	Lung and ear damage Cutting by thin high-pressure jets Shock
		Warming cryogenic liquids in a closed or inadequately vented system Impact Blast	Leaks in lines and equipment designed for lower pressures
		Failure or improper release of connectors	Blowout of seals and gaskets Permanent deformation of metals
		Inadequate restraining devices High acceleration of liquid system Deep submersion Water hammer (hydraulic shock)	Excessively rapid motion of hydraulically or pneumatically activated equipment
Low Pressure	Vacuum systems High altitude	Compressor failure Increased altitude without pressure relief	Unbalanced forces Pressure vessel collapse Inadequate air for respiration

Hazard	Occurrence	Possible Cause	Possible Effects
		Increase in altitude without suitable respiratory equipment	Bursting of pressurized vessels
			Physiological damage (atelectasis)
		Inadequate design against implosion forces	Increased leakage if differential increases
		Rapid condensation of gas in a closed system	
		Decrease in gas volume by combustion	
		Cooling of hot gas in a closed system	
Pressure Changes	High-altitude vehicles Space vehicles Underwater vehicles Gas expansion systems Compressing or pumping equipment	Rapid expansion of gas High gas compression Rapid changes of altitude Loss of cabin pressurization at high altitudes or in space	Joule-Thomson cooling Compressive heating Explosive decompression Physiological disturbances (aeroembolism, dysbarism, cramps, the bends)
	Airfoils Carburetors	Meteoroid damage at extremely high altitudes or in space	Condensation of moisture
		Blowout of window or hatch on high-altitude or space vehicle	
		Rapid rise toward surface from underwater	
RADIATION Thermal Infrared	Any heat producing body or process. (See High Temperature under HEAT AND TEMPERATURE)	Flames Highly heated surface Solar or nuclear radiation	Undesirable heat gain or temperature rise
			Overheating Skin burns Charring of organic materials
Electromagnetic	Radar equipment Communications equipment	Radar equipment operation Communications equipment operation	Initiation of ordnance devices Interference with operation of other electronic equipment
Ionizing	Radioactive materials X-ray equipment Radar equipment Communications equipment Nuclear weapons Space environment	Inadequate containment of radioactive materials

Excessive exposure to ionizing source | Tissue damage Degradation of electronic components and changes in their characteristics

Degradation of material strength |

Hazard	Occurrence	Possible Cause	Possible Effects
Ultraviolet	Certain light sources	Sunshine Electric welding arcs Germicidal lamps	Decomposition of chlorinated hydrocarbons Ozone or nitrogen oxide generation Vision damage Deterioration of materiel, especially rubber and other polymers Color fading Increased temperature in enclosures
STRUCTURAL DAMAGE OR FAILURE	Any part, piece of equipment, vehicle,	Shock by impact Blast overpressures Inadequate design strength for expected loads Rough handling Object dropped on a hard surface Hard object dropped on a vulnerable part Moving object hitting a vulnerable part Collision between moving vehicles or vessels Grounding of ships Inadequate care of metal surfaces during manufacture or handling Overloading Reduction of strength by corrosion Crimping of metal sheet Rotating part hitting stationary object Excessively high centrifugal force Overpressures due to internal or external fluid	Bending or distortion that causes an object to fail in: • Its function • Mating with another part • Alignment of parts. In rotating equipment damage to other parts, vibration, noise, or shock may result • Disassembly from another part Cracking or initial surface or edge failure that causes: • Stress concentrations and their effects • Irregular surfaces • Regions where contaminants may accumulate • Regions where corrosion may take place Breaking or complete failure of an object by separation into two or more parts: • Cable, chain, or sling failure • Rupture of pressure vessels

Hazard	Occurrence	Possible Cause	Possible Effects
		Poorly fitted or inadequately tightened parts	• Tearing of thin materials • Shearing of metal or plastic parts or their connections
		Overtorquing of nuts and bolts	
		Loss of strength with temperature under load	• Twisting and shearing of shafts, nuts, bolts, or pins
		Thermal expansion and distortion of parts	• Shattering of brittle materials
		Loss of ductility, and brittleness produced by cold	• Splitting away of a portion or extension of a body from its main mass
		Inadvertent exposure to aerodynamic loads	
		High accelerations and decelerations	
		Fatigue due to vibration or thermal cycling	
		Cutting or punching by sharp pointed objects	Crimping or creasing or cutting into a metal sheet, wire, cable, or pipe:
		Bird strikes	
		Stress concentration: • Residuals created by manufacturing processes such as machining, grinding, extruding, drawing	• Reducing cross section and strength, permitting easy breakage • Creating a high resistance point in a conductor
		• Scratches and gouges due to lack of care in handling	• Reducing or blocking flow of fluid
		• Sharp corners, especially at right angles where two planes meet	• Leakage of fluid Crushing or collapse of containers or structures
		• Surface treatment, such as shot peening, cold working, plating	Delaminations of layered material
		• Assembly stresses caused by shrink or press fits, torquing	

Hazard	Occurrence	Possible Cause	Possible Effects
		• Surface roughness due to corrosion, chemical action, abrasion, erosion (blowing sand)	
		• Openings, such as rivet or bolt holes	
		• Sharp bends or crimping	
		• Welding arc starts or other spark indentations	
		• Cyclic changes in stresses from tension to compression	
		• Changes in internal stresses due to changes in temperature	
		Stress reversals: • Vibrating or oscillating equipment • Flexing panels or reeds • Cyclic changes in stress from tension to compression • Temperature changes due to starting and stopping thermal equipment, or diurnal changes • Change from high pressure to vacuum (or vice versa) without suitable equalization	
TOXICITY	Any substance whose presence in relatively small amounts will produce physiological damage or disturbance Any situation where a lack of oxygen for breathing may exist	Toxic gases or liquids Fine metal or other particulate matter Inadequate oxygen for respiration due to: • High altitudes • Dilution by inert gases • Combustion, which consumes oxygen	Irritation of eyes, nose, throat, or respiratory passages Damage to: • Respiratory system • Blood system • Body organs • Skin damage (dermatitis)

Hazard	Occurrence	Possible Cause	Possible Effects
	Polluted atmosphere, especially in terrain depressed below its surroundings, during a temperature inversion, or both	• Insufficient ventilation in occupied, enclosed space • Atmospheric pollution by industrial, automobile, or other exhausts	Effects on nervous system (narcosis, anesthesia, paralysis, nerve damage) Annoyance or nausea caused by foul odors
		Lack of respiratory protection	Reduction in personnel efficiency or capabilities
		Lack of skin protection Inadequate personal cleanliness	Destruction of vegetation
		Ingestion of toxic or contaminated materials or food	
		Outgassing of gases at low pressures in confined spaces	
VIBRATION AND NOISE	Any type of operating mechanical equipment, parts, or vehicle	Reciprocating motion equipment	Cracking and breaking of brittle materials
		Irregular motion of rotating parts	Loosening of bolts or other fastened parts
		Irregular or cyclic motion during transportation	Breakage of lead wires, filaments, and supporting parts
		Rocket motor or jet engine exhaust	Personnel fatigue Inability to read instruments or to activate controls
		Aerodynamic surface flutter or buzz	
		Pneumatic or hydraulic shock (water hammer)	Damage to hearing Interference with communications
		Vibrating tools Misaligned equipment in motion	Decreased corrosion resistance Metal fatigue and other changes in crystalline structure
		Lack of vibration isolators	
		Loose or undersized mountings	Involuntary reaction to sudden loud noise
		Bottoming or failure of shock mounts	Static electricity generated between susceptible surfaces

Hazard	Occurrence	Possible Cause	Possible Effects
		Pump or blower cavitation	Chattering of spring type contacts, valves, and pointers
		High-velocity fluid hitting a surface or object that can vibrate	
			Loss of calibration of monitoring devices and other instruments
		Sonic booms and other shock waves	Possible false readings on pointer-type devices
		Explosion and violent ruptures	
			Crazing and flaking of finishes
		Scraping of hard surfaces against each other	
		Lack or failure of sound isolation devices such as mufflers	
		Escaping high-velocity gas	
WEATHER AND ENVIRONMENT	Any out-of-doors location	Moisture and humidity: dew, rain, clouds, fog, hail	High-humidity conditions Low-humidity conditions Icing of carburetors, aerodynamic surfaces, instruments, or controls
		Extreme cold or heat Temperature inversions Solar radiation Cosmic radiation Ionizing radiation Temperature changes Airborne salts, dust, sand, dirt, fungi	Ultraviolet radiation effects Infrared radiation effects High-temperature effects Low-temperature effects Temperature change effects
		Lightning Submarine pressures	Possibility of or acceleration of corrosion Contamination by sand, dirt, moisture, or fungi
		Reduced pressures at high altitudes	
		Space vacuum Meteoroids Industrial plant discharges Tides, floods, and currents	Structural overloads, movement, or toppling caused by pressure effects of wind on large surfaces
			Loss of visibility due to fog, clouds, or condensation
			Sudden acceleration due to turbulence and gusts
			Impact damage by hail

Hazard	Occurrence	Possible Cause	Possible Effects
			Possible reflections of noise or vibration by inversions
			Concentration of toxic gases, smog, or particulate matter caused by inversions
			Short circuits, inadvertent activations, or disruptions of electrical systems caused by moisture condensation in electrical devices
			Surface friction for traction or braking reduced by wet surfaces
			Stopping of a vehicle prevented by hydroplaning
			Skidding and loss of control of vehicle caused by wet surfaces
			Energized power lines torn down by wind
			Flooding of facilities and shops
			Loss of bouyancy of vessels, such as ships and submarines
			Washing away of foundations and equipment
			Drowning of personnel
			Abrasion or scratching of surfaces by sand.
			Electrical conductivity of water increased by salt, thus reducing insulation value and permitting galvanic coupling between adjacent dissimilar metals
			Snow-blindness or difficulty in guiding a vehicle or in reading dials and meters caused by strong sunlight

INDEX

A

Bioenvironmental engineering, 150, 182–185
Blocking elements, 230–237
Boccardo, James F., 13
Boeing Company, 238
Boiler Code, 25
Boolean logic, 226, 229, 230, 238
Bruchey, W. J., 219
Bubble charts, 118, 121
Buddy system, 267, 317
Buick Company, 18
Burn-in screening, 282–283

C

Canale, S., 160
Campus, F., 136
Capabilities, man versus machine, 75–81
Care, due, 22
Cardozo, Benjamin, 18
Checklists, 113–115
Code for Unfired Pressure Vessels, 25
Codes, 23–26
Coffin, Lorenzo, 3
Confidence levels, 277
Containment, 287–289
Contingency analysis, 166, 198, 200–209, 292, 294
  procedure, 203–208
  response times, 201–203
  results, 208–209
Contributory error, 69
Contributory hazard, 64
Corrective actions, 45
Costs
  accident, 7–8
  of human life, 9–12
  military fatalities, 3–4
  safety program, 55–59
  versus risk, 58–59
Crashworthiness, 288, 291, 293–294
Criteria review and analysis, 111–115
  procedure, 112–115
Critical component analysis, 226
Critical hazard, 64
Critical incident technique, 187–192
  procedure, 190–192
Critical items, 299–300
Critical processes, 302–307
Criticality analysis, 156–159

D

Daedalus, 108–109
Damage
  defined, 62
  minimization and containment, 287–289
Danger, defined, 62
Decision making, and logic, 246–249
Decision redundancy, 284
Defense, Department of, 3–4, 24, 54, 74
Derating, 279
Design errors, 69–71
Designers, responsibilities of, 68–69, 311–312
Destruct system, 232–237
Detailed analyses
  criticality, 156–159
  energy, 159–164
  failure modes and effects, 148–156, 226, 294
  flow, 168–170
  interface, 164–168
  prototypes, 170–180
  subsystem, 143–148
Detailed safety studies, 101, 103–104
Discovery, process of, 26–28
Drills, 255
Due care, 22

E

Electrical hazards, 65, 71, 111, 132, 168, 255–258
Emergencies
  equipment, 290–295
  procedures, 200–209, 294–295
Encapsulation, 303–305
Energy analysis, 156, 159–164
  procedure, 163–164
Engineering
  bioenvironmental, 150, 182–185
  practices, 26
  System Safety, 38
Environmental analysis, 138–140
  procedure, 137–138
Environmental hazards, 67, 94, 131
Environments
  artificial, 135
  closed, 135–136
  controlled, 134–135
  free, 135

Environments (*cont.*)
    induced, 132, 134
    natural, 130–132
Equipment
    emergency, 290–295
    personal protective, 289–291, 318–319
Equivalency, TNT, 160–163
Escape, 291–294
Error
    design, 69–71
    maintenance and repair, 71, 308–309
    operations, 71, 74
    personnel, 68–69
    production, 71
Explosive hazards and effects, 160–163

F

Fail-safe designs, 237, 259–261
    fail-active, 260
    fail-operational, 260
    fail-passive, 260
Failure investigation, 52–54
Failure minimization, 261–287
    failure rate reduction, 278–283
    monitoring, 262–268
    redundancy, 283–287
    safety factors and margins, 273–278
    warnings, 268–273
Failure modes and effects analysis, 148–157, 226, 294
    limitations, 155–156
    procedure, 150–155
Failure Modes, Effects and Criticality Analysis (FMECA), 148, 157
Failure plotting, 124–126
Failure rate reduction, 262, 278–283
    derating, 279
    redundancy, 283–287
    screening, 281–283
    timed replacements, 279–281
Fault Hazard Analysis (FHA), 148
Fault Tree Analysis, 155, 226, 238–246
    limitations, 244–246
Federal Aviation Agency (FAA), 8, 10, 24, 261
Federal government, safety requirements, 5, 23–24
Ffield, P., 136
Fitts, P. M., 188–189

Flags and streamers, as warning, 271
Flow analysis, 168–170
    procedure, 170
Foreseeability, 22, 69

G

Garnerin, Andre Jacques, 2
Gates and connectives logic, 229–230
Geise, John, 191
Goldberg v. *Kollsman Instrument Corporation, 1959,* 29

H

Haasl, David, 240
Harris, N. D., 4
Hazard analysis
    fundamentals of, 86–105
    types of
        postdesign, 87–88
        predesign, 87–88
        qualitative, 88
        quantitative, 89–95
Hazards
    and accidents, 83–84
    basic concepts of, 62–84
    catastrophic, 64
    categories of, 67–68
    contributory, 64
    critical, 64
    defined, 62
    determining existence of, 64–66
    environmental, 67, 94, 131
    initiating, 64
    level limitation, 254–256
    man and, 68–74
        design errors, 69–71
        maintenance and repair errors, 71, 308–309
        operations errors, 71, 74
        production errors, 71
    primary, 64
    review check lists, 113–115
Heat, 136, 163, 256–257
Helicopters
    accidents and, 3, 8, 126–128

Index

349